Unaccusativity

Linguistic Inquiry Monographs

Samuel Jay Keyser, general editor

1. *Word Formation in Generative Grammar*, Mark Aronoff
2. *X̄ Syntax: A Study of Phrase Structure*, Ray Jackendoff
3. *Recent Transformational Studies in European Languages*, Samuel Jay Keyser, editor
4. *Studies in Abstract Phonology*, Edmund Gussmann
5. *An Encyclopedia of AUX: A Study in Cross-Linguistic Equivalence*, Susan Steele
6. *Some Concepts and Consequences of the Theory of Government and Binding*, Noam Chomsky
7. *The Syntax of Words*, Elisabeth Selkirk
8. *Syllable Structure and Stress in Spanish: A Nonlinear Analysis*, James W. Harris
9. *CV Phonology: A Generative Theory of the Syllable*, George N. Clements and Samuel Jay Keyser
10. *On the Nature of Grammatical Relations*, Alec Marantz
11. *A Grammar of Anaphora*, Joseph Aoun
12. *Logical Form: Its Structure and Derivation*, Robert May
13. *Barriers*, Noam Chomsky
14. *On the Definition of Word*, Anna-Maria Di Sciullo and Edwin Williams
15. *Japanese Tone Structure*, Janet Pierrehumbert and Mary Beckman
16. *Relativized Minimality*, Luigi Rizzi
17. *Types of Ā-Dependencies*, Guglielmo Cinque
18. *Argument Structure*, Jane Grimshaw
19. *Locality: A Theory and Some of Its Empirical Consequences*, Maria Rita Manzini
20. *Indefinites*, Molly Diesing
21. *Syntax of Scope*, Joseph Aoun and Yen-hui Audrey Li
22. *Morphology by Itself: Stems and Inflectional Classes*, Mark Aronoff
23. *Thematic Structure in Syntax*, Edwin Williams
24. *Indices and Identity*, Robert Fiengo and Robert May
25. *The Antisymmetry of Syntax*, Richard S. Kayne
26. *Unaccusativity: At the Syntax–Lexical Semantics Interface*, Beth Levin and Malka Rappaport Hovav

Unaccusativity

At the Syntax–Lexical Semantics Interface

Beth Levin and
Malka Rappaport Hovav

The MIT Press
Cambridge, Massachusetts
London, England

Second printing, 1996

© 1995 Massachusetts Institute of Technology

The verb lists in Appendix A are reprinted by permission of the publisher from Beth Levin. *English Verb Classes and Alternations: A Preliminary Investigation.* Chicago, Ill.: University of Chicago Press. © 1993 by The University of Chicago.

This book was set in Times Roman by Asco Trade Typesetting Ltd., Hong Kong and was printed and bound in the United States of America.

Library of Congress Cataloging-in-Publication Data

Levin, Beth, 1955–
  Unaccusativity: at the syntax-lexical semantics interface / Beth
  Levin and Malka Rappaport Hovav.
      p.   cm.—(Linguistic inquiry monographs; 26)
  Includes bibliographical references and index.
  ISBN 0-262-12185-9.—ISBN 0-262-62094-4 (pbk.)
  1. Grammar, Comparative and general—Transitivity. 2. Grammar,
Comparative and general—Syntax. 3. Semantics. I. Rappaport Hovav, Malka.
II. Title. III. Series.
P281.L48   1995
415—dc20   94-17439
                                                        CIP

Contents

Series Foreword

We are pleased to present this monograph as the twenty-sixth in the series *Linguistic Inquiry Monographs*. These monographs will present new and original research beyond the scope of the article, and we hope they will benefit our field by bringing to it perspectives that will stimulate further research and insight.

Originally published in limited edition, the *Linguistic Inquiry Monograph* series is now available on a much wider scale. This change is due to the great interest engendered by the series and the needs of a growing readership. The editors wish to thank the readers for their support and welcome suggestions about future directions the series might take.

Samuel Jay Keyser
for the Editorial Board

Acknowledgments

This book represents the results of a long-standing collaboration. It is therefore fitting, we think, to thank those people who helped us to get this collaboration started and those who facilitated its continuation despite the fact that the Atlantic Ocean separated us almost from the first.

Starting at the beginning, we would like to thank Morris Halle, who suggested that we work together back in 1984, as well as Ken Hale and Jay Keyser, the directors of the MIT Lexicon Project, funded by a grant from the System Development Foundation, under whose auspices we carried out our initial collaborative research.

Moving next to the final stages of this work, we give our warm thanks to the members of the Department of Linguistics at Rutgers University, who, by letting us spend our leaves there in the fall of 1993, provided us with the first opportunity in years to be in the same place for more than a couple of weeks at a time. During this time we were able to put the finishing touches on this book.

We have discussed various parts of this work with many people over the years, and a number of people have provided us with comments after reading different portions of the manuscript. We thank them all, and we hope that we have not left anyone out. They are Sue Atkins, Betty Birner, Joan Bresnan, Strang Burton, Chris Collins, Edit Doron, David Dowty, Martin Everaert, Adele Goldberg, Jane Grimshaw, Ken Hale, Ray Jackendoff, Mary Laughren, Lori Levin, Talke Macfarland, David Pesetsky, James Pustejovsky, Tova Rapoport, Betsy Ritter, Susan Rothstein, Grace Song, Natsuko Tsujimura, Robert J. Van Valin, Jr., and Annie Zaenen. We also appreciate the comments and suggestions offered by the two reviewers of an earlier version.

Almost all of the material in this book has been presented at one time or another at too many conferences, workshops, and colloquia to mention individually here. We are grateful to the audiences for their questions and comments. We would also like to extend our thanks to the students in classes at Bar Ilan University, Northwestern University, Rutgers University, and the Dutch National Ph.D. Courses in Nijmegen in December 1992. We have benefited greatly from the many opportunities to present this material.

We thank the following people for their help with data: Peter Ackema and Martin Everaert (Dutch), Henri Béjoint (French), Beatrice Santorini (German), Edit Doron and Bnayahu Hovav (Hebrew), Höskuldur Thráinsson (Icelandic), Nicoletta Calzolari, Alessandra Giorgi, and Vieri Samek-Lodovici (Italian), Mutsumi Imai and Natsuko Tsujimura (Japanese), and Boris Katz (Russian).

We would also like to comment briefly on the English data used throughout this book and to thank those who have helped us obtain them. The tokens of the locative inversion construction are taken from a corpus of over 2,000 such constructions collected by Betty Birner, Beth Levin, and Gregory Ward, with contributions from Georgia Green and Lori Levin. Olivia Chang, Steven Forsythe, Alice Rusnock, and Kirsten Winge are to be thanked for their help in compiling the corpus of locative inversions. Ken Church, Don Hindle, John Wickberg, and David Yarowsky have all at various times carried out searches for us over large on-line text corpora, and we are grateful for their efforts. Examples labeled "AP Newswire 1990" are from searches of the AP newswire for 1990; those labeled "Brown Corpus" are from searches of the Brown Corpus (Kučera and Francis 1967). Examples labeled "Oxford Corpus" are taken from a corpus owned by Oxford University Press. Full bibliographic citations for all the other short references after examples from texts are listed at the end of the book in the section entitled "Sources of Examples."

Olivia Chang deserves very special thanks for helping with numerous facets of the preparation of this manuscript. We thank Anne Mark for her splendid copyediting job.

This research was supported in part by grants to Levin: a Northwestern University Research Grant and NSF grants BNS-8919884 and DBS-9221993.

Finally, this book would never have been completed without the unfailing support of our friends and colleagues, and most important of all our families. We thank Mr. and Mrs. Rappaport for their hospitality on numerous occasions, allowing us to brainstorm in the same room instead of via transatlantic e-mail. Bnayahu Hovav deserves a special mention for support, understanding, infinite patience, and a willingness to make sacrifices. We thank him, the extended Hovav family, and the Rappaports for their baby-sitting services at various points over the years. Hadas and Yair Hovav, who, although unaware of this book, had to compete with it for attention, are to be blessed for being their lovable, wonderful selves.

Chapter 1

Introduction

The hypothesis that the syntactic properties of verbs are determined by their meaning has long intrigued researchers in linguistics and related fields. The most striking illustration of the role of meaning in the determination of syntax is the tendency for arguments bearing certain semantic roles to be associated with particular syntactic expressions. These tendencies were noted by traditional grammarians dating at least as far back as Pāṇini, and they are encoded, for example, in the "subjectivalization" rule proposed by Fillmore (1968), stated in terms of deep case relations. Following Carter (1988), we call the regularities in the association of arguments bearing certain semantic roles to particular syntactic expressions *linking regularities*, and the rules that effect such associations *linking rules*. To the extent that the semantic role of an argument is determined by the meaning of the verb selecting it, the existence of linking regularities supports the idea that verb meaning is a factor in determining the syntactic structure of sentences. The striking similarities in the linking regularities across languages strongly suggest that they are part of the architecture of language.

Although linking regularities are widely acknowledged to exist, many unresolved issues must be confronted in order to develop a full theory of the mapping between lexical semantics and syntax. Not least among them is the determination of the extent to which the syntactic expression of arguments is predictable and cross-linguistically regular. Another, equally important issue concerns the nature of the lexical semantic representation, since the linking rules are formulated in terms of elements in this representation. A theory of linking, therefore, must be built on a fully articulated theory of lexical semantic representation, yet there is little consensus regarding the nature of this representation.

The resolution of these issues has become all the more urgent because of certain recent developments in syntax. As a result of efforts to develop a constrained theory, various theories of syntax harness idiosyncratic properties of verbs, particularly their meanings, to explain certain properties of the syntactic configurations in which they are found (for discussion, see Wasow 1985). These theories share the assumption that aspects of the syntax of a sentence are determined by the meaning of the verb in that sentence. This assumption is implicit in early formulations of the Projection Principle (Chomsky 1981), and it finds explicit expression in the theory first proposed by Pesetsky (1982), and later adopted by Chomsky (1986b), that s-selection (semantic selection) determines c-selection (categorial selection). (Although as we discuss in section 5.4 and the afterword, several researchers have recently argued for a very different relationship between lexical and syntactic structure.)

Over the past fifteen years, the relationship between lexical semantics and syntax has received substantial attention in the context of the Unaccusative Hypothesis (Perlmutter 1978). This hypothesis proposes that the class of intransitive verbs is not homogeneous, but consists of two subclasses, each associated with a distinct syntactic configuration. There appear to be striking semantic regularities in the composition of the two classes of intransitives, regularities that are manifested across languages in impressive similarities in verb classification. Because of the convergence of semantic and syntactic properties that characterize it, unaccusativity provides fertile ground for exploring the relationship between lexical semantics and syntax. The importance of the Unaccusative Hypothesis is that, if correct, it allows us to use unaccusativity as a means of identifying aspects of verb meaning that are relevant to the syntax and of appropriately formulating at least some of the linking rules. Besides representing an extended investigation into the nature of unaccusativity, this book is intended as a contribution to the development of a theory of lexical semantic representation and to the elucidation of the mapping from the lexical semantic representation to syntax.

1.1 Unaccusativity Introduced

The Unaccusative Hypothesis, as first formulated by Perlmutter (1978) within the context of Relational Grammar and later adopted by Burzio (1986) within the Government-Binding (GB) framework (Chomsky 1981),[1] is a syntactic hypothesis that claims that there are two classes of intransitive verbs, the *unaccusative* verbs and the *unergative* verbs, each associated with a different underlying syntactic configuration. For example, from a GB perspective—the approach we use in this book—an unergative verb takes a D-Structure subject and no object, whereas an unaccusative verb takes a D-Structure object—be it clausal or a simple NP—and no subject. Thus, the members of the two classes are associated with the D-Structure syntactic configurations schematized in (1).[2]

(1) a. Unergative verb: NP [$_{VP}$ V]
    b. Unaccusative verb: _____ [$_{VP}$ V NP/CP]

Alternatively, in argument structure terms, an unergative verb has an external argument but no direct internal argument, whereas an unaccusative verb has a direct internal argument but no external argument.[3]

There is another syntactic characteristic associated with this verb class. As reflected in the name given to the class, an unaccusative verb is unable to take an object with accusative case (or in GB terms, it is unable to assign structural Case to its object). Burzio (1986) has studied this facet of unaccusativity extensively, noting a correlation between the ability of a verb to take an external argument and its ability to assign structural Case. Given the statement of this correlation, which has come to be known as Burzio's Generalization,[4] an alternative definition is sometimes adopted for an unaccusative verb: an unaccusative verb is one that does not take an external argument (i.e., is unable to assign a θ-role to its subject). For the most part the two definitions pick out the same range of verbs as unaccusative, making it unnecessary to choose between them.[5] Nevertheless, in this book we have chosen to use the definition involving Perlmutter's characterization of the class: an unaccusative verb is one that takes an internal argument but no external argument. On this definition, unaccusative verbs are identical in D-Structure configurational terms to passive verbs, which also have a direct internal argument but no external argument.

Since the introduction of the Unaccusative Hypothesis, a wide range of phenomena in various languages have been studied that purport to distinguish between unaccusative and unergative verbs (see Grimshaw 1987 for an overview, as well as the entry on unaccusativity in Dubinsky and C. Rosen's (1987) Relational Grammar bibliography). We refer to these phenomena as *unaccusative diagnostics*. Since the Unaccusative Hypothesis claims that the two classes of intransitive verbs are syntactically defined, it appeals to the difference in syntactic configuration to explain many of the diagnostics that reveal differences in behavior between the classes. Only apparent diagnostics whose ability to discriminate between the two classes can be explained in this way are *actual* unaccusative diagnostics. It turns out that not every phenomenon that appears to distinguish between two classes of intransitive verbs is actually an unaccusative diagnostic in this strong sense.

Much of the initial research on unaccusativity was directed toward establishing the syntactic aspect of unaccusativity, that is, toward proving that there are verbs with the syntactic properties attributed to unaccusative verbs by the Unaccusative Hypothesis. Originally, little attention was paid to the relation between the meaning of intransitive verbs and their membership in the unaccusative or unergative class, although the paper in which Perlmutter introduced the Unaccusative Hypothesis includes a first attempt at delineating the set of semantically defined verb classes that are expected to show unaccusative or unergative behavior. In fact, the Unaccusative Hypothesis was introduced by Perlmutter in the context of the broader Universal Alignment Hypothesis, which suggests that the syntactic expression of arguments is always determinable on the basis of the meaning of the verb. Indeed, the impressive similarity between the verbs selected by unaccusative diagnostics cross-linguistically suggests that there are important semantic facets to the distinction. It has been proposed that the postulation of the Unaccusative Hypothesis permits the statement of a single simple linking generalization that covers transitive and intransitive verbs alike: agent arguments are D-Structure subjects and patient/theme arguments are D-Structure objects (B. Levin 1983, Marantz 1984, C. Rosen 1984, among others). Thus, although the Unaccusative Hypothesis claims that the distinction between the two classes of verbs is syntactically *represented*, it was originally assumed that the distinction is fully semantically *determined*.

1.2   Approaches to Unaccusativity

Once more attention was paid to the relationship between the lexical semantics and the syntax of unaccusativity, it became clear that linguistic reality is more complicated than the simple linking generalization mentioned above suggests. This situation is reflected in the existence of what have become known as *unaccusative mismatches* (L. Levin 1986): cases in which there seems to be an imperfect match between the verbs expected to be selected on semantic or syntactic grounds as unaccusative or unergative by various diagnostics and the verbs actually selected by those diagnostics. Below we will distinguish between two kinds of mismatches, one that has led to the *syntactic approach* to unaccusativity, which denies that unaccusativity is fully semantically predictable, and another that has led to the *semantic approach* to unaccusativity, which denies that unaccusativity is syntactically encoded. In essence, this book is an extended attempt to meet the challenges that the mismatches present to Perlmutter's original hypothesis that unaccusativity is both syntactically encoded and semantically predictable. The original thesis will be defended throughout the book. In the remainder of this section we lay out the essentials of the syntactic and semantic approaches to unaccusativity and discuss the problems with these two approaches. At the same time we highlight the methodological considerations that are relevant to meeting the challenges that these approaches pose.

1.2.1 The Syntactic Approach
The existence of phenomena that suggest that the classification of verbs as unaccusative or unergative cannot be completely determined semantically has led to the development of the syntactic approach to unaccusativity, first systematically defended by C. Rosen (1984). On this approach, all that unaccusative verbs have in common is a particular syntactic configuration, although Rosen and other proponents of this approach do not deny that there tend to be certain correspondences between the meanings of verbs and their classification as unaccusative or unergative. In this section we discuss the phenomena that Rosen cites in favor of the syntactic approach in order to show that they do not necessarily warrant the conclusions she draws from them.

First, Rosen makes much of the fact that there is no single semantic property common to all unaccusative verbs selected by all diagnostics in all languages (see also Baker 1983, DeLancey 1985, among others). However, the hypothesis that the classification of verbs as unergative or unaccusative is predictable on the basis of meaning in no way implies that all unaccusative verbs or all unergative verbs represent a unified semantic class. Although this point should be obvious, it is worth stressing since often researchers strive to find a uniform semantic characterization for the unaccusative class. But given the many-to-one character of the mapping from lexical semantics to syntax, there is no reason to assume that all verbs that have the syntactic properties attributed to unaccusative verbs will form a semantically homogeneous class. There is no more reason to assume that the unaccusative class is semantically homogeneous than there is to assume the same about the class of transitive verbs. And one of the points that will emerge from our study of unaccusativity, particularly in chapters 3 and 6, is precisely that the class is not unified semantically. We will show that this assumption has far-ranging consequences since the members of the different subclasses of the unaccusative verb class differ in certain aspects of their behavior; nevertheless, they can all be shown to be legitimate members of the class.

Second, Rosen shows that verbs with similar meanings in and across languages may be classified differently with respect to unaccusativity. For example, she claims that the verb corresponding to *die* acts like an unaccusative verb in Italian, but like an unergative verb in Choctaw (although see Martin 1991 and section 1.2.3 for further discussion of the Choctaw data). Within Italian itself, verbs of bodily process diverge in their behavior: the verb *russare* 'snore' manifests unergative properties, whereas the verb *arrossire* 'blush' manifests unaccusative properties.

Third, Rosen discusses the existence of individual verbs that appear to be classified as both unaccusative and unergative by the same diagnostic. For example, as Rosen points out, certain Italian intransitive verbs are found with both the auxiliary *avere* 'have' and the auxiliary *essere* 'be'. (For reasons of consistency and clarity, glosses of some quoted examples have been expanded or slightly modified.)

(2) a. Mario ha continuato. (*è)
       Mario has continued   is
       'Mario continued.'
    b. Il dibattito è continuato. (*ha)
       the debate is continued   has
       'The debate continued.'
       (C. Rosen 1984:45, (21))

(3) correre 'to run', saltare 'to jump', volare 'to fly', vivere 'to live',
    suonare 'to toll', fiorire 'to bloom' (Centineo 1986:220, (o), (q))

The pattern of auxiliary selection is problematic since with intransitive verbs the selection of *essere* 'be' is considered to be a signal of unaccusative status, whereas the selection of *avere* 'have' is considered to be a signal of unergative status (Burzio 1986, Perlmutter 1989, C. Rosen 1981, among others). Consequently, Rosen concludes from the existence of dual auxiliary verbs that the distinction between the unaccusative and unergative classes is not completely characterizable in terms of meaning alone.[6]

Before we discuss each of the problems just mentioned individually, we provide a brief general evaluation of the syntactic approach. There is no question that in comparison with the syntax, the lexicon is the domain of the idiosyncratic. But the heightened attention that has been paid to lexical matters in recent years has revealed that although many idiosyncratic phenomena are lexical in nature, much of the lexical knowledge that speakers have of their language is systematic, most likely reflecting deep principles of grammar. In fact, aspects of what Chomsky (1986b) has termed "Plato's problem" are as evident in the domain of the lexicon as in the domain of syntax. That is, it is fairly clear that speakers acquire complex knowledge concerning lexical items for which it is hard to argue that they receive direct evidence.

To illustrate this point, we preview a contrast that we discuss at length in chapter 5. This contrast involves the behavior of agentive verbs of manner of motion in the English resultative construction. As the examples show, verbs of manner of motion can appear in two forms of the resultative construction: one involving no object, as in (4a), and one involving a reflexive object, as in (4b).

(4) a. Jump clear of the vehicle!
    b. Don't expect to swim yourself sober!

As we show in chapters 2 and 5, the objectless resultative is an unaccusative diagnostic, whereas the form with a reflexive object signals that the verb in the construction is unergative. These examples show, then, that agentive verbs of manner of motion can appear in the resultative construction in the pattern expected of unaccusative verbs, as in (4a), or in the pattern expected of unergative verbs, as in (4b). Examples such as these may at first glance be taken to illustrate the idiosyncratic nature of verb classification; that is, agentive verbs of manner of motion can be classified as either unaccusative or unergative. But on closer examination, the opposite turns out to be true. The examples in (4) are not idioms or fixed expressions; furthermore, it can be shown that despite surface appearances the presence or absence of the reflexive is not random.

(5) a. *Jump yourself clear of the vehicle!
    b. *Don't expect to swim sober!

An in-depth examination of the phenomenon in chapter 5 will show that the judgments of native speakers concerning the grammaticality and interpretation of such constructions are subtle and consistent. If the seemingly unpredictable behavior of agentive verbs of manner of motion is by hypothesis expected to be principled, we are forced to seek a principled explanation for it. In chapter 5 we will show that it is possible to predict precisely when agentive verbs of manner of motion will appear in the resultative construction in the guise of unergative verbs and when in the guise of unaccusative verbs.

The resultative example illustrates that unless we take as our starting point the hypothesis that the behavior of verbs is indeed principled, we can easily take the sentences in (4) to be evidence for their idiosyncratic behavior. We acknowledge that there is room for idiosyncrasy in the lexicon, so that in languages where there is explicit evidence for the classification of verbs as unaccusative or unergative (such as, for example, from morphological properties), the classification may not be entirely predictable; nonetheless, it is methodologically most useful to assume that the class membership of each verb is for the most part predictable and to test the limits of this hypothesis. After all, taking the assumption that all is chaos as the starting point of our investigation is not likely to lead us to a better understanding of the interface between lexical semantics and syntax.

Furthermore, there are language acquisition considerations that raise clear problems for the syntactic approach. Assuming that a language such as English, which lacks morphological clues that could distinguish between unaccusative and unergative verbs, does encode this distinction syntactically, then learnability considerations dictate that the distinction must be fully determined by the semantics. For example, in chapter 2 we present extensive evidence involving the resultative construction that the distinction between unaccusative and unergative verbs must be syntactically represented in English, even though the overt evidence for this distinction is rather slim. It is unlikely that every child learning English will necessarily have access to evidence concerning the behavior of each intransitive verb acquired with respect to the kinds of phenomena that force the postulation of an unaccusative or unergative classification for that verb. If Universal Grammar allows both unaccusative and unergative D-Structure configurations for intransitive verbs, then how does the language learner know how to classify newly learned verbs? There are two options: either (i) the choice is predictable on the basis of the meaning of the verb being acquired, or (ii) there must be some way, on the basis of simple data, to determine what class a given verb belongs to. Since option (ii) appears not to be correct for English, then, if the Unaccusative Hypothesis holds, a verb's class membership must be completely determined on the basis of its meaning. It is possible, however, that in languages with overt morphological markers of unaccusativity, membership in the unaccusative or unergative class may be grammaticalized; since there are overt indicators of class membership, the members of the classes may show some deviation from the semantic criteria for class membership.

Let us now briefly consider how the mismatches that Rosen discusses can be dealt with. As we note elsewhere (B. Levin and Rappaport 1989, B. Levin and Rappaport Hovav 1991, 1992), the existence of verbs with similar meanings but different classifications need not have the implications for the Unaccusative Hypothesis that Rosen suggests. The key to dealing with these mismatches is the recognition that certain aspects of verb meaning are relevant to the syntax and other aspects of meaning are not, a point also made forcefully by Pinker (1989). It is only after the syntactically relevant aspects of meaning are isolated that it is possible to evaluate whether two verbs are expected to have the same classification with respect to the Unaccusative Hypothesis. Consider once again Rosen's example concerning the varied classification of Italian verbs of bodily process. The behavior of these verbs is only problematic for the Unaccusative Hypothesis if the verbs belong to the same syntactically relevant semantic class. In fact, it is unclear whether the notion "bodily process" can be used to define such a class. There are other ways of classifying these verbs according to meaning, and some of these alternative semantic classifications do not necessarily put all bodily process verbs into the same class. The concept denoted by the English verb *snore* can be classified as an activity, whereas that denoted by the English verb *blush* is open to an activity or change-of-state interpretation, depending on one's perspective. What is interesting is that the Italian verb *arrossire* 'blush' literally means 'become red', suggesting that in Italian this verb can be considered a verb of change of state.[7] Several recent studies have converged on the conclusion that semantic notions such as "activity" and "change of state" are aspects of meaning that are relevant to the classification of verbs (Dowty 1991, Pinker 1989, Pustejovsky 1991b, Tenny 1987, 1992, Van Valin 1990, among others); if so, there is no reason to expect the verbs *snore* and *blush* to pattern in the same way. In general, a comparison of the status of two apparently similar verbs either in a single language or in two different languages is only valid if the comparison is made with respect to components of meaning relevant to the determination of unaccusativity. We devote much of chapters 3, 4, and 5 to isolating those aspects of meaning that figure in the classification of verbs and to uncovering exactly how these components of meaning contribute to verb classification.

The same considerations lead to a solution for the problem posed by verbs, such as the agentive verbs of manner of motion, that select two auxiliaries. Work by various researchers (see, among other works, Hoekstra 1984, L. Levin 1986, Van Valin 1990) has revealed that for at least a subset of the dual auxiliary verbs, the choice of auxiliary is associated with systematic differences in meaning (see section 5.1.1). As we show in chapter 5, dual auxiliary verbs are just one instance of the more general phenomenon of verbs that show multiple classification with respect to a variety of syntactic phenomena. We term such verbs *variable behavior verbs*. In chapter 5 we investigate several types of variable behavior verbs, including certain dual auxiliary verbs, and demonstrate that each type of variable behavior verb is associated with two meanings differing precisely in those elements of meaning that we have found to be syntactically relevant. If such correlations can be shown to hold more generally, then the existence of verbs with multiple classifications does not present a problem for the hypothesis that unaccusativity is semantically determined; rather, it shows yet again the importance of pursuing the search for syntactically significant components of verb meaning. Furthermore, it is fruitful methodologically to make variable behavior verbs a focus of study since contrasting the meaning of a verb when it shows one type of syntactic behavior with the meaning of the same verb when it shows another type of syntactic behavior will aid in the isolation of just those aspects of meaning that are relevant to the syntactic classification of verbs.

1.2.2   The Semantic Approach

The syntactic approach can be contrasted with the semantic approach to unaccusativity. The claims of the semantic approach are that the two classes of intransitive verbs can be differentiated on semantic grounds and that the semantic characterization of the two classes obviates the need to attribute different syntactic representations to the verbs they contain. This approach can be contrasted with ours since, although it assumes that unaccusativity is semantically determined, it denies that it is syntactically encoded. The most thorough attempt at developing and justifying the semantic approach to unaccusativity is presented by Van Valin (1990). Van Valin claims that "the phenomena which the Unaccusative Hypothesis (UH) strives to explain in syntactic terms are better explained in semantic terms" (1990:221). We will not review Van Valin's theory here, since we do so in section 2.4.2.1. Here we discuss some properties of the semantic approach in general and also point out some problems that it faces.

Recall that on the syntactic approach to unaccusativity, unaccusative and passive verbs are found in the same D-Structure syntactic configuration. And indeed there are syntactic and morphological phenomena that class unaccusative verbs and passive verbs together. For instance, as we discuss in chapter 2, in English resultative phrases can be predicated of the S-Structure subjects of passive and unaccusative verbs but not of those of unergative and transitive verbs. Prenominal perfect/passive participles may modify the S-Structure subjects of passives (*a badly written letter*) and unaccusatives (*a recently appeared book*) but not those of unergatives (**a hard-worked lawyer*) and transitives (**a much-painted artist*) (B. Levin and Rappaport 1986, Rappaport Hovav and B. Levin 1992). In contrast, *-er* nominals refer to the S-Structure subjects of unergatives and transitives but not to those of unaccusatives and passives (B. Levin and Rappaport 1988). Similarly C. Rosen (1981) and Perlmutter (1989), among others, argue that Italian participial absolutes can be predicated of S-Structure subjects of unaccusative and passive verbs but not of S-Structure subjects of transitive and unergative verbs. C. Rosen (1984) also mentions voice marking in Albanian, citing Hubbard (1980): unaccusative and passive verbs share a voice-marking morpheme, which is lacking on transitive and unergative verbs. The existence of such phenomena provides strong support for the syntactic approach, since, by hypothesis, unaccusative verbs and passive verbs appear in the same syntactic configurations, and it is difficult to find a semantic property shared by all passive and unaccusative verbs, a point also emphasized by Burzio (1986). Proponents of the semantic approach would have to claim that the objects of transitive verbs and the subjects of unaccusative verbs share a single semantic property. On Van Valin's semantic approach to unaccusativity, all such phenomena make reference to verbs taking an argument with the macrorole undergoer, but with no argument taking the macrorole actor. Van Valin shows that the notion "undergoer" is not equivalent to the notion "direct object," since, for example, the object of a multiargument activity verb such as *eat* is a direct object but not an undergoer. Be this as it may, it seems to us misleading to claim that the notion "undergoer" is semantic, since it cannot be reduced to any single semantic notion.

Rather, it can be characterized as a generalization over a number of specific semantic roles; the undergoer is chosen based on an algorithm that makes reference to these specific semantic roles. Therefore, it seems to us that such phenomena strongly support the syntactic approach.

But the semantic approach has been motivated by a second kind of unaccusative mismatch, which highlights the fact that most unaccusative diagnostics do not single out the sole argument of all unaccusative verbs and the D-Structure objects of all passive verbs. This kind of mismatch involves the existence of two or more apparent unaccusative diagnostics that single out distinct (but not necessarily disjoint) semantically coherent classes of verbs. This type of mismatch can be exemplified with data from Dutch. Zaenen (1993) shows that two purported diagnostics of unaccusativity in Dutch turn out to be sensitive to two different semantic features. Prenominal perfect participles are usually said to modify the S-Structure subjects of unaccusative verbs, as in (6), but not unergative verbs, as in (7).

(6)   de gevallen/(pas) gearriveerde jongen
      the fallen/(just) arrived   boy
      (Zaenen 1993:140, (42))

(7)   *de gewerkte/getelefoneerde man
       the worked/phoned   man
      (Zaenen 1993:140, (41))

It turns out, however, that according to Zaenen these participles may modify the subjects of telic intransitive verbs, a set of verbs that turns out to be a subclass of the unaccusative verbs, but not the subjects of atelic intransitive verbs. (English shows a similar pattern (B. Levin and Rappaport 1989).) Thus, the following example involving an atelic verb that is classified as unaccusative by other diagnostics is unacceptable:

(8)   *De gebleven jongen
       the remained boy
      (Zaenen 1993:141, (45a))

On the other hand, in Dutch impersonal passivization is supposed to be impossible with unaccusative verbs (Perlmutter 1978), but Zaenen argues that only verbs whose subjects do not show "protagonist control," a term introduced by McLendon (1978:4), fail to undergo impersonal passivization, whether they are independently considered to be unaccusative, as in (9), or unergative, as in (10), on the basis of other diagnostics.

(9) *In dat ziekenhuis werd er   (door veel patienten) gestorven.
    in that hospital   was there by many patients   died
    'In that hospital there was died by many patients.'
    (Zaenen 1993:131, (8b))

(10) *Er werd (door de man) gebloed.
     there was by the man   bled
     'There was bled by the man.'
     (Zaenen 1993:131, (7b))

If the explanation for these two diagnostics lies in the syntactic configuration required by the verbs, then such diagnostics are not expected to distinguish between semantically coherent subclasses of verbs. From mismatches of this sort, some researchers have concluded that a syntactically encoded distinction between unaccusative and unergative verbs is unnecessary and that the distinction between unaccusative and unergative verbs is purely semantic, and not syntactic; see, for example, Napoli 1988 for discussion along these lines with respect to English.

On the semantic approach, the nonhomogeneous behavior of intransitive verbs stems from the fact that some constructions are compatible with verbs with certain types of meanings, and others are compatible with verbs with other types of meanings. The bifurcation in the intransitive class, then, does not reduce to any syntactic feature of the verbs, but follows from the compatibility of different semantically defined verb classes with the semantic constraints on the different constructions. In this respect, intransitive verbs are no different from transitive verbs, some of which are compatible with certain constructions and others of which are not. Moreover, the same kind of bifurcation is expected *within* the unaccusative class. Since each construction is associated with its own semantic constraints, there is no reason to assume that all diagnostic constructions should differentiate among the intransitive verbs in the same way. One construction may distinguish telic from atelic verbs; a second may distinguish agentive from nonagentive verbs. Therefore, a single verb may be classfied as "unaccusative" by one diagnostic but as "unergative" by another. In this way, the semantic approach explains why most diagnostics single out semantically coherent subclasses of verbs, while allowing for certain types of mismatches. (See also Dowty 1991 for related discussion.)

On our approach to unaccusativity, it is not surprising that the verbs selected by various diagnostics can receive a proper semantic characterization. After all, we argue that the syntactic classification of verbs is semantically determined. But the fact that the verb classes can be given a semantic characterization does not preclude the attribution of common syntactic properties to all unaccusative verbs. In fact, the original motivation for the Unaccusative Hypothesis was the recognition that some diagnostics are *explained* by the postulation of two syntactically distinct subclasses of the intransitive verbs, an aspect of the syntactic approach that proponents of the semantic approach largely ignore.

The choice between the two approaches rests on showing whether there is any need to postulate a syntactic difference between the unaccusative and unergative verbs. For the proponents of the semantic approach, this means demonstrating an explanatory connection between the semantic classification of a verb and the diagnostics, thus obviating the need for a syntactic encoding of the distinction between unaccusative and unergative verbs. At the heart of the semantic approach is the proposal that certain constructions, by virtue of their meaning, "select" for verbs belonging to certain semantic classes. But in order to show that the semantic approach is to be preferred over the syntactic approach, it is not sufficient to show that the class of verbs selected by each of the diagnostic constructions can be given a semantic characterization; it must also be shown that the semantic characterization will explain the compatibility of the members of a verb class with that construction. For example, in chapter 3 we argue that although the verbs that participate in the causative alternation can be characterized semantically, there is a syntactic component to the explanation of why just these verbs participate in the alternation as they do; if this account is correct, it constitutes support for the syntactic approach. The presence of syntactic and semantic components to the explanations of several of the diagnostics we examine in this book suggests that a verb's ability to be found in the unaccusative syntactic configuration may be a necessary, but not a sufficient, condition for the verb to manifest some property. This reflects the fact that many constructions are also associated with their own semantic constraints. For example, although resultative phrases in English may be predicated of subjects of unaccusative, but not unergative, verbs, there is a semantically defined subset of unaccusative verbs whose subjects cannot have resultative phrases predicated of them for independent reasons, as we show in section 2.3.2.

Moreover, the semantic properties of the verb may be a necessary, but not a sufficient, condition for passing an unaccusative diagnostic. Such a case is provided by auxiliary selection in Dutch. Both Van Valin (1990) and Zaenen (1993) discuss auxiliary choice as a diagnostic that is sensitive to a semantic property, namely, telicity. The claim is that all and only telic verbs select the auxiliary *zijn*, the Dutch equivalent of English *be*. Although the connection between the syntactic properties of unaccusative verbs and their selection of the *be* auxiliary in several languages is not well understood (Grimshaw 1987; though see Burzio 1986, Vikner 1991, among others, for some proposals), Everaert (1992) points out that even on a descriptive level the generalization linking auxiliary selection to telicity, as close as it is to being correct, is not entirely accurate. Everaert shows that, at least in Dutch, a sentence that meets the criterion of telicity can nonetheless contain the auxiliary *hebben*, the Dutch counterpart of English *have* and Italian *avere*, if the sentence contains either a light verb construction, as in (11a), or an idiom that involves a verb plus object, as in (11b).

(11) a. Het vliegtuig heeft een landing gemaakt.
         the plane   has   a landing   made
         'The plane has made a landing.'
         (Everaert 1992:4, (12a))
     b. Hij heeft zich uit de voeten   gemaakt.
        he   has   self out of the feet made
        'He fled.'
        (Everaert 1992:7, (24b))

The contrast between the selection of the auxiliary *hebben* 'have' in the light verb construction in (11a) and the selection of the auxiliary *zijn* 'be' in a near paraphrase involving a simple verb with the same meaning in (12) illustrates this point.

(12) Het vliegtuig is geland.
     the plane   is landed
     'The plane has landed.'
     (Everaert 1992:4, (11a))

Therefore, even if telicity is the meaning component relevant to auxiliary selection, it is applicable only if the verb phrase is intransitive in a purely *syntactic* way. That is, it is necessary, but not sufficient, that a verb be telic if it is to select *zijn* 'be'.[8]

Summarizing the difference between the syntactic and semantic approaches to unaccusativity, the syntactic approach takes unaccusativity to be a unified phenomenon: all unaccusative verbs, no matter what their semantic class, share certain syntactic properties (the selection of a direct internal argument, the lack of an external argument, and the inability to assign accusative Case). Not all unaccusative verbs are expected to give positive results with respect to all unaccusative diagnostics, because, as we mentioned above, an unaccusative classification is often a necessary, but not a sufficient, condition for a verb to test positive with respect to certain unaccusative diagnostics. Despite these differences, all unaccusative verbs share a particular set of syntactic properties. On the semantic approach, in contrast, unaccusativity is not a unified phenomenon, and a single verb can test as "unaccusative" according to one diagnostic and as "unergative" according to another diagnostic, a point also discussed by Dowty (1991).

1.2.3 Further Methodological Considerations

The discussion of the syntactic and semantic approaches to unaccusativity underscores that, as in any area of linguistics, there are various methodological considerations that must be kept in mind in making claims about the viability of a particular approach to unaccusativity. The complexity of unaccusative phenomena coupled with the fact that unaccusative phenomena involve the interface between lexical semantics and syntax means that care is especially necessary in this respect. In particular, it is difficult to make claims about unaccusativity in a given language unless both the syntax and the lexical semantics of the language are well understood. In this section we mention some additional methodological considerations that must be taken into account in investigating the nature of unaccusativity.

First—and possibly most obviously—in making a claim about the unaccusative or unergative status of a given verb, the diagnostic used to make the classification must be a legitimate diagnostic. A valid unaccusative diagnostic is one that tests for a syntactic property whose explanation is tied to the unaccusative syntactic configuration. (Furthermore, even diagnostics that receive a syntactic explanation need to be carefully evaluated to be sure that they test for what they are claimed to test for.) After all, unaccusativity as we define it is a syntactic property, even if we do claim that it is semantically predictable. It is precisely because we are using unaccusativity to explore the mapping between lexical semantics and syntax that it is important that we provide a syntactic means of identifying unaccusative verbs, so that we have an independent check on the hypotheses we present concerning the nature of the semantic determination of unaccusativity.

Some purported unaccusative diagnostics, especially those with no inherent connection to direct objecthood, may turn out not to be diagnostics for unaccusativity. For instance, C. Rosen (1984), drawing on Davies 1981, cites verb agreement as an unaccusative diagnostic in the Muskogean language Choctaw. On this basis, she points out that the Choctaw counterpart of English *die* is unergative. Martin (1991), on the basis of a thorough study of agreement in another Muskogean language, Creek, argues that the evidence that had been used to link verb agreement to underlying grammatical relations is not strong. Instead, he argues that it simply tests for a semantic property of the verb.[9] He concludes that verb agreement should not be considered a valid unaccusative diagnostic and that therefore the Choctaw data do not pose a problem for the Unaccusative Hypothesis.

It is important, then, to reevaluate purported diagnostics before using them to draw conclusions about verb classification. In this book we will reevaluate three diagnostics in depth, rejecting one of them in the process. We will also use several other diagnostics whose status we believe to have been well established, recognizing that ideally these too should receive further scrutiny.

There is one more point we want to make in this section. Although it is desirable to look at a range of languages to test the generality of claims being made about unaccusativity, and although our understanding of unaccusativity has benefited immensely from cross-linguistic studies, it is equally important when undertaking a study of the interface between lexical semantics and syntax to restrict the discussion to languages the researcher is familiar with. Because of the subtle judgments about verb meanings that are required to uncover the syntactically relevant components of verb meaning and the intricate patterns of behavior that need to be examined as part of this process, a knowledge of the languages under consideration that goes beyond what most dictionaries and reference grammars offer is necessary. For this reason, we have focused our investigation on a few languages we are familiar with and have given the most weight to data from English. We hope that our study will establish a general research strategy that can be extended to other languages as well.

1.3 Deep versus Surface Unaccusativity

Research on unaccusativity initially focused on the fact that the single arguments of some intransitive verbs show object-like properties despite being expressed like subjects of transitive verbs at S-Structure. Subsequent research revealed purported unaccusative constructions in which the single argument of certain intransitive verbs not only shows object-like properties but also is apparently expressed like the object of a transitive verb. In Italian, for example, there is evidence that the sole argument of an unaccusative verb can appear as a direct object at S-Structure (Belletti 1988, Belletti and Rizzi 1981, Burzio 1986, among others). The evidence comes from a number of grammatical phenomena, including *ne*-cliticization. For example, in Italian the single argument of an unaccusative verb such as *arrivare* 'arrive' can appear either before the verb, as in (13a), or after the verb, as in (13b).

(13) a. Molti esperti arriveranno.
         many experts will arrive
         'Many experts will arrive.'
     b. Arriveranno molti esperti.
         will arrive   many experts
         'Many experts will arrive.'
         (Burzio 1986:21, (4i))

Verbs such as *arrivare* 'arrive' permit *ne*-cliticization to apply to their sole argument, but only when it appears after the verb—that is, only if it remains in what appears to be surface direct object position.

(14) a. Ne   arriveranno molti.
         of them will arrive   many
         'Many of them will arrive.'
         (Burzio 1986:22, (5i))
     b. *Molti ne   arriveranno.
         many of them will arrive
         (Burzio 1986:23, (7c))

Ne-cliticization, then, is a diagnostic that applies only if the argument of the unaccusative verb remains in a postverbal position throughout the derivation. It contrasts with a diagnostic such as auxiliary selection, which applies regardless of the surface position of the argument. For example, the verb *arrivare* 'arrive' selects the auxiliary *essere* 'be' independently of the surface position of its argument.

(15) a. Gianni è già   arrivato.
         Gianni is already arrived
         'Gianni has already arrived.'

b. È arrivato Gianni.
   is arrived Gianni
   'Gianni has arrived.'

As this discussion suggests, the unaccusative diagnostics themselves are of two types. We call diagnostics such as *ne*-cliticization *diagnostics of surface unaccusativity* and those such as auxiliary selection *diagnostics of deep unaccusativity*. In English surface unaccusativity is manifested only in the *there*-insertion construction (*There appeared a ship on the horizon*) and the locative inversion construction (*Into the room came a man*). In both constructions the single argument of an intransitive verb appears to be in the syntactic position of the object of a transitive verb (see, among others, Burzio 1986, Hoekstra and Mulder 1990, and L. Levin 1986 for discussion of *there*-insertion, and Bresnan 1993, Bresnan and Kanerva 1989, Coopmans 1989, Hoekstra and Mulder 1990, and L. Levin 1986, as well as chapter 6, for discussion of locative inversion). Among the unaccusative diagnostics posited for English, the resultative construction qualifies as a diagnostic of deep unaccusativity. It is the D-Structure status of the argument of an intransitive verb that determines whether or not that verb will be found in this construction (see chapter 2 for an extensive discussion of this construction). An explanatory theory of unaccusativity should predict which unaccusative diagnostics work in which way. In chapter 6 we suggest that phenomena involving discourse function and relations involving quantifier scope will show properties of diagnostics of surface unaccusativity, since these are relations that are set at S-Structure. Diagnostics that rest on properties like θ-role assignment or the building of compositional semantics will show properties of deep unaccusativity.

But there is another property of surface unaccusative diagnostics that needs to be emphasized. The constructions that are sensitive to surface unaccusativity are typically restricted to a subclass of the unaccusative verbs: verbs of existence, such as *exist, remain*, and *thrive*, and verbs of appearance, such as *appear, arise*, and *emerge* (see Kimball 1973, Milsark 1974, Penhallurick 1984, among others, and chapter 6 for discussion of this restriction as it applies to locative inversion and *there*-insertion). For example, verbs of change of state, which we argue in chapters 3 and 4 to be unaccusative, are rarely compatible with the English surface unaccusative constructions.

(16) a. *On the streets of Chicago melted a lot of snow.
     b. *There melted a lot of snow on the streets of Chicago.

This property is not all that surprising since many unaccusative diagnostics are restricted to semantically coherent subsets of the unaccusative class. However, what is problematic is that, as we will show in chapter 6, many unergative verbs also appear in the locative inversion construction in English. There we argue that the appearance of unergative verbs in the locative inversion construction is not due to what we have termed variable behavior. Thus, the dual classification of some verbs as both unaccusative and unergative cannot be used to resolve the problem of unergative verbs in the locative inversion construction.

In chapter 6 we argue that there is in fact little evidence that locative inversion actually diagnoses unaccusativity in English, and that there are problems with considering this construction to be an unaccusative diagnostic. Instead, we attribute the restrictions on the verbs found in this construction, which are reminiscent of, but not exactly like, those associated with unaccusative diagnostics, to the discourse function of the construction. Essentially, the discourse function requires a verb with a single argument in postverbal position. We show that this assumption helps explain certain properties of the construction that are otherwise left unexplained. In the conclusion to chapter 6 we speculate that all diagnostics of surface unaccusativity are not true unaccusative diagnostics, but are simply sensitive to certain postverbal subjects of intransitive verbs. Discourse considerations determine both the S-Structure position of the subject and the classes of verbs that can appear in such constructions. This suggestion stems from the observation that phenomena in other languages that qualify as diagnostics of surface unaccusativity tend to be restricted to the same subclasses of unaccusative verbs as locative inversion, while at the same time being open to a range of unergative verbs.[10]

1.4 Assumptions about Lexical Representations

In this section we set out the assumptions about the structure of the lexicon and the nature of lexical representation that we presuppose throughout this book. Rather than attempting to develop a full theory of the lexicon, we make only those assumptions that are necessary for the issues under investigation. We assume that each verb is associated with two lexical representations: a lexical semantic representation and a lexical syntactic representation. The lexical semantic representation, sometimes called a *lexical conceptual structure* (Hale and Keyser 1986, 1987, Jackendoff 1990) or simply a *conceptual structure* (Jackendoff 1983), encodes the syntactically relevant aspects of verb meaning, whereas the lexical syntactic representation—typically called an *argument structure*—encodes the syntactically relevant argument-taking properties of a verb. We discuss each representation in more detail below. Given that our goal is to show that unaccusativity is semantically determined but syntactically represented, we are particularly interested in those aspects of the lexical semantic representation that are relevant to the statement of the linking rules.

We begin with a brief discussion of the lexical syntactic representation. As just stated, we assume that each verb is associated with an argument structure that encodes the syntactically relevant argument-taking properties of that verb, and that this argument structure is *not* a representation of the verb's meaning. The conception of argument structure that we adopt is set out in Rappaport and B. Levin 1988. In particular, we assume that these representations allow distinctions to be made between the external argument and the internal arguments of a verb (Williams 1981), with a further distinction among the internal arguments according to whether they are direct or indirect (Marantz 1984). The external argument is expressed in the syntax external to the VP headed by the verb selecting that argument, and the internal arguments are projected inside the VP; the direct internal argument is realized as the argument that is the sister of, and hence governed by, the verb.[11] Following much current work (Grimshaw 1990, Rappaport and B. Levin 1988, Zubizarreta 1987, among others), we assume that the positions in argument structures are not referred to by θ-role (semantic role) labels since the argument structure is a purely syntactic representation. For instance, the argument structure we would posit for the verb *put* would be as follows:

(17) $e, x \langle y, P_{loc} z \rangle$

The three variables in this structure indicate that *put* is a triadic verb. The variable outside the brackets represents the external argument; the variables inside the brackets represent the internal arguments. The first internal argument is the direct internal argument; the other is an indirect internal argument, which is assigned its θ-role by a locative preposition (represented as P_{loc}). We assume that the argument structure contains an "event" position, as proposed, for example, by Higginbotham (1985), Rothstein (1983), and Schein (1985), following ideas of Davidson's (1967); this position is the e in (17). We assume, in addition, that the information in a verb's argument structure, together with the Projection

Principle and the θ-Criterion, determine the syntactic configuration that a verb is found in. Thus, we see the relation between argument structure and the D-Structure syntactic representation as being "trivial." In this last point we differ, for example, from Grimshaw (1990), who proposes that argument structure is not isomorphic to D-Structure.

There is no substantial consensus on the nature of a lexical semantic representation, either with respect to its form or with respect to the elements that it needs to represent. We do not try to articulate a complete theory of lexical semantic representation here; however, we do make some important assumptions about the nature of lexical organization, which the lexical semantic representation must be chosen to accommodate. We review these below.

One of the more striking properties of the lexicon is that many aspects of a verb's behavior, including the possible expressions of its arguments, appear to be determined by its membership in semantically coherent verb classes (for discussion, see Fillmore 1971, Guerssel et al. 1985, B. Levin 1993, Pinker 1989, among others). Given this observation, it is only reasonable to assume that many of the properties of verbs need not be learned verb by verb but can be learned for a particular verb class as a whole. However, the verb classes cross-classify in intricate ways in terms of their syntactic behavior, and this extensive cross-classification suggests that verb classes themselves are not primitive, but arise because their members share certain basic components of meaning. These are the syntactically relevant components of meaning we have already referred to. The generalizations that implicate semantically coherent verb classes are probably best stated in terms of these components of meaning, just as phonological rules are stated in terms of the basic building blocks of distinctive features. Any lexical semantic representation that is adopted must be able to accommodate these properties of verbs and the classes that they belong to.

Explicit representations of verb meaning have generally been of two types: semantic role lists and predicate decompositions (B. Levin 1994). In the former, the meaning of a verb is reduced to a list of semantic roles that the arguments bear to the verb. In the latter, a verb's meaning is represented in terms of a fixed set of primitive predicates; the semantic roles can be identified with particular argument positions associated with these predicates. It appears that the syntactically relevant components of meaning can be better expressed in predicate-centered approaches to lexical semantic representation (for additional discussion, see Gropen et al. 1991,

Jackendoff 1987, Pinker 1989, Rappaport and B. Levin 1988, among others). In order to make our discussion more concrete, many of the properties that we require in a lexical semantic representation are illustrated here with a representation that takes the form of a predicate decomposition, but it is not clear that this is the only type of representation that would meet our requirements. Any lexical semantic representation will be consistent with our approach if it recognizes that verb meanings include certain common elements that tie verbs together into semantically defined classes, but at the same time allows for the cross-classification of verbs. These considerations impose certain requirements on the "grain size" of these elements: they must be neither so finely chosen as to prevent the identification of the relevant verb classes, nor so coarsely chosen as to prevent the cross-classification of verbs. In addition, the representation must provide for the encoding of the localized differences in meaning that distinguish among the members of the classes.

A lexical semantic representation that takes the form of a predicate decomposition involves two basic types of primitive elements: primitive predicates and constants. A verb's meaning is represented using members of a fixed set of primitive predicates, together with constants—typically chosen from a limited set of semantic types—that either fill argument positions in these predicates or act as modifiers of these predicates. A verb's arguments are represented by the open argument positions associated with these predicates. As an illustration of these points, consider the possible predicate decomposition given in (19) for the intransitive, noncausative use of the verb *break* illustrated in (18).

(18) The window broke.

(19) Noncausative *break:* [y BECOME *BROKEN*]

In this representation BECOME represents a potential primitive, and *BROKEN* is a constant that represents the element of meaning that sets the state of being broken apart from other states. On this approach, the semantic relations between verbs and their arguments are defined with respect to the subcomponents in the decomposition (see, for example, Jackendoff 1972, 1987). Typically, predicate decompositions are selected so that verbs belonging to the same semantic class have common substructures in their decompositions. (This assumption also allows the set of primitive predicates used to be restricted in size; ideally, the same primitive predicates might recur in different combinations as well.) For example, all verbs of change of state have in common the substructure consisting of the primitive BECOME, with a constant naming a particular state filling the second argument of BECOME.

(20) Noncausative verb of change of state: $[y$ BECOME $STATE]$

Such templates are what Pinker (1989) calls "thematic cores"; we will refer to them as *lexical semantic templates*. Pinker identifies a dozen or so of these templates.

To take another example, denominal verbs such as *pocket* and *butter* are said to share the same basic decompositional structure—the structure associated with a verb of putting, illustrated in (21)—but to differ in both the choice of constants and the positions that they fill, as shown in (22) (Carter 1976, Jackendoff 1983, 1990).[12]

(21) Verb of putting: $[x$ CAUSE $[y$ BECOME $P_{loc}\ z]]$

(22) a. *butter:* $[x$ CAUSE $[BUTTER$ BECOME $P_{loc}\ z]]$
   b. *pocket:* $[x$ CAUSE $[y$ BECOME $P_{loc}\ POCKET]]$

Alternatively, the constant can represent a manner modifier to a predicate. For instance, consider verbs of manner of motion. The verb *amble* has the basic predicate decomposition associated with such a verb, but this decomposition includes a manner modifier that represents what makes this verb different from other verbs of manner of motion such as *stroll* and *wander*. We do not give an example of such a representation; but see Pinker 1989 for one illustration of how such modifiers could be included in predicate decompositions. Pinker (1989) and Jackendoff (1983, 1990) discuss the types of constants that can be found in predicate decompositions. Not only can these constants be elements representing entities in the world, but they can also be what Jackendoff (1990) refers to as "3-D model structures." These structures can be used not only to encode objects but also to represent what Jackendoff calls "action patterns."

Much of the research on lexical semantic representation has stressed the basic structures defined by the primitive predicates. Such structures effectively define semantic classes of verbs and determine the syntactic properties of the members of the verb classes. For example, by abstracting away from the templates in (22), we can set out the basic templates that would be characteristic of other verbs in the same classes as *butter* and *pocket*.

(23) a. $[x$ CAUSE $[STUFF$ BECOME $P_{loc}\ z]]$ (cf. (22a))
   b. $[x$ CAUSE $[y$ BECOME $P_{loc}\ LOCATION]]$ (cf. (22b))

The constant in a verb's lexical semantic representation is what distinguishes that verb from other verbs of the same semantic type (i.e., verbs sharing the same lexical semantic template). The constant also determines —or, maybe more accurately, restricts—the verb's semantic class membership in the sense that certain constants have features that make them compatible only with certain positions in particular lexical semantic templates; we have indicated this by the labels *STUFF* and *LOCATION* in (23), which are intended to represent the restrictions on these particular open positions. For instance, if the constant represents a physical object that serves as a container, such as a pocket, then it is likely to turn up in templates of the type in (23b), rather than those of the type in (23a). Given this function of the constant, it is not surprising that the "name" of a verb—the phonological form used to label a verb's meaning—is often morphologically derived from or identical to the name of the constant itself. As pointed out by Carter (1976), the use of constants provides the decompositional approach to lexical semantic representation with much of its power. It is precisely by allowing for constants to fill selected positions in a decomposition that it is possible to give a finite characterization of the possible verb meanings that might be found in a language, while allowing for the fact that new verbs can be coined.

We believe that studying the ways in which a language allows verbal lexical semantic templates to be paired with phonological forms provides the key to understanding the variable behavior verbs mentioned in section 1.2.1. There are many departures from a one-to-one association between a meaning and a phonological form: sometimes one meaning is associated with several phonological forms (synonymy), and more often—and more relevant to our concerns—several meanings are associated with one form (polysemy). We are not interested in instances of accidental polysemy (homonymy), but in instances of more systematic polysemy, what Apresjan (1973, 1992) has called *regular polysemy*. This kind of polysemy is the source of variable behavior verbs. In the remainder of this section we raise some issues concerning how the different verb meanings that a particular theory of lexical semantic representation makes available come to be associated with verb names—that is, how certain phonological forms come to be attached as labels to particular verbal semantic concepts, including how some phonological forms come to be attached to more than one verbal semantic concept.[13]

The question of the pairing of verb meanings and verb names is not often systematically or explicitly discussed (the work by Talmy (1975,

1985, 1991) is an exception). When it is discussed, it surfaces in work on polysemy where the following question is being raised: what are the meanings associated with a particular verb name? Is there in fact more than one meaning? We believe that a better understanding of how verb names and verb meanings are paired can be achieved by asking the reverse question: given the verb meanings that a theory of lexical semantic representation makes available, what principles, if any, constrain the ways in which names can be attached as labels to these meanings? For example, which meanings are compatible with a monomorphemic name? Which meanings may—or even must—be associated with a morphologically complex name? Do languages differ regarding the lexical semantic representations that they can associate names with? (This last question is the one that Talmy asks in his important work on lexicalization patterns.) And finally, there is the question that is of particular interest here given the existence of variable behavior verbs: when can two meanings be associated with the same name? We cannot provide a full treatment of these questions, since this is relatively unexplored territory. We attempt only to make some preliminary suggestions about the forms that their answers might take as they pertain to the goal of this book. We hope to investigate these issues further in future research.

A fully articulated theory of lexical semantic representation should be a generative theory that allows for the characterization of all possible verb meanings (see Carter 1976 and Pustejovsky 1991a for discussion of this conception of the lexicon). Many of these possible meanings will be meanings of actual verbs in a language. Those meanings that are actualized need to be associated with a verb name. Putting sound symbolism aside, the association of a morphologically simple phonological form with a particular verbal semantic concept is to a large extent an arbitrary process; for example, there seems to be no reason why the phonological form of the verb *buy* couldn't have been associated with the meaning associated with the verb *sell* and vice versa.[14] Nevertheless, it appears that there are some constraints involved both in determining the choice of names and in governing when two lexical semantic representations can share the same name.

As noted earlier, it is the constants in the lexical semantic representation that differentiate among members of a particular semantic class of verbs. In some sense, the constants serve to identify a particular member of a verb class. There are whole classes of verbs whose members differ in meaning precisely with respect to the choice of constant, and it is therefore not surprising that in such cases the verb name is derived from that constant. With respect to English, this can be illustrated in several ways.

First, many English verbs are zero-related to nouns that actually denote the content of the constant. For instance, the words *whistle* and *creak* name not only verbs of sound emission but also the nouns that denote the particular sounds that distinguish one of these verbs of sound emission from the other and that presumably serve as the constant in the lexical semantic representation of such verbs. Similarly, many verbs of change of state, such as *dry*, *empty*, and *warm*, are deadjectival, taking their name from the adjective denoting the state whose change typifies that verb, as illustrated in the sample lexical semantic representations for the noncausative, intransitive uses of such verbs in (24), which are all instances of the lexical semantic template in (20), repeated here as (25).

(24) a. *dry:* $[y$ BECOME $DRY]$
     b. *empty:* $[y$ BECOME $EMPTY]$
     c. *warm:* $[y$ BECOME $WARM]$

(25) Noncausative verb of change of state: $[y$ BECOME $STATE]$

Second, English has a word formation process known as zero-derivation or conversion; this is the process that creates the verb *modem* from the noun *modem*. This process is a way of associating names with new verbs whose meanings are of certain semantic types: meanings in which the nouns that the verbs take their name from appear as constants in certain designated lexical semantic templates. We do not try to characterize these lexical semantic templates here. What is important is that the meanings of such verbs all involve conventional uses of the entity denoted by the noun, and, as described by Clark and Clark (1979), these conventional uses are determined by the ontological status of the noun—whether it denotes a location, a profession, an instrument, stuff, and so on. It is clearly the nouns, which presumably serve as the constants, that determine verb names. More often than not when there is a verb that has a meaning of the appropriate type, it takes its name from the constant, but there are exceptions (e.g., *drive* rather than **car*, *row* rather than **oar*).

Overt morphological markers may be involved in the creation of certain types of verb names. In English, for example, the prefix *de-* combines with a noun to form a name for a verb that involves the removal of the entity denoted by that noun from a location, as in *deice a plane* or *defuzz a sweater*. (Not all verbs of this type are created with the prefix *de-*; conversion can be used to create verbs of removal from certain nouns, when there is an inalienable possession relationship between the location and located entity, as in *bone* or *core*.)

Sometimes, because of its properties, a single constant can plausibly be associated with more than one lexical semantic template, and to the extent that verbs often take their name from the constant in their lexical semantic representation, the result is that more than one lexical semantic representation will have the same name. The association of a single name with multiple lexical semantic representations due to a common constant is the source of polysemous verbs. These are the variable behavior verbs that we have been discussing. To take a simple example involving the formation of denominal verbs, the same noun might denote an entity that is conventionally either added to or removed from a surface; accordingly, that entity might give its name to either the action of adding or the action of removing that entity. As an illustration, consider an instrument that can be used to put or remove stuff from locations; such an instrument can give its name to the actions involving its use to either add or remove stuff from a surface. The verb *shovel*, for example, shows these two uses; it can be used either as a verb of removal (*shovel the snow off the walk*) or as a verb of putting (*shovel the sand into the truck*). The lexical semantic templates associated with a single verb name can be quite different; the two senses of *shovel* are "opposites," although both senses of the verb involve changing the location of a substance with respect to some location. In some instances the association of a constant with more than one lexical semantic template may be idiosyncratic, but in others a whole class of constants may qualify for association with more than one template because of their inherent nature. Thus, the association of *shovel* with two templates is not an accident, since there are other verbs like it, including *ladle*, *rake*, *spoon*, and *sponge*.

As these examples show, the members of a set of lexical semantic representations that involve different lexical semantic templates but the same constant can have the same name. In contrast, we are not aware of any instances in which a single name is associated with multiple instantiations of a single lexical semantic template that differ in the choice of constant. Interestingly, it is verbs that share a lexical semantic template but differ in the associated constant that form classes whose members show the same expression of arguments. For example, all verbs of removal share the same lexical semantic template and express their arguments like the verb *shovel* in its removal sense. In contrast, when a single verb name is associated with several lexical semantic representations that are based on different lexical semantic templates but share the same constant, each of the pairings of a particular verb name with a lexical semantic representation is associated with its own distinct argument expression. For instance, *shovel* expresses its arguments one way when it is a verb of removal and another way when it is a verb of putting.

What will emerge from our study of variable behavior verbs in chapter 5 is that there are general patterns of multiple association of lexical semantic templates with verb names. In particular, whole classes of verbs tend to be associated with the same range of multiple meanings. These patterns can be described by statements of the following form:

(26) A verb in semantic class x is also a member of semantic class y.

Partly in response to earlier versions of this work, this approach has been criticized by a number of linguists (A. Goldberg 1994a, Grimshaw 1993, 1994, Hoekstra 1992, Hoekstra and Mulder 1990, S. Rosen 1993, among others), since these researchers would like to see these multiple associations effected without recourse to lexical rules. We discuss this issue at greater length in chapter 5. The approach we take here is that it is necessary to have some lexical statement indicating the patterns of multiple association between verb names and lexical semantic templates that a language allows. We show that this lexical approach makes slightly different predictions from the nonlexical approach, and our initial investigations suggest that the evidence favors the lexical approach. However, it would clearly be preferable if these lexical statements did not refer to semantic verb classes because, by hypothesis, verb classes themselves are not primitive, but are derived from the combinations of more basic lexical semantic substructures. We will show in chapter 5 that there is evidence for this, since lexical statements in terms of more basic meaning components make real predictions about the patterns of variable behavior verbs attested across languages, predictions that appear to be borne out. Although we are fairly certain that the correct approach to the lexical statements governing multiple verb classification will avoid explicit reference to verb classes, we do not develop a theory of these lexical statements, since it is beyond the scope of this book. We hope that our initial investigations of the phenomenon of variable behavior verbs will provide an impetus for further investigations.

In concluding the discussion of the relationship between verb names and verb meanings, we want to point out that there is also an important cross-linguistic dimension to the naming of verb meanings, which a full account of this relationship cannot ignore. Languages seem to have different constraints on the kinds of verb meanings that can have morphologically simple names associated with them. This issue has been investigated most thoroughly in Talmy's (1985, 1991) work on *lexicalization patterns*, generalizations concerning the types of meaning that can be associated with the verbs of a language, whether morphologically simple or not. We will briefly discuss some cross-linguistic divergences in chapter 5 in the context of our discussion of variable behavior verbs. We hope once again that this discussion, though brief, will stimulate further research on this topic.

1.5   Overview of the Book

The goal of this book is to provide support for Perlmutter's hypothesis that unaccusativity is syntactically represented but semantically determined. To achieve this goal, we provide evidence bearing on both parts of this hypothesis. To show that unaccusativity is syntactically represented, we demonstrate the existence of certain syntactic phenomena whose explanation rests on the unaccusative syntactic configuration. To show that unaccusativity is semantically determined, we introduce a set of linking rules that identify the components of verb meaning that give rise to an unaccusative or an unergative classification.

We begin in chapter 2 by giving evidence for the syntactic encoding of unaccusativity. This chapter provides an extended study of one unaccusative diagnostic, the English resultative construction. In this chapter we examine the diagnostic carefully and show that the postulation of a syntactic difference between unaccusative and unergative verbs can indeed explain the difference in the way the two types of verbs pattern in this construction. We also take a careful look at the available semantic analyses of the construction and show that they cannot explain the patterns of behavior with the same success. Two more unaccusative diagnostics that we study in detail are the causative alternation in chapter 3 and locative inversion in chapter 6. In the first instance we show that there is a syntactic component to the account of this diagnostic; in the second we show that the evidence for taking the construction to be a diagnostic is not convincing.

In chapters 3 and 4 we look more closely at the lexical semantics–syntax interface as it pertains to unaccusativity, providing evidence pertinent to the semantic factors that determine unaccusativity. We argue for the validity of the causative alternation as an unaccusative diagnostic, while providing for a lexical semantic characterization of the verbs that participate in the alternation. We show that unergative verbs that show up in causative pairs do not represent the same phenomenon as the alternating unaccusative verbs. Finally, we show that there are two major subclasses of the unaccusative verbs, which have distinct lexical semantic characterizations.

In chapter 4 we present a set of linking rules that classify verbs from the various semantic classes that we have examined as unaccusative or unergative. In this chapter we also discuss the ordering relations between these rules, and we compare the meaning components that figure in these linking rules with those that have figured in other analyses of the semantic underpinnings of unaccusativity.

Building on the results of chapters 3 and 4, we turn in chapter 5 to the problem of variable behavior verbs, a set of verbs that pose an apparent problem for the semantic determination of unaccusativity because they show characteristics of both unaccusative and unergative verbs. We show that in most instances such verbs have two distinct meanings, one associated with an unaccusative and the other with an unergative analysis, and the syntactic behavior of these verbs corresponds to their predicted classification. In this chapter we distinguish between two sources for such variable behavior.

In chapter 6 we turn to locative inversion, a purported unaccusative diagnostic, which differs from the other diagnostics considered in this book in being a surface unaccusative diagnostic. It also differs from the other diagnostics in singling out verbs of appearance and existence rather than verbs of change of state. Even more problematic, it is also found with a wide range of unergative verbs. Although some researchers have maintained that locative inversion is nevertheless an unaccusative diagnostic, we argue that the evidence for its diagnostic status is not convincing. We propose instead that it favors verbs of appearance and existence because of its discourse function. We then show that under certain circumstances, some unergative verbs can fulfill the same discourse function as verbs of appearance and existence, explaining their occurrence in locative inversion. We conclude this chapter with some speculations concerning the nature of apparent diagnostics of surface unaccusativity in general.

Chapter 2

The Anatomy of a Diagnostic: The Resultative Construction

In this chapter we investigate whether there is evidence for the syntactic encoding of the distinction between unaccusative and unergative verbs in English through a close examination of the resultative construction. We examine whether the data involving this construction are better handled by a syntactic account that relies on the syntactic encoding of unaccusativity or a semantic account that does not.

First, we review studies that show how this construction can be used to argue for the syntactic encoding of unaccusativity. These studies have shown that a unified restriction on all resultative constructions, which we call the Direct Object Restriction (DOR), can be maintained assuming an unaccusative analysis of certain intransitive verbs. We then elaborate on both the syntactic and the semantic aspects of previous analyses. We show how the effects of the DOR can be derived from a particular formulation of a familiar linking rule that maps from semantic structure to syntactic structure.

We investigate the distribution of resultative phrases and the syntax of resultative constructions based on transitive, unergative, and unaccusative verbs. A striking fact that emerges from this examination is that the syntax of the resultative construction based on verbs from these three classes is just the syntax of these types of verbs in isolation (assuming unaccusativity), except for the addition of the resultative phrase. We show that our form of the syntactic approach is preferable to the alternative set out by Hoekstra (1988, 1992), which is unable to account for this property of the construction. We also contrast the syntactic approach with two semantic analyses of the resultative construction. These semantic analyses are similar in many respects to our own analysis, which has a substantial semantic component. However, it turns out that there are certain aspects of the construction that have no obvious semantic explanation, although they have a natural syntactic explanation. Furthermore, the semantic account does not predict the syntactic differences between the resultative constructions based on the three syntactic classes of verbs, because, as we will show, the syntax of the construction is not projected from the syntax of the verbs in isolation on the semantic account. We conclude that the syntactic approach, which relies on the syntactic encoding of unaccusativity, provides a more explanatory account of the phenomenon. We also consider why some unaccusative verbs do not appear with resultative phrases, contrary to what is predicted given the DOR.

2.1 The Distribution of Resultative Phrases

A resultative phrase is an XP that denotes the state achieved by the referent of the NP it is predicated of as a result of the action denoted by the verb in the resultative construction. The basic insight that emerges from work on the resultative construction is that a resultative phrase may be predicated of the immediately postverbal NP, but may not be predicated of a subject or of an oblique complement. We call this generalization the *Direct Object Restriction*.[1] The relevance of the resultative paradigm to unaccusativity was first pointed out by Simpson (1983a), as part of a systematic exploration of the properties of the resultative construction. A more recent systematic discussion of resultative constructions with respect to a variety of verb classes is found in the work of Carrier and Randall (1992, in press). Drawing on this and other previous work, we present a complete typology of resultative constructions in English, while simultaneously establishing the validity of the DOR.

2.1.1 Resultative Constructions Based on Transitive Verbs

Resultative phrases may appear with a variety of transitive verbs. Such phrases may be predicated only of the object of a transitive verb, never the subject.

(1) a. Woolite safely soaks all your fine washables clean. (ad)
     b. ... a 1,147 page novel that bores you bandy-legged ... [P. Andrews, "Abandoned in Iran," 28]
     c. ... while she soaps me slippery all over ... [D. Pryce-Jones, *The Afternoon Sun*, 186]
     d. And when her father finally did come home and kiss them, he was like the handsome prince, thought Laura, kissing them all alive. [D. Smith, *Remember This*, 28]

e. The music is violent and mindless, with a fast beat like a crazed parent abusing a child, thrashing it senseless. [B. A. Mason, "A New-Wave Format," 227]

f. Absently, she dipped a finger into the peanut butter and licked it clean. [M. Thurm, *The Way We Live Now*, 66]

Although XPs may be predicated of the subject of a transitive verb, they receive not a resultative interpretation, but what is referred to as a *depictive* interpretation, a term originally due to Halliday (1967). That is, *Julia burned the cookies dirty* cannot mean that Julia got dirty as a result of burning the cookies, but only that she burned the cookies when she was dirty. We are not aware of any counterexamples to the DOR that involve transitive verbs.

2.1.2   Resultative Constructions Based on Unergative Verbs

The DOR predicts that if a verb has no object, then it cannot appear with a resultative phrase. Indeed, unadorned unergative intransitive verbs cannot take resultative phrases, so that (2) cannot mean that Dora got hoarse as a result of shouting.

(2) *Dora shouted hoarse.

It is striking that this meaning can be expressed through the addition of what Simpson (1983a) calls a *fake reflexive* object: (3) means precisely what (2) cannot mean.

(3) Dora shouted herself hoarse.

Unergative verbs cannot be followed by reflexive NPs in the absence of a following resultative phrase (*Dora shouted herself*). As Simpson (1983a) points out, the fake reflexive NP could be viewed as a syntactic device for allowing a resultative phrase to be interpreted as if it were predicated of the subject of an unergative verb, while still conforming to the DOR. That is, the resultative phrase is predicated of a fake reflexive NP, which is itself coreferential with the subject. (4) and (5) illustrate this use of the fake reflexive.

(4) a. We searched the woods and cliffs, yelled ourselves hoarse and imagined you drowned ... [M. Wesley, *A Sensible Life*, 327]

b. Well, the conclusion was that my mistress grumbled herself calm. [E. Brontë, *Wuthering Heights*, 78]

c. The compère stands by grinning awkwardly and the other officers laugh themselves helpless. [P. Lively, *Moon Tiger*, 112]

(5) a. *We yelled hoarse.
    b. *My mistress grumbled calm.
    c. *The officers laugh helpless.

Unergative verbs are also found in a second type of resultative construction where the resultative phrase is again predicated of a postverbal NP; but in this type of construction the NP is not a reflexive pronoun.

(6) a. I ... ruthlessly roused Mr. Contreras by knocking on his door until the dog barked him awake. [S. Paretsky, *Blood Shot*, 183]
    b. You may sleep it [= the unborn baby] quiet again ... [E. Bagnold, *The Squire*, 285]
    c. ... the system does not "hallucinate" arbitrary meanings into an expression ... [D. Stallard, "The Logical Analysis of Lexical Ambiguity," 184]

The resultative phrases in (6) describe the state achieved by the referent of the postverbal NP as a result of the action denoted by the verb, just as they do in the transitive verb plus resultative phrase examples in (1). The difference between these examples based on unergative verbs and the examples in (1) based on transitive verbs is that the postverbal NPs found with the former are not arguments of the verbs, as shown by the unacceptability of the examples in (7).

(7) a. *The dog barked him.
    b. *You may sleep it.
    c. *The system hallucinates meanings.

The resultative constructions in (6) are similar in this respect to those involving unergative verbs followed by fake reflexives, such as those in (3) and (4). Both types of constructions involve resultative phrases predicated of nonsubcategorized NPs, differing only in whether the resultative phrase is predicated of a reflexive pronoun or some other NP.

Related to these two types of resultative constructions based on unergative verbs is a third type in which the NP following the unergative verb is a nonsubcategorized inalienably possessed NP (generally denoting a body part), where the possessor is coreferential with the subject of the verb.

(8) a. Sylvester cried his eyes out.
    b. Sleep your wrinkles away. (ad)
    c. Valentino ... winds up strutting his life away in the town square with his sister's blessing. [A. Cancogni, "A Widow's Dream," 31]

    d. ... you need not stitch your poor fingers to the bone ... [G. Eliot,
      Daniel Deronda, 247]

Again the postverbal NP in such examples is not subcategorized by the
verb.

(9) a. *Sylvester cried his eyes.
    b. *Sleep your wrinkles.
    c. *Valentino strutted his life.
    d. *You need not stitch your fingers. (on the interpretation intended
      in (8d))

These constructions are intermediate between the first two types. The NP
in postverbal NP position is not a reflexive pronoun, as in (3) and (4);
however, it does include a possessive pronoun understood to be coreferential with the subject, establishing a relation between the subject and
the resultative phrase as in the resultative constructions with the fake
reflexive.[2]

2.1.3 Resultative Constructions Based on Unspecified Object Verbs

Resultative phrases predicated of either fake reflexives or nonsubcategorized NPs (whether possessive or not) are also found with a certain class
of transitive verbs. The class includes those verbs that, like *eat*, allow
intransitive uses with an unspecified object interpretation (*Sylvia ate*), as
well as transitive uses (*Sylvia ate the grapes*).

(10) a. Sudsy cooked them all into a premature death with her wild
      food. [P. Chute, *Castine*, 78]
    b. 'I'm glad you didn't stay at the Club drinking yourself dottier.'
      [W. Muir, *Imagined Corners*, 62]
    c. Having ... drunk the teapot dry ... [E. Dark, *Lantana Lane*, 94]
    d. Drive your engine clean. (Mobil ad)

Although these verbs are also found in resultative constructions where the
postverbal NP is selected by the verb, as shown for *cook* in (11), the
resultative constructions in (10) involve postverbal NPs that are not selected by the verb in the construction, as shown by the contrast between
(10) and (12).

(11) "It is the heat," complained another old auntie. "Cooking all your
    flesh dry and brittle." [A. Tan, *The Joy Luck Club*, 71]

(12) a. *Sudsy cooked them. (on the interpretation intended in (10a))
    b. *You drank yourself.

    c. *They drank the teapot.

    d. *Drive your engine.

The resultative constructions in (10) are based on the unspecified object form of the verb in each construction. The sentences in (10) are interpreted in the same way as those based on unergative verbs and include the three types of postverbal NPs illustrated with unergative verbs in (3), (6), and (8). In contrast, as pointed out by Carrier and Randall (1992, in press), transitive verbs that do not independently allow the omission of an unspecified object cannot be found in resultative constructions with postverbal NPs that are not selected by the verb.

(13) a.   The bombing destroyed *(the city).

      b. *The bombing destroyed the residents homeless.

(14) a.   The bears frightened *(the hikers). (C&R 1992:187, (35a))

      b. *The bears frightened the campground empty. (C&R 1992:187, (37a))

(15) a.   The magician hypnotized *(the volunteers). (C&R 1992:187, (35c))

      b. *The magician hypnotized the auditorium quiet. (C&R 1992:187, (37c))

Several researchers (see, among others, Jackendoff 1990, Sato 1987) have suggested that at least some resultative constructions based on unergative verbs and unspecified object verbs do involve "arguments," because the fake reflexives or nonsubcategorized NPs bear the same semantic relation to the base verb in the resultative construction as the object of the preposition heading an oblique PP complement that can be found with this verb. For example, such PPs are selected by the verbs *bark* and *drink*.

(16) a.   The dog barked at them. (cf. (6a))

      b. They drank from the teapot. (cf. (10c))

However, this solution will not extend to all resultative constructions based on unergative and unspecified object verbs. It is difficult to imagine such a source for many of the fake reflexives or nonsubcategorized NPs. For example, consider what type of PP could be the source of the postverbal NPs in (6c) or (8b), repeated in (17).

(17) a.   ... the system does not "hallucinate" arbitrary meanings into an expression ... [D. Stallard, "The Logical Analysis of Lexical Ambiguity," 184]

   b. Sleep your wrinkles away. (ad)

We follow Carrier and Randall (1992, in press) in claiming that nonsub-categorized NPs are found only after verbs that can independently be intransitive (i.e., the verb is unergative or may take an unspecified object). (See section 2.4.1 for a discussion of the analysis presented in Hoekstra 1988, 1992, which explicitly denies this claim.)

2.1.4   Resultative Constructions with Passive and Unaccusative Verbs

The primary potential counterexamples to the DOR involve passive and unaccusative verbs. Passive and unaccusative verbs may appear with re-sultative phrases predicated of their surface subjects, as in (18) and (19), respectively.[3]

(18) a. The floor had also been swept quite clean of debris ... [P. Klass, *Other Women's Children*, 165]
   b. In marked contrast with the outside land which had been eaten bare by goats and horses, the enclosed area was almost massed with native shrubs and grasses ... [A. W. Upfield, *Sinister Stones*, 172]
   c. She was shaken awake by the earthquake.

(19) a. The river froze solid.
   b. The prisoners froze to death.
   c. The bottle broke open.
   d. The gate swung shut.
   e. This time the curtain rolled open on the court of the Caesars ... [Olivia (D. Bussy), *Olivia*, 35]

However, given a movement analysis of passives, the DOR can be main-tained: the surface subject of a passive verb is an underlying object. Simi-larly, with unaccusative verbs the DOR can be maintained if the surface subject of an unaccusative verb, like the subject of a passive verb, is ana-lyzed as a derived subject and an underlying object.

In contrast to unergative verbs, unaccusative verbs cannot appear with resultative phrases predicated of either fake reflexives or nonsubcatego-rized NPs.

(20) a. *During the spring thaw, the boulders rolled the hillside bare.
   b. *The rice slowly cooked the pot black. (meaning: the pot became black as a result of the rice cooking)
   c. *The snow melted the road slushy.

This observation is supported by corpus evidence. There are no examples of unaccusative verbs followed by either a fake reflexive or a nonsubcategorized NP and a resultative phrase in the entire corpus of resultative constructions that we have been collecting over the last several years.

Within the GB framework, these facts receive an explanation in the context of Burzio's Generalization (Burzio 1986), which states that unaccusative verbs cannot assign Case (see also section 1.1). In general, unaccusative verbs contrast with unergative verbs in not being able to take any surface objects, including cognate objects. Compare the ability of unergative verbs to take cognate objects (*Louisa slept a restful sleep, Malinda smiled her most enigmatic smile*) with the inability of unaccusative verbs to take such objects (**The glass broke a crooked break, *The actress fainted a feigned faint*). Although there is no generally accepted satisfactory explanation of Burzio's Generalization, the correlation it describes is nonetheless considered to be well established, at least in English. As discussed in B. Levin and Rappaport 1989, Burzio's Generalization is implicated in the explanation of the ungrammaticality of (20), since these structures, on the syntactic account of the resultative construction, involve two postverbal NPs at D-Structure. One of these NPs can receive Case by movement to subject position, but there is no way for the second NP to receive Case.[4]

As pointed out by Carrier and Randall (1992, in press), middles pattern with unaccusative and passive verbs in that resultative phrases can be predicated of the surface subject of a middle (*This table wipes clean easily*). They claim that this fact supports a movement analysis of middles, as proposed, for example, by Keyser and Roeper (1984), Roberts (1987), and Stroik (1992). They also note that resultative phrases can be found in adjectival passives, as in *the spun-dry clothes*. At the same time, they adopt B. Levin and Rappaport's (1986) analysis of the formation of adjectival passives that involves lexical externalization of the verb's direct internal argument. There seems to be a conflict between an analysis of adjectival passive formation that involves nonderived subjects for adjectival passives and the use of resultative phrases as a diagnostic for derived subjects. Carrier and Randall (1992) avoid this problem by claiming that adjectival passive formation creates a new adjective consisting of the adjectival passive participle and the resultative phrase (e.g., *wiped clean*) with its own argument structure. It is important, however, to point out that whether or not adjectival passives pose a problem for the DOR depends on the explanation given for the DOR. Therefore, we defer addressing this question until note 8, that is, until after we have provided our explanation for the DOR.

2.1.5   Resultative Phrases and Obliques
The DOR also predicts that resultative phrases cannot be predicated of VP-internal NPs that are not direct objects, such as obliques. And as noted by Simpson (1983a), among others, this prediction is borne out. Consider, for example, the following contrasts:

(21)   a.   John loaded the wagon full with hay.
         b.   *John loaded the hay into the wagon full.
              (Williams 1980:204, (2a,d))

(22)   a.   John was shot dead.
         b.   *John was shot at dead.
              (Simpson 1983a:147, (27a,b))

(23)   a.   The silversmith pounded the metal flat.
         b.   *The silversmith pounded on the metal flat.

The DOR, therefore, is precisely a restriction involving postverbal NPs; other VP-internal arguments cannot have resultative phrases predicated of them.

2.1.6   The Distribution of Resultative Phrases: A Summary
To summarize, this survey of resultative constructions shows that the distribution of resultative phrases can be simply characterized by the DOR together with the assumption that English has a class of unaccusative verbs.

2.2   The Syntax of the Resultative Construction

We have shown, then, that the DOR descriptively captures the basic generalizations concerning the resultative construction and accounts for the contrasting behavior of unergative and unaccusative verbs: unaccusative verbs can appear with resultative phrases without the mediation of a fake reflexive, whereas unergative verbs cannot. At this point, the DOR is merely a generalization. The success of a syntactic account of the distribution of resultative phrases depends on the extent to which the DOR can be shown not to be a mere stipulation but to follow from independently motivated principles of grammar. We offer such an explanation in this section, after establishing certain facts about the syntax of the construction.

2.2.1 The Argument Structure of Verbs in the Resultative Construction

Besides providing an explanation for the DOR, an analysis of the resultative construction must also establish what lexical relations exist between the NPs and the predicates of the construction. In particular, it must predict when the postverbal NP is an argument of the verb and when it is not.

We noted in the previous section that unergative verbs (and unspecified object verbs) in resultative constructions can be followed by NPs that are not arguments of the verb and hence are not θ-marked. This point is illustrated in (6), repeated here as (24).

(24) a. I ... ruthlessly roused Mr. Contreras by knocking on his door until the dog barked him awake. [S. Paretsky, *Blood Shot*, 183]
  b. You may sleep it [= the unborn baby] quiet again ... [E. Bagnold, *The Squire*, 285]
  c. ... the system does not "hallucinate" arbitrary meanings into an expression ... [D. Stallard, "The Logical Analysis of Lexical Ambiguity," 184]

Evidence that the postverbal NPs are not arguments of the verb came from the ungrammaticality of sentences such as those in (7), repeated here as (25).

(25) a. *The dog barked him.
  b. *You may sleep it.
  c. *The system hallucinates meanings.

However, these sentences show that the relevant NPs are nonsubcategorized only on the assumption that the verb in the resultative construction has the same lexical representation and, in particular, the same argument structure as it has when it appears in isolation. This assumption is by no means self-evident, and it is explicitly denied in a number of analyses, including those of B. Levin and Rapoport (1988), L. Levin, Mitamura, and Mahmoud (1988), and Hoekstra (1988, 1992). The first two works cited assume that the lexical semantic representation of a verb in the resultative construction is different from that of the verb in isolation. Hoekstra's work assumes that, although the verb has the same lexical semantic representation whether or not it is found in the resultative construction, it projects arguments of distinct semantic and syntactic types in the resultative construction than it does outside of it. Our analysis differs from both these types of analyses; we will discuss the differences in section 2.4.

In this section, however, we cite syntactic evidence that the lexical representation of a verb in the resultative construction does *not* differ from that of the same verb in isolation, and that the verb projects the same argument structure as it does in isolation. The evidence is drawn from Carrier and Randall's (1992, in press) extensive studies of the syntax of the resultative construction, and particularly from their (1992) evaluation of competing syntactic analyses of the construction. They show that the postverbal NP in a transitive-based resultative construction behaves like an argument of the verb, whereas the postverbal NP in an unergative-based resultative construction does not behave like an argument of the verb. This pattern is exactly what one would expect if a verb has the same lexical representation (including argument structure) in the resultative construction as it has in isolation.

Carrier and Randall (1992) examine the behavior of postverbal NPs in middle constructions, adjectival passives, and nominalizations. The postverbal NP in a resultative construction based on a transitive verb can be externalized by middle formation and adjectival passive formation, as illustrated in the (a) examples in (26) and (27), as well as by (28). This behavior contrasts with that of the postverbal NP in resultative constructions based on unergative verbs, as shown in the (b) examples in (26) and (27).[5]

(26) a. This table wipes clean easily.
      This metal pounds flat easily.
   b. *This type of pavement runs thin easily. (C&R, in press, (69a))
      *This baby ticks awake easily.
      *This teapot drinks dry in no time at all.

(27) a. a wiped-clean table
      pounded-flat metal
   b. *the run-thin pavement (C&R, in press, (73c))
      *a ticked-awake baby
      *a drunk-dry teapot

(28) The pounded-thin beef ... was so unlike the thick, chewy London broil we ate on most nights. [D. Leimbach, "Wunderbar!" 69]

The adjectival passives and middles involving resultative constructions based on unergative verbs contrast in this respect with verbal passives based on the same resultative constructions, which are fully acceptable.

(29) a. The pavement in Central Park has been run thin by all the jogging enthusiasts.

 b. The baby was ticked awake by the loud clock.

 c. The teapot was drunk dry by the thirsty workers.

Before we consider the consequences of these data for the analysis of the resultative construction, a comment on the status of the adjectival passive data is in order. Jackendoff (1990) disagrees with Carrier and Randall's acceptability judgments for examples of the type given in (27a), finding examples such as *a swept-clean room* and *squashed-flat grapes* "at best marginal" (1990:236) and examples such as *washed-clean clothes* and *watered-flat tulips* unacceptable. He suggests that resultative phrases cannot in general be found in adjectival passives. Other English speakers agree with his judgments. There is evidence, however, that the unacceptability of the examples in (27a) should be treated differently from that of the examples in (27b). Although some English speakers may question the acceptability of examples of this type and may not find them as good as simple adjectival passives, the examples in (27a) are significantly better than those in (27b). We attribute the less-than-perfect status of the examples in (27a) to the fact that such adjectival passives violate the Head-Final Filter (Williams 1982), since the passive participle, which is the head of the adjectival passive, is to the left of the resultative phrase. The effects of the Head-Final Filter in prenominal position can be avoided by forming an adjectival passive where the order of the resultative phrase and the passive participle is reversed, as in *a clean-shaven man* or the examples in (30).

(30) a. Judy Ryan, Grandmother's servant-girl, always had my dinner ready for me on the white-scrubbed table that stood against the wall ... [M. Laverty, *Never No More*, 15]

 b. In those few undertoned words of Grandcourt's she felt as absolute a resistance as if her thin fingers had been pushing at a fast-shut iron door. [G. Eliot, *Daniel Deronda*, 311]

 c. There were extensive lanes of short-cropped, fortified-green lawns ... [J. Bailey, *Bagged*, 170–71]

This is the structure that is derived when the passive participle is made into the head of a compound. It is unclear to us why this option is not more generally available; most such structures sound unacceptable (*flat-watered tulips*).

This approach gains support from adjectival passives based on resultative constructions in Icelandic. In addition to having a resultative construction like the English one in which an adjective is predicated of a postverbal NP, Icelandic regularly forms compound verbs with result-denoting adjectives incorporated to the left of the verb. The following examples illustrate the availability of the two options:

(31) a. Þeir máluðu húsið   hvítt.
        they painted house the white
     b. Þeir hvítmáluðu   húsið.
        they whitepainted house the

(32) a. Ég bað   þá   að mala kaffið   fínt.
        I   asked them to grind coffee the fine
     b. Þeir fínmöluðu kaffið   fyrir mig.
        they fineground coffee the for   me

As we would predict, the adjectival passives based on the compound resultative verbs are fine since the Head-Final Filter is not relevant here.

(33) a. Hún býr í hvítmálaða   húsinu.
        she lives in whitepainted house the
     b. Fínmalað kaffi er betra.
        fineground coffee is better

Another way the effects of the Head-Final Filter can be avoided in English is by placing the adjectival passive in other than prehead modifier position within an NP. One such position, which is known to be a diagnostic environment for adjectives, and hence for adjectival passives, is as the complement to verbs such as *seem*, *remain*, and *feel* (Wasow 1977). In this environment the Head-Final Filter is inapplicable, so that adjectives, including adjectival passives, may be followed by their complements as the syntax dictates. And in such environments, adjectival passives based on the resultative construction are impeccable when they involve transitive verbs.

(34) I remember feeling rubbed raw in the wake of Kent State. [M. R. Drake, "A Message from the Director," 17]

But even in such environments, where the Head-Final Filter is irrelevant, adjectival passives based on resultative constructions involving unergative verbs are still impossible.

(35) a. *The pavement looked run thin.
   b. *The insomniac remained ticked awake night after night.
   c. *The pitcher looked drunk dry.

Assuming, then, that the data involving the interaction of the resultative construction with both middles and adjectival passives are valid, these data can be used as evidence that the postverbal NP is an argument in transitive-based resultative constructions and a nonargument in unergative-based resultative constructions. Since both adjectival passive formation and middle formation can externalize only arguments, as shown for adjectival passives by Wasow (1977) and for middles by Keyser and Roeper (1984) and Carrier and Randall (1992, in press), the unacceptability of middles and adjectival passives with resultative constructions based on unergative verbs suggests that the postverbal NP in such resultative constructions is not an argument.

Carrier and Randall (1992, in press) also note the following contrasts in nominalizations, which again support differing syntactic analyses of transitive-based and unergative-based resultative constructions:

(36)   The watering of tulips flat is a criminal offense in Holland.
       The Surgeon General warns against the cooking of food black.
       (C&R 1992:201, (74a))

(37)   *The drinking of oneself sick is commonplace in one's freshman
       year.
       *The jogging craze has resulted in the running of a lot of pairs of
       Nikes threadbare.
       (C&R 1992:201, (74b))

As pointed out by Chomsky (1970) and Stowell (1981), the posthead NP in a nominalization cannot be marked by the preposition *of* if it is the argument of an embedded clause. Thus, the unacceptability of the nominalizations involving resultative constructions based on unergative verbs is consistent with the nonargument status of the posthead NP in such nominalizations.

Further evidence that the postverbal NP in resultative constructions based on unergative verbs is not an argument of the verb, in contrast to the corresponding NP in resultative constructions based on transitive verbs, is presented by Rothstein (1992). The argument is based on the contrasting behavior of the two types of NPs with respect to extraction from *wh*-islands. Chomsky (1986a) notes that in general extraction of a θ-marked NP from a *wh*-island results in a Subjacency violation, whereas extraction of an NP that is not θ-marked from a *wh*-island results in a severer violation—a violation of the Empty Category Principle (ECP). Bearing this in mind, note the contrast in the acceptability of extraction from resultative constructions based on transitive and unergative verbs.

(38) a. ?Which people do you wonder whether he punched senseless?
   b. ?Which counter do you wonder whether the cook wiped clean?

(39) a. ??Which pavements do you wonder whether they ran thin?
   b. ??Which neighbors do you wonder whether the dog barked awake?

Carrier and Randall (1992) deny that there is a difference in acceptability between extractions from the two kinds of constructions; however, the fact that some speakers do detect a difference, finding extractions from the unergative-based resultative constructions worse than those from the transitive-based constructions, can be considered evidence that strengthens the point that has already been made using the other diagnostics.[6]

We will, then, make the crucial assumption that the arguments of a verb are expressed in the same way in the resultative construction as they are when the verb appears in isolation. All that the formation of a resultative construction involves is the addition of a resultative XP (and sometimes, as we discuss below, a subject for that XP). The syntactic properties of the construction should follow from this assumption and from general principles of syntax. We discuss this point and its ramifications further in section 2.2.3.

In resultative constructions based on unergative verbs, the addition of a postverbal NP is required in order that the resultative XP can satisfy the predication requirement on its head. We have been assuming that the postverbal NP is not θ-marked by the verb. We may ask, however, what the syntactic position of that NP is. In some theories, the fact that the postverbal NP in unergative-based resultative constructions is not an argument of the verb must be reflected in the syntax. If so, the NP in these instances is not a direct object, but the subject of a small clause, as schematized in (40).

(40) The dog barked [$_{SC}$ him awake].

This assumption is consistent with the claim made by Chomsky (1986a) that only an argument NP may be the sister of a verb. This move would obviously require a change in the formulation of the DOR, since on this analysis, the resultative XP, although always predicated of the postverbal

NP, is in some instances not predicated of a direct object. However, there are theories that do countenance a direct object that is not assigned a θ-role by the verb, and hence such theories do not require a small clause in these instances (see, for example, Williams 1983). Theories making extensive use of small clauses usually assume that any predication relation must be represented by a clausal structure in syntax. Since in the case of the transitive resultative constructions we are allowing a predication relation to be expressed without a syntactic clausal structure, the predication relation between the resultative phrase and the postverbal NP in the unergative construction does not force us to posit a small clause there either. Our syntactic analysis would be consistent with a theory in which the structural conditions on predication are those outlined by Williams (1983); the subject of the predicate must be outside the maximal projection of the predicate, and the two must be in a relation of mutual c-command. Such a position is taken by Carrier and Randall (1992), who give all resultative constructions a ternary-branching analysis. We will not take a stand on this issue, however, and will just stress that it is important for us that the postverbal NP is not an argument of the verb in resultative constructions based on unergative verbs, although it is in resultative constructions based on transitive verbs. (See section 2.4.1 for a discussion of the analysis presented by Hoekstra (1988, 1992), which takes all resultative constructions to be based on small clauses.) Below we will show that our explanation for the DOR is consistent with both approaches to the syntactic representation.

2.2.2 Explaining the Direct Object Restriction

Having established the lexical relations between the NPs and predicates in the resultative construction, we give our explanation of the DOR. First, however, we show that a commonly cited purely syntactic explanation of the DOR based on mutual c-command is not tenable.

It has often been argued that the DOR can be reduced to a mutual c-command requirement on predication (Williams 1980, Rothstein 1983). The argument goes as follows. Verbs impose various semantic restrictions on the resultative phrases that can appear with them (for discussion, see Carrier and Randall, in press, Rapoport 1990, Simpson 1983a, among others), and hence resultative phrases can be considered to be selected by the verb. As selected constituents, they must appear inside the VP (or perhaps inside the V′) headed by the verb. If so, resultative phrases can be predicated neither of subjects nor of objects of prepositions, since they cannot be in a relation of mutual c-command with such constituents. Only if they are predicated of direct objects is the mutual c-command requirement met.

This argument does not go through, however, a point also discussed by Carrier and Randall (1992). The fact that a resultative phrase or some other XP inside the VP does not c-command the subject of the VP does not preclude the possibility that the XP can be predicated of the subject. Depictive phrases show precisely this property. As shown by Andrews (1982), and more recently by Rapoport (1987) and Roberts (1988), traditional constituency tests indicate that depictive phrases are inside the VP, but as noted above, depictive phrases can be predicated of subjects.[7] Therefore, another explanation for the DOR must be found.

Various syntactic tests for VP constituency such as *do so*–substitution and VP-preposing show that resultative phrases are VP-internal and are attached at the same bar level as subcategorized PPs (the (a) sentences in (41) and (42)), whether the resultative construction is headed by a transitive verb (the (b) sentences) or an unergative verb (the (c) sentences).

(41) a. *Jason put the book on the table, and Bill did so on the floor.
   b. *Bill fastened the shutters open, and May did so shut.
   c. *The joggers ran the pavement thin, and the runners did so
      smooth.

(42) a. *Jason said that he would put the book on the table, and put the
      book he did on the table.
   b. *Bill said that he would fasten the shutters open, and fasten
      them he did open.
   c. *The joggers thought that they would run the pavement thin,
      and run the pavement they did thin.

In this respect, resultative phrases contrast with depictive phrases, which do not show the same pattern of behavior as subcategorized PPs with respect to these constituency tests.

(43) Jason wiped the table tired and May did so wide awake.

(44) Jason said that he would even wipe the table tired, and wipe the
   table he did tired.

The behavior of resultative phrases with respect to these tests suggests that the state denoted by the resultative XP is part of the core eventuality described in the VP. In fact, as noted by many researchers (see, for example, Dowty 1979, Hoekstra 1988, 1992, Pustejovsky 1991b, Tenny 1987,

1992, Van Valin 1990), resultative phrases often derive accomplishments from activities. Accomplishments are usually analyzed as complex eventualities consisting of an activity and a state, where the activity results in the bringing about of the state (see, for example, Dowty 1979, Grimshaw and Vikner 1993, Pustejovsky 1991b). Accomplishments, then, describe causative changes of state. Although accomplishments have a complex internal structure, there are simple nonderived verbs, such as *build, construct, destroy,* and *kill,* that are accomplishments. With such verbs, the result state is lexically specified, whereas the activity that causes the result state is left unspecified. For example, consider the verb *destroy:* there are many ways to destroy something, but no matter how the destruction is accomplished, the result is that that thing no longer exists. The resultative construction differs from lexically simple accomplishments in that both the activity and the result state are lexically specified, each by a different predicate: the former by the verb and the latter by the resultative XP. For example, in *Terry wiped the table clean,* the verb *wipe* specifies the activity and the AP *clean* specifies the result state.

Resultative constructions denote a change of state even when the verb in the construction does not denote a change of state when used in isolation. Verbs of contact by impact such as *pound, beat,* and *hammer* illustrate this point. Sentence (45a) does not necessarily entail a change in the state of the metal; in fact, the pounding may have no effect at all on the metal. The addition of a resultative phrase, as in (45b), produces an eventuality that specifies a change in the state of the metal: it becomes flat.

(45) a. The blacksmith pounded the metal.
      b. The blacksmith pounded the metal flat.

As discussed in B. Levin and Rapoport 1988 and Rapoport 1990, this shift in *pound*'s semantic type explains why *pound* can participate in the middle alternation, which is manifested by verbs of change of state (Hale and Keyser 1986, 1987, 1988), only when accompanied by a resultative phrase.

(46) a. *Metal pounds easily.
      b.   Metal pounds flat easily.

As is well known, the NP that denotes an entity that changes state is always expressed as a direct object. This generalization is often formalized in a linking rule that states that arguments bearing the patient or theme semantic roles—the semantic roles typically associated with such NPs—are expressed as direct objects (Anderson 1977, Marantz 1984, among others). We can assume that this linking rule applies to the NP denoting the entity that undergoes the change of state in a resultative construction as well. The linking rule could take one of the two forms in (47). (This linking rule is really a subcase of the Directed Change Linking Rule, which we formulate in section 4.1.2.)

(47) *The Change-of-State Linking Rule*
      Version (a): An NP that refers to the entity that undergoes the change of state in the eventuality described in the VP must be governed by the verb heading the VP.
      Version (b): An NP that refers to the entity that undergoes the change of state in the eventuality described in the VP must be the direct object of the verb heading the VP.

As we mentioned earlier, it is not important for our purposes whether the postverbal NP in unergative resultative constructions is a direct object or the subject of a small clause. Depending on which option turns out to be correct, the rule could be formulated to make reference either to the NP governed by the verb, as in version (a), or to the direct object of the verb, as in version (b). The version (a) formulation will be necessary if the postverbal NP in a resultative construction based on an unergative verb is not the direct object of the verb, but the subject of a small clause. Both direct objects of verbs and subjects of postverbal small clauses are governed by the verb. Throughout this section our discussion takes both versions of the linking rule into account.

If this linking rule is correct, then it is clear why resultative phrases can only be predicated of direct objects or NPs governed by the verb. Resultative phrases specify the state that is brought about as the result of the action described in the VP. Following our assumption that the expression of a verb's arguments does not change with the addition of a resultative XP, then each resultative construction must simultaneously meet two requirements on argument expression: the verb's arguments must be expressed according to the lexical specifications of the verb and in accordance with the general linking rules, and the NP denoting the entity that changes state must be the verb's direct object or governed by the verb.[8] In addition, this NP must be in the appropriate structural relation— presumably mutual c-command—with the resultative XP.

The transitive-based resultative construction *Terry wiped the table clean* meets all the requirements: the arguments of *wipe* are appropriately expressed according to the linking rules, *Terry* as subject and *the table* as direct object, and *clean* is predicated of the direct object, satisfying the mutual c-command relation on predication. This example cannot receive the interpretation 'Terry became clean as a result of wiping the table', because, under that interpretation, the argument of *wipe* denoting the entity undergoing the change of state is not governed by the verb.

The same analysis applies to resultative constructions based on unaccusative verbs, such as *The door rolled open.* Assuming the unaccusative analysis of *roll* (see chapter 4), the argument of the verb is appropriately expressed as a D-Structure object and an S-Structure subject. The resultative phrase *open* predicates a change of state of *the door*, which as a D-Structure object is governed by the verb, satisfying either version of the Change-of-State Linking Rule. If the single argument of an unaccusative verb were a D-Structure subject, then this argument would not meet the requirement that the argument undergoing a change of state be a direct object or governed by the verb. For the same reasons, since the single argument of an unergative verb is a D-Structure subject, the Change-of-State Linking Rule would be violated if a resultative phrase were predicated of this argument directly.

Thus, if nothing more is added to the grammar of English, we would assume that resultative phrases cannot be added to unergative verbs. In fact, according to Doron (1991), this is the situation in Modern Hebrew. As the sentences in (48) show, a resultative phrase can be added to unaccusative verbs and passive verbs, but, as shown in (49), not to unergative verbs.

(48) a. Ha-kad nišbar le-xatixot.
         the-vase broke to-pieces
         'The vase broke to pieces.'
    b. Moše huka   la-mavet.
         Moshe was beaten to the-death
         'Moshe was beaten to death.'

(49) a. *Ha-cevaot nilxemu le-xatixot.
          the-armies fought   to-pieces
          'The armies fought each other to pieces.'
    b. *Rina raca la-mavet.
          Rina ran to the-death
          'Rina ran herself to death.'

However, English (and, as reported by Hoekstra (1988), Dutch as well) allows unergative verbs to be followed by a resultative phrase that expresses a change of state in an entity denoted by an NP that is not an argument of the verb. That is, English allows resultative constructions of the form in (50).

(50) The joggers ran the pavement thin.

A resultative construction based on an unergative verb, such as that in (50), meets all the syntactic requirements on the construction. The single argument of the verb is expressed appropriately, and the NP that denotes the entity undergoing a change of state is either the direct object of the verb or (if the analysis where this NP is the subject of a small clause is adopted) at least governed by the verb, as required by the Change-of-State Linking Rule. This NP is also a sister of the resultative phrase that is predicated of it, so that the predication requirement is satisfied. Finally, since this NP is governed by the verb, it can also be assigned Case by the verb.

Once structures such as these are allowed by the grammar, then structures with fake reflexives are immediately allowed as well. The only difference between a resultative construction with a fake reflexive and structures such as (50) is that in the former, but not in the latter, the nonsubcategorized NP is coreferential with the matrix subject. With either the direct object analysis of the postverbal NP or the small clause analysis, the postverbal NP, being coreferential with the matrix subject and also governed by the verb, is expressed as a reflexive. However, nonsubcategorized NPs, as illustrated in (20), will not be available for resultative constructions based on unaccusative verbs. This property is explained, as mentioned in section 2.1.4, by the Case-assigning properties of unaccusative verbs.

On this analysis, the fake reflexive is not a pleonastic element introduced simply to ensure that in some narrow sense the DOR is satisfied. It functions as a "subject" for the predicate heading the resultative phrase. Its introduction is forced by the Change-of-State Linking Rule, because without it the resultative phrase would not be predicated of an element to which the linking rule could apply. (Presumably the Change-of-State Linking Rule could not force the appearance of a pleonastic element.) At the same time it allows the predicate to meet the linking rule without any change in the verb's lexical properties. (Body part objects fulfill the same function.)

2.2.3 Ramifications

The analysis just presented is based on the assumption that the lexical representation of a verb, and hence the way it maps its arguments to the syntax, does not change when the verb is in a resultative construction. Given this assumption, the resultative phrase on our account is not licensed by the lexical representation of the verb. Rather, the interpretation of the resultative construction is compositionally derived: specifically, it is derived from the meaning of the verb plus that of the resultative XP.[9] The only additional aspect of meaning associated with the resultative construction that is not explicitly represented in the syntax is the causal relation between the action described by the verb and the state denoted by the resultative XP, to which we return immediately. Therefore, since the verb and the resultative phrase are expressed as distinct predicates, and the meaning of neither changes, the null hypothesis would postulate no change in lexical representation. Since the predicates are distinct constituents in syntax, each imposes its own requirements on the expression of its arguments. To make this point somewhat differently, a language learner knows not to postulate a different lexical representation for the verb in the resultative construction precisely because the resultative construction is interpreted compositionally.

Support for this hypothesis comes from phenomena that at first glance appear to pose a problem for the approach developed here. In chapter 5 we will show that the syntax of some verbs *does* change in the resultative construction. But it turns out that this happens only when there is independent evidence that the verbs have a dual classification, that is, when there is an independent lexical rule that allows the verbs to be associated with more than one syntactic configuration. In effect, this is evidence that the resultative construction does make use of independently existing lexical entries. See chapter 5 for illustration of this point.

As just mentioned, the causal relation between the eventuality described by the verb and the result state must be accounted for. That is, in *Terry wiped the table clean* the fact that the clean state of the table is a *result* of Terry's wiping the table must be derived. In addition, the derived change-of-state reading for verbs such as *pound*, *hammer*, and *roll* in the resultative construction must be accounted for. We offer the following analysis. The resultative XP must be licensed and integrated into the semantic representation of the sentence. If the resultative XP is added at the lowest bar level within the VP, then it must be integrated into the core eventuality named by the verb. There is a limited ontological typology of eventuality types. The only type of eventuality with a state following any kind of process is an accomplishment. As we have already shown, accomplishments always describe causative changes of state. Therefore, an XP denoting a state that follows an activity verb can only be interpreted as denoting the result state of an accomplishment. The causal relation between the activity and the change of state follows from the interpretation of the eventuality as an accomplishment. If the resultative XP is added to a verb that is already an achievement or an accomplishment, then, once again, given the typology of basic eventuality types, it can only be interpreted as further specifying an already encoded change of state (see section 2.3.2). The analysis falls out from the natural assumption that the eventualities created by the composition of predicates can only belong to types for which there are underived lexical items. As mentioned above, the event type of *wipe the table clean* is essentially the same as the event type of *build a house*. A similar account is offered by Pustejovsky (1991b), who draws on earlier versions of this work.

These suggestions answer the question of how the resultative phrase is interpreted, although it is not projected from the lexical representation of the verb. We now turn to the question of how the resultative phrase is syntactically licensed. This question must be asked since on our analysis it is not the Projection Principle that licenses the phrase. Here, we extend to the resultative construction a suggestion made by Rapoport (1991) concerning the licensing of depictives. Rapoport suggests that the syntactic licensing of depictives involves identifying two event positions: (i) the event position in the argument structure of the verb whose argument the depictive is predicated of and (ii) the event position in the argument structure of the head of the depictive phrase. This identification ensures the proper semantic interpretation of the depictive. As support for this account, Rapoport points out that only stage-level verbs are found with depictives, and also that only stage-level adjectives can be used to head depictives; according to Kratzer (1989), only stage-level predicates have argument structures with an event position. As also noted by Hoekstra (1992) and Rapoport (1990), similar constraints apply to the resultative construction: stative verbs—a class that subsumes individual-level verbs —are not found in this construction (see section 2.3.3), and the resultative phrase cannot be headed by an individual-level predicate (*The witch frightened the children intelligent*), suggesting that Rapoport's account can be extended to the resultative construction.[10]

2.3 Semantic Restrictions on the Resultative Construction

We turn next to certain semantic restrictions on the resultative construction. The DOR or its reformulation in terms of the Change-of-State

Linking Rule would lead us to expect that resultative phrases should be able to appear with all unaccusative verbs, since the S-Structure subject of these verbs is an underlying direct object. However, resultative phrases are not compatible with all unaccusative verbs. We argue that the Change-of-State Linking Rule imposes a necessary, but not a sufficient, condition on resultative constructions, and that there are independently motivated semantic restrictions that prevent resultative phrases from occurring with certain unaccusative verbs. This point is important methodologically, since, as mentioned in chapter 1, the fact that not all unaccusative verbs uniformly pass all unaccusative tests has been taken by some as evidence undermining the Unaccusative Hypothesis. We discuss in turn the two classes of unaccusative verbs that may not appear with resultative phrases: stative verbs such as *remain* and verbs of inherently directed motion such as *come*, *go*, and *arrive*. Although such verbs may be found with XPs inside the VPs they head, these XPs may only be interpreted as depictive phrases. Sentence (51a) cannot mean that Carla became bored by remaining in the country, and (51b) cannot mean that Willa became breathless as a result of arriving.

(51) a. Carla remained in the country bored.
     b. Willa arrived breathless.

2.3.1 Resultative Phrases as Delimiters

The restriction on resultative phrases with unaccusative verbs of inherently directed motion such as *come*, *go*, and *arrive* can be understood in the context of the function of resultative phrases as delimiters, in conjunction with Tenny's (1987, 1992) Aspectual Principles of Argument Structure.

Aspectual classifications of eventualities distinguish between *telic* (*delimited* in Tenny's terminology, which we adopt) eventualities—those that are bounded in time—and *atelic* (*nondelimited*) eventualities—those with no specific temporal delimitation (Declerck 1979, Dowty 1979, among others). Some verbs such as *break*, *ripen*, *build*, and *devour* describe eventualities that are inherently delimited. Brinton (1988:26) describes a delimited (telic) eventuality as

one which necessarily includes a goal, aim, or conclusion. The goal is an inherent part of the situation, without which the situation could not be what it is. Thus, a telic situation, such as fruit ripening, necessarily implies a final state of ripeness; if that end state is not attained, then the fruit cannot be said to have ripened. If the fruit is eaten before it is ripe, then the process of ripening is terminated rather than concluded.

A delimited eventuality can be differentiated from a nondelimited one by a variety of tests. For instance, a nondelimited, but not a delimited, eventuality can occur with durative phrases.

(52) Sylvia ran for an hour.

(53) *Karen built the house for an hour.

As pointed out in the literature on verbal aspect (Declerck 1979, Dowty 1979, among others), there are various syntactic processes that serve to produce delimited eventualities involving verbs that are inherently activity verbs and would otherwise name nondelimited eventualities. If the verb in a sentence does not describe an inherently delimited eventuality, then some verbs allow the eventuality to be delimited (i) by a particular choice of direct object, or (ii) by an appropriate choice of XP internal to the VP. We illustrate the first possibility with verbs of consumption and creation, which Dowty (1991) describes as verbs with incremental themes, and the second with goal phrases and resultative phrases.

Verbs of consumption such as *eat* and *drink* and verbs of creation such as *paint* and *knit* describe nondelimited activities, as indicated by their ability to cooccur with durative phrases.

(54) Patricia ate (grapes) for an hour.

When the direct object of these verbs is an NP that denotes a specific quantity, as in (55), the eventuality described becomes delimited, as indicated by the sentence's compatibility with a nondurative time adverbial.

(55) Patricia ate a bunch of grapes in/*for an hour.

Sometimes the direct object does not serve to delimit the eventuality, but some other constituent inside the VP—for example, a PP—does. This situation holds with verbs of exerting force, such as *push* and *pull*.

(56) a. Martha pushed the cart.
      b. Martha pushed the cart to the shed.

The eventuality in (56a) is nondelimited, whereas the addition of the PP in (b) provides an endpoint, thus delimiting the eventuality.

Resultative phrases resemble the goal phrases found with verbs like *push* and *pull*, in that they too serve to delimit an eventuality; in fact, this insight might be behind L. Levin and Simpson's (1981) analysis of both *to* phrases and resultative phrases as goals. Most resultative phrases do not specify an achieved location but rather specify an achieved state. The delimiting function of resultative phrases can be seen by examining the effect of adding a resultative phrase to a sentence that in the absence of such a phrase may receive a nondelimited interpretation. This property is observed in sentences with verbs such as *wipe*, as illustrated in (57a), where both the delimited and nondelimited interpretations are available in the absence of an explicit delimiter. But the addition of a resultative phrase affects the interpretation: (57b), in contrast to (57a), has only a delimited interpretation.

(57) a. The waiter wiped the table (in/for two minutes).
     b. The waiter wiped the table dry (in/*for two minutes).

With verbs that are lexically delimited, the resultative phrase provides a further specification of the achieved state, as in sentences like *The river froze solid* and *The climbers froze to death*.

2.3.2 The Incompatibility of Resultative Phrases with Verbs of Inherently Directed Motion

We return now to the question of the incompatibility of resultative phrases with verbs of inherently directed motion. Verbs of inherently directed motion are achievement verbs; they specify an achieved endpoint—an attained location. Tenny suggests that an eventuality may have only one delimitation: "There may be at most one 'delimiting' associated with a verb phrase" (1987:190).[11] This is a grammatical constraint, since there is nothing incoherent in a proposition such as *Willa became breathless as a result of arriving*, which is what a resultative interpretation of (51b), repeated as (58), would be intended to convey.

(58) Willa arrived breathless.

As mentioned earlier, the delimitation of an eventuality in a sentence may be a consequence of the meaning of the verb in the sentence, if the verb is inherently delimited, or the eventuality may be explicitly delimited through the use of a PP or other XP that functions as a delimiter. Given that verbs of inherently directed motion are lexically delimited, since their meaning involves an achieved change of location, they may not take a second syntactically encoded delimiter specifying a change of state. Thus, these verbs can appear with goal phrases only if they serve to specify further the endpoint inherent in the verb's meaning, as in (59).

(59) We arrived at the airport.

Support for this approach comes from verbs of manner of motion such as *run*, *swim*, and *walk*. These verbs, which do not describe inherently delimited eventualities, can appear with resultative phrases, but only in the absence of a goal phrase, a restriction that arises because both types of phrases act as delimiters.

(60) a.   We ran the soles off our shoes.
     b.   *We ran the soles off our shoes into the town. (meaning: we
          wore our soles down as a result of running into town)

Additional support comes from the incompatibility of resultative phrases with transitive verbs such as *bring* and *take*, whose meanings, like those of the verbs of inherently directed motion, involve an inherently specified direction (Simpson 1983a). Like the verbs of inherently directed motion, these verbs allow only a depictive interpretation of an XP.

(61) *Sharon took/brought Willa breathless.

Still more support derives from the contrast in behavior with respect to the resultative construction between verbs of inherently directed motion and a second class of unaccusative achievement verbs, verbs of change of state such as *break* in their intransitive use, as in *The window broke*. The verb of change of state *break*, like the verb *arrive*, is lexically delimited; however, unlike *arrive, break* describes the attainment of a state, not the attainment of a location. Despite the lexical delimitation, *break* can occur with a resultative phrase.

(62) The bottle broke open.

The resultative phrase in (62) can be seen as a further specification of the inherent state that is part of *break*'s meaning, in the sense that something can break without breaking open, so that breaking open is a very specific type of breaking, which contrasts, for example, with breaking apart. The resultative phrase in (62), then, does not describe a second result state in addition to the state inherently specified by *break;* therefore, it is not prohibited from occurring with the verb.[12]

The XP found with a verb of inherently directed motion can sometimes be understood as specifying an achieved state, as in (63), but when the XP receives this interpretation, the verb no longer describes physical displacement, and the construction is no longer a resultative construction. That is, (63) does not mean 'the child came to be asleep/silent as a result of a change of position'; rather, it simply means that 'the child came to be asleep/silent'.

(63) The child fell asleep/silent.

It appears that the component of meaning in the verb that is incompatible with the change of state has been lost, and only the notion of achievement inherent in the meaning of the verb is preserved; that is, the verb means something like 'become' or 'come to be', with the XP specifying the achieved state. An XP can be understood as specifying an achieved state with a verb of inherently directed motion if the verb loses its motion sense, as the prohibition against two delimitations suggests. To cite another example, a sentence such as *The letter came open* is only two-ways ambiguous. It can mean either 'the letter arrived without having been sealed', where the AP receives a depictive interpretation, or 'the letter came to be unsealed', where the AP is interpreted as an achieved state. This sentence cannot receive the interpretation that would have been expected if it involved a resultative construction: it cannot mean 'the letter became unsealed as a result of coming'. That is, *open* cannot be understood as a delimiter, if *come* retains its displacement sense.

An example cited by A. Goldberg (1991), *We broke the walnuts into the bowl* (Goldberg's (41)), poses a potential problem for the claim that there may be at most one delimiter per clause, as do the similar examples in (64).

(64) a. The cook cracked the eggs into the glass.
     b. Daphne shelled the peas onto the plate.

These examples describe both a change of state and a change of location. However, the noun heading the postverbal NP in these examples is of a very special type. The noun *walnut* can refer to the nut as a whole (i.e., both the nutshell and the nutmeat) or to the nutmeat alone; the nouns *egg* and *peas* also have two senses showing a similar relation. In Goldberg's example, the nut is broken (a change of state) and the nutmeat goes into the bowl (a change of location). This suggests that the restriction may be that only one change per entity may be expressed in a single clause. In most instances, this amounts to a restriction of one change per clause, because the entity that undergoes the change must be expressed as the direct object. There is no way to predicate a change of more than one entity, since only one argument can be expressed as a direct object. In the examples under discussion here, the NP can be understood to refer "inherently" to two entities, each of which can have a change predicated of it. We assume that examples such as *slice the mushrooms into the bowl*, which might appear problematic since mushrooms differ from peas, eggs, and nuts in not having a shell and contents, should actually be handled in the same way, in that the noun *mushrooms* can be used to refer to the whole mushrooms or to the cut-up mushrooms. NPs that do not have this property cannot appear in this kind of resultative construction (*I broke the mirror into the garbage pail*); that is, pieces of a mirror are not generally referred to as "mirrors." Goldberg makes the interesting point that the verbs that appear in these kinds of sentences all describe changes of state that are typically accompanied by a change in position. A similar analysis can be applied to a type of example discussed by Parsons (1990), *I emptied the tank into the sink*, where, as discussed by Apresjan (1973, 1992), Ostler and Atkins (1991), and others, container nouns such as *tank* regularly refer to both the container and its contents.

2.3.3 Resultative Phrases and Stative Unaccusative Verbs

The incompatibility of resultative phrases with stative unaccusative verbs such as *remain* is subsumed under the more general fact that resultative phrases are incompatible with all statives, whether expressed by transitive or unaccusative verbs, as pointed out by Carrier and Randall (in press) and Hoekstra (1992).

(65) a. *The appraisers felt the rug threadbare through their shoes.
     b. *The botanist smelled the moss dry from across the room.
        (C&R, in press, (255b,c))

(66) a. *The Loch Ness monster appeared famous.
     b. *The POWs survived into frustration.
        (C&R, in press, (257))

The postverbal AP in (65b) cannot be interpreted as a resultative phrase; that is, the interpretation where the smelling actually dries out the moss is unavailable. Compare this example to the identical example where the verb has been replaced by *sniff*—a nonstative verb of perception using the sense of smell.

(67) The botanist sniffed the moss dry. (C&R, in press, (256c))

We attribute the absence of such resultative constructions to the typology of ontological categories of eventualities: there is no such eventuality type as a delimited state. In Vendler's (1957) classification of eventuality types, as well as in the subsequent classifications based on his work, there are two categories of delimited eventualities: accomplishments and achievements. Both of these are nonstative. There is also a systematic relation between activities and accomplishments, in that accomplishments are merely delimited activities. In English there appears to be a productive relation between activities and accomplishments. For almost any activity, a corresponding accomplishment can be formed. Resultative formation can be seen as an instance of this strategy. The addition of a resultative phrase can be used to map an activity into an accomplishment. However, since there is no eventuality type of delimited state, resultative phrases cannot be used to create eventualities of this type from stative verbs.

2.4 Alternative Accounts of the Resultative Construction

The salient features of our analysis are that the DOR is given a quasi-syntactic explanation, with unaccusativity being represented syntactically, and that the arguments of verbs are projected in the resultative construction in the same way as they are when the verb is found in isolation. In this section we compare our account with accounts that differ in both respects. First, we compare our account with one that, although it also assumes unaccusativity is syntactically represented, also assumes the arguments of the verb are projected differently in the resultative construction. Then, we compare our syntactic account with a number of accounts that are purely semantic in that they do not appeal to the syntactic properties of unaccusative verbs in order to explain the difference between the behavior of unaccusative and unergative verbs in the resultative construction.

2.4.1 A Comparison with Hoekstra's Account
In sections 2.2.2 and 2.2.3 we provided a syntactic explanation for why the DOR holds and showed that our proposal has interesting ramifications for the nature of lexical representation. Here we compare our explanation of the DOR with the rather different syntactic explanation presented by Hoekstra (1988, 1992). Hoekstra's account assumes a uniform syntactic structure for all resultative constructions independent of the type of verb; thus, it rejects the central assumption in our account, that the verb in the resultative construction projects its arguments in exactly the same way as it does when it is in isolation. Although either position could potentially be correct, we will show that the syntactic properties of the resultative construction favor our approach over Hoekstra's. In addition, we will argue that the examples that appear to support Hoekstra's uniform structure assumption are actually not instances of the resultative construction.

The central feature of Hoekstra's analysis is the assumption that the resultative phrase and the NP that it is predicated of always form a small clause no matter what type of verb is found in the resultative construction. This approach is consistent with the theory first put forth by Stowell (1981)—but challenged by others (see, for example, Williams 1983, Schein 1982, Rothstein 1983, Rapoport 1987, Carrier and Randall 1992)—that the predication relation is always encoded syntactically in a clausal structure. In Hoekstra's account, most of the syntactic properties of the resultative construction are reduced to properties of the small clause structure assigned to these constructions. (Semantic constraints on the construction are generally reduced to aspectual properties as they are in our account.)

Consider first constructions based on transitive or intransitive unergative verbs, which, as illustrated in (68), are given identical structures.

(68) a. Terry [$_{VP}$ wiped [$_{SC}$ the table clean]].
     b. She [$_{VP}$ slept [$_{SC}$ her wrinkles away]].

In this account, the crucial property of the small clause in both instances is that it is L-marked by the verb in the terminology of Chomsky (1986a). Since the small clause denotes the state resulting from the activity described by the verb, it serves to delimit the eventuality described by the VP. The delimiting function of the small clause is what licenses its appearance in the sentence, and also what allows the relation between the verb and the small clause to be one of L-marking. Since the small clause is L-marked, it is transparent to government, allowing the subject of the small clause to be either a lexical NP, as it is in (68a–b), or an NP-trace, as it is when the verb in the construction is a passive or unaccusative verb.

(69) a. The table$_i$ was [$_{VP}$ wiped [$_{SC}$ t_i clean]].
     b. The gate$_i$ [$_{VP}$ swung [$_{SC}$ t_i open]].

The inability of resultative phrases to be predicated directly of unergative verb subjects follows from the assumption that even in such instances the resultative phrase would have to be part of a postverbal small clause. Since small clauses must have subjects and since the single argument of an unergative verb will not qualify, a PRO must be introduced as the subject of the small clause. The single argument of the unergative verb—its subject—would presumably control the interpretation of this PRO, giving rise to the intended interpretation. This structure is schematized in (70).

(70) *Dora$_i$ [$_{VP}$ talked [$_{SC}$ PRO$_i$ hoarse]].

This structure is unacceptable because the small clause is governed by the verb, but PRO is precluded from appearing in this position by the PRO Theorem (Chomsky 1981). The use of a fake reflexive in resultative constructions based on unergative verbs allows this problem to be circumvented.[13]

In Hoekstra's approach to the resultative construction, transitive verbs do not project their arguments in the resultative construction in the same way as they do when they appear in isolation, since in the resultative construction, they appear without an NP direct object, selecting a small clause instead, as shown in (68a). Hoekstra tries to motivate this analysis by claiming that all activity verbs—and many transitive verbs found in the resultative construction are activity verbs (e.g., *pound* and *wipe*)—can become accomplishments by the appropriate projection of arguments. In particular, activity verbs have the option of projecting a small clause that denotes a state resulting from the activity; this small clause delimits the activity described by the verb, turning it into an accomplishment.

This solution, however, runs into problems precisely because, as we showed in section 2.2.1, the facts seem to indicate that verbs project their arguments in the resultative construction in the same way as they do in isolation. So, for example, the fact that resultative constructions based on transitive and intransitive verbs differ with respect to middle formation, adjectival passive formation, nominalization, and extraction, as noted in section 2.2.1, receives no explanation on Hoekstra's account. Stated in a slightly different way, Hoekstra's analysis essentially claims that the post-verbal NP in a resultative construction based on a transitive verb is not an argument of the verb. As Carrier and Randall (1992) stress, this analysis is therefore unable to account for the fact that in (68a), for example, the table becomes clean as a result of Terry's wiping the table itself, and not as the result of her wiping something other than the table. Contrast the interpretation of such transitive-based resultative constructions with that of constructions based on unergative intransitive verbs, where the post-verbal NP has a greater degree of freedom in interpretation. As we showed in section 2.1.2, the postverbal NP in the latter may correspond to an argument of the verb loosely speaking, as in examples such as (6a), repeated here as (71), which Jackendoff (1990), among others, would take to be related to *The dog barked at him*.

(71) I ... ruthlessly roused Mr. Contreras by knocking on his door until the dog barked him awake. [S. Paretsky, *Blood Shot*, 183]

But there are also examples of such resultative constructions where the postverbal NP cannot be taken to be a participant in the event that the verb denotes on its own; one such case is (6c), repeated here as (72).

(72) ... the system does not "hallucinate" arbitrary meanings into an expression ... [D. Stallard, "The Logical Analysis of Lexical Ambiguity," 184]

As mentioned in section 2.2.2, our analysis makes a different prediction: the postverbal NP following a transitive verb needs to correspond to the regular direct object of the verb. The only exception is when the verb independently allows intransitive uses because it permits unspecified objects, as in (10c), repeated here.

(73) Having ... drunk the teapot dry ... [E. Dark, *Lantana Lane*, 94]

However, Hoekstra cites some examples that do not conform to this prediction, including those listed in (74).

(74) a. He washed the soap out of his eyes. (Hoekstra 1988:116, (35a))
        (cf. *He washed the soap.)
        (cf. *He washed—acceptable on wrong interpretation)
     b. He shaved his hair off. (Hoekstra 1988:116, (35b))
        (cf. *He shaved his hair.)
        (cf. *He shaved—acceptable on wrong interpretation)
     c. He rubbed the tiredness out of his eyes. (Hoekstra 1988:116, (35d))
        (cf. *He rubbed the tiredness./*He rubbed.)

Additional similar examples can be constructed.

(75) a. The weaver rinsed the dye out of the material.
        (cf. *The weaver rinsed (the dye).)
     b. The builder scraped the putty off the window frames.
        (cf. *The builder scraped (the putty)—acceptable on wrong interpretation)
     c. Sylvia filed the serial number off. (B. Levin and Rapoport 1988:276, (3a))
        (cf. *Sylvia filed (the serial number)—acceptable on wrong interpretation)

Hoekstra takes such examples to be representative of resultative constructions based on transitive verbs and formulates his analysis so that it can account for them. The consequence is that he is unable to account for the data that do not conform to this pattern—the data suggesting that the postverbal NP in transitive constructions is an argument of the verb. Since we take these other examples to be representative of the nature of the construction and have built our analysis on the pattern they suggest, it is incumbent upon us to provide an explanation for the examples that suggest that the postverbal NP in a transitive-based resultative construction need not be an argument of the verb.

Our claim is that these problematic examples, which we will refer to as the *wash* sentences, should not be considered instances of the resultative construction. Rather, they involve an alternate projection of the arguments of certain verbs into the syntax that comes about because verbs from a variety of semantic classes (usually, but not exclusively, verbs of contact through motion such as *wipe* and *rub*) can also become verbs of removal, a phenomenon we describe in detail in B. Levin and Rappaport Hovav 1991.[14] This is an instance of the more general phenomenon of meaning shifts described at greater length in chapter 5. We must, however, show that there is a principled reason for assuming that the *wash* sentences require a different treatment, since otherwise our argument is vacuous. We would be claiming that since there is an alternative analysis for the examples that do not conform to the predictions of our theory, there is no way to come up with counterexamples to our theory. It is not simply sufficient to claim that the *wash* sentences can receive an alternative analysis; we must also show that there is good reason to favor this analysis.

As evidence that the *wash* sentences are not instances of the resultative construction, we will show not only that the phenomenon is restricted in scope, but also that it is possible to delimit its scope rather precisely. To begin with, all the *wash* sentences involve a verb-of-removal interpretation. In all the relevant examples the purported resultative phrase is a PP describing the location that something is removed from; it is never an AP: **I washed the soap slippery, *I filed my parents edgy*. Furthermore, the object of the preposition in each instance is an NP that would otherwise be the "normal" direct object of the verb. For example, the NP *his eyes* bears roughly the same semantic relation to the verb in both *He washed the soap out of his eyes*, where it is the object of a preposition, and *He washed his eyes*, where it is the direct object. These properties of the problematic transitive examples are in striking contrast with the resultative constructions based on unergative or unspecified object verbs, where the resultative phrase can be either an AP or a PP, as shown in (76), and, if it is a PP, the object of the preposition does not have to correspond to anything that is normally considered an argument of the verb, as shown in (77).

(76) a. The clock ticked the baby awake.
     b. The phone rang me out of my slumber.

(77) a. The phone rang me out of my slumber.
       (cf. *The phone rang my slumber.)
     b. The system doesn't hallucinate meanings into the text.
       (cf. *The system doesn't hallucinate the text.)

In fact, it is likely that the *wash* sentences must include a PP since that is the only way to "bring in" the original object of the verb. If the original object is not actually present, as in *She washed the soap out*, then, as in this example, it is implied. In fact, the verbs found in the *wash* sentences cannot be found in resultative constructions that do not meet these properties.

(78) *Phil rubbed the cloth dirty. (on the interpretation where Phil causes the cloth to become dirty by rubbing things with it)

Our suggestion is that the verbs in the *wash* sentences have indeed undergone a meaning shift, becoming verbs of removal, and they therefore project their arguments differently. Thus, these verbs qualify as variable behavior verbs in the sense introduced in section 1.2.1 (see also the further discussion in section 5.1). The pattern of argument expression exhibited by these verbs is associated with the class of *wipe* verbs in B. Levin and Rappaport Hovav 1991; in fact, many of the verbs in the *wash* sentences are included on the list of members of the *wipe* verb class. In that paper we analyze the alternative expression of arguments shown by the *wipe* verbs, and we argue that it reflects a meaning shift, with the alternative argument expressions arising from the expression of arguments typical of each meaning. For instance, we suggest there that the verb *scrape* has undergone a meaning shift in the purported resultative sentence (75b), from a verb of contact through motion to a verb of removal by contact, an analysis for which we provide independent support.

These properties also correlate with the very important fact that the postverbal NP in the *wash* sentences *can* be the derived subject of the related middle, suggesting that the NPs are in fact arguments of the verb.

(79) This dye rinses/washes out easily.

It can also become the external argument of an adjectival passive.

(80) a. the rinsed-out/washed-out soap
     b. All the soap seemed washed out of my hair.

On the basis of the properties discussed here, it appears that the post-verbal NP in these examples is indeed an argument of the verb, and that in these instances the verb does have more than one option of projecting its arguments. The striking differences between these constructions and true resultative constructions based on unergative verbs suggest that these constructions were wrongly included among the resultative constructions and that there are therefore no instances of resultative constructions based on transitive verbs where the postverbal NP is not an argument of the verb. If so, we can maintain our assumption that the verb retains its argument structure in the resultative construction and that a uniform syntactic analysis of all resultative constructions, such as the one Hoekstra suggests, is unwarranted.

Before ending this section, we would like to address one more type of evidence that Hoekstra cites as favoring his analysis. Following Kayne (1984), Hoekstra suggests that the small clause analysis of the resultative construction receives support from so-called Subject Condition effects. *Subject Condition effect* is the name given to the unacceptability that typically results when a subpart of a constituent in subject position is extracted (Chomsky 1973). The following examples illustrate this effect:

(81) a. *Who$_i$ would [[for John to visit t_i] bother you]?
     b. Who$_i$ would it bother you [for John to visit t_i]?
         (Stowell 1991:191, (22a–b))

Subject Condition effects associated with extractions from a postverbal NP have often been taken as evidence for a postverbal small clause, as in (82); it is for this reason that such effects are of interest in studies of the resultative construction.

(82) ??Which politician$_i$ do you consider [$_{SC}$ [the book about t_i]
     scandalous]?

As Stowell points out, although Subject Condition effects may be an indication that a postverbal NP is the subject of a small clause, depending on the explanation given for the Subject Condition effects themselves, they may also merely indicate that a postverbal NP is not L-marked by the verb unless it is the subject of a small clause. This second option of course depends in part on which theory of the syntactic encoding of the predication relation is adopted. In any event, on our analysis of the resultative construction, the postverbal NP in a resultative construction based on a transitive verb is not the subject of a small clause, nor is it not L-marked by the verb. Therefore, if a Subject Condition effect associated with a postverbal NP is a valid diagnostic for nonargument status and if this effect shows up in all resultative constructions, we would have to provide an explanation.

Acceptability judgments involving extractions intended to test for the Subject Condition effect in resultative constructions are not all that clear. In soliciting such judgments, we have found a clear preference for extractions out of transitive-based resultative constructions over those out of unergative-based resultative constructions.

(83) a.   Which tables did you wipe the tops of clean?
     b.   Which gang did you shoot the leader of dead?

(84) a.   ?Which shoes did you run the soles of thin?
     b.   *Which man did the dog bark the neighbors of awake?

This pattern would seem to indicate that, consistent with the analysis we have been developing, the postverbal NP is an argument of the verb in the resultative construction only if it is an argument of the verb in isolation. However, Carrier and Randall (1992) present a different set of judgments, claiming that there is no distinction in acceptability in the two types of resultative constructions. Therefore, since the judgments in these instances do not yield clear results and since the rest of the evidence conforms to our analysis, we do not take the purported Subject Condition effects to argue against our analysis. If the judgments we have solicited reflect a general pattern, it is likely that the Subject Condition effects actually support our analysis.

2.4.2 Semantic Accounts

Some researchers have argued for a purely semantic account of the distribution of resultative phrases rather than the mixed syntactic/semantic account we have presented here. In this section we review and discuss three semantic analyses of the resultative construction. One explains the DOR by appeal to aspectual notions, a second appeals to notions of thematic roles, and the third essentially stipulates the DOR. We then show that the mixed syntactic/semantic analysis presented here is better equipped to describe and explain the range of data associated with the resultative construction than these alternatives.

2.4.2.1 Van Valin's Aspectual Account   As mentioned in chapter 1, Van Valin (1990) claims that all unaccusative diagnostics can receive a semantic explanation. Within the context of this general assertion, he provides an account of the resultative construction in terms of Aktionsart—lexical aspect. This account is supposed to explain the difference in behavior of unaccusative and unergative verbs without attributing different syntactic representations to the two kinds of verbs. As should be clear from our analysis in the previous section, we also take the Aktionsart of the resultative construction into consideration in explaining some of its properties. Therefore, at first glance, Van Valin's account may seem similar to our own. However, we will show that careful scrutiny of the behavior of a variety of verb classes in the resultative construction indicates that there are both syntactic and semantic aspects to the explanation of the properties of the construction, and that some of the syntactic facts are best explained by appeal to the syntactic properties of unaccusativity.

Van Valin's account is couched in terms of Role and Reference Grammar (RRG; Foley and Van Valin 1984, Van Valin 1990, 1993). In this framework, the mapping between the semantic representation of a predicate (its "logical structure" or LS) and the morphosyntactic expression of its arguments is mediated by the assignment of two macroroles—actor and undergoer—to the arguments. The linking rules and many morphosyntactic rules, such as passive, are formulated in terms of these macroroles. Van Valin claims that the DOR can be replaced with a restriction that refers to the notion "undergoer" instead of the notion "direct object."[15] He writes (1990:254–55),

The argument of which the resultative phrase is predicated is an undergoer in every case. The direct object restriction proposed by Levin and Rappaport is captured in RRG in terms of a restriction to undergoers. This correlates naturally with the Aktionsart of the construction, since constructions allowing resultatives are either accomplishments (53a,e) [= *Terry wiped the table clean; He talked himself hoarse*] or achievements (53c) [= *The river froze solid*], all of which code a result state as part of their inherent meaning. Activity verbs, which are inherently atelic and therefore cannot in principle code a result state or have an undergoer argument, do not take resultative phrases.

RRG's LS uses predicate decompositions based on those proposed by Dowty (1979) as a lexical semantic representation. The elements in these decompositions are motivated on the basis of Aktionsart and capture the properties of and the interrelationships between the various Vendler (1957) verb classes. Van Valin's explanation of the resultative construction essentially claims that the resultative phrase is always predicated of the argument of the predicates BECOME (STATE) in the LS of the verb. Because only achievements and accomplishments have this substructure in their LS, resultative constructions are possible only with achievements and accomplishments. With achievements and accomplishments, the state is always predicated of an undergoer argument; hence the undergoer restriction. A resultative phrase cannot be directly predicated of an unergative verb such as *talk*, because unergative verbs are typically activity verbs that have no state in their LS and thus lack an undergoer for the resultative phrase to be predicated of. On the other hand, unaccusative verbs, such as *freeze*, are typically achievement verbs that code a result state predicated of an undergoer.

Van Valin must also provide an explanation of the fake reflexive in resultative constructions such as *talk oneself hoarse*. Van Valin's claim is that such constructions no longer describe activities, but instead describe accomplishments, and the fake reflexive serves to signal the change in Aktionsart and not to fulfill a syntactic requirement. However, this last claim merely begs the question of why the fake reflexive is needed for deriving an accomplishment from an unergative activity verb, since the fake reflexive is not needed to derive an accomplishment from an activity with transitive and unaccusative verbs. There are transitive activity verbs and unaccusative activity verbs, and both can be turned into accomplishments through the addition of resultative phrases but without the use of fake reflexives. In isolation, the transitive verb *pound* and the unaccusative verb *roll* are atelic and therefore do not have undergoers or encode a result state. The question is why resultative phrases can be added directly to these verbs without the mediation of a fake reflexive, thereby changing their Aktionsart, whereas the same option is not available for unergative verbs such as *talk*. This contrast is precisely what the syntactic account explains.[16]

The purely aspectual account also fails to explain the restriction, noted in section 2.1.4, against adding a nonsubcategorized NP and resultative phrase to an unaccusative verb as in (20), repeated here.

(85) a. *During the spring thaw, the boulders rolled the hillside bare.
  b. *The rice slowly cooked the pot black. (meaning: the pot became black as a result of the rice cooking)
  c. *The snow melted the road slushy.

Van Valin (personal communication) suggests that this restriction is derived from the fact that Dowty's decomposition system allows LSs of the form in (86) but not (87).

(86)   [activity LS] CAUSE [achievement LS]

(87)   *[achievement LS] CAUSE [achievement LS]

Since unaccusative verbs are typically achievements, the presence of an additional result state predicated of a second NP is ruled out since this situation would give rise to the problematic LS in (87). However, this explanation cannot be extended to unaccusative verbs such as *roll, bounce,* and *cook* (on the appropriate interpretation). These verbs are all atelic, as their ability to appear with durative phrases indicates, so that a resultative construction with these verbs could not take the form in (87).

(88) a. The ball rolled for two minutes.
     b. The ball bounced for a full minute.
     c. The stew cooked for almost an hour.

Furthermore, this restriction cannot be reduced to Tenny's principle against two delimiters per VP (or, in Van Valin's terms, against two undergoers), since some of these atelic unaccusative verbs, such as *roll* and *bounce*, do not describe a change of state and do not, in isolation, take undergoers.

2.4.2.2   A Thematic Account of the Resultative Construction   Although we know of no comprehensive published account along these lines, a semantic analysis of the resultative construction can also be formulated in terms of an analysis of verb meaning based on thematic roles. If such an approach is taken, the DOR restriction or the Change-of-State Linking Rule would be replaced with a restriction stated in terms of thematic roles. Here we develop and critique as complete an analysis as we can along these lines, building on the analysis presented by L. Levin, Mitamura, and Mahmoud (1988), which in turn draws on B. Levin and Rapoport 1988. In order to bring out the problems facing such an account, we elaborate on it more fully than we might otherwise, filling in some details that have been left unexplored.

Suppose that the DOR is replaced by the following thematic restriction: a resultative phrase can be predicated only of an argument bearing the *theme* role (i.e., following Anderson (1977), Gruber (1965), and Jackendoff (1972), an entity that undergoes a change of state or position or whose state or position is described). Although the use of thematic role labels such as "theme" is eschewed in much recent work (Grimshaw 1990, Rappaport and B. Levin 1988, Zubizarreta 1987), let us assume for the sake of argument that some appropriately defined notion of theme can be found. L. Levin, Mitamura, and Mahmoud (1988) present such an analysis, which assimilates resultative constructions to directed motion constructions with goal phrases. On this analysis, both *We floated the bottle into the cave* and *We hammered the nail flat* are associated with the thematic structure ⟨*agent, theme, goal*⟩, where both the *into* phrase and the resultative phrase are analyzed as goals. (We showed in section 2.3 that both kinds of phrases are delimiters, justifying to some extent the common thematic analysis.) Typically, goals appear only with themes, and, if there is a thematic restriction allowing resultative phrases only to be predicated of themes, then this restriction could be used to distinguish between the grammaticality of *The river froze solid*, in which the resultative phrase is predicated of a theme, and the ungrammaticality of **Dora shouted hoarse*, which lacks a theme that the resultative phrase could be predicated of.[17]

The appearance of fake reflexive postverbal NPs with unergative verbs must also receive an explanation. Given that the verbs that appear with fake reflexives do not select direct objects, it might seem that these fake reflexives cannot bear any thematic role at all, let alone the role of theme. L. Levin, Mitamura, and Mahmoud (1988) suggest that the appearance of fake reflexives can be explained, while preserving the theme restriction. They propose that this will be possible if the lexical semantic representation of a verb in the resultative construction differs from that of the same verb when it appears without a resultative phrase in a way that requires the presence of a fake reflexive with unergative verbs.

This approach takes the resultative construction to be both lexically specified and lexically derived, rather than derived by compositional means in the syntax as we have been suggesting in this chapter. It essentially assimilates verbs in the resultative construction to other instances of variable behavior verbs, taking them all to involve a meaning shift, accompanied by a shift in syntactic behavior. The particular mode of representing the meaning shift that L. Levin, Mitamura, and Mahmoud adopt is the one sketched in B. Levin and Rapoport 1988, called there "lexical subordination."

L. Levin, Mitamura, and Mahmoud and B. Levin and Rapoport propose that lexical subordination relates the meaning of a verb in the resultative construction to the simple meaning of the same verb. Consider the transitive verb *pound*, which is basically a verb of contact by impact. When this verb is found in a resultative construction such as *Pam pounded the metal flat*, the verb means 'cause to change state by means of contact-by-impact *pound*'. The original meaning of *pound* is subordinated under a causative change-of-state predicate, as sketched in the lexical semantic representation in (89).

(89) *pound* (resultative): $[x \text{ CAUSE } [y \text{ BECOME } z] \text{ BY } [x \text{ } POUND \text{ } y]]$

Support for considering that the verb in the resultative construction has an extended meaning comes from the fact that *pound* behaves like a verb of change of state when followed by a resultative phrase, even though it does not in the absence of a resultative phrase (see also section 2.2.2).

According to accounts of lexical subordination, the newly created verb derives its syntactic properties from the "main clause" of its lexical semantic representation (i.e., the clause to the left of BY in (89)), and its "name" is derived from the subordinated clause (Laughren 1988, Rappaport and B. Levin 1988). In this case the causative main clause will dictate a transitive syntax. But the fact that the sentence *Pam pounded the metal flat* means that the metal became flat *as a result of* Pam's pounding is not explicitly represented in the syntax in this approach. The lexical semantic representation in (89) makes this aspect of the sentence's interpretation explicit.

Neither L. Levin, Mitamura, and Mahmoud nor B. Levin and Rapoport give an explicit representation for resultative constructions with unaccusative verbs. A potential lexical semantic representation of an unaccusative verb such as intransitive *freeze* when it is found in a resultative construction such as *The river froze solid* is given in (90).

(90) *freeze* (resultative): $[x \text{ BECOME } y \text{ BY } [x \text{ } FREEZE]]$

However, L. Levin, Mitamura, and Mahmoud consider the appearance of the fake reflexive with an unergative verb and attribute its presence to the causative nature of the "main clause." Suppose that the verb *shout*, when found in a sentence like *Dora shouted herself hoarse*, has the representation in (91).

(91) *shout* (resultative): $[x \text{ CAUSE } [x \text{ BECOME } y] \text{ BY } [x \text{ } SHOUT]]$

On this analysis, the reflexive is not a "fake" reflexive, but the reflex of the second occurrence of the variable x in the main clause of the lexical semantic representation in (91): the occurrence of x that is the left argument of BECOME. The analysis extends naturally to unergative verbs followed by a nonsubcategorized NP and a resultative phrase. *The joggers ran the pavement thin* will be associated with the following extended lexical semantic representation for *run:*

(92) $[x$ CAUSE $[y$ BECOME $z]$ BY $[x$ $RUN]]$

In each instance it seems that the thematic approach relies crucially on the assumption that the verb in a resultative construction does not have the same lexical semantic representation as the same verb in isolation. Certain aspects of the meaning of the construction, which are not reflected directly in the syntax, are projected from the lexical semantic representation associated with the extended meaning of the verb.

However, this approach faces a significant limitation: it assigns all transitive and unergative verbs in resultative constructions a lexical semantic representation with the same main clause substructure. This substructure is shown in (93).

(93) $[x$ CAUSE $[y$ BECOME $STATE]]$

As a consequence, this approach loses the insight discussed in section 2.2 that the syntax of the resultative construction is determined by the syntax of the verb in isolation. In particular, this analysis does not account for the fact that the NP corresponding to the y variable in (93) behaves like an argument of the verb when the subordinated verb is transitive, but not when the subordinated verb is intransitive. Recall from section 2.2.1 that the postverbal NP in *Terry wiped the table clean* behaves like an argument of the verb, whereas the postverbal NP in *The joggers ran the pavement thin* does not. If the postverbal NP in both instances corresponds to the same variable in the same substructure of the lexical semantic representation, then a significant syntactic insight is lost.

On the thematic approach, one way to deal with the difference in syntax is to assume that resultative constructions based on transitive verbs do not have the lexical semantic representation associated with the extended meaning, whereas those based on unergative verbs do. Then a representation of the verb in *Dora shouted herself hoarse* could be assumed to give rise to a syntactic structure in which the postverbal NP is part of a small clause, whereas a representation for *Terry wiped the table clean* would give rise to a regular transitive syntactic structure. This approach is unsatisfactory, however, since it precludes a unified account of resultative constructions. The lexical semantic representation associated with the extended meaning is designed to capture certain aspects of meaning that are

present in resultative constructions based on both transitive and unergative verbs (for example, the fact that the state denoted by the resultative
XP is achieved as a result of the action described by the verb and the fact
that all verbs in resultative constructions have a change-of-state reading).
But if the lexical semantic representation of a resultative construction
based on a transitive verb does not involve a meaning shift, then, at
least for transitive verbs, these aspects of the meaning of the construction
would have to be derived in some other way, for example, along the lines
we suggested in section 2.2.3. If these aspects of meaning are derived
compositionally for the transitive-based resultatives, then there would
seem to be little motivation for retaining the thematic approach at all.

2.4.2.3 Jackendoff's Account   Jackendoff (1990) presents an analysis of
the resultative construction in the context of what he calls "superordinate
adjunct rules." These adjunct rules are rather similar to the rule of "lexical
subordination" found in B. Levin and Rapoport 1988, in that they subordinate the meaning (and the syntax) of the verb to a newly introduced
predicate. The newly introduced predicate is what Jackendoff refers to as
a "superordinate adjunct."

Conceptually, Jackendoff conceives of the resultative construction as a
"constructional idiom," in that the conceptual structure and the syntactic
structure of the entire construction are lexically given, and the conceptual
structure of the verb is "plugged in" as a variable. Jackendoff offers two
rules for the construction. The rule for resultative constructions based on
transitive and unergative verbs is given in (94), and the rule for unaccusative verbs is given in (95).

(94) *Resultative Adjunct Rule* (version 3: constructional idiom)

$[_{VP} \, V_h \, NP_j \, AP_k]$ may correspond to

$$
\begin{bmatrix}
\text{CAUSE } ([\alpha], [\text{INCH } [\text{BE}_{\text{Ident}} \, ([\beta], [\text{AT } [\quad]_k])]]) \\
\text{AFF}^- \, ([\quad]^\alpha_i, [\{\alpha\}]^\beta_j) \\
[\text{BY } [\text{AFF}^- \, ([\alpha], \{[\beta]\})]_h]
\end{bmatrix}
$$

(Jackendoff 1990:231, (48))

(95) *Noncausative AP Resultative Adjunct Rule*

$[_{VP} \, V_h \, AP_k]$ may correspond to

$$
\begin{bmatrix}
\text{INCH } [\text{BE}_{\text{Ident}} \, ([\alpha], [\text{AT } [_{\text{Property}} \quad]_k])] \\
\text{AFF } ([\quad]^\alpha_i, \quad) \\
[\text{BY } [\text{AFF}^- \, (\quad , [\alpha])]_h]
\end{bmatrix}
$$

(Jackendoff 1990:239, (73))

These rules stipulate the meaning and the syntax of the construction in each instance, as well as the correspondence between the arguments of the subordinated verb and the syntactic positions. The first line of the structures enclosed in the large square brackets in (94) and (95) sets out the basic meaning of the constructions. The material on the remaining two lines sets out certain semantic restrictions on the verbs that can appear in each structure.

Although these rules capture the semantics of the construction quite accurately, there are two major problems we see with this approach. First, it is similar to the approach of L. Levin, Mitamura, and Mahmoud (1988) that we just reviewed in that the syntax of the verb in the construction is subordinated to the syntax of the entire construction. Therefore, it cannot in principle distinguish between resultative constructions based on transitive verbs and those based on unergative intransitive verbs. In fact, Jackendoff explicitly claims that "even in the transitive cases . . . , the direct object as well as the predicate AP is actually an adjunct—not part of the verb's argument structure" (1990:228). This, we showed, is simply not true, since it disregards the syntactic properties of the postverbal NP in resultative constructions based on transitive verbs. In fact, it needs to be stipulated in the appropriate rule that the object of the main clause is identical to that of the subordinated clause. This property falls out naturally, without stipulation, in the account we gave.

The second problem is the way in which Jackendoff derives the fact that unergative and unaccusative verbs appear in different types of resultative constructions. Jackendoff accounts for this difference by stipulating that the verb in the intransitive (objectless) resultative constructions must take an undergoer or patient, whereas the verb in the resultative constructions containing a fake reflexive takes only an actor. Although this statement perhaps accurately captures the distinction required here, it is essentially a stipulation. For instance, could English have been different only in that unergative verbs appeared in the intransitive structure? Essentially, our analysis, which preserves the syntax of the verb and derives the semantics of the structure compositionally based on general rules of syntax and semantic composition, derives the same results as Jackendoff's, while capturing the syntactic properties of the construction more accurately. In fact, Marantz (1992) levels a criticism along the same lines against Jackendoff's analysis of the similar *X's way* construction, introduced in chapter 4 and more extensively discussed in section 5.1.3.

2.5 Conclusion

In this chapter we have explored whether there is evidence for unaccusativity in English through a study of the resultative construction, a construction that has been claimed to be sensitive to the unaccusative/unergative distinction. We have presented a mixed syntactic/semantic approach to the resultative construction in which unaccusativity is syntactically represented and have argued that this approach is to be preferred over semantic ones.

Chapter 3

The Causative Alternation: A Probe into Lexical Semantics and Argument Structure

In the previous chapter we argued at length in favor of the existence of a class of verbs with the syntactic properties attributed to unaccusative verbs by the Unaccusative Hypothesis: the selection of a direct internal—but no external—argument and, concomitantly, the inability to assign accusative Case. In this chapter and the next two, we will examine the lexical properties of unaccusative verbs in order to get at the essence of this class of verbs. We will approach the issue from two related perspectives: the basic adicity of unaccusative verbs and their lexical semantic characterization. Establishing basic adicity and uncovering those aspects of meaning that determine syntactic classification are fundamental to the development of a theory of the lexical semantic representation of unaccusative verbs.

In this chapter we use the much-studied causative alternation (see B. Levin 1993 for references), illustrated in (1), as a probe for uncovering these properties.

(1) a. Pat broke the window./The window broke.
    b. Antonia opened the door./The door opened.
    c. Tracy sank the ship./The ship sank.

In English verbs that participate in this alternation show transitive and intransitive uses such that the transitive use has roughly the meaning 'cause to V-intransitive'. In some languages the alternation is characterized by morphologically related rather than identical forms of the verb in the two variants, though the same semantic relationship between the variants is maintained.

The semantic relationship between the two variants is reflected in the fact that the subject of the intransitive variant and the object of the transitive variant bear the same semantic role. The causative alternation has been claimed to be an unaccusative diagnostic (Burzio 1986, C. Rosen 1981, among others) precisely because this sharing of a semantic role can be explained if the verb in the intransitive variant is unaccusative, so that its subject is a D-Structure object. In fact, unaccusative analyses of the intransitive variant, such as the one presented by Hall (1965), antedate Perlmutter's formulation of the Unaccusative Hypothesis.

Many of the verbs cited as prototypical unaccusatives—specifically, verbs of change of state, such as the English verbs *break*, *dry*, and *open*, as well as their counterparts in other languages—participate in the causative alternation.[1] Indeed, participation in the causative alternation has been considered to be a hallmark of a verb of change of state (e.g., Fillmore 1970). In contrast, verbs that are considered prototypical unergatives such as *laugh*, *play*, and *speak* do not participate regularly in the alternation, at least not in English, French, Italian, and Russian.[2]

(2) a.   The children played.
    b. *The teacher played the children.
        (cf. The teacher made the children play.)

(3) a.   The actor spoke.
    b. *The director spoke the actor.
        (cf. The director made the actor speak.)

(4) a.   The crowd laughed.
    b. *The comedian laughed the crowd.
        (cf. The comedian made the crowd laugh.)

Thus, there appears to be good reason to use the causative alternation as a probe into the nature of unaccusativity. If, as previous studies suggest, a verb's ability to participate in the causative alternation correlates strongly with an unaccusative classification of that verb, then one way to arrive at the semantic characterization of the unaccusative class is by asking what element of meaning sets causative alternation verbs like *break* apart from nonalternating verbs like *speak*.

Since unaccusative and unergative verbs are both intransitive, the difference between them is usually considered to be a difference in semantic characterization that does not involve a difference in basic adicity. For example, it has been proposed that verbs of change of state are unaccusative, whereas agentive verbs are unergative (Perlmutter 1978). However, Chierchia (1989), noting the participation of unaccusative verbs in the causative alternation, suggests that unaccusative verbs are derived from basically dyadic causative verbs, whereas unergative verbs are basically monadic. The semantic characterization of the difference between the two classes of verbs is then reflected in a difference in their basic adicity. In claiming that unaccusative verbs are underlyingly causative and thus dyadic, Chierchia's analysis departs from many others, which take these verbs to be basically monadic, the causative alternation arising from the addition of an argument (see, for example, Brousseau and Ritter 1991, Lakoff 1968, 1970, Williams 1981).

In this chapter we argue that a causative lexical semantic analysis is valid for a large class of unaccusative verbs, although in section 3.3 we argue that it is not valid for all of them. In section 3.1 we introduce our version of the causative analysis and present evidence for its validity. In section 3.2 we consider what element of meaning distinguishes between intransitive verbs that do and do not participate in the causative alternation, since this element will play an important part in the semantic determination of unaccusativity. Although, as noted above, the notions of change of state and agentivity have figured in previous accounts, we show that these notions are too coarse. We propose that a semantic distinction between what we refer to as "internally" and "externally" caused eventualities can be used to characterize when a superficially intransitive verb is basically dyadic. In section 3.2.5 we show that apparent causative pairs involving unergative verbs do not instantiate the same phenomenon as the causative pairs involving verbs of change of state.

In section 3.3 we show that the causative alternation can also be used to argue for the existence of two major semantically defined subclasses of unaccusative verbs. Specifically, we show that in English and other languages verbs of existence and appearance, though cited as bona fide unaccusative verbs, are like unergative verbs in generally lacking causative uses. The causative analysis of unaccusative verbs, then, cannot be extended to the whole class of unaccusatives. This should not be surprising since, as mentioned in chapter 1, we do not take finding a unified lexical semantic representation for all unaccusative verbs to be a goal of this work. Given the many-to-one mapping between lexical semantics and syntax, there is no more reason to believe that the class of unaccusative verbs is homogeneous than there is to believe that all transitive verbs constitute a single semantic class. With respect to the question we address in this chapter, there is no reason to believe that all unaccusative verbs have the same adicity and argument structure.

What emerges from the investigation in this chapter, then, is a correlation between certain lexical semantic properties, basic adicity, and the argument structure associated with intransitive verbs, where the lexical semantic properties have an explanatory relation to adicity and argument structure. We conclude that intransitive verbs can be divided into (at least) three distinct classes with respect to their lexical semantic representation. The first is the class of unaccusative verbs whose lexical semantic representation is basically that of a causative (dyadic) verb and whose argument structure consists of a single direct internal argument. The second is also a class of unaccusative verbs, but these unaccusative verbs are not related to "more basic" causative verbs. The members of this second class are shown to have two internal arguments. The last class consists of the unergative verbs, a set of verbs that in terms of their lexical semantic representation are basically monadic and in terms of their argument structure take a single external argument. In the course of this chapter, we introduce most of the semantically defined intransitive verb classes that we will be analyzing further in the remainder of the book. (Full lists of the members of the major intransitive verb classes that we discuss are included in appendix A.) As we do this, we sketch the semantic characterization of the three classes of intransitive verbs that need to be distinguished on the basis of argument structure. In the next chapter we elaborate on the lexical semantic properties of the various classes of verbs and formulate the linking rules that give rise to the syntactic properties of these verb classes. In this chapter, as in the last, we take the unaccusative and unergative status of certain verbs for granted, without justifying their syntactic status through the use of unaccusative diagnostics. We do this in chapters 4 and 5.

3.1 A Causative Analysis of Alternating Unaccusative Verbs

The observation that many of the verbs cited as unaccusatives are paired with morphologically related, if not identical, causative transitive counterparts in a variety of languages has led Chierchia (1989) and, in his footsteps, Reinhart (1991) to argue that all unaccusative verbs are basically causative. We assume that the alternating unaccusative verbs are basically causative, although we differ from Chierchia and Reinhart in not extending this analysis to the nonalternating unaccusative verbs for reasons that we set out in section 3.3. More specifically, we assume that the alternating unaccusative verbs have a single lexical semantic representation associated with both their unaccusative and transitive forms, and that this is a causative lexical semantic representation. Thus, in terms of its lexical semantic representation the verb *break* of *The window broke* is a dyadic causative verb, just as the verb *break* of *Pat broke the window* is. This analysis departs from the analyses that are typically found in other studies, which assume that the intransitive variant of a causative alternation verb is basic and the transitive variant derived. This assumption probably stems from the fact that the typical definition given for the meaning of the verb in the transitive variant of the causative alternation includes that of the verb in the intransitive variant: whereas transitive *break* means something like 'cause to become broken', intransitive *break* appears to mean simply 'become broken'. In contrast, on our analysis those intransitive verbs that do not participate in the causative alternation are inherently monadic predicates, whereas the alternating verbs are inherently dyadic causative predicates. Causative verbs detransitivize only under specific circumstances; we discuss the circumstances that license the nonexpression of the cause in section 3.2.3. But we stress that on our analysis causative verbs do not arise from a process of causativization—they are inherently causative—but instead undergo a process of detransitivization under certain conditions.

The following lexical semantic representations for the two types of verbs illustrate the kind of distinction we propose.

(5) *break:* [[x DO-SOMETHING] CAUSE [y BECOME *BROKEN*]]

(6) *laugh:* [x *LAUGH*]

A verb like *break* on both its transitive and intransitive uses has a complex lexical semantic representation involving the predicate CAUSE; it represents the meaning of such verbs as involving two subevents, each an argument of CAUSE. The analysis of CAUSE that we are adopting, then, is the "biclausal" or "bievent" analysis argued for by Dowty (1979) and Parsons (1990), among others, and adopted in the work of a number of researchers including Pustejovsky (1991b) and Van Valin (1990) (see also D. Wilkins and Van Valin 1993). The two subevents can be characterized as the *causing* subevent and, following Hale and Keyser (1987), the *central* subevent—the event that specifies the change associated with the verb. Each of the arguments of the verb is associated with a distinct subevent: the causer argument is associated with the causing subevent, and the passive participant—that is, the argument that undergoes the change, which is often referred to as the *patient* or *theme*—with the central subevent (see

Grimshaw and Vikner 1993 for evidence for such an analysis). In some instances the external argument of such a verb corresponds to the entire causing subevent, as in *Will's banging shattered the window*. More often, however, the external argument of such a verb is simply a participant in the causing subevent. This participant can be viewed as representing the entire causing subevent via a process of metonymy, as discussed by D. Wilkins and Van Valin (1993), who call the projection of one of the arguments of the causing subevent to stand in for the whole event "metonymic clipping." It is due to the nature of this process that such verbs may have external arguments that can be agents, instruments, or natural forces (e.g., *The boy/The rock/The earthquake broke the window*).

The lexical semantic representation associated with a nonalternating intransitive verb such as *laugh* does not involve the predicate CAUSE; its representation has only one subevent, and it is taken to be basically monadic. The lack of a causative variant for such verbs is a reflection of the fact that these verbs do not have the predicate CAUSE and the accompanying causing subevent in their lexical semantic representation.[3]

The linking rules that determine the syntactic expression of the arguments in these lexical semantic representations are presented in chapter 4; however, whatever their formulation, it is clear that the intransitive form of *break* must arise from an operation that prevents the causer argument from being projected to the lexical syntactic representation (the argument structure).[4] We discuss this operation in section 3.2. Thus, we take the lexical semantic representation of the intransitive form of the verb *break* to be causative and dyadic, but we follow standard analyses in assuming that the intransitive form of the verb is monadic at argument structure, the level of representation that determines the projection of arguments into the syntax. The unaccusativity of intransitive *break* will follow from the fact that the same linking rule applies to the passive participant whether or not the causer is projected onto the syntax.

We now present some evidence in support of the causative analysis we have just sketched. We begin with evidence involving selectional restrictions. It is almost a defining property of the causative alternation as we have described it that the subject of the intransitive use of the verb bears the same semantic relation to the verb as the object of the transitive use. The shared semantic relations are typically reflected in the existence of common selectional restrictions, a property of these verbs noted by some researchers (see, for instance, Fillmore 1970, Hall 1965). The examples in (7) and (8) suggest that the set of possible objects of transitive *break* and the set of possible subjects of intransitive *break* do indeed coincide; specifically, only certain types of physical objects can break.

(7) a. Antonia broke the vase/the window/the bowl/the radio/the toaster.
    b. The vase/The window/The bowl/The radio/The toaster broke.

(8) a. *Antonia broke the cloth/the paper/the innocence.
    b. *The cloth/The paper/The innocence broke.

On closer examination, however, it turns out that the selectional restrictions on the subject of intransitive *break* and the object of transitive *break* are not identical. For instance, there are senses of the verb *break* where the overlap in selectional restrictions is not complete, as in the examples in (9), which were inspired by similar French examples in Brousseau and Ritter 1991.

(9) a. He broke his promise/the contract/the world record.
    b. *His promise/The contract/The world record broke.

It appears that across senses transitive *break* allows a wider range of objects than intransitive *break* allows subjects.

This phenomenon is more general. It is not difficult to find alternating verbs where the selectional restrictions on the subject of the intransitive variant and the object of the transitive variant are not identical.[5] Consider another verb of change of state, *open*. It appears that some of the possible objects of transitive *open* cannot be subjects of intransitive *open*. As with *break*, this happens, for example, with some of the extended uses of the verb, as in (11).

(10) a. Jean opened the door/the window.
     b. The door/The window opened.

(11) a. This book will open your mind.
     b. *Your mind will open from this book.

The differences do not only show up with less "literal" uses of verbs. Consider the verb *clear*, a deadjectival verb that presumably means 'cause to become clear$_{Adj}$' or 'become clear$_{Adj}$'. This verb is found in causative pairs, as in (12); yet, although one can clear a table, the table can't "clear," as shown in (13).

(12) a. The wind cleared the sky.
     b. The sky cleared.

(13) a.   The waiter cleared the table.
     b.   *The table cleared.

In this instance, once again an alternating verb when used transitively is found with a set of objects that is larger than the set of subjects that the same verb allows when used intransitively. As a final example, consider the verb of change of state *lengthen*, which also demonstrates the same pattern of selectional restrictions: there are things that can be lengthened, but that do not lengthen.

(14) a.   The dressmaker lengthened the skirt.
     b.   *The skirt lengthened.

(15) a.   The mad scientist lengthened the days.
     b.   The days lengthened.

If these examples are representative, they suggest that a close examination of a wide range of alternating verbs will reveal that the selectional restrictions on the object of the transitive use and the subject of the intransitive use do not coincide for any verb. However, there is still a generalization that ties all the examples cited here together: the set of possible subjects for the intransitive use of a verb appears to be a subset of the set of possible objects for the transitive use of the same verb.

The asymmetry in the selectional restrictions is significant since it provides a guide to which variant is basic. We assume that the basic use of the verb will impose less stringent restrictions on its arguments, so that in those instances where there are different selectional restrictions on the transitive and intransitive uses, the use with the looser selectional restrictions, if there is one, will be basic. We do not make the alternative assumption that the basic form of the verb is the one that imposes more stringent restrictions since then it would not be easy to derive the variant with the looser restrictions in a plausible way. That is, if intransitive *clear* were the basic form of this verb, it would be difficult to derive the transitive use in *The waiter cleared the table*, which has no intransitive counterpart, short of asserting that the transitive and intransitive uses of a verb like *clear* are not related. Taking this interpretation of the selectional restriction patterns together with data discussed in (12)–(13), then the transitive use of the verb *clear* is basic. A similar assumption about selectional restrictions is made by Junker (1988) in an investigation of the basic transitivity of deadjectival verbs in French; overall, the results of Junker's study support the results of our study. Selectional restriction data, then, support the claim that certain unaccusative verbs have a causative lexical semantic representation.

The next argument for the causative analysis, which is morphological in nature, is drawn from Chierchia 1989. Chierchia points out that an unaccusative verb that lacks a paired transitive causative use is exceptional on the causative analysis and would be expected to acquire such a use because it derives from a causative predicate and is thus basically dyadic. Chierchia suggests that an unaccusative verb like *come*, for example, which lacks a causative use, is related to a causative verb meaning something like *bring*, but that this causative verb either is not lexicalized or is marked as being lexicalized by a verb that is not related to the intransitive verb morphologically. Citing a personal communication from C. Rosen, Chierchia points out that unaccusative verbs tend to have what he calls "unstable valency." That is, "[t]hey tend to oscillate in valence from transitive to intransitive and vice versa, both diachronically and across dialects" (Chierchia 1989:23). For example, Chierchia cites the Italian verb *crescere* 'grow', which in standard Italian is only intransitive, though there are dialects where it has a transitive causative use with the meaning 'raise (children)'. As an illustration of this point from English, consider the verb *deteriorate;* this verb is generally used only intransitively (*Over the years the roof deteriorated*), but B. Levin once heard her landlord say *The pine needles were deteriorating the roof.* In contrast, Chierchia points out, similar variation is not expected of unergative verbs, since they are basically monadic. Unergative verbs like English *cry* and *sweat*, or their Italian counterparts *piangere* and *sudare*, respectively, are in fact "stable" in their intransitivity in the sense that they are not regularly paired with causative transitive counterparts. (As we will discuss throughout this chapter, Chierchia's discussion is only a beginning; there is in fact much more to be said about when intransitive verbs are expected to be paired with causative uses. We will show that the lack of a causative variant is often more principled than Chierchia's discussion suggests.)

Certain facts concerning the formation of causatives across languages presented by Nedjalkov (1969) are not surprising in light of our analysis of the adicity of alternating and nonalternating intransitive verbs. Nedjalkov looks at the morphological relation between the causative and noncausative uses of the verbs *break* and *laugh* (as well as two other verbs) in sixty languages. Nedjalkov finds that in most of his sample, the transitive causative form of the verb *break* is morphologically unmarked, the intransitive form being identical to the transitive form (19 out of 60 languages) or derived from this form (22 out of 60 languages). If verbs such as *break* are appropriately characterized as inherently causative verbs, then the monadic use is in some sense derived, and indeed morphological marking has a function: it is needed to indicate the nonexpression of the external cause.[6]

Nedjalkov also considers the verb *laugh*. What is striking is that Nedjalkov does not cite any languages in which this verb has a causative transitive use identical in form to or morphologically less complex than the intransitive use.[7] Nedjalkov reports that in 54 of the 60 languages surveyed, the causative form of *laugh* is morphologically more complex than the noncausative form (see also Hale and Keyser 1987 for discussion of similar data). This is in sharp contrast to the verb *break* and consistent with our proposal that *laugh* is basically a monadic verb, whose lexical semantic representation does not involve a causative predicate.

One final piece of evidence in favor of the causative analysis of unaccusative verbs, also drawn from Chierchia 1989, involves an issue of interpretation. Since the intransitive use of a verb like *break* is analyzed as containing a cause argument at some level of representation, it might be expected that some kind of adverbial modifier could be found that would reflect the presence of this cause. Chierchia suggests that the Italian phrase *da sè* 'by itself' (in the sense of 'without outside help') is such an adverbial. Returning to the alternating verbs, in Italian they are compatible with this adverbial in their intransitive uses, as (16a–b) show.

(16) a. La porta si è aperta da sè.
     the door opened   by itself
     'The door opened by itself.'
     (Chierchia 1989, (42a))
   b. La barca è affondata da sè.
     the boat sank   by itself
     'The boat sank by itself.'
     (Chierchia 1989, (42b))

The English counterpart of the Italian adverbial, the adverbial *by itself*, has two interpretations: 'without outside help' and 'alone'. Only the first interpretation is relevant to Chierchia's point, and, in fact, this interpretation is found with the intransitive use of the English alternating verbs.

(17) a. The plate broke by itself.
   b. The door opened by itself.

This adverbial appears to be modifying a cause, which, given its ana-
phoric nature, it identifies as the theme argument itself. It is striking that
the intransitive verbs that do not participate regularly in the causative
alternation do not appear with the adverbial. For instance, the most natural interpretation of the sentence *Molly laughed by herself* is that Molly
laughed unaccompanied rather than without outside help.

3.2   A Closer Look at the Causative Alternation

Having reviewed some reasons for proposing a causative analysis of certain unaccusative verbs—the alternating verbs—our next step is to provide a more precise semantic characterization of these verbs. Such a
characterization will help us to identify the semantic determinants of unaccusativity, given our claim that verbs like *break* have a causative lexical
semantic representation but allow both transitive and unaccusative expressions of their arguments. Our goal is to find an explanatory relationship between a facet of the meaning of a verb and its ability to participate
in the causative alternation. The adicity of the verb as represented in the
lexical semantic representation (5) would then be a direct reflection of a
semantic property of the verb. Although the class of alternating verbs can
most obviously be described as verbs of change of state and has in fact
been characterized precisely in these terms, it will emerge from the study
in section 3.2.1 that not all intransitive verbs of change of state have
transitive causative variants; furthermore, as we discuss in section 3.2.3,
not all transitive causative verbs of change of state have intransitive variants, and some intransitive verbs that are not verbs of change of state
have causative transitive uses. Instead, we introduce a distinction between
verbs describing "internally" and "externally" caused eventualities, arguing that this distinction more accurately predicts which verbs do and do
not participate in the causative alternation. Specifically, we claim that this
distinction determines which verbs are basically dyadic causative verbs. In
section 3.2.3 we investigate which dyadic causative verbs will have an
intransitive unaccusative variant, since not all causative verbs alternate.
That is, we ask what distinguishes alternating verbs like *break* from verbs
like *cut* and *write*, which have only transitive, but not intransitive, uses. In
section 3.2.5 we investigate some intransitive verbs that satisfy the semantic characterization of unergative verbs but have transitive uses that mean
roughly 'cause to *V*-intransitive'. We argue that in each instance the causative relationship is not the same as the one characteristic of verbs like

break. Rather, in these instances there is evidence that the intransitive variant is basic. Thus, the apparent counterexamples to our analysis actually turn out to support it.

3.2.1   Internal versus External Causation

Our task is to semantically characterize verbs such as *break* and *open* that have transitive causative uses as well as intransitive noncausative uses. In order to do this, we compare verbs such as *break* and *open* that participate in the causative alternation—and thus show both transitive and intransitive uses—with verbs such as *laugh*, *play*, and *speak* that show intransitive uses but never show transitive causative uses (except perhaps under very special circumstances). We ask what makes verbs like *break* and *open* different from those verbs that are not regularly paired with a transitive causative counterpart. In answering this question, we take as our starting point Smith's (1970) insightful discussion of the semantic factors that play a part in determining which verbs that are used intransitively have transitive causative uses.

Smith characterizes the difference between those intransitive verbs that do and do not have transitive causative uses by means of a notion of control. Verbs like *break* and *open*, Smith proposes, describe eventualities that are under the control of some external cause that brings such an eventuality about. Such intransitive verbs have transitive uses in which the external cause is expressed as subject. Verbs like *laugh*, *play*, and *speak* do not have this property: the eventuality each describes "cannot be externally controlled" but "can be controlled only by the person engaging in it"; that is, control "cannot be relinquished" to an external controller (Smith 1970:107). Smith takes the lack of a causative transitive use for these verbs (and other verbs such as *shudder*, *blush*, *tremble*, *malinger*, and *hesitate*) to be a reflection of the presence of "internal control"; we return in section 4.1.1.3 to the question of why verbs of internal control should have this property.

(18) a.   Mary shuddered.
     b.   *The green monster shuddered Mary.
     c.   The green monster made Mary shudder.
        (Smith 1970:107, (35a–c))

Similar distinctions have been recognized in other work on English (e.g., Hale and Keyser 1987) and other languages (e.g., Guerssel 1986 on Berber, Labelle 1990, 1992 on French).

For reasons we explain below, we do not use Smith's notion of control. Rather, we use a slightly different notion, distinguishing between *internally* and *externally caused* eventualities. With an intransitive verb describing an internally caused eventuality, some property inherent to the argument of the verb is "responsible" for bringing about the eventuality. For agentive verbs such as *play* and *speak*, this property is the will or volition of the agent who performs the activity. Thus, the concept of internal causation subsumes agency. However, an internally caused verb need not be agentive. For example, the verbs *blush* and *tremble*, which take animate—though nonagentive—arguments, can nevertheless be considered to describe internally caused eventualities, because these eventualities arise from internal properties of the arguments, typically an emotional reaction. These verbs, which do not participate in the causative alternation, also exemplify why the notion of control is inappropriate: neither trembling nor blushing is generally under a person's own control, as shown by the acceptability of examples such as *Carla couldn't help blushing whenever her name was called.*

Verbs with an inanimate—and thus clearly nonagentive—single argument may also describe internally caused eventualities in the sense that these eventualities are conceptualized as arising from inherent properties of their arguments. In particular, the notion of internal causation can be straightforwardly extended to encompass a class of nonagentive single argument verbs that we refer to as *verbs of emission*. This set subsumes the verbs that Perlmutter describes as verbs of "[n]on-voluntary emission of stimuli that impinge on the senses" (1978:163). The verbs of emission can be divided into four subclasses according to what is emitted: sound, light, smell, or substance.[8]

(19) a. Sound: burble, buzz, clang, crackle, hoot, hum, jingle, moan, ring, roar, whir, whistle, . . .
   b. Light: flash, flicker, gleam, glitter, shimmer, shine, sparkle, twinkle, . . .
   c. Smell: reek, smell, stink
   d. Substance: bubble, gush, ooze, puff, spew, spout, squirt, . . .

The class of verbs cited by Perlmutter (1978) includes members of only three of these subclasses (the verbs of sound, light, and smell emission); however, since the overall behavior of these three types of verbs resembles that of the members of the subgroup identified here as "verbs of substance emission," all four sets of verbs will be treated as belonging to a single larger class of verbs of emission.

The eventualities described by such verbs come about as a result of internal physical characteristics of their argument. Consequently, only a limited set of things qualify as arguments of any specific verb of emission, as reflected in the strong restrictions that these verbs impose on possible subjects. For example, only embers, lights, and certain substances glow since only they have the necessary properties, and the same holds of other verbs of emission. Consistent with their classification as internally caused verbs, verbs of emission generally do not have causative counterparts, as illustrated in (20). (We return in section 3.2.5 to instances in which they do.)

(20) a. The jewels glittered/sparkled.
     b. *The queen glittered/sparkled the jewels.

(21) a. The stream burbled/roared.
     b. *The rocks burbled/roared the stream.

(22) a. The stew bubbled.
     b. *The cook bubbled the stew.

Verbs of emission, then, pattern with other verbs without causative counterparts even though it seems inappropriate to attribute control to the argument of a verb of emission—the inanimate emitter. Consequently, we prefer the internally/externally caused verb distinction to the internal/external control distinction. (For conciseness, we will refer to internally or externally caused verbs, although it is more accurate to say that a verb describes an eventuality that can be conceptualized as either internally or externally caused.)

Unlike internally caused verbs, externally caused verbs by their very nature imply the existence of an "external cause" with immediate control over bringing about the eventuality described by the verb: an agent, an instrument, a natural force, or a circumstance. Thus, consider the verb *break*. Something breaks because of the existence of an external cause; something does not break solely because of its own properties (although it is true that an entity must have certain properties in order for it to be breakable). Although it might be possible to conceive of something as breaking spontaneously, even so, it is most natural to describe such a situation by a sentence like *The vase broke by itself*, where, as mentioned in section 3.1, the external cause is being overtly identified with the theme itself. In contrast, internally caused verbs such as *glow*, *sparkle*, *shudder*, and *tremble* cannot appear with the phrase *by itself* in the 'without outside help' sense, consistent with the absence of an external cause.[9]

(23) a. *The diamond glowed by itself.
     b. *Jane trembled by herself.

Some externally caused verbs such as *break* can be used intransitively without the expression of an external cause, but, even when no cause is specified, our knowledge of the world tells us that the eventuality these verbs describe could not have happened without an external cause. We thus assume that the intransitive verbs that regularly have transitive causative uses are externally caused, and those intransitive verbs that do not are internally caused. (In section 3.2.5 we will show that some internally caused intransitive verbs do have transitive causative uses, but we conclude that such pairs are instances of a different phenomenon.) A closer look at the class of alternating verbs will bear out this suggestion.

The core class of causative alternation verbs are the verbs of change of state, which typically describe changes in the physical shape or appearance of some entity. Jespersen (1927) suggests that the class of verbs that are found in the causative alternation can be characterized as the "move and change" class, because it includes a variety of verbs of change of state and verbs of motion. The list of alternating verbs can easily be divided into two subclasses along these lines.

(24) a. bake, blacken, break, close, cook, cool, dry, freeze, melt, open,
        shatter, thaw, thicken, whiten, widen, ...
     b. bounce, move, roll, rotate, spin, ...

Relatively few verbs of motion participate in the causative alternation; those that do are not necessarily agentive when used intransitively, consistent with our claim that alternating verbs are externally caused. (In section 3.2.5 we examine the causative uses of agentive verbs of manner of motion such as *walk* and *swim*, which because of their agentiveness must be internally caused verbs, and we argue that these causatives represent a distinct phenomenon.) To the extent that the alternating verbs of motion involve a change of position (though not necessarily a translation through space), the set of "move and change" verbs might be given the unified characterization *verbs of change*. There are, however, many more verbs of change of state than verbs of change of position among the alternating verbs, probably because there are few verbs of change of position that need not be agentive, a prerequisite for the classification of these verbs as externally caused.

The difference between internally and externally caused verbs is also reflected in the general pattern of selectional restrictions on the cause argument of the two kinds of verbs. Many nonagentive internally caused verbs exert strong restrictions on their single argument. For instance, as mentioned above, only a limited set of things qualify as the arguments of any specific verb of emission, so that only embers, lights, and certain substances glow, since only they have the necessary properties; similar restrictions hold of other verbs of emission. Although this property might seem to make the single argument of an internally caused verb resemble the argument of the noncausative use of alternating externally caused verbs such as *break*, which is also subject to strong restrictions arising from the nature of the change of state described by the verb, the appropriate comparison is between the external cause argument of an externally caused verb and the single argument of an internally caused verb. Unlike most internally caused verbs, most externally caused verbs do not impose restrictions on their external cause argument, taking agents, natural forces, and instruments as the external cause. This difference reflects the nature of internal causation, which involves causation initiated by, but also residing in, the single argument and hence dependent on its properties. In contrast, with externally caused verbs, the external cause argument sets the eventuality in motion, but it is not necessarily involved in seeing it through (verbs differ in this respect).

We return now to the lexical semantic representations for the alternating and nonalternating intransitive verbs proposed in (5) and (6), repeated here.

(25) *break:* $[[x$ DO-SOMETHING$]$ CAUSE $[y$ BECOME $BROKEN]]$

(26) *laugh:* $[x$ $LAUGH]$

As we stated in section 3.1, our proposal concerning the basic adicity of the alternating verbs influenced the choice of representation; the representation is also intended to reflect the fact that such verbs are externally caused verbs, involving two subevents. Abstracting away from the lexical semantic representations suggested for the verbs *break* and *laugh*, we propose that the lexical semantic templates associated with externally and internally caused verbs are as in (27a) and (27b), respectively.

(27) a. $[[x$ DO-SOMETHING$]$ CAUSE $[y$ BECOME $STATE]]$
　　 b. $[x$ $PREDICATE]$

It is in the nature of internally caused verbs as we have described them that they are inherently monadic predicates. Similarly, externally caused verbs are inherently dyadic predicates, taking as arguments both the external cause and the passive participant in the eventuality. The adicity of a verb is then a direct reflection of a lexical semantic property of the verb, namely, the number of open positions in the lexical semantic representation.[10]

The proposed analysis of externally caused verbs predicts that there should be no externally caused verbs without a transitive variant. An examination of the range of verb classes in B. Levin 1993 suggests that this is indeed so. That is, all externally caused verbs have a transitive causative use, but not all of them have an intransitive use in which the external cause is unspecified, as illustrated in (28)–(31) with the verbs *cut*, *sterilize*, *write*, and *murder*.

(28) a.   The baker cut the bread.
     b.   *The bread cut.

(29) a.   The nurse sterilized the instruments.
     b.   *The instruments sterilized.

(30) a.   Anita Brookner just wrote a new novel.
     b.   *A new novel wrote.

(31) a.   The assassin murdered the senator.
     b.   *The senator murdered.

The English suffix *-ize* is particularly interesting, as is the suffix *-ify*. These suffixes are used to form novel externally caused verbs from adjectives and nouns. We have collected a list of recently coined words with these suffixes (e.g., *windowize a computer*, *Aspenize Jackson Hole*, *securitize planes*), and these coinages support the prediction that there are no externally caused verbs without a transitive variant. As shown by the example in (29), many *-ize* and *-ify* verbs are only transitive, and none of the new verbs we have found are exclusively intransitive.

In English adjectives are used to describe states, and not surprisingly, many alternating verbs of change of state are deadjectival, as shown by the examples in (32), taken from Levin 1993:28. These deadjectival verbs have been divided into two groups, one in which the verbs are zero-related to adjectives, as in (32a), and a second in which the verbs are formed from adjectives through the use of the suffix *-en*, as in (32b).

(32) a. brown, clean, clear, cool, crisp, dim, dirty, dry, dull, empty,
         even, firm, level, loose, mellow, muddy, narrow, open, pale,
         quiet, round, shut, slack, slim, slow, smooth, sober, sour, steady,
         tame, tan, tense, thin, warm, yellow, ...

b. awaken, blacken, brighten, broaden, cheapen, coarsen, dampen, darken, deepen, fatten, flatten, freshen, gladden, harden, hasten, heighten, lengthen, lessen, lighten, loosen, moisten, neaten, quicken, quieten, redden, ripen, roughen, sharpen, shorten, sicken, slacken, smarten, soften, steepen, stiffen, straighten, strengthen, sweeten, tauten, thicken, tighten, toughen, waken, weaken, whiten, widen, worsen, . . .

What is relevant for us is that the adjectives that form the base for alternating verbs of change of state support the proposal that such verbs are externally caused. As pointed out by Dixon (1982), deadjectival verbs of this type tend to be related to adjectives that describe physical characteristics, color, and temperature. More generally, these verbs are related to stage-level adjectives and not to individual-level adjectives. The distinction between stage-level and individual-level predicates is introduced by Carlson (1977). Stage-level predicates describe temporary properties or transitory activities of entities; they contrast with individual-level predicates, which describe permanent properties (see also Diesing 1992, Kratzer 1989). The observation that deadjectival verbs are based on stage-level adjectives supports the claim that only externally caused verbs are found in the causative alternation: individual-level properties typically cannot be externally caused, whereas stage-level properties could be. (We do not address a larger question that is raised by these data: whether both oppositions are necessary.)

The verb *smarten* provides a particularly interesting illustration of the constraints on the adjectives that can serve as the base for alternating verbs. Although the adjective *smart* has two senses, 'intelligent' and 'well and fashionably dressed', the verb *smarten* is related to the second adjectival sense, reflecting the fact that it is typically only in this sense that the adjective describes a stage-level property, and, hence, a property that might be caused to change. Dowty (1979:129, n. 4) discusses several deadjectival verbs that do not show some of the senses of their base adjective. For example, he notes that although the adjective *tough* can mean either 'difficult' or 'resistant to tearing', the verb *toughen* cannot mean 'make difficult'. It seems to us that the stage-level versus individual-level distinction could be responsible for the set of senses available to *toughen*, as well as for those available to some of the other verbs that Dowty cites.

The interaction between the stage-level/individual-level predicate contrast and the internal/external causation contrast can also be used to explain why there is sometimes a verb related to only one member of a pair of antonymous adjectives. For instance, although there are verb pairs such as *harden* and *soften* or *widen* and *narrow* based on antonymous adjectives, corresponding to the verb *tame* there is no verb *wild* or *wilden*. Our analysis suggests that the absence of this verb is no accident. Rather, it follows because the adjective *wild*, unlike the adjective *tame*, necessarily describes an individual-level predicate and thus cannot be the basis for an externally caused verb of change of state.

Although the major class of causative alternation verbs can be characterized as verbs of change, it is important to point out that external causation cannot be equated with change of state or position. There are verbs of change of state that lack a transitive causative variant whatever the nature of the external cause argument, as the following examples show:

(33) a.   The cactus bloomed/blossomed/flowered early.
     b.   *The gardener bloomed/blossomed/flowered the cactus early.
     c.   *The warm weather bloomed/blossomed/flowered the cactus early.

(34) a.   The logs decayed.
     b.   *The rangers decayed the logs.
     c.   *The bad weather decayed the logs.

These verbs are set apart from the alternating verbs of change of state because they describe internally caused changes of state. That is, the changes of state that they describe are inherent to the natural course of development of the entities that they are predicated of and do not need to be brought about by an external cause (although occasionally they can be, and in such instances causative uses of these verbs are found). This class includes verbs such as *flower*, *bloom*, *blossom*, and *decay*, all cited above, and in some languages *blush*, as well as *grow*.[11] The class of internally caused verbs of change of state is much smaller than the large class of externally caused verbs of change of state.

The distinction between internally and externally caused eventualities is also relevant to verbs that are not verbs of change. For example, it explains the behavior of the members of a class of verbs that we call *verbs of spatial configuration* with respect to the causative alternation. This class includes verbs such as *hang*, *sit*, and *stand*, which specify the position of an entity that bears a particular spatial configuration with respect to that position; we discuss these verbs in more detail in section 3.3.3. Certain verbs of spatial configuration allow a transitive causative use; these include *hang*, *lean*, *lie*, *sit*, and *stand*.

(35) a. The laundry hung on the clothesline.
     b. Tracy hung the laundry on the clothesline.

(36) a. The ladder leaned against the wall.
     b. I leaned the ladder against the wall.

Other verbs in this class, including *slouch*—though rather close in meaning to *lean*—and *loom*, do not.

(37) a. The surly youth slouched against the wall.
     b. *I slouched the surly youth against the wall.

(38) a. The bear loomed over the sleeping child.
     b. *The giant loomed the bear over the sleeping child.

The distinction between internally and externally caused eventualities appears to provide the key to their differing behavior. Looming and slouching are postures that are necessarily internally caused, unlike hanging, leaning, sitting, or standing, which are postures that can be brought about by an external cause. These examples show yet another way in which the correlation between external causation and change of state is not perfect: there are externally caused verbs that are not verbs of change of state.

We conclude our introduction of the distinction between internally and externally caused verbs by relating it to the unaccusative/unergative distinction, previewing the discussion in chapter 4. The distinction between internally and externally caused verbs corresponds roughly to the distinction between unaccusative and unergative verbs. As we show in chapter 4, internally caused verbs are generally unergative, whereas many unaccusative verbs are derived from externally caused verbs. There are two reasons for saying that there is only a rough correspondence between the internally/externally caused verb distinction and the unaccusative/ unergative distinction. First, as we show in section 3.3, there are unaccusative verbs that are not derived from causative verbs; these are the verbs of existence and appearance. Second, as we have just shown, there is a class of internally caused verbs of change of state, and, as we show in section 4.2.1, these verbs are unaccusative.

3.2.2 Consequences of the Internally versus Externally Caused Distinction

The distinction between internally and externally caused eventualities is a distinction in the way events are conceptualized and does not necessarily correspond to any real difference in the types of events found in the world. In general, the relation between the linguistic description of events and the events taking place in the real world is mediated by the human cognitive construal of events, which is what we take our lexical semantic representations to represent.

Often there are events that are compatible with more than one cognitive construal, as Pinker (1989) and Grimshaw (1993, 1994) have stressed in their research. If the distinction between internal and external causation is indeed implicated in the way humans conceive events, then we predict that verbs that fall squarely into one or the other of these two categories will be stable in their syntactic behavior. For example, verbs that are clearly agentive will be internally caused monadic verbs and will not be found in the causative alternation. However, there are some events in the world that can be construed as either internally or externally caused. Our account predicts variation both within and across languages with respect to whether verbs describing such events are classified as internally or externally caused.

Consider the verb *deteriorate*, mentioned in section 3.1, which is classified as both an internally caused and an externally caused verb in B. Levin 1993. The change of state specified by this verb can be construed as either internally or externally caused. There may even be variation among speakers regarding whether a given eventuality that could be described by this verb should be conceptualized as internally or externally caused. For example, as already mentioned, B. Levin once heard her landlord say *The pine needles were deterioriating the roof*. Although to our ears this sentence is unacceptable, probably because we conceive of deterioration as always being internally caused, it appears that the landlord's conceptualization was different. In fact, Pinker (1989) also includes two causative uses of *deteriorate* in a list of novel causatives, noting that these examples, like the other examples in the list, "sound quite unusual" (1989:153).

(39) a. UL-approved outdoor lighting sets are weatherproofed so that water will not deteriorate the sockets. (Pinker 1989:153, (4.44a))

b. He said that the Agnew and Watergate affairs have tended to deteriorate confidence in the American system. (Pinker 1989:153, (4.44b))

In a follow-up to Nedjalkov's (1969) study discussed in section 3.1, Haspelmath (1993) discusses verbs that tend not to show consistent patterns of behavior across languages. For example, the morphologically simple form of the verb corresponding to English *melt* tends to be transitive in most languages, the intransitive form being the morphologically derived form, but a few languages show the opposite pattern. It is likely that this cross-linguistic variation arises because the meaning of a verb such as *melt* is consistent with its describing either an internally or an externally caused eventuality. In fact, it should be possible to verify this prediction by looking at the range of subjects found with *melt* in various languages; presumably, in languages where *melt* is internally caused, it will only be found with ice or ice cream or other substances that melt at room temperature as its subject when intransitive. What is important is that the nature of the externally versus internally caused verb distinction leads to expectations about where fluctuation with respect to verb classification both within and across languages may be found. It is precisely verbs such as *melt*, whose classification with respect to the syntactically relevant meaning components is in some way ambiguous, that would be expected to manifest cross-linguistic variation. If certain aspects of meaning determine syntactic behavior, then isolation of the correct syntactically relevant meaning components will help predict which types of verbs are most likely to exhibit cross-linguistic variation. Since the predictions made by the distinction between externally and internally caused eventualities seem to be correct, we take this as corroboration for our approach.

A language could choose to have two verbs whose meanings are the same in every respect except that one describes the eventuality as internally caused and the other as externally caused. An example of this possibility may be provided by a pair of verbs whose contrasting behavior was pointed out to us by A. Kroch. The verbs *shudder* and *shake* at first glance appear to be synonymous, but only *shake*, and not *shudder*, shows a transitive causative use. Given the differing behavior of these verbs with respect to the causative alternation, *shake* should be externally caused and *shudder* internally caused. This proposal receives support from an examination of the things that can shake and shudder. Not only is the set of things that shudder to a large extent a subset of the set of things that shake, but it is a subset precisely in a way that is consistent with the classification of *shudder* as describing an internally caused eventuality. Things that shudder usually can be thought of as having a "self-controlled" body; they include people, animals, and, perhaps by forced extension, the earth, engines, machinery, and vehicles. In contrast, leaves, teacups, and furniture, none of which can be said to have a "self-controlled" body, can only shake. This distinction is relevant because the type of movement characteristic of shaking or shuddering can be internally caused only with those things that have self-controlled bodies. The narrower restrictions on things that shudder reflect the classification of *shudder* as an internally caused verb. Interestingly, agentivity has nothing to do with the difference between these two verbs.

Given the importance of the nuances in meaning that are central to disentangling the varying behavior of verbs like *deteriorate* and *melt*, the survey-based studies of causatives presented by Haspelmath (1993) and Nedjalkov (1969) are of limited value. It is difficult to get the required level of detail from most grammars and dictionaries or from perfunctory data solicitation from informants. In fact, the Modern Hebrew data that Haspelmath provides are incomplete in a way that is crucial to the point that Haspelmath is investigating. The verb he cites as the Hebrew counterpart of English *burn*, *saraf*, which shows the morphological causativization pattern expected of an externally caused verb, actually means 'burn' in the 'consume by fire' sense. This verb can be predicated of leaves or paper, but not flames or candles. There is another Hebrew verb, *ba'ar*, which means 'burn' in the sense of 'blaze' or 'emit heat or light'. This verb can be predicated of fire, flames, and candles; it is true that some of these entities, such as candles, might sometimes be consumed in the process, but this is incidental. This second verb shows the morphological causativization pattern expected of an internally caused verb. (See section 3.2.5 for more on the causativization patterns of Hebrew verbs.) Indeed, this difference in causativization patterns is what is expected since consumption by fire is an externally caused eventuality, whereas the emission of heat or light by a candle or flame is presumably an internally caused eventuality. In fact, in English too, the verb *burn* shows the causative alternation only in the 'consume by fire' sense.

(40) a. The leaves burned.
　　 b. The gardener burned the leaves.

(41) a. The fire burned.
　　 b. *The campers burned the fire.

Nedjalkov, like Haspelmath, also examined the verb *burn*, finding that its behavior with respect to causative formation across languages is significantly more variable than that of *break* and *laugh*. It may be precisely because they failed to control for the subtleties in the meaning of *burn* that both Nedjalkov and Haspelmath found considerable cross-linguistic variation in the morphological causativization patterns of this verb.

3.2.3   When Can Externally Caused Verbs "Detransitivize"?

In the previous section we proposed that all externally caused verbs are basically dyadic. However, although we proposed that the intransitive form of an alternating verb like *break* is derived from the causative form, only a subset of externally caused verbs have such intransitive uses.

(42) a.   The baker cut the bread.
      b.   *The bread cut. (on the interpretation 'The bread came to be cut')

(43) a.   The terrorist killed/assassinated/murdered the senator.
      b.   *The senator killed/assassinated/murdered.

(44) a.   Anita Brookner just wrote a new novel.
      b.   *A new novel wrote.

Furthermore, alternating verbs often show the intransitive form only for some choices of arguments, as discussed in section 3.1. In this section we address the following question: when can externally caused verbs turn up as intransitive verbs, and why is this possibility open to some verbs only for certain choices of arguments? We continue to draw on the insights in Smith 1970 to reach an understanding of this phenomenon, which, in turn, is crucial to understanding unaccusativity, given our proposal that a large class of unaccusative verbs are basically causative dyadic verbs.

Smith proposes that the verbs of change that may be used intransitively are precisely those in which the change can come about independently "in the sense that it can occur without an external agent" (1970:102). Smith's observation can also be recast as follows: the transitive causative verbs that detransitivize are those in which the eventuality can come about spontaneously without the volitional intervention of an agent. In fact, among the transitive verbs that never detransitivize are verbs that require an animate intentional and volitional agent as subject. Consider some verbs that never detransitivize, such as the verbs *murder* and *assassinate* or the verbs of creation *write* and *build*. These particular verbs require an animate intentional and volitional agent as subject.

(45) a.   The terrorist assassinated/murdered the senator.
      b.   *The explosion assassinated/murdered the senator.

(46) a.   Pat wrote a letter to the editor of the local newspaper.
      b.   *My anger wrote a letter to the editor of the local newspaper.

(47) a.   A local architect built the new library.
      b.   *The windstorm built a sand dune.

Since these verbs have meanings that specify that the eventuality they describe must be brought about by a volitional agent, the change they specify obviously cannot come about independently. In contrast, the change specified by alternating verbs such as *break* can come about without the intervention of a volitional agent. Consequently, alternating verbs allow natural forces or causes, as well as agents or instruments, as external causes, and, hence, as subjects.

(48) The vandals/The rocks/The storm broke the windows.

Next consider the verb *cut*. As shown in (42), this verb cannot be used intransitively to describe the coming about of a separation in the material integrity of some entity. The behavior of this verb can be understood in the context of the proposed constraint since what characterizes its meaning is a specification of the means or manner involved in bringing about the action described by that verb; this specification, in turn, implies the existence of a volitional agent. The very meaning of the verb *cut* implies the existence of a sharp instrument that must be used by a volitional agent to bring about the change of state described by the verb. If the same change of state were to come about without the use of a sharp instrument, then it could not be said to have come about through cutting. A verb like *cut* demonstrates that the set of verbs that do not detransitivize is not the same as the set of verbs that restrict their subjects to volitional agents. The verb *cut* allows instruments or agents as subjects; however, *cut* does not allow natural force subjects.[12]

(49) a.   The baker/That knife cut the bread.
     b.   *The lightning cut the clothesline.

The proposed constraint on detransitivization may explain the behavior of the verb *remove*, which does not have an intransitive form. Its non-existence might seem somewhat surprising since to a first approximation this verb's meaning might be paraphrased as 'cause to become not at some location'. However, a closer look at its meaning reveals that the eventuality it describes is brought about by a volitional agent, as shown by the oddness of the examples in (50), which have inanimate nonvolitional subjects.

(50) a.   ??The wind removed the clouds from the sky.
          (cf. The wind cleared the clouds from the sky.)
     b.   ??The water removed the sand from the rocks.
          (cf. The water washed the sand from the rocks.)

In B. Levin and Rappaport Hovav 1994 we show that the approach developed here can explain why verbs formed with the suffixes -*ize* and -*ify* cannot typically detransitivize, as the data in (51)–(52) illustrate, even though these affixes have been characterized as "causative" (see, for example, the discussion of these suffixes in Marchand 1969).

(51) a.   The farmer homogenized/pasteurized the milk.
     b.   *The milk homogenized/pasteurized.

(52) a.   Carla humidified her apartment.
     b.   *Her apartment humidified.

Most of these morphologically complex verbs cannot detransitivize, we propose, because they describe eventualities that cannot come about spontaneously without the external intervention of an agent. In contrast, those -*ify* and -*ize* verbs that allow for this possibility appear to be precisely the ones that do detransitivize.

(53) a.   I solidified the mixture./The mixture solidified.
     b.   The cook caramelized the sugar./The sugar caramelized.

Again, the -*ify* and -*ize* verbs that resist detransitivization show a narrower range of subjects than those verbs that permit detransitivization; specifically, they appear to exclude natural force subjects.

(54) a.   *The weather humidified the apartment.
     b.   The intense heat caramelized the sugar.

The constraint on detransitivization also explains why some verbs have intransitive uses only for certain choices of the argument that changes state: it is only for these choices that the change can come about without the intervention of an agent. For instance, in section 3.1 we noted the following contrasts involving the verb *clear*:

(55) a.   The waiter cleared the table.
     b.   *The table cleared.

(56) a.   The wind cleared the sky.
     b.   The sky cleared.

Our knowledge of the world tell us that tables are things that are cleared (typically, of dishes) through the intervention of an animate agent. The sky, however, can clear through the intervention of natural forces, such as the wind. Hence the difference in the possibility of intransitive counterparts.

In this context, we can also understand the contrast presented in section 3.1, and repeated here, involving the verb *lengthen*.

(57) a.   The dressmaker lengthened the skirt.
     b.   *The skirt lengthened.

(58) a.   The mad scientist lengthened the days.
     b.   The days lengthened.

Skirts can only be lengthened through the intervention of an agent; hence, the verb *lengthen* as applied to skirts is not typically used intransitively. Days, on the other hand, become longer as the earth progresses through a certain part of its orbit around the sun, something that happens without the intervention of an animate agent. And *lengthen* as applied to days is typically used intransitively, although in a science fiction context where artificial manipulation of the length of days is possible, transitive uses might be found, as in (58a).

We can return here to the instances of *break*, cited in (9) and repeated here, which do not detransitivize.

(59) a.   He broke his promise/the contract/the world record.
     b.   *His promise/The contract/The world record broke.

Again, this verb does not detransitivize for these choices of object because the eventuality it describes cannot come about without the intervention of an agent for these choices. The examples in (55)–(59) show once again that detransitivization is possible precisely where an externally caused eventuality can come about without the intervention of an agent. In this sense, detransitivization is a productive process, since it appears to be possible wherever this condition is met.

Our study of the factors that influence a verb's transitivity suggests that verbs can be classified according to whether or not they describe an externally caused eventuality and according to whether or not they describe an eventuality that can occur spontaneously. If the eventuality described by a verb has an external cause, the verb is basically transitive; moreover, if this eventuality can occur without the direct intervention of an agent, then the external cause does not have to be expressed in the syntax. Given the similarities between these two notions, the question arises whether they might be collapsed. In fact, Haspelmath (1993) has independently developed an analysis that resembles the one presented here, except that he does not make a clear distinction between the two notions. Haspelmath links the likelihood of spontaneous occurrence to intransitivity, and although he is not explicit about this, it appears that he takes spontaneous occurrence to be the opposite of external causation, so that if a particular event does not occur spontaneously, then it is externally caused and thus expressed with a transitive verb. For Haspelmath, those verbs that describe eventualities that are likely to occur spontaneously will have an intransitive form, and those that are not likely to occur spontaneously will have only a transitive form. Thus, the verbs *wash* and *decapitate* will have only a transitive form, and the verbs *break* and *laugh* will both have intransitive forms.

It seems to us that there is evidence that favors the use of both spontaneous occurrence and external causation in the determination of transitivity, as in our approach. The evidence comes from an observation that Haspelmath himself makes. He notes that across languages certain intransitive verbs like *break* tend to be the morphologically marked member of a causative alternation verb pair, whereas others like *laugh* tend to be the morphologically unmarked member. It turns out, as he notes, that those verbs which like *break* describe eventualities that are both spontaneously occurring and externally caused are the ones that tend to have the intransitive form as the morphologically marked one. Those which like *laugh* describe eventualities that occur spontaneously and are internally caused tend to have the transitive member of a causative alternation pair morphologically marked. That is, among verbs describing spontaneously occurring eventualities, it is the status of the eventuality as internally or externally caused that determines the morphological shape of the verb. This difference justifies the recognition of both notions as contributing to a verb's syntactic behavior and morphological shape. In some sense, Haspelmath's study provides cross-linguistic corroboration of the results we obtained from our in-depth study of English.

3.2.4   The Derivation of the Intransitive Use of Externally Caused Verbs

In this section we propose an account of how the intransitive use of an externally caused verb arises. As a first step, we refine and reformulate the constraint on detransitivization. In the previous section we observed that alternating verbs do not usually exert any restrictions on the external cause argument: it can be an agent, instrument, circumstance, or natural force. As for verbs that do exert restrictions on the external cause argument—that is, the nonalternating verbs—they appear to exert a rather limited range of restrictions on it. Parsons (1990) observes that there appears to be no verb that is lexically specified to take only an instrument as subject. All verbs that allow an instrument as subject also allow an agent, and some allow natural forces as well. Taking Parsons's observation further, there is also, as far as we know, no verb describing an externally caused eventuality that takes only a natural force as subject. Thus, the only restrictions exerted by verbs on the external cause seem to involve agency in some way.

However, a closer look at causative verbs provides an even deeper insight into this. Causative verbs are generally classified as accomplishments in Vendler's (1957) terms, and, as mentioned in chapter 2, accomplishments are standardly analyzed as complex predicates involving a causing event that brings about some change of state or location (Dowty 1979, Grimshaw and Vikner 1993, Pustejovsky 1991b). We mentioned in chapter 2 that resultatives are expressions in which both the causing event and the change of state are specified, each by a different predicate. In contrast, morphologically simple accomplishment verbs usually specify either the causing event or the result state; for example, the verb *break* specifies the result state, but leaves the causing event unspecified. In *Pat broke the window*, it is only the change in the state of the window that is specified by the verb; Pat could have brought this change about by any of a wide variety of activities. On the other hand, the verb *cut* specifies both the change of state and something about the event leading up to this change of state.[13] What characterizes the class of alternating verbs is a complete lack of specification of the causing event. Thus, the fact that a wide variety of subjects are possible with the alternating verbs is just a reflection of the fact that the causing event is left completely unspecified. Therefore, we can reformulate the condition sanctioning detransitivization: an externally caused verb can leave its cause argument unexpressed only if the nature of the causing event is left completely unspecified.

There is one advantage to the reformulation. If the restriction were against detransitivizing a verb with an agent, we would expect that even a verb like *break*, when used agentively, could not be used in the intransitive form. But this is clearly not the case, as shown by the acceptability of *I threw the plate against the wall, and it broke*. If, however, we say that the property of *break* that allows it to detransitivize is that it specifies something about the change of state in the passive participant but nothing about the causing event, then the example conforms to our generalization.[14]

We have suggested that the lexical semantic representation of verbs describing externally caused eventualities consists of two subevents, the causing subevent and the central subevent. As we discussed in section 1.1, the external cause argument of such a verb in some sense stands in for the causing subevent. Suppose that the intransitive form of externally caused verbs arises from binding the external cause within the lexical semantic representation, where this binding is interpreted as existential quantification. The intransitive form will then be interpreted as asserting that the central subevent came about via some causing subevent, without any specification of its nature. Suppose, however, that if the verb lexically specifies something about the nature of the external cause, then it cannot be lexically bound, and the intransitive form of the verb would not be attested.

We suggest that the binding of the external cause takes place in the mapping from the lexical semantic representation to argument structure. Just as the binding of a position in argument structure prevents that position from being projected onto the syntax, so the binding of a position in the lexical semantic representation prevents the projection of that position to argument structure. Since the position is not projected into argument structure, there is no argument associated with this position in the syntax. We can schematize the proposed relation between the lexical semantic representation (LSR below) of *break* and the argument structure of both its transitive and intransitive forms as follows:

(60) *Intransitive* break

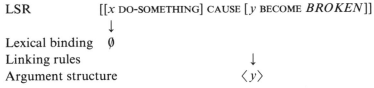

LSR $[[x$ DO-SOMETHING$]$ CAUSE $[y$ BECOME $BROKEN]]$
                               ↓
Lexical binding $\emptyset$
Linking rules   ↓
Argument structure $\langle y \rangle$

(61) *Transitive* break

LSR $[[x$ DO-SOMETHING$]$ CAUSE $[y$ BECOME $BROKEN]]$
Linking rules   ↓   ↓
Argument structure x $\langle y \rangle$

There is evidence that the operation of binding the external cause must take place before argument structure. This evidence comes from comparing certain properties of the intransitive form of causative alternation verbs and passive verbs. As described by Grimshaw (1990), for example, the operation that derives the passive form of a verb from an active one involves binding a position in the lexical syntactic representation of a verb—its argument structure—thereby preventing the expression of that argument in the syntax. Thus, it contrasts with the operation of binding the external cause of a verb such as *break*, which we propose involves its lexical semantic representation. Although the lexically bound argument of a passive verb cannot be directly expressed in the syntax, there is well-known evidence that the argument is present, nonetheless, in argument structure. Specifically, its presence is manifested in the sanctioning of *by* phrases and the control of purpose clauses, as discussed by Roeper (1987), who cites work by Manzini (1983) as the source of the evidence involving purpose clauses.

(62) a. The ship was sunk by Bill. (Roeper 1987:268, (2b))
　　 b. The boat was sunk to collect the insurance. (Roeper 1987:268, (3b))

(63) a. The window was broken by Pat.
　　 b. The window was broken to rescue the child.

In contrast, the lexically bound external cause cannot license a *by* phrase or control a purpose clause, as is also well known.

(64) a. *The ship sank by Bill. (Roeper 1987:268, (2a))
　　 b. *The boat sank to collect the insurance. (Roeper 1987:268, (3a))

(65) a. *The window broke by Pat.
　　 b. *The window broke to rescue the child.

In closing this section, we raise a question that requires further investigation: the relationship between detransitivization and the unexpressed unspecified objects permitted by verbs such as *eat* and *read*. It has been proposed that the unspecified objects understood in sentences such as *The child ate* arise through existential quantification of the object at some level of linguistic representation (see Bresnan 1980 and Dowty 1981 for proposals along these lines, and Fodor and Fodor 1980 for arguments against such an account). This phenomenon may appear to be problematic for our analysis since, as we discuss immediately below, under what appear to be similar circumstances an argument can be left unexpressed with unspecified object verbs, whereas an argument cannot be left unexpressed with verbs like *break*. However, despite the similarity in the analyses proposed for them, the phenomena themselves appear to be different. We have proposed that in order for a causative verb to detransitivize, the verb must not impose any lexical specification on the causing subevent, so that in its noncausative intransitive use the external cause argument of the verb is understood as not being lexically specified. In the noncausative use of a verb like *break*, the claim is that the external cause can be left unexpressed, whatever its nature. On the other hand, the unexpressed argument of the unspecified object construction is probably best characterized as being interpreted as the "prototypical" choice for that argument. It does not seem correct to characterize this argument as not being lexically specified since the unexpressed argument must do more than meet the general selectional restrictions on that argument; it must be the most typical argument that meets those restrictions, and in this sense it is predictable rather than not lexically specified. We think that being a prototypical argument is quite different from not being lexically specified. Prototypicality is determined by real-world knowledge; it is not linguistic knowledge. We leave additional investigation of this question for further research.

3.2.5   Apparent Instances of the Causative Alternation

We have characterized causative alternation verbs as externally caused verbs that meet the criteria for detransitivization. Thus, such verbs have a causative lexical semantic representation, the unaccusative use arising when the criteria for detransitivization are met. In section 3.1 we also mentioned the observation cited by Chierchia (1989) that unergative verbs appear to be stable in their intransitivity, a property in part attributable to their monadic lexical semantic representation. However, there are pairs of morphologically identical verbs in English consisting of an internally caused intransitive verb and a transitive verb that means roughly 'cause to *V*-intransitive'. The existence of such pairs might seem to be problematic for our analysis. In this section we examine several instances of this phenomenon and argue that each represents a different phenomenon from what we have described as the causative alternation. Specifically, we argue that in such causative pairs the relationship between the transitive and intransitive uses is not the same as the one characteristic of causative alternation verbs like *break*. From now on we reserve the term *causative alternation* for the alternation shown by verbs like *break;* we will use the term *causative pair* to refer to any pair of morphologically related transitive and intransitive verbs such that the transitive verb means approximately 'cause to *V*-intransitive'.

First, we investigate certain agentive verbs that appear in causative pairs, as illustrated in (66)–(68).[15]

(66) a. The soldiers marched to the tents.
     b. The general marched the soldiers to the tents.

(67) a. The horse jumped over the fence.
     b. The rider jumped the horse over the fence.

(68) a. The mouse ran through the maze.
     b. We ran the mouse through the maze.

Although these pairs, like those observed with verbs like *break*, involve transitive and intransitive uses of verbs that differ with respect to the notion "cause," there is evidence that the pairs shown in (66)–(68) do not involve the causative alternation. This phenomenon is exhibited by members of a semantically coherent subgroup of the agentive verbs: agentive verbs of manner of motion. These verbs of motion, which we discuss in more detail in sections 4.1.4 and 5.1.1, describe the manner in which motion takes place, contrasting with verbs of inherently directed motion like *come* and *go*, which describe the direction but not the manner of motion. Various researchers have commented that the causative use of agentive verbs of manner of motion is qualitatively different from that shown by verbs such as *break* (see, for example, Cruse 1972, 1973, Hale and Keyser 1987). Some of them have pointed out that the referent of the direct object in sentences such as (66)–(68) maintains a degree of agentiveness that is uncharacteristic of the objects of verbs that usually participate in the causative alternation or the objects of transitive verbs in general.

The proposal that we are dealing with two distinct phenomena receives further support from another fact, which to our knowledge has never been accounted for in the literature, although it is mentioned briefly by Pinker (1989): the directional phrases that are optional in the intransitive use of the agentive verbs of manner of motion are obligatory in their transitive use.[16]

(69) a. The soldiers marched (to the tents).
     b. The general marched the soldiers to the tents.
     c. ??The general marched the soldiers.

(70) a. The horse jumped (over the fence).
     b. The rider jumped the horse over the fence.
     c. ?The rider jumped the horse.

(71) a. The mouse ran (through the maze).
     b. We ran the mouse through the maze.
     c. *We ran the mouse.

This distinctive property of the agentive verbs of manner of motion is highlighted when these verbs are contrasted with nonagentive verbs of manner of motion such as *roll* and *bounce*—Jespersen's (1927) "move" verbs—which, as shown in (72), do not require a directional phrase in either their transitive or intransitive use.

(72) a. The ball bounced/rolled (into the room).
     b. The boys bounced/rolled the ball (into the room).

Additional evidence that a distinct phenomenon is involved comes from the observation that the "cause" argument in such causatives can only be an agent in the true sense, never an instrument or a natural force, as pointed out by Cruse (1972) and Reinhart (1991).

(73) a. *The downpour marched the soldiers to the tents.
     b. *The tear gas marched the soldiers to the tents.

(74) a. *The lightning jumped the horse over the fence.
     b. *The firecracker jumped the horse over the fence.
     c. *The whip jumped the horse over the fence.

Given the fundamentally different properties of the causative pairs involving agentive verbs of manner of motion and those involving causative alternation verbs like *break*, we conclude that there is no need to abandon our proposal that only externally caused verbs show the causative alternation. But what about the causative pairs involving internally caused verbs? Our analysis does not preclude the existence of such pairs; it simply predicts that they cannot represent the same phenomenon as the causative pairs associated with verbs like *break* since they could not have been derived in the same way. Specifically, since internally caused verbs, unlike externally caused verbs, are not causative verbs basically, the noncausative use cannot be derived from detransitivizing the causative use. However, there is no reason not to assume that the agentive verbs of manner of motion, like other internally caused verbs, are basically monadic noncausative verbs and that the transitive members of the pairs in (66)–(68) are actually derived by a process of causativization. We propose that this is the case.[17] (We return in section 5.1.1.2 to the question of why the directional phrase is needed in the English causative uses.)

Evidence for a causativization analysis comes from the morphological relationship between the members of the causative pairs with agentive verbs of manner of motion. If, as we have been assuming, the morphologically marked member of a causative pair is the derived member, then in languages that, unlike English, differentiate the members of causative pairs morphologically, it should be possible to verify the causativization analysis. We would expect that in such languages the causative member of a causative pair involving an internally caused verb should be morphologically marked. Investigations of several languages of this type suggest that the prediction is borne out.

Consider first Modern Hebrew, where verbs are formed from triconsonantal roots. A single root can give rise to up to seven basic verb patterns, many of which show strong semantic correlates (Berman 1978, Bolozky 1982, Bolozky and Saad 1983, Glinert 1989, among others). The most productive morphological pattern for intransitive/transitive causative pairs with externally caused verbs, particularly verbs of change of state, is for the transitive causative verb to be in the Pi'el pattern and the intransitive verb to be in the derived Hitpa'el pattern, as in the pairs in (75) and (76).

(75) a. Hu kimet   et   ha-bad.
        he creased ACC the-material
        'He creased the material.'
     b. Ha-bad   hitkamet.
        the-material creased
        'The material creased.'

(76) a. Hu kirer   et   ha-oxel.
        he cooled ACC the-food
        'He cooled the food.'
     b. Ha-oxel hitkarer.
        the-food cooled
        'The food cooled.'

The intransitive form of verbs with causatives in the Pi'el pattern always involves the Hitpa'el pattern (Bolozky 1982, Rappaport 1979). In fact, the Pi'el-Hitpa'el pairing is used for all semantically appropriate new coinages; see Berman 1980 for evidence for this point from child language acquisition and Bolozky and Saad 1983 for evidence involving the coining of novel denominal verbs. Morphologically, the Hitpa'el pattern is derived from the Pi'el pattern by affixation of the prefix *hit-*; the vowel change accompanying the affixation is due to a regular phonological process (Prince 1975). Berman (1980) also argues that the Pi'el pattern is basic and the Hitpa'el pattern is derived.

Modern Hebrew differs from English in allowing to a certain extent the formation of causatives of verbs describing internally caused eventualities, including some agentive verbs of manner of motion. What is striking is that the morphological relationship between the causative and noncausative uses of such verbs is invariably different from that associated with verbs describing externally caused eventualities. With internally caused verbs, the noncausative form is the underived form, appearing in the Pa'al pattern, and the causative form is the derived form, appearing in the Hif'il pattern. The examples in (77)–(80) illustrate this point, which also emerges from the discussion in Bolozky 1982.[18]

(77) a. Hu rakad.
        he danced
        'He danced.'
     b. Ha-nagan   hirkid   oto.
        the-musician made dance him
        'The musician made him dance.'

(78) a. Hu rac.
        he ran
        'He ran.'
     b. Ha-meamen heric   oto.
        the-coach   made run him
        'The coach made him run.'

(79) a. Hu kafac.
        he jumped
        'He jumped.'
     b. Ha-ra'aš hikpic   oto.
        the-noise made jump him
        'The noise made him jump.'

(80) a. Ani caxakti.
        I   laughed
        'I laughed.'
     b. Ha-yeled hicxik   oti.
        the-boy made laugh me
        'The boy made me laugh.'

Since the Modern Hebrew process involves causative morphology, its scope is wider than the scope of the English process. The Hebrew process is found with a range of other internally caused verbs; the English process is productive only with a semantically coherent subset of the internally caused verbs (see section 5.1.1.2).

Hale and Keyser (1987) cite similar evidence from Berber, Navajo, Warlpiri, and Winnebago. They write, "In Athapaskan languages, for example, the ergative alternation [the causative alternation] is marked in the simplest manner, by choice of the so-called 'classifier' (an element appearing in immediate prestem position correlating very roughly with transitivity), while the transitivization of 'unergative' verbs like *walk* and *run* involves not only this classifier element but special causative prefix morphology as well" (1987:25), pointing the reader to entries in Young and Morgan's (1980) dictionary of Navajo.

Agentive verbs of manner of motion are not the only internally caused verbs that show causative uses in English. Apparent instances of the causative alternation are found sporadically throughout the class of nonagentive internally caused verbs, as in (81) from Smith 1970, although they are observed most frequently, but not exclusively, among the verbs of emission, especially among the verbs of sound emission.

(81) a. The baby burped.
    b. The nurse burped the baby. (Smith 1970:107, (36a))

(82) a. The doorbell buzzed/rang.
    b. The postman buzzed/rang the doorbell.

(83) a. The flashlight beamed/shone.
    b. We beamed/shone the flashlight.

We will show that these are also not instances of the causative alternation as we have defined it. The pair in (81) is what we term an *idiosyncratic* pair, in the sense that it is a one-of-a-kind pair that is not representative of any sort of regular type of causativization. The pairs in (82) and (83) are what we call *spurious* causative pairs; by "spurious" we mean that what appears to be a causative pair involves two distinct verb meanings— one of them causative—that are not derivationally related.

Consider first the *burp* example in (81). As Smith (1970) points out, the verb *burp* enters into such causative pairs only for certain highly specific choices of objects for the transitive use.

(84) a. The baby burped.
    b. The nurse burped the baby. (Smith 1970:107, (36a))

(85) a. The doctor burped.
    b. *The nurse burped the doctor. (Smith 1970:107, (36c))

Not only are there restrictions on the transitive object, but *burp* is one of two verbs of bodily process that show this phenomenon. The other is the verb *bleed*, which is used in the sense of 'cause to *bleed*-intransitive' in a very restricted way. For instance, it is not possible to use *bleed* as a causative if one cuts one's hand on a knife.

(86) a. The patient bled.
     b. The doctor bled the patient.

Furthermore, as expected if they are internally caused verbs, other verbs of bodily process do not show causative uses at all.

(87) a. Kay coughed./*The doctor coughed Kay.
     b. Pat yawned./*The sleeping pills yawned Pat.
     c. Tony sneezed./*The pollen sneezed Tony.

As there is no evidence that the causative uses of *bleed* and *burp* represent a regular process of causativization as applied to a particular verb class, we suggest that they represent idiosyncratic instances of causativization. We propose that the sporadic causative coinages that turn up in everyday speech, such as the examples in (88), represent the same phenomenon.

(88) a. What's fussing her? [A Grandpa wondering why baby is crying] (Pinker 1989:153, (4.44l))
     b. "He lunched me to-day in terrific style ..." [G. B. Stern, *The Matriarch*, 261]

Consider next the examples of verbs of emission in (82) and (83). Some, though by no means all, verbs of emission can be found in causative pairs. Among the verbs of light emission, besides the verbs *beam* and *shine*, the verb *flash* is found in causative pairs. Similarly, among verbs of sound emission, besides the verbs *buzz* and *ring*, a range of verbs are found in causative pairs, including *clatter*, *clink*, *jingle*, *rattle*, *rustle*, and *toll*.

Unlike the agentive verbs of manner of motion, the nonagentive internally caused verbs, including the verbs of emission, do not require co-occurring directional phrases in their causative use. However, the causative uses of verbs of emission resemble the causative uses of the agentive verbs of manner of motion in one respect: they also do not permit instrument or natural force subjects.

(89) a. *The short circuit rang the bell.
     b. *The dishwasher clattered the dishes.

In this respect, both of these classes contrast with the causative uses of verbs like *break*.

The relationship between the causative and noncausative uses of verbs of emission also differs from that associated with the causative and noncausative uses of causative alternation verbs. With a causative alternation verb, the causative use entails the noncausative use, so that if someone breaks something, then that thing breaks. In contrast, verbs of emission do not demonstrate this pattern. Not only do they show causative uses only for a very restricted range of emitters, as the examples in (90)–(93) show, but the relationship between the causative and noncausative uses is different from that shown by the *break* verbs. For example, if someone buzzes a doorbell or flashes a light, it is odd to describe the very same event by saying that the doorbell buzzed or the light flashed. In contrast, if someone breaks a window, then it is possible to describe the same event with the sentence *The window broke.*

(90) a.   The doorbell buzzed.
     b.   The postman buzzed the doorbell.

(91) a.   The bees buzzed.
     b.   *The postman buzzed the bees.

(92) a.   The light flashed.
     b.   The stagehand flashed the light.

(93) a.   The lightning flashed.
     b.   *The cloud seeding flashed the lightning.

This difference supports treating the causative pairs involving verbs of emission as representing a phenomenon other than the causative alternation.

How can this pattern of properties be explained? We proposed in section 3.2.2 that certain verbs have meanings that allow them to describe either an internally caused or an externally caused eventuality. Although in section 3.2.1 we proposed that verbs of emission describe internally caused eventualities, we suggest that some verbs of emission are actually compatible with a dual classification as either internally or externally caused verbs. The transitive causative uses of verbs of sound and light emission in (82) and (83), we argue in B. Levin and Rappaport Hovav 1994, represent the externally caused option, and the intransitive uses they are paired with represent the internally caused option.

Consider, for example, the verb *buzz*. When used as a verb that describes a particular animal sound, this verb clearly describes an internally caused eventuality since the sound is emitted under the emitter's own control. It also describes an internally caused eventuality when used to describe the sound emitted by certain devices, such as doorbells and buzzers, which can in some circumstances be conceptualized as emitting the sound under their own control. However, certain devices—many of them the same ones that can be conceptualized as self-controlled—can be made to emit the sound known as a *buzz* by a person who manipulates the device; this is the externally caused option. To the extent that the set of emitters that can be manipulated to emit a particular sound and the set of emitters that can be conceptualized as emitting the same sound under their own control overlap, the verb describing the emission of that sound will show internally and externally caused uses with the same emitters. Consequently, apparent causative pairs, such as the one in (90), arise. When an emitter belongs to only one of these two sets, then the verb shows only one of the two options for that emitter. As an illustration, consider the pair in (91): bees cannot be externally caused to emit a buzz, so that there is no externally caused use of *buzz*, such as *The postman buzzed the bees*, paired with the internally caused use of *buzz* in *The bees buzzed*.

There are several factors that limit the number of apparent causative pairs with verbs of sound emission. Most important, there are restrictions on the set of verbs that can be found in such pairs. The sounds associated with some verbs of sound emission, such as the verb *burble*, are necessarily internally caused, and, thus, these verbs will not show externally caused uses at all. In general, externally caused uses are found with verbs describing sounds emitted through contact between two surfaces, such as *jingle*, *rattle*, and *rustle*. It is a matter of real-world knowledge whether the emission of a particular type of sound involves internal or external causation. The number of apparent causative pairs is further limited because even when a verb of sound emission permits an externally caused use, such uses can arise only with certain emitters. In the externally caused use, the relevant sound must be emitted by manipulable entities such as coins, dishes, keys, papers, doorbells, and buzzers under direct manipulation. If the emitters are not manipulable, then the emission of the sound cannot be externally caused.

The relationship between the two members of the causative pairs with verbs of emission can be made explicit using the lexical semantic representations introduced in chapter 1. The constant associated with each verb of emission represents what is distinct about that verb; for example, for a verb of sound emission it would be the characteristic sound associated with that verb. Suppose that the constant associated with a verb of emission showing causative and noncausative uses is compatible either with the lexical semantic template of an internally caused verb or with that of an externally caused verb. If so, a causative pair associated with such a verb of emission involves two distinct lexical semantic representations that happen to share a single constant and thus the same "name." They are not, however, related by any productive rule. It is for this reason that we labeled these "spurious" causative pairs. Our initial investigations suggest that the causative pairs involving verbs of emission merit further study, showing behavior that is more complicated and less uniform than the data presented here suggest; however, we believe that their behavior patterns can all be understood in terms of the discussion here and in sections 5.1.2.2 and 5.3.

Summarizing this section, English has two types of regularly formed causative pairs. The first, and by far more pervasive, involves externally caused verbs, which, although basically dyadic, in specific circumstances undergo a process of detransitivization. English has a more restricted phenomenon of causativization of agentive verbs of manner of motion in the presence of a directional phrase. We return to these alternations in the next two chapters, where we provide an explanation for why internally caused verbs cannot be causativized, except in special conditions.

3.3 Verbs of Existence and Appearance

So far in this chapter we have focused on the causative alternation as a device for better understanding how unaccusative verbs differ from unergative verbs. In this section we introduce a fundamental division within the class of unaccusative verbs that is motivated by behavior with respect to the causative alternation. Specifically, we show in section 3.3.2 that the arguments used in favor of a causative lexical semantic analysis of one class of unaccusative verbs indicate that the causative analysis is inappropriate for another class of unaccusative verbs. Verbs of existence such as *exist*, *flourish*, and *thrive* and verbs of appearance such as *appear*, *emerge*, and *arise*, although all bona fide unaccusative verbs, do not participate in the causative alternation. We show that this property is not characteristic only of English, but is typical of a variety of languages. We show that they are nevertheless dyadic even though they do not have the causative lexical semantic representation we attributed to the alternating externally caused verbs. In chapter 4 we establish that they are unaccusative, taking two internal arguments. In section 3.3.3 we introduce a subclass of the verbs of existence, the simple position verbs, and show that although many of them have a causative use, they also do not participate in the causative alternation, as narrowly defined in section 3.2.5.

3.3.1 Verbs of Existence and Appearance Introduced

As argued in many studies (Clark 1978, Kimball 1973, Lyons 1967, and works cited therein), there is a relationship between existence and location. For instance, noting the deictic origin of English *there* and similar elements that characterize existential sentences in European languages, Lyons writes that "it might appear reasonable to say that all existential sentences are at least implicitly locative (the term 'locative' being taken to include both temporal and spatial reference)" (1967:390). We follow these studies in taking verbs of existence to be verbs having two arguments: one describing the entity that exists and the other describing the location at which this entity exists. Thus, we claim that verbs of existence are basically dyadic, although, since we argue in chapter 4 that they are unaccusative, we propose that they take two internal arguments rather than an internal and an external argument like verbs of change of state.

More recently, Hoekstra and Mulder (1990) and Mulder and Wehrmann (1989) have also explored the properties of verbs of existence. Mulder and Wehrmann recognize that verbs of existence describe eventualities that involve two participants: a theme (i.e., an entity whose existence is asserted) and a location. However, Mulder and Wehrmann, and following them Hoekstra and Mulder, treat these verbs as monadic verbs taking a small clause internal argument, which itself contains theme and location arguments. We discuss a problem with the small clause account in section 6.7 in the context of our investigation of locative inversion. Here we merely emphasize that there is general agreement that verbs of existence are associated with a theme and a location.

Verbs of appearance and verbs of existence are related semantically. A verb of appearance can be viewed as a verb of coming into existence. Alternatively, a verb of existence can be seen as a verb that describes the state resulting from the appearance of some entity; in fact, Kimball writes, "The concept of existence is, I claim, formed semantically (and grammatically) as the perfective of coming into being" (1973:267). It is unclear to us which of the two characterizations is correct or whether both are plausible, and it is beyond the scope of this book to determine this. All that matters for our purposes is the existence of a semantic relationship between the two. Verbs of disappearance, such as *disappear* and *vanish*, also belong in the larger class of verbs of existence and appearance, since they can be considered to be verbs of coming not to exist.

Support for treating the verbs of appearance, the verbs of disappearance, and the verbs of existence together comes from the fact that these three types of verbs share a variety of properties, although for some purposes the classes need to be kept distinct. First, all three types of verbs require a location argument—and, if there is no overt location argument, one is understood. Second, verbs of existence and appearance are the verbs most commonly found in the locative inversion construction, which we discuss in detail in chapter 6, and the *there*-insertion construction, which we discuss briefly in chapter 4; as we note in these discussions, verbs of disappearance are independently excluded from these constructions.

(94) a. In front of her appeared a fabulous sight.
     b. In the desert flourished a utopian community.

(95) a. There appeared a ship on the horizon.
     b. There exists a solution to that problem.

Finally, all three types of verbs consistently lack causative variants. This property will be central to our consideration of whether the causative analysis proposed for externally caused verbs of change of state is also applicable to these verbs.

(96) a. My mother lived in Boston.
     b. *Her job lived my mother in Boston.

(97) a. A picture appeared (on the screen).
     b. *The programmer appeared a picture (on the screen).

(98) a. The bicycle disappeared (from the garage).
     b. *The thief disappeared the bicycle (from the garage).

3.3.2 Evidence against a Causative Analysis

With this background, we turn now to evidence that the causative analysis is inappropriate for the verbs of existence and appearance. We do this by reviewing those arguments previously used to support the causative analysis of the alternating intransitive verbs that would be expected to extend to the verbs of existence and appearance. For instance, given the lack of a causative form, the argument from selectional restrictions is inappropriate and is not considered.

First, consider the phenomenon that Chierchia terms "unstable valency." It is striking that this property does not extend to verbs of appearance and existence, even though they are also considered to be unaccusative. The examples in (99)–(102) illustrate the inability of such verbs to participate in the causative alternation in several languages that we are familiar with.[19]

(99)   *English*
     a. i.   A star appeared in the sky.
       ii. *The darkness appeared a star in the sky.
     b. i.   An explosion occurred.
       ii. *The gas leak occurred an explosion.
     c. i.   A solution exists.
       ii. *The mathematician existed a solution.

(100) *Modern Hebrew*
     a. i.   Koxav hofia.
           star   appeared
           'A star appeared.'
       ii. *Ha-xošex   hofia   koxav.
           the-darkness appeared star
     b. i.   Er'a   hitpocecut.
           happened explosion
           'An explosion happened.'
       ii. *Dlifat ha-gaz er'a   hitpocecut.
           leak   the-gas happened explosion
     c. i.   Ha-pitaron nimca   be'amud 90.
           the-solution is found on page 90
           'The solution is found on page 90.'
       ii. *Ha-mexaber himci   et   ha-pitaron be'amud 90.
           the-author   made be found ACC the-solution on page 90
       iii. Ha-mexaber maca et   ha-pitaron be'amud 90.
           the-author   found ACC the-solution on page 90
           'The author found the solution on page 90.' (wrong interpretation)

(101) *Italian*
     a. i.   È apparsa una stella.
           is appeared a   star
           'A star appeared.'

ii. *La notte a   apparso una stella.
     the night has appeared a   star
b. i. Accadono delle cose   strane qui.
       happen   some things strange here
       'Some strange things are happening here.'
ii. *Il vento accade delle cose   strane qui.
     the wind happens some things strange here
c. i. La risposta si   trova a   pagina 90.
       the answer REFL finds on page   90
       'The answer is found on page 90.'
ii. Lo scrittore ha trovato la risposta a   pagina 90.
     the writer   has found the answer on page   90
     'The writer found the answer on page 90.'   (wrong interpretation)

(102) *Russian*
   a. i. Zvezda pojavila-s'   na nebe.
          star   appeared-REFL in sky
          'A star appeared in the sky.'
     ii. *Noč' pojavila zvezdu na nebe.
          night appeared star   in sky
   b. i. Proizošël vzryv.
          occurred explosion
          'An explosion occurred.'
     ii. *Utěčka gaza proizošla vzryv.
          leak   gas occurred explosion
   c. i. Suščestvuet rešenie.
          exists   solution
          'A solution exists.'
     ii. *Matematik   suščestvil rešenie.
          mathematician existed   solution
   d. i. Rešenie ètoj zadači   naxodit-sja na stranica 90.
          solution this assignment finds-REFL on page   90
          'A solution to this assignment is found on page 90.'
     ii. Student našël rešenie ètoj zadači   na stranica 90.
          student found solution this assignment on page   90
          'The student found the solution to this assignment on page
          90.' (wrong interpretation)

Those verbs listed above that are morphologically related to transitive
verbs, such as the Modern Hebrew verb *nimca* 'be found' (related to *maca*

'find') or its Russian and Italian counterparts *naxodit'sja* 'be found' and *trovarsi* 'be found' (related to *naxodit'* 'find' and *trovare* 'find'), cannot be related to them by the semantic relation that characterizes the transitive and intransitive variants of a verb such as *break*. Specifically, these intransitives are stative, unlike the intransitive form of verbs such as *break*. Consequently, there is no reason to believe that *The solution is found on page 90* is semantically derived from *Something caused the solution to be found on page 90*, as the causative analysis would predict. (Although it is striking that three languages have similar pairs, suggesting that there is more to be said here.)

Chierchia (1989) suggests that unaccusative verbs without a transitive causative form are idiosyncratically marked for the nonlexicalization of this form. However, since a semantically coherent subset of the unaccusative verbs consistently lacks this form in a variety of languages, this phenomenon does not seem to be idiosyncratic at all, casting doubt on an analysis that takes these verbs to have a causative lexical semantic representation.

The morphological shape of the verbs of existence and appearance also does not provide any support for a causative analysis, further distinguishing these verbs from the causative alternation verbs. As we have pointed out several times, the intransitive form of a causative alternation verb is morphologically complex in many languages, being derived from the causative form. Often it is derived from the causative form via a reflexive affix (Chierchia 1989, Marantz 1984, Nedyalkov and Silnitsky 1973, among others). That is, this variant is associated with the morphological form used to derive the intransitive *dress* of *She dressed* (meaning 'She dressed herself') from transitive *dress*. This is the case, for instance, in French, Italian, Modern Hebrew, and Russian. A perusal of the morphological shape associated with the verbs of existence and appearance listed in (99)–(102) shows that there is no general pattern suggesting a transitive causative source—even a nonlexicalized one—for these verbs. In particular, there is no association of reflexive morphology with these verbs. For example, in Modern Hebrew the verbs in these classes typically show the patterns Pa'al, Nif'al, or Hif'il, which are never associated with a reflexive interpretation, unlike the Hitpa'el pattern used for the causative alternation verbs (see section 3.2.5). In the Romance languages hardly any of these verbs have the reflexive morpheme (*se/si*). We have found only one such verb, which interestingly has a counterpart with this morphological shape in Russian; this is the verb glossed as 'be found'.

(103) a. trovarsi 'be found'/trovare 'find' (Italian)
       b. se trouver 'be found'/trouver 'find' (French)

In Russian verbs of existence and appearance vary in their morphological shape. Some have the reflexive morpheme -*sja*, though they are rarely related to transitive verbs lacking this morpheme, as the examples in (104) illustrate, whereas others do not have the reflexive morpheme (e.g., *suščestvovat'* 'exist', *proizidti* 'occur').[20]

(104) a. pojavit'sja 'appear'/*pojavit'
       b. slučit'sja 'occur'/*slučit' (exists, but with the wrong meaning)
       c. naxodit'sja 'exist/be found'/naxodit' 'find'
       d. okazat'sja 'turn out'/*okazat' (transitive)
       e. ostat'sja 'remain'/*ostat' (transitive)

Even when such verbs *do* have reflexive morphology, as in the case of Russian *naxodit'sja* 'be found', Italian *trovarsi* 'be found', and French *se trouver* 'be found', the interpretation of the verb makes it clear that it is not plausibly related to the transitive form, if one exists, by a process of "decausativization." And in many instances there is no related transitive form, again setting these verbs apart from the verbs like *break*. In general, then, there appears to be no general systematic morphological pattern associated with verbs of existence and appearance that would suggest that they are related to a more basic transitive causative form.

Next, consider the adverbial modifier *by itself*, which is claimed to bring out the presence of the cause argument that would be expected if the causative analysis were appropriate. As discussed in section 3.1, Chierchia suggests that the Italian phrase *da sè* 'by itself' (in the sense of 'without outside help') is such an adverbial. Although this adverbial can be found with verbs of change of state, it is striking that the English counterpart of the Italian adverbial cannot appear with verbs of existence and appearance, and, where it does appear, it receives a completely different interpretation: 'alone'.

(105) a. Cassie appeared by herself. ('alone', not 'without outside help')
       b. My mom lived by herself. ('alone', not 'without outside help')
       c. *The solution existed by itself.

Once again verbs of existence and appearance behave differently from verbs of change of state, which permit the 'without outside help' interpretation of the adverbial. Thus, this adverbial does not provide evidence for positing a cause argument for verbs of existence and appearance. The unambiguous 'alone' interpretation of the adverbial would not be surprising if these verbs simply had no cause argument.[21]

In summary, the arguments in favor of a causative lexical semantic representation for the alternating unaccusative verbs do not hold up for the verbs of existence and appearance. These verbs do not participate in the causative alternation, as the examples in (99)–(102) demonstrate, nor do they show other evidence of a causative analysis. In light of our analysis of the causative alternation in section 3.2, we propose that this behavior reflects the absence of an external cause in the lexical semantic representation of these verbs. However, unlike internally caused verbs such as *laugh* and *cry*, which also lack an external cause, these verbs are among the prototypical unaccusative verbs of many languages, as we show in chapter 4. In English, for example, these verbs cannot assign accusative Case, and in Italian they typically select the auxiliary *essere* 'be', the auxiliary found with unaccusative verbs. Furthermore, these properties suggest that these verbs are not internally caused verbs either, since then they would most likely be classified as unergative by the linking rules. Rather, we propose that these verbs belong to a class of verbs for which the notions of external and internal causation are apparently not relevant. Given this characterization, the unaccusativity of these verbs must have a different source from the unaccusativity of those externally caused verbs such as *break*, which undergo a process of detransitivization. We formulate a linking rule to handle this in chapter 4. In chapter 6, where we discuss verbs of existence and appearance in greater detail, we show that this class of verbs is distinguished from the externally caused verbs of change of state in a variety of ways.

3.3.3   Verbs of Spatial Configuration

Hoekstra and Mulder (1990) include verbs such as *sit*, *stand*, and *lie* in the class of verbs of existence. Although this treatment appears to be well motivated, these verbs show some properties that at first glance are rather unexpected if this classification is correct.

Before we can offer a fuller treatment of the verbs of spatial configuration, we need to set out the range of meanings associated with them in English and other languages. What is distinctive about verbs such as *sit*, *stand*, and *lie* is that each is associated with a specific spatial configuration. Languages associate up to three types of noncausative meanings and one type of causative meaning with a particular spatial configuration.

Only one of the noncausative meanings is relevant to determining whether verbs such as *sit* are verbs of existence; therefore, we need to present the possible meanings in order to ensure that we are considering the relevant one in our discussion.

The first noncausative meaning available to verbs of spatial configuration is agentive and can appropriately be called the *maintain position* sense. This meaning describes the maintenance of a particular spatial configuration by an animate being, as in *Yvonne stood alone (in the hallway) for six hours*. The locative phrase is optional when the verb is used in this sense. Another agentive noncausative meaning can be referred to as the *assume position* sense; it describes an animate being coming to be in a particular position under his or her own control, as in *Yvonne stood (up)*. Again a location phrase is not required when the verb is used in this meaning. It is likely that the location phrases found with these two meanings are adjuncts. As we discuss in Rappaport Hovav and B. Levin, in press, the two agentive meanings can be distinguished from each other: in the assume position meaning, but not the maintain position meaning, verbs associated with spatial configurations often cooccur with completive particles in the simple past tense, as illustrated in (106).[22]

(106) a. Holly sat up/down.
     b. Denise lay down.
     c. The audience all stood up.

The third noncausative meaning is nonagentive. In this meaning, the verb is typically predicated of inanimates (or animates "viewed" as inanimates) and describes the location of the entity it is predicated of, as in *The papers lay on the desk;* we refer to this meaning as the *simple position* meaning. The locative phrase is obligatory with this meaning, as illustrated in (107).

(107) a. The statue stood *(in the corner).
     b. The purse lay *(on the table).
     c. The picture is hanging *(on the wall).

Languages differ about whether they use a single verb form to label all four verb meanings associated with a particular spatial configuration; see Talmy 1985 for some discussion of the possibilities. English often allows the three noncausative verb meanings associated with a particular spatial configuration to be associated with a single verb form; sometimes, as we discuss below, the same form may also be used for the causative meaning. This verb form can be said to take its name from the spatial configuration.

Given the theory of meaning/form association set out in section 1.4, each of the verb meanings can be viewed as involving a distinct lexical semantic template, with particular spatial configurations used to fill the constant associated with these templates. The result is a set of lexical semantic representations with a shared constant, and hence in English, more often than not, these representations are associated with a shared name. When we refer to verbs that take their name from a spatial configuration apart from one of the specific meanings that can be associated with such verbs, we will refer to them as *verbs of spatial configuration*. When we are discussing particular senses associated with verbs of spatial configuration, we will refer to the verb according to its meaning.

It is the simple position sense of verbs of spatial configuration that is relevant to the discussion of verbs of existence; we return to the other senses in chapter 4. We propose that the simple position verbs are verbs of existence. These verbs pattern in many respects like verbs of existence. They describe the existence of an entity at a particular location, each particular verb contributing information about the particular spatial configuration involved. Like verbs of existence, these verbs require a locative phrase in this sense. Furthermore, in chapter 4 we present cross-linguistic evidence that the simple position verbs, like verbs of existence, are unaccusative. In chapter 6 we show that, like verbs of existence, the simple position verbs participate in locative inversion.

If the simple position verbs are verbs of existence, then one aspect of their behavior is somewhat unexpected. As noted earlier, many of these verbs have transitive causative variants, unlike verbs of existence in general.

(108) a. The bicycle leaned against the fence.
      b. I leaned the bicycle against the fence.

(109) a. A statue of Jefferson stood on the pedestal.
      b. They stood the statue of Jefferson on the pedestal.

However, if simple position verbs, like other verbs of existence, are not externally caused verbs, then all we need to show is that such causative pairs do not represent the same phenomenon as the causative pairs involving externally caused verbs like *break*. There is indeed evidence that this is so.

We begin with a variety of morphological evidence that these causative pairs should be set apart from the causative pairs involving verbs like *break*. The morphological relationship between the causative and noncausative senses of the simple position verbs is not always completely regular.

For example, although the verb *sit* can be used to describe the location of animate or inanimate entities, the causative sense of this verb is appropriate for describing the position of animates only, *set* being used as the causative when describing the position of inanimates and sometimes animates.

(110) a. The usher sat the guests in the first row.
     b. We set/*sat the books on the table.

On the other hand, the verb *lie* is used as a simple position verb but not as a causative; the related causative meaning is expressed with the verb *lay*.

(111) a. The dressmaker laid/*lay the dress carefully in a box.
     b. Sally laid/*lay her baby down for a nap.

The irregularity of the pattern is also evident in the behavior of another subset of the verbs of spatial configuration. The members of this subset appear not to have the simple position sense available. They cannot be used intransitively with an inanimate subject; instead, the adjectival passive participle based on their causative sense is used to express the comparable meaning.[23]

(112) a.   We balanced the load on the wagon.
     b.   *The load balanced on the wagon.
     c.   The load was balanced on the wagon.

(113) a.   The designer mounted the photograph on the bulletin board.
     b.   *The photograph mounted on the bulletin board.
     c.   The photograph was mounted on the bulletin board.

(114) a.   We perched the picture on the piano.
     b.   *The picture perched on the piano.
     c.   The picture was perched on the piano.

To take another example of the irregularity, compare the behavior of the apparently synonymous verbs *hang* and *suspend*. *Hang* behaves like *stand*, allowing the simple position sense and the related causative sense, whereas *suspend* patterns like *balance*.

(115) a.   The cook hung the dried herbs from the rafters.
     b.   The dried herbs hung from the rafters.
     c.   The dried herbs were hung from the rafters.

(116) a.   The cook suspended the dried herbs from the rafters.
     b.   *The dried herbs suspended from the rafters.
     c.   The dried herbs were suspended from the rafters.

Irregular morphological relationships between the causative and non-causative forms of such verbs are also displayed in other languages. In Dutch the verbs *zitten* 'sit' and *liggen* 'lie' have the intransitive simple position sense, but cannot be used as transitive causatives; instead, the phonologically related verbs *zetten* 'sit' and *leggen* 'lay' are used. In Russian the pattern of morphological relations between the forms is even more complicated, although there is evidence of a common root (for further discussion, see Townsend 1970, Gołab 1968, Gladney 1993). What is relevant is that this pattern is different from the regular pattern associated with the causative pairs involving the Russian counterparts of verbs like *break*. In true causative alternation pairs, the causative verb is morphologically simple and the noncausative verb is morphologically complex, being derived by affixation of the reflexive suffix *-sja* (*-s'* after vowels) to the morphologically simple verb.

(117) a. Anna otkryla dver'.
Anna opened door
'Anna opened the door.'

     b. Dver' otkryla-s'.
door opened-REFL
'The door opened.'

In general, a range of lexicalization patterns are observed across languages for expressing the various verbal meanings associated with a given spatial configuration, as briefly reviewed by Talmy (1985). We expect that further study will reveal some subregularities, although we do not pursue this issue here. All that matters is that these irregularities are in clear contrast with the very regular morphological relation that obtains between the members of the causative pairs involving externally caused verbs of change of state.

The semantic relationship between the causative and noncausative uses of verbs of spatial configuration is also not the same as the relationship between the causative and noncausative uses of externally caused verbs of change of state like *break*. With alternating verbs like *break*, the intransitive use can be described as "inchoative"; it means something like 'come to be in the state lexicalized by the verb'. In fact, many of the alternating verbs, such as *cool*, *dry*, and *harden*, are morphologically related or identical to adjectives that name this state. Therefore, it is possible to derive the inchoative variant from the causative variant via a process that lexically binds (or existentially quantifies over) the first argument of the CAUSE predicate, as suggested in section 3.2.4. In contrast, verbs of spatial configuration are never morphologically deadjectival. Rather than being inchoative, the intransitive simple position sense of a verb of spatial configuration like *hang* is stative and means something like 'be in the spatial configuration designated by the verb'. (Marantz (1984) provides one of the few discussions of causative pairs that acknowledges that in some instances the intransitive member of the pair is stative.) Of the possible senses associated with a given verb of spatial configuration, the one that comes closest to having an inchoative interpretation is the assume position sense, but it is unlikely that the causative sense of the verbs of spatial configuration is related to this sense. With the exception of the verb *sit*, in the causative sense the theme does not have to be animate, unlike the entity that assumes a position in the assume position sense; nor does the theme of the causative sense have to be able to assume a position under its own control, again contrasting with the assume position sense.

Carter (1976, 1978) argues that all causative verbs should be analyzed as causatives of verbs of change. If so, the causative verbs of spatial configuration would have roughly the same lexical semantic representation as the causative verbs of change of state. That is, this representation would take a form along the lines in (118). (In this representation we use /*SPATIAL-CONFIG* to indicate the spatial configuration that is particular to a given verb; we also intend this notation to encode the modificatory function that this constant serves within the lexical semantic representation.)

(118) [[*x* DO-SOMETHING] CAUSE [*y* BECOME AT *z* /*SPATIAL-CONFIG*]]

The process of lexical binding of the first argument of the CAUSE predicate, which was used to derive the intransitive use of an externally caused verb such as *break*, would not derive the simple position use of a verb of spatial configuration from its causative use. The simple position use is stative, but the central subevent in the representation in (118) is that of a verb of change, and the process of binding will not effect any changes in the representation of the central subevent. In fact, it is unclear what kind of rule could derive the lexical semantic representation of a stative verb from that of a verb of change.

As suggested above, we propose that the causative and simple position senses do not involve a single lexical semantic representation, as we proposed for the two uses of *break*, where the intransitive use arises from the lexical binding of an argument in the lexical semantic representation that is common to both uses. In contrast, causative pairs involving verbs of spatial configuration involve the association of a single constant specifying a particular spatial configuration with two distinct lexical semantic templates. There are thus two verbs, belonging to two semantic classes, that happen to involve the same constant and therefore may have the same name. (Obviously, nothing precludes the association of distinct names with two lexical semantic representations involving distinct templates but the same constant.) Intransitive *hang*, for example, belongs to the class of simple position verbs, whereas transitive *hang* belongs to the same class as causative *put*, except that it lexicalizes the spatial configuration of the placed entity. B. Levin (1993) calls the class of verbs that includes *hang* "verbs of putting in a spatial configuration." The fact that these two verbs *hang* share the same "name" is due to the fact that they both involve the same spatial configuration. The relationship between the two uses of *hang* is illustrated with the lexical semantic representations in (119); compare this relationship to the one that holds between the lexical semantic representations for transitive and intransitive *break* given in (60) and (61).

(119) a. $[x \text{ BE AT } z / HANG]$
       b. $[[x \text{ DO-SOMETHING}] \text{ CAUSE } [y \text{ BECOME AT } z / HANG]]$

Why, then, don't all verbs of spatial configuration have causative uses? As discussed in section 3.2.1, some, like *loom* and *slouch*, take their name from spatial configurations whose very nature makes them compatible only with meanings associated with internally caused eventualities. These constants, therefore, cannot be associated with the lexical semantic template of externally caused verbs. Consequently, the verb forms naming such spatial configurations will not be associated with a transitive causative use for the same reason that verbs like *laugh* and *talk* are not. Only those spatial configurations that can be externally caused may be associated with a causative lexical semantic template.

To summarize, causative pairs of the type exhibited by verbs like *break* involve two distinct argument structures associated with a single lexical semantic representation. In contrast, with the verbs of spatial configuration causative pairs arise because two distinct lexical semantic representations, one causative and one not, share the same constant. Furthermore, the morphological relationship between the two members of such causative pairs is not necessarily uniform across the entire class within any particular language, and the morphological expression of the relationship is often different from the one that signals the relationship between the members of the *break*-type causative pairs. Moreover, there is greater cross-linguistic variability in the way languages express the relation between the members of these pairs. Thus, these causative pairs are spurious pairs in the sense defined in section 3.2.5, and their presence does not detract from the inclusion of the simple position verbs among the verbs of existence and appearance.

3.4 Conclusion

In this chapter we have isolated three broad classes of verbs, defined in terms of their lexical semantic representation and their associated argument structure, and hence in terms of their syntactic configuration. The first set of verbs can be characterized as externally caused verbs; this set includes many verbs of change of state. In terms of their lexical semantic representation, these verbs are basically dyadic causative verbs that need not express their cause argument under certain circumstances, giving rise to what we show in chapter 4 is an unaccusative intransitive use. The second set of verbs includes internally caused verbs; these verbs are monadic in terms of their lexical semantic representation and, as we show in chapter 4, unergative. The third set includes the verbs of existence and appearance, which are dyadic; as we show in chapter 4, these verbs are unaccusative verbs with two internal arguments.

Chapter 4

The Linking of Arguments

In the previous chapter we investigated the basic adicity of a range of intransitive verbs and began to isolate certain lexical semantic distinctions relevant to determining a verb's argument structure. We sketched properties of the argument structures of various types of intransitive verbs, but not in any systematic way. In this chapter we focus on the explicit formulation of the linking rules that are responsible for determining the argument structures of a wide variety of intransitive verbs and, hence, the syntactic expression of their arguments. In section 4.1 we lay out the four linking rules we will make use of. In section 4.2 we examine the interactions between these rules. In section 4.3 we compare our approach with other proposals concerning the lexical semantic determinants of argument expression.

4.1 The Linking Rules

4.1.1 The Immediate Cause Linking Rule

In the previous chapter the distinction between internally and externally caused verbs was shown to be pertinent to determining basic adicity. The notions of internal and external causation allow the identification of the participant in an eventuality that is the immediate cause of the eventuality, if there is such a participant. We call such a participant the *immediate cause*, and we suggest that the linking rule that determines which argument of a verb is its external argument makes reference to this notion.[1]

(1) *Immediate Cause Linking Rule*
    The argument of a verb that denotes the immediate cause of the eventuality described by that verb is its external argument.

The Immediate Cause Linking Rule will apply to both internally and externally caused verbs and to both transitive and intransitive verbs. We begin by illustrating its applicability to a variety of internally caused verbs, showing that it correctly predicts their unergative status. We will then discuss how this linking rule is applicable to externally caused verbs.

For intransitive verbs, the Immediate Cause Linking Rule captures the generalization that internally caused verbs typically receive an unergative classification since their sole argument is the immediate cause (although we will show in sections 4.2.1 and 5.1 that not all internally caused verbs —and specifically not all agentive verbs—are unergative). It is well known that a large subclass of unergative verbs are agentive. Since, as we have already shown, agentivity is subsumed under internal causation, agentive monadic verbs will generally be classified by this linking rule as unergative. Because the unergative status of agentive monadic verbs has been illustrated so frequently in the literature, we will only briefly justify this classification here. Agentive verbs figure prominently on the list of verbs that C. Rosen (1984) has shown to be unergative in Italian; some of these verbs are cited in the perfect in (2) to show that they take the auxiliary *avere* 'have', an indicator of their unergative status.

(2) ha sorriso 'smiled', ha leticato 'quarreled', ha viaggiato 'traveled',
    ha scherzato 'joked', ha chiacchierato 'chatted', ha telefonato
    'telephoned', ... (C. Rosen 1984:44, (19))

In English evidence for the unergative classification of monadic agentive verbs is provided by the resultative construction. These verbs are found with resultative phrases predicated of a surface direct object, rather than predicated directly of their surface subject, as would be the case with unaccusative verbs.

(3) a. They were fluent and brilliant talkers; they could said Rachel
       "chat a dormouse out of its winter sleep" ... [J. Aiken, *Jane
       Fairfax*, 97]
    b. "Miss Bates, are you mad to let your niece sing herself hoarse in
       this manner ..." [J. Aiken, *Jane Fairfax*, 200]
    c. I ... ruthlessly roused Mr. Contreras by knocking on his door
       until the dog barked him awake. [S. Paretsky, *Blood Shot*, 183]

Agentive monadic verbs are found not only in the unergative resultative pattern, but also in a related construction, exemplified in (4), known as the *X's way construction* (see A. Goldberg 1994a, 1994b, Jackendoff 1990, Marantz 1992, Salkoff 1988, and section 5.1.3 for further discussion).

(4) a. ... three dozen Hare Krishnas danced and sang their way
       through Gorky Park on Sunday ... [AP Newswire 1990,
       29138379]
    b. ... corporate executives wined, dined and golfed their way to a
       record 4.98 trillion yen or about $36.5 billion ... [AP Newswire
       1990, 45776417]
    c. As soon as we had smiled our way out of our new friends' sight
       ... [L. Haire-Sargeant, *H.*—, 277]

This construction takes its name from the NP *X's way*, which appears
following the verb. As in the resultative construction, a result XP is predicated of this NP; however, in this construction, unlike in the resultative
construction, the noun that heads the postverbal NP is invariant. This
construction has been argued to be a diagnostic for unergative verbs
(Marantz 1992). Unergative verbs have the ability to assign accusative
Case (Burzio 1986), and, furthermore, English allows the marked option
of accusative Case assignment to nonsubcategorized objects. Together
these two properties give rise to the *X's way* construction, by allowing an
unergative verb to be found with the phrase *X's way* as a postverbal NP,
while retaining its original syntactic classification. Unaccusative verbs do
not appear in this construction, presumably because they lack the ability
to assign Case to a postverbal NP. As discussed by Burzio (1986), the
ability to assign Case correlates with the presence of an external argument, a property of unergative, but not unaccusative, verbs.

The Immediate Cause Linking Rule will also classify verbs such as
cough, shiver, sleep, snore, tremble, and *yawn* as unergative, although they
are more often than not nonagentive, since as shown in chapter 3, such
verbs can nonetheless be considered internally caused. In English these
verbs do not have lexical causative variants, suggesting that they indeed
are properly classified as internally caused verbs. Evidence for their unergative classification comes from Italian, where these verbs all select the
auxiliary *avere* 'have' (Perlmutter 1989, C. Rosen 1984, among others).[2]

(5) ha tossito 'coughed', ha dormito 'slept', ha russato 'snored', ha
    tremato 'trembled', ... (C. Rosen 1984:44, (19))

In English support for classifying these verbs as unergative comes from
the resultative construction and the related *X's way* construction. Not
only are they found in the unergative, and not the unaccusative, resultative pattern, as shown in (6), but they are also found in the *X's way*
construction, as shown in (7).

(6) a. ... poor Sam had been wretchedly ill and had coughed himself
       into a haemorrhage ... [J. Aiken, *Jane Fairfax*, 98]

    b. You ... have not slept yourself sober. [1839 Dickens, Nich.
       Nickl., 738; cited in Visser 1963:584]

(7) a. I was about to cough my way out the door, when this man crept
       to the podium. [B. Pesetsky, *The Late Night Muse*, 24]

    b. ... while the half-child half-young-woman shivered her way
       through the dangerous memory ... [ThEdge; Oxford Corpus]

    c. ... when Tony had yawned his happy way to bed ... [B.
       Lehmann, *Rumour of Heaven*, 135]

4.1.1.1 Verbs of Emission A more interesting illustration of the scope
of the Immediate Cause Linking Rule involves the verbs of emission introduced in chapter 3. On the basis of their meaning, it is not immediately
apparent whether these verbs are best classified as unaccusative or unergative. The semantic criteria that are most frequently considered to be indicators of class membership are not pertinent to them. Unlike the single
argument of most unergative verbs, their single argument is usually not
agentive and does not show protagonist control. Nor does the argument
of a verb of emission undergo a change of state like the single argument
of many unaccusative verbs. In addition, most of these verbs do not describe eventualities that are temporally bounded. (There are exceptions
like the verbs *flash* and *hoot*, which can describe one flash or hoot or a
series of flashes or hoots.)

However, if, as we suggested in chapter 3, the verbs of emission are
internally caused, then they are predicted to be unergative since the Immediate Cause Linking Rule should apply to their argument, which is the
emitter. Indeed, the evidence from unaccusative diagnostics overwhelm-
ingly suggests that these verbs are unergative. In English the most convincing evidence comes from the ability of these verbs to be found not
only in the unergative resultative pattern, but also in the *X's way* construction, as exemplified in (8)–(11) using members of the different subclasses.

(8) The beacons flared the news through the land. [Henderson I 92; cited
    in Lindkvist 1976:89, sec. 233, 4]

(9) a. The phone rang me out of a dreamless oblivion at seven-fifteen.
       [C. Brennan, *Headhunt*, 82]

    b. Each morning the train groans and creaks its way out of the 20th
       century into a world that differs little from what Ottoman

passengers saw from their carriages a century ago. [C. Hedges, "Heavy Snow in Israel Helps the Trains, Sort Of," 6]

c. Then he watched as it gurgled its way into a whiskey tumbler. [M. Grimes, *The Five Bells and Bladestone*, 200]

(10) a. The skunk stank us out of house and home.
      b. He stank his smelly way home.

(11) At Victoria Falls the Zambezi is rife with tumult, boiling and bubbling its way through basalt gorges . . . [P. L. Brown, "Dodging Hippos on the Zambezi," 14]

Another type of evidence that suggests that in English the verbs of emission are unergative involves derivational morphology. In English -*er* nominals are typically formed from unergative, but not unaccusative, intransitive verbs (B. Levin and Rappaport 1988, Rappaport Hovav and B. Levin 1992). The existence of -*er* nominals related to many verbs of emission is also consistent with an unergative classification.

(12) beeper, buzzer, clicker, ringer, squeaker, . . . ; blinker, flasher, sparkler, . . . ; stinker; bubbler, gusher, . . .

Furthermore, as we point out in B. Levin and Rappaport 1988, there is evidence that these verbs are unergative in other languages as well. These verbs behave like unergative verbs with respect to auxiliary selection in Italian, Dutch, and Basque. The Italian counterparts of these verbs invariably select the auxiliary *avere* 'have', rather than the unaccusative auxiliary *essere* 'be'.

(13) ha scintillato 'sparkled', ha puzzato 'stank', ha brillato 'shone'
      (C. Rosen 1984:64, (77))

Similar examples can be constructed for Dutch, where the verbs of emission take the auxiliary *hebben* 'have'.

(14) a. De zon heeft geschenen.
          the sun has   shined
          'The sun shone.'
      b. De cello heeft geglansd, maar hij is nu   oud, en dof
          the cello has   gleamed but   he is now old and dull
          geworden.
          become
          'The cello gleamed, but it is old now, and has become dull.'

   c. De air-conditioning heeft gebromd/gezoemd
      the air conditioning has   hummed
      (maar nu niet meer).
      (but not any more)
      'The air conditioning hummed (but not any more).'
   d. De sleepboot heeft eenmaal getoeterd.
      the tugboat   has   once   hooted
      'The tugboat hooted once.'
   e. De kerkkloken hebben geluid.
      the church bells have   rung
      'The church bells rang.'
   f. Het afval   heeft gestonken.
      the garbage has   stunk
      'The garbage stank.'
   g. De fontein   heeft geborreld.
      the fountain has   bubbled
      'The fountain bubbled.'

Basque also has two auxiliaries: *izan* 'be', which is used only with unaccusative verbs, and *ukan* 'have', which is used elsewhere (B. Levin 1989). The list of single-argument verbs taking *ukan* rather than *izan* cited in Lafitte's (1979) grammar of Basque includes a few verbs of emission.

(15) argitu 'shine', dirdiratu 'shine', disdiratu 'sparkle'

The small number of verbs of emission included in Lafitte's list is not surprising given that the intransitive verb class of Basque is almost exclusively made up of unaccusative verbs, the class of unergative intransitive verbs in Basque being much smaller than that of other languages. The Basque counterparts of the most commonly cited agentive unergative verbs of other languages are expressed periphrastically in a light verb construction headed by the verb *egin* 'do/make' together with a noun. For example, the Basque counterparts of English *laugh* and *work* are *barre egin* 'laugh do' and *lan egin* 'work do'. The verb *egin*, like other transitive verbs, takes the auxiliary *ukan* 'have'. Interestingly, the Basque counterparts of some English verbs of emission take the form of a noun plus the verb *egin* 'do/make', as illustrated in (16).

(16) giltz-zarata egin 'jingle', kirrinka egin 'creak', orroe egin 'roar',
     tik-tak egin 'tick'; diz diz egin 'shine, glow, sparkle', ñirñir egin
     'sparkle, twinkle, flicker, glimmer' (Aulestia and White 1990)

Thus, Basque makes use of the same device for expressing the counterparts of verbs of emission as it does for expressing the counterparts of agentive monadic verbs, supporting the classification of verbs of emission as unergative.

Before concluding this section, we comment on the analysis of the verbs of emission presented by Perlmutter (1978), who included these verbs among the unaccusative verbs because of their failure to undergo impersonal passivization in Dutch. There are, however, independent reasons for this property, so that it need not preclude an unergative classification of these verbs.

Because Perlmutter (1978) assumed that the existence of an impersonal passive signaled unergative classification and its nonexistence signaled unaccusative classification, he concluded that verbs of emission were unaccusative. The impersonal passive diagnostic has been the subject of some controversy in the literature on unaccusativity. Zaenen (1993), for example, claims that it cannot be used as an unergative diagnostic, proposing that compatibility with impersonal passivization in Dutch is determined by the semantic notion of protagonist control (see also chapter 1). She points out that some Dutch verbs that are clearly unergative cannot appear in impersonal passives, citing examples such as (17), attributing their behavior to the fact that they are not protagonist control verbs.

(17) *Er   werd (door de man) gebloed.
     there was (by the man)   bled
     'There was bled (by the man).'
     (Zaenen 1993:131, (7b))

Moorcroft (1985), Shannon (1987), and others also cite an agentivity requirement on German impersonal passives. Nevertheless, we take impersonal passivization to be an unaccusative diagnostic, following Hoekstra and Mulder (1990), Perlmutter (1978), Marantz (1984), and others, but we take its sensitivity to protagonist control to be an indication that it is a necessary but not a sufficient condition that a verb be unergative for it to permit impersonal passivization. That is, only unergative verbs—although not all unergative verbs—will be found in this construction.[3]

Given the semantic restriction on impersonal passivization, this diagnostic can only be used to provide information about monadic verbs whose arguments are animate and hence could show protagonist control. Since the arguments of verbs of emission are typically inanimate, these verbs could not be expected to show impersonal passives even if they were unergative, so that this diagnostic cannot be used to classify them. But if one of these verbs took an appropriate argument that is capable of protagonist control, then given their unergative classification, we might expect them to show an impersonal passive. In fact, Zaenen (1993) points out that (18), cited by Perlmutter (1978) as evidence that verbs of emission do not allow impersonal passives, is only ruled out on a nonagentive interpretation (where *krengen* is understood as 'carcasses'), but is acceptable if the emission of the stimulus is understood to be intentional (i.e., if *krengen* is understood as 'nasty women', giving a protagonist control interpretation).

(18) Er   werd door de krengen   gestonken.
     there is   by the nasty women/carcasses stunk
     'There is stunk by the nasty women/*carcasses.'
     (Zaenen 1993:139, (37), Perlmutter 1978:171, (71b))

4.1.1.2 Verbs of Spatial Configuration The Immediate Cause Linking Rule will also apply to the verbs of spatial configuration in their maintain position sense, since they are internally caused in this sense, making them unergative. We single out this class for mention since the exact aspectual classification of these verbs is a matter of debate in the literature on aspect (see, for example, Dowty 1979 and note 14 of this chapter). It is clear, however, that these verbs can be considered internally caused when they are agentive, as they are in the maintain position sense.

As discussed briefly in section 3.3.3, the verbs of spatial configuration show complex behavior, allowing both agentive and nonagentive monadic noncausative uses. When nonagentive, these verbs describe the position of their subject with respect to some location. When agentive, they can describe either the assumption or the maintenance of a position. We thus distinguished between the simple position sense, the maintain position sense, and the assume position sense. In this section we will not be concerned with the assume position sense (but see the discussion in section 4.2.3). What is relevant is that the other two senses, which are both monadic, differ according to whether or not they involve internal causation. We predict that the Immediate Cause Linking Rule should apply to these verbs in their maintain position sense, classifying them as unergative, since it is this sense that involves internal causation. (Another linking rule will determine their classification on the simple position reading. They will be classified as unaccusative on this reading; see section 4.1.3.)

The claim about class membership can be tested in English and Dutch. Hoekstra and Mulder (1990), for example, provide evidence from Dutch that these verbs are found in the unergative resultative pattern when they take animate subjects, suggesting an unergative analysis.

(19) a. dat hij zijn rug door   gelegen heeft
        that he his back through lain   has
        'that he lay his back sore'
        (Hoekstra and Mulder 1990:12, (20a))
     b. dat hij een gat in de stoel gezeten heeft
        that he a   hole in the chair sat   has
        'that he sat a hole in the chair'
        (Hoekstra and Mulder 1990:12, (20b))

In English the resultative construction is not an appropriate diagnostic to apply to these verbs since in English this construction is preferred with nonstative verbs (Carrier and Randall, in press; see also the discussion in section 2.3.3); nevertheless, we find the constructed example in (20) is not entirely unacceptable.

(20) ?She knelt her knees sore scrubbing the marble floors.

Actually, as Hoekstra and Mulder themselves note, and as M. Everaert also informs us, not all Dutch speakers accept the resultatives in (19). It is likely that the stativity restriction that applies to English resultative constructions applies in Dutch as well, with speakers differing in their classification of agentive verbs of spatial configuration as state or activity verbs in these examples. Moving beyond the resultative construction, even in English verbs of spatial configuration on the maintain position sense can sometimes appear with nonsubcategorized objects, as in (21), an indication of unergative status.

(21) Carla impatiently sat the meeting out.

Further evidence that the maintain position sense receives an unergative classification in English comes from the prepositional passive construction, sometimes also known as the "pseudopassive," proposed as an unaccusative diagnostic by Perlmutter and Postal (1984). Perlmutter and Postal present evidence that prepositional passivization in English, like impersonal passivization in languages such as Dutch and Turkish (Perlmutter 1978), is possible only with unergative verbs. Prepositional passives also resemble impersonal passives in showing an animacy restriction: it appears that only those unergative verbs that take an animate subject are eligible for this construction.[4] Verbs such as *sit* and *stand* are readily found in the prepositional passive construction with the maintain position interpretation, as shown in (22); therefore, these verbs must be unergative on this interpretation.

(22) a. This platform has been stood on by an ex-president.
     b. These chairs have been sat on by the Queen's children.

As part of a study of Dutch verbs of spatial configuration, Mulder and Wehrmann (1989) demonstrate that verbs of spatial configuration with animate subjects are found in the Dutch middle construction, a construction that they say is possible with unergative and transitive, but not unaccusative, verbs.

(23) Het zit makkelijk   in deze stoel/met je benen over elkaar.
     it   sits comfortably in this chair/with your legs crossed
     (Mulder and Wehrmann 1989:119, (45b))

This behavior, they note, supports the unergative classification of these verbs.

4.1.1.3   Other Consequences of the Immediate Cause Linking Rule   As mentioned above, the Immediate Cause Linking Rule also applies to transitive verbs in externally caused eventualities. The external cause in such instances can be considered an immediate cause, and therefore the Immediate Cause Linking Rule determines that the argument denoting such an external cause will be an external argument. For example, the Immediate Cause Linking Rule applies to the external arguments of verbs such as transitive *break*, transitive *hang*, and *destroy*.[5]

The Immediate Cause Linking Rule has another advantage: it explains why internally caused verbs are unable to undergo lexical causativization. The Immediate Cause Linking Rule associates the single argument of this type of verb—an "internal cause"—with the external argument position in the argument structure. The causative counterpart of such a verb would involve the introduction of an external cause, which itself must be the external argument of the causative verb by the Immediate Cause Linking Rule. Since the linking of the internal cause argument would not be affected by the introduction of the external cause, the external cause would compete for the single external argument slot in the argument structure with the verb's own argument. The unavailability of sufficient positions for the two causes would prevent the existence of lexical causative uses of internally caused verbs.

Pinker (1989) proposes another explanation for why internally caused verbs do not have causative uses in English. He points out that transitive verbs in English can only express direct causation. The introduction of an external cause for internally caused verbs cannot yield a lexical semantic representation of the type associated with direct causation, since by its very nature an internally caused eventuality cannot be construed as being directly caused. We agree that this property is probably implicated in the noncausativizability of such verbs. We argue in section 4.2.1 that there are internally caused unaccusative verbs—that is, internally caused verbs whose immediate cause is a direct internal argument. Although there would be no competition for the external argument position if a causative was formed from such a verb, nevertheless, these verbs do not have lexical causatives presumably for the reasons suggested by Pinker. However, as we have shown in section 3.2.5, there are certain internally caused verbs that do causativize regularly under specific syntactic conditions (the presence of a directional PP). These are the agentive verbs of manner of motion. This lexical process of causativization must indeed be marked, given the observation that transitive verbs in English can only express direct causation. But if we are correct in suggesting, as we do in chapter 5, that the presence of the directional PP syntactically licenses the causativization process, then it appears that syntactic factors do enter into the explanation of the general lack of lexical causatives of internally caused verbs.

In the absence of lexical causatives, the causative of an internally caused verb is expressed periphrastically using whatever mechanism a language makes available for the productive formation of causatives, whether by the use of a causative verb or a causative morpheme. Following Baker (1988a), Marantz (1984), and S. Rosen (1989), among others, we assume that such causative verbs or morphemes have their own argument structure, so that general principles involving the merger of predicates will determine which of the competing arguments will be expressed as subject. We then make an interesting prediction that is easily tested: only languages with causative morphemes will allow unergative verbs to undergo a productive lexical process of causativization. We do not know of any counterexamples and leave it for further research to investigate this prediction more fully.

4.1.2 The Directed Change Linking Rule
Next we introduce a linking rule that has substantial responsibility for the linking of internal arguments.

(24) *Directed Change Linking Rule*
The argument of a verb that corresponds to the entity undergoing
the directed change described by that verb is its direct internal
argument.

Most obviously, this rule is intended to apply to verbs of change of state
such as *break;* hence, it can be viewed as subsuming and replacing the
Change-of-State Linking Rule from chapter 2.[6] The Immediate Cause
Linking Rule ensures that when a verb like *break* is used transitively, the
external cause will be the external argument, and the Directed Change
Linking Rule ensures that the passive participant will be the direct internal argument. When a verb like *break* is used intransitively, only the
passive participant is projected into the argument structure since the external cause is lexically bound (see section 3.2.4). The Directed Change
Linking Rule will again apply, and this argument will be the direct internal argument. This linking is consistent with the observation that these
verbs behave like unaccusatives when they take a single argument; we
review the data for considering such verbs to be unaccusative below. Since
in English these verbs have S-Structure subjects when they take a single
argument, this argument, although a direct internal argument and hence
linked to the D-Structure object position, must assume the subject relation at S-Structure, presumably as a consequence of independent syntactic
principles. The typical GB account of the expression of the arguments of
such verbs makes reference to the Case Filter, Burzio's Generalization,
and the Extended Projection Principle (Burzio 1981, Rothstein 1983); we
do not go into details here. (See Bresnan and Zaenen 1990 for an account
within LFG's Lexical Mapping Theory.)

When their external cause is left unspecified under the conditions described in chapter 3, the verbs of change of state are among the prototypical unaccusative verbs, as predicted by the Directed Change Linking
Rule. There is plenty of evidence in favor of this classification. We have
already shown that these verbs are among the canonical causative alternation verbs, and we have argued that the causative alternation is an unaccusative diagnostic. These verbs also pattern like unaccusatives with
respect to the resultative construction.

(25) a. The bag broke open.
      b. The toast burned black.
      c. The ice froze solid.

In addition, in languages that show a distinct auxiliary for unaccusative verbs, the counterparts of these verbs take the unaccusative auxiliary. For example, in Italian they take the auxiliary *essere* 'be', as shown in (26), and in Basque they take the auxiliary *izan* 'be', as shown in (27).

(26) a. Gianni ha aperto la porta.
Gianni has opened the door
'Gianni opened the door.'
   b. La porta si   è aperta.
the door REFL is opened
'The door opened.'

(27) a. Miren-ek   atea   ireki du.
Miren-ERG door (ABS) open 3sABS-have-3sERG
'Miren opened the door.'
   b. Atea   ireki da.
door (ABS) open 3sABS-be
'The door opened.'

Finally, consistent with an unaccusative classification, these verbs are not attested with cognate objects or with nonsubcategorized objects with resultative phrases predicated of them (see section 2.1.4).

(28) a. *The mirror broke a jagged break.
   b. *The toast burned its crust black.

The Directed Change Linking Rule is meant to capture a parallel between verbs of change of state such as *break* and *open*, and verbs of inherently directed motion such as *fall* and *come*, characterizing both types of change as "directed." As already mentioned, there is a distinction among verbs of motion between verbs like *roll*, *walk*, *swim*, and *bounce*, which specify a manner of motion but not a direction of motion, and verbs like *arrive*, *come*, *go*, *rise*, and *fall*, which specify a direction (be it deictic, as in the case of *come*, or not, as in the case of *rise*) but not a manner (Hoekstra 1984, B. Levin and Rappaport 1989, B. Levin and Rappaport Hovav, 1992, L. Levin 1986, C. Rosen 1984, Schlyter 1978, 1981). Consider, for example, the verb *come:* someone might come somewhere by running, walking, skipping, or jogging.[7] The Directed Change Linking Rule is intended to apply to verbs of inherently directed motion, classifying them as unaccusative. It will not apply to the verbs of manner of motion because, although the action described by a verb of manner of motion inherently involves a kind of change, it is not directed. It turns out that nonagentive verbs of manner of motion such as *roll* and *bounce* are indeed unaccusative, but we will argue in section 4.1.4 that their unaccusativity arises from a yet-to-be-introduced linking rule. In that section we also argue that agentive verbs of manner of motion such as *run* and *swim* are unergative, as expected given the Immediate Cause Linking Rule.

There is evidence that the verbs of inherently directed motion are unaccusative. For example, the Italian verbs in (29) take the unaccusative auxiliary *essere* 'be', and the Basque verbs in (30) take the unaccusative auxiliary *izan* 'be'.

(29) andare 'go', venire 'come', entrare 'enter', partire 'leave'

(30) etorri 'come', joan 'go'

In English these verbs are not acceptable with cognate objects, consistent with an unaccusative classification.

(31) a. *She arrived a glamorous arrival.
     b. *The apples fell a smooth fall.

We cannot use the resultative construction to test for the status of these verbs, because, as discussed in section 2.3.2 and Simpson 1983a, the resultative construction is incompatible with verbs of inherently directed motion. However, these verbs are also unable to occur in the *X's way* construction even though there are different restrictions on this construction than on the resultative construction, suggesting that the verbs are unaccusative.

(32) a. *The oil rose its way to the top.
     b. *The apples fell their way into the crates.
     c. *She arrived her way to the front of the line.

The unacceptability of the *X's way* example in (32b) cannot be attributed to the nonagentive inanimate subject, since instances of this construction with such subjects are attested (see, for example, (9b), (9c), and (11)).

4.1.3   The Existence Linking Rule

In this section we turn to the linking of the theme argument of verbs of existence and appearance. In chapter 3 we argued that verbs of existence and appearance form a linguistically significant class of verbs with a characteristic pattern of behavior that sets them apart from monadic verbs of change of state, although the members of both classes have been classified as unaccusative verbs. We also suggested in section 3.3 that some of the distinctive properties of the verbs of existence and appearance might arise because the notions of internal and external causation do not seem relevant to their semantic characterization. In this section we present evidence in support of their unaccusative classification. Having established this, we propose a linking rule to account for their classification and discuss its relationship with the Directed Change Linking Rule.

We begin by reviewing the evidence for considering verbs of appearance and existence to be unaccusative. Most obvious is the inclusion of the verbs in (33) among the Italian verbs that take the unaccusative auxiliary *essere* 'be', of the verbs in (34) among the Basque verbs that take the unaccusative auxiliary *izan* 'be', and of the verbs in (35) among the Dutch verbs that take the unaccusative auxiliary *zijn* 'be'.

(33) apparire 'appear', rimanere 'remain', stare 'stay/be', ...

(34) agertu 'appear', egon 'stay/be', gertatu 'happen', sortu 'arise', ...

(35) blijven 'remain, stay', gebeuren 'happen', verschijnen 'appear', ontstaan 'come into existence', ... (Hoekstra 1984: 178)

The strongest evidence that the verbs of appearance and existence in English are unaccusative comes from their behavior in the *there*-insertion construction. Although it is debatable whether all instances of this construction can be used to diagnose the unaccusative syntactic configuration, those instances of this construction that take the form "*there* V NP PP," where the PP is selected, have been argued to diagnose unaccusativity (Burzio 1986). The reason for this claim is that if the NP appears to the left of (i.e., "inside") a selected PP, then that NP is presumably in the S-Structure object position, and hence the verb must be unaccusative since movement to object position—something that would be required if the verb were unergative—is not permitted. Such instances of *there*-insertion are what Milsark (1974) calls "inside verbals"; he contrasts them with what he calls "outside verbals," instances of *there*-insertion of the form "*there* V PP NP," where the NP is to the right of (i.e., "outside") the PP. As Burzio (1986) points out, outside verbals—also called "presentational" *there*-insertion by Aissen (1975)—need not be related to unaccusative verbs. In fact, the list of verbs found as outside verbals is much larger than the list of verbs found as inside verbals, resembling the list of verbs found in locative inversion (a construction that we discuss at length in chapter 6). What is important here is that verbs of existence and appearance are attested in instances of *there*-insertion that qualify as inside verbals, supporting an unaccusative classification of these verbs.

(36) a. There arose dissension between them, concerning a head wound
        suffered by a cow ... [A. W. Upfield, *Man of Two Tribes*, 79]
     b. There remained three documents on his blotter when he pressed
        his desk bell. [A. W. Upfield, *The Bachelors of Broken Hill*, 11]

Also consistent with an unaccusative classification of these verbs is their
inability to take any form of object. For instance, they are not found with
cognate objects.

(37) a. *Karen appeared a striking appearance at the department party.
     b. *Phyllis existed a peaceful existence.

The *X's way* construction is of mixed value as a diagnostic with these
verbs. It is not relevant to verbs of existence since, like the resultative
construction, it has a stativity restriction (see Jackendoff 1990), as shown
by the unacceptability of the example in (38) involving a stative verb;
therefore, as would be expected, an existence verb such as *remain* is not
possible in this construction.

(38) *Sylvia is knowing her way to first prize.

(39) *Jill remained her way to a ticket to the show.

Nevertheless, the *X's way* construction is not acceptable with verbs of
appearance, even though these verbs are nonstative. There may be independent grounds for excluding these verbs. As Jackendoff (1990) notes,
this construction is generally incompatible with intransitive achievement
verbs. The question is whether this restriction arises because achievement
verbs are semantically incompatible with this construction, or whether it
simply reflects the syntactic fact that intransitive achievement verbs are
unaccusative. Jackendoff points out that in the *X's way* construction the
process described by the verb can be a repeated bounded event, as in *She
yawned her way into the study;* nonetheless, the verb in the construction
cannot be a verb of appearance, even if such a verb is used to describe the
iteration of a bounded event.

(40) a. *Andrea appeared her way to fame.
     b. *The explosions occurred their way onto the front page.

Finally, further evidence for the unaccusativity of verbs of appearance
comes from their ability to form adjectival perfect participles (Hoekstra
1984, B. Levin and Rappaport 1986).

(41) a recently appeared book, a newly emerged scandal

Although such participles are formed only from telic intransitive verbs (B. Levin and Rappaport 1989), if B. Levin and Rappaport (1986) are correct, adjectival perfect participles are nevertheless an unaccusative diagnostic since the explanation for the derivation of such participles from unaccusative and passive verbs appeals to the syntactic properties of the verbs. Because of the telicity restriction, this test also is inapplicable to verbs of existence.

We have argued that verbs of spatial configuration on the simple position sense should also fall into the class of verbs of existence and appearance (that is, essentially when they take nonagentive arguments), and if so, we would expect them also to be unaccusative. In Italian it is difficult to establish the unaccusativity of these verbs because of the very different way in which the senses associated with verbs of spatial configuration in English are lexicalized. The Italian counterparts of most English verbs of spatial configuration have only an assume position monadic reading. The simple position interpretation that is available to these verbs in English can be expressed in Italian only through the use of the copula when the argument is inanimate and through either the use of the copula alone or the use of the copula plus a deverbal adjective formed from an assume position verb when the argument is animate.

(42) Giovanni/La sedia era sotto l'albero.
     'Giovanni/the chair was under the tree.'

(43) Giovanni era seduto sotto l'albero.
     'Giovanni was sitting under the tree.'

Mulder and Wehrmann (1989) look at evidence from Dutch regarding the classification of the simple position verbs and suggest that they are unaccusative; however, as a reviewer has pointed out to us, not only are the data that they examine quite subtle, but there are problems with their application of the diagnostics.

Returning to English, the strongest evidence for an unaccusative classification of the simple position verbs once again comes from their behavior in the *there*-insertion construction. These verbs appear in instances of this construction of the form "*there* V NP PP," that is, with the NP inside the PP.

(44) a. Meaning that it had not happened yet for there stood Buffy in the driveway staring after them her hand raised in a wan farewell. [J. C. Oates, *Black Water*, 142]

    b. Throughout the war years there stood six statues of the martyrs
       on the palace lawn.

Although (44a) describes the location of a person, it still seems to us that
this example involves the simple position and not the maintain position
use of the verb *stand;* in other words, the verb has a nonagentive interpretation. In fact, this must be so, since as Kirsner (1973:110) has pointed
out, *there*-insertion sentences never receive an agentive interpretation. To
illustrate this, he shows that *There remained three men in the room* does
not permit the agentive interpretation available in *Three men remained in
the room*—that is, the interpretation in which the men deliberately chose
to stay in the room.

    In addition, consistent with their unaccusative classification the simple
position verbs do not take cognate objects.

(45) a. *The statue stood a heroic stance in the middle of the common.
     b. *The city sprawled an extensive sprawl around the bay.

It is difficult to find other evidence bearing on the status of these verbs in
English for the same reason that it is difficult to find other evidence that
bears on the status of verbs of existence: most of the tests are inapplicable
for one reason or another.

    We propose that the unaccusative status of verbs of existence and ap-
pearance results from the following linking rule:

(46) *Existence Linking Rule*
    The argument of a verb whose existence is asserted is its direct
    internal argument.

This rule will apply to the theme argument of both types of verbs. With
verbs of appearance, the theme argument comes to exist, whereas with
verbs of existence it already exists. This rule would also apply to certain
dyadic and triadic verbs, specifically verbs of creation such as *make* and
build and verbs of putting such as *put* and *place*, since the object of these
verbs is in one instance an entity that comes to exist and in the other an
entity whose existence at a new location is asserted. In fact, the relationship between these classes of transitive verbs and the verbs of existence
and appearance is brought out by their behavior with respect to locative
inversion. Verbs of creation and verbs of putting are two of the classes of
transitive verbs that are particularly well represented in this construction
in their passive form; verbs of existence and appearance are considered
to be the canonical locative inversion verbs. See section 6.4.5 for more
discussion.

Although we have focused on verbs of existence and appearance, verbs of disappearance also pattern with these verbs, as noted in section 3.3.1. We assume that the theme argument of these verbs would become their direct internal argument by the Existence Linking Rule. If so, a slight reformulation of the linking rule would be required, so that it would apply to arguments whose existence is "denied" as well as "asserted."

(47) *Existence Linking Rule* (revised)
    The argument of a verb whose existence is asserted or denied is its direct internal argument.

The evidence that verbs of disappearance should be classified as unaccusative comes from many of the same sources that were used to argue for the unaccusative classification of verbs of appearance. For instance, the Italian counterpart of *disappear*, the verb *sparire*, takes the unaccusative auxiliary *essere* 'be'. In English these verbs are found as adjectival perfect participles, although some of these have been nominalized, as in (48).

(48) a. vanished civilizations, an expired contract, the deceased, . . .
    b. . . . if you don't blink you may be able to see . . . lingering up there in the void . . . just the faintest remnant of an evanesced cat . . . smile. [R. Baker, "The '92 Follies," 59]

The *there*-insertion construction cannot be used to show the status of these verbs because of a constraint against verbs of disappearance (Kimball 1973, among others; see also chapter 6).

Depending on how the notion of directed change is defined, verbs of appearance may fall under the Directed Change Linking Rule as well as the Existence Linking Rule, since appearance could be regarded as a directed change. However, this possibility does not detract from our analysis. There is no reason why more than one linking rule may not apply to a single argument. In fact, this is precisely what happens in Dowty's (1991) proto-role approach to linking, where several of the entailments associated with a particular proto-role may apply to a particular argument. The observation that verbs of appearance are particularly stable in their unaccusativity could even be taken as support for this possibility. That is, no matter which linking rule these verbs fall under, they are predicted to be unaccusative. This constant expression is to be contrasted, for example, with the expression of the experiencer arguments of psychological predicates, as discussed by Dowty. Since these arguments have a single Proto-Agent entailment (sentience) and a single Proto-Patient entailment (change of state), they qualify for expression as either subject or object.

The existence of verbs like *fear* and verbs like *frighten*, which differ in the expression of their experiencer arguments, shows that experiencers actually vary in the type of expression they manifest.

4.1.4 The Default Linking Rule

The three linking rules introduced so far do not account for the behavior of all single-argument verbs. They apply only to internally caused verbs, verbs of directed change, and verbs of existence and appearance. But there are monadic verbs that satisfy none of these properties. Here we assume that the default assignment for an otherwise unassigned argument is as a direct internal argument, as set out in the following linking rule:

(49) *Default Linking Rule*

An argument of a verb that does not fall under the scope of any of the other linking rules is its direct internal argument.

We address in section 4.2 the reasons for introducing a "default" linking rule in addition to the other two linking rules that involve the notion of direct internal argument. In that section we present several types of evidence that argue against dispensing with the other linking rules. In this section we simply introduce this additional linking rule, focusing, for illustrative purposes, on its role in the linking of the theme argument of certain verbs of motion.

The assumption behind the Default Linking Rule is that, unless otherwise specified, a verb will take an internal argument before taking an external argument. This, in turn, suggests that the hierarchical organization of argument structure reflects the order of semantic composition of a verb with its arguments. We cannot provide full support for this assumption in this book, but we sketch its underlying motivation. Belletti and B. Levin (1985) examined a wide range of intransitive verbs taking PP complements (e.g., *depend on, talk to, know of*) and found strong reasons to believe that such verbs also take a direct internal argument. This property was taken as evidence that a verb can take a PP only if it already has a direct argument. Belletti and B. Levin studied several subcases of this construction and identified several ways of meeting this requirement. In particular, some verbs taking PP complements meet this requirement by being unaccusative, and others meet it by taking some sort of direct internal argument—possibly, one that is not expressed. If this generalization is correct, then, when taken together with the fact that transitive and unaccusative verbs have direct internal arguments, it suggests that the default is for a verb to have a direct argument. Belletti and B. Levin make the further proposal, which we do not adopt, that even typical unergative verbs take direct internal arguments. In fact, Hale and Keyser (1993) make a similar proposal as part of an attempt to characterize the range of possible English unergative verbs.

The Default Linking Rule will apply to a subclass of the verbs of manner of motion. As already mentioned in section 4.1.2, verbs such as *jog*, *run*, *stroll*, *swim*, and *walk*, which are typically used with animate agentive arguments, show unergative behavior since, as internally caused verbs, they fall under the scope of the Immediate Cause Linking Rule. We have previously referred to such verbs as agentive verbs of manner of motion since they are typically used with animate agentive arguments; however, they might be more accurately characterized as internally caused verbs of manner of motion since some permit inanimate arguments if these arguments have "self-controlled" bodies (*A battered boat was sailing on Lake Michigan, A lot of planes fly over Chicago*). We contrast this class with a second class of verbs of manner of motion that are usually nonagentive; this class includes *bounce*, *roll*, and *spin*. For purposes of simplicity, in this section we refer to the agentive and nonagentive verbs of manner of motion as the *run* and *roll* verbs, respectively. When the *roll* verbs are used nonagentively, they are externally caused. Their passive participant does not fall under the scope of the Directed Change Linking Rule, since the change it undergoes is not directed. Instead, it is linked by the Default Linking Rule. The result is that the *roll* verbs, when the external cause is left unexpressed, are unaccusative. There is in fact abundant evidence (some of which is presented in B. Levin and Rappaport Hovav 1992) that the class of verbs of manner of motion is not homogeneous and that the *run* verbs fall under the Immediate Cause Linking Rule, whereas the *roll* verbs fall under the Default Linking Rule. The members of the two classes of verbs show the expected differences in behavior with respect to unaccusative diagnostics.

Once again the resultative construction affords some of the clearest evidence that English treats verbs like *roll* and verbs like *run* differently. In this construction the *run* verbs are found in the unergative pattern and the *roll* verbs are found in the unaccusative pattern, as illustrated in (50)–(53). (Although see section 5.1.1 for a fuller picture of the *run* verbs in the resultative construction.)

(50) a. The jogger ran his soles thin.

    b. Don't expect to swim yourself sober!

(51) a. *The jogger ran sore.
     b. *Don't expect to swim sober!

(52) a. The door rolled open.
     b. The shutter swung shut.

(53) a. *The door rolled itself open.
     b. *The shutter swung itself shut.

Furthermore, the *run* verbs, but not the *roll* verbs, are found in the *X's way* construction.

(54) a. The jogger ran his way to better health.
     b. Swim your way to a new you!

(55) a. *The pebbles rolled their way into the stream.
     b. *The ball bounced its way into the street.

The causative alternation can also be used to support the proposal that not all verbs of manner of motion are classified alike. Consistent with the proposed classifications, verbs from the *roll* class exhibit this alternation, which is associated with unaccusative verbs.

(56) a. The ball rolled/bounced.
     b. The child rolled/bounced the ball.

Hale and Keyser (1987) note that across languages verbs from the *run* class are not typically found in this alternation, as illustrated for English in (57) and (58), consistent with their proposed unergative classification.

(57) a. The runners jogged all day.
     b. *The coach jogged the runners all day.

(58) a. The tourists wandered around the Roman ruins.
     b. *The guide wandered the tourists around the Roman ruins.

As discussed in section 3.2.5, some members of the *run* class exhibit transitive causative uses in English in the presence of a directional phrase; but these uses were shown to differ in several respects from the transitive causative uses of prototypical causative alternation verbs such as *break* and thus do not weaken our claim that these verbs are unergative. We discuss these uses further in section 5.1.1.2.

Additional evidence from English regarding the classification of verbs of manner of motion comes from the prepositional passive construction, which (as discussed in section 4.1.1.2) is manifested by unergative verbs that allow protagonist control. The *run* verbs behave like other unergative verbs in being found in this construction.

(59) a. This track has been run on by our finest young athletes.
　　 b. This pool has been swum in by the last three world record holders.

This construction does not provide conclusive evidence concerning the status of the *roll* verbs, since verbs with nonagentive subjects are never candidates for this construction.

(60) a. *This golf course has been rolled on by only the best golf balls.
　　 b. *This floor has been bounced on by every type of ball imaginable.

Italian also provides support for the different classification of the *roll* and *run* verbs. In Italian the members of the two classes can to some extent be distinguished from each other in terms of their morphological shape. When used intransitively, members of the *roll* class often take the reflexive clitic *si*, and some verbs in this class must take this clitic. When they take this clitic, like all monadic *si* verbs in Italian (Burzio 1986, C. Rosen 1981, among others), they display unaccusative behavior; for instance, they take the auxiliary *essere* 'be'.

(61) I　 bambini si　 sono rotolati sul　 prato.
　　 the children REFL is　 rolled　 on the meadow
　　 'The children rolled on the meadow.'

However, it is striking that in Italian none of the verbs in the *run* class ever takes the clitic *si* while maintaining basically the same sense.

(62) a. *Giovanni si　 è corso.
　　　 Giovanni REFL is run
　　 b. *Maria si　 è nuotata.
　　　 Maria REFL is swum

This property is consistent with an unergative classification of the *run* verbs. Finally, the *roll* verbs can select the unaccusative auxiliary *essere* 'be' even when they are found without the clitic *si* or without a directional phrase; the *run* verbs cannot select the auxiliary *essere* in these circumstances.

(63) a. La palla è rotolata sul　 prato.
　　　 the ball is rolled　 on the meadow
　　　 'The ball rolled on the meadow.'

b. *Gianni è corso.

    Gianni is run

To summarize the discussion of verbs of manner of motion, the members of the two subclasses of this larger class receive a different classification in accordance with their meanings and the linking rules. Both classes of verbs will be discussed further in chapter 5.

We conclude our discussion of the Default Linking Rule by pointing out that it is also likely that once the range of data studied is broadened to include transitive verbs, the Default Linking Rule will apply to a variety of arguments that do not clearly fall under any other linking rule, and, consequently, they will be direct internal arguments. It is well known that although verbs in which an agent acts on and affects a patient are transitive, there are also many transitive verbs that do not fit this mold, typically because their nonagent argument is not a patient. The Default Linking Rule would also apply to such nonpatient arguments, resulting in their expression as objects.

4.2 Ordering the Linking Rules

Now that we have introduced a set of linking rules, another question needs to be addressed: are all the linking rules relevant to direct internal argument—the Directed Change Linking Rule, the Existence Linking Rule, and the Default Linking Rule—necessary? In particular, given that one of the linking rules for direct internal argument has been formulated as a default rule, could it subsume the other rules that apply to direct arguments, the Directed Change and Existence Linking Rules? For example, one might suggest that the Default Linking Rule be applied to verbs like *fall* and *break*, obviating the need for the Directed Change Linking Rule. One way of demonstrating that the Directed Change Linking Rule is needed is by examining the behavior of verbs that fall under both the Immediate Cause Linking Rule and the Directed Change Linking Rule. We will show that such verbs consistently exhibit unaccusative behavior in English, Italian, and Dutch. This suggests that, at least in these languages, the Directed Change Linking Rule takes precedence over the Immediate Cause Linking Rule. If the Default Linking Rule were responsible for the expression of arguments denoting entities undergoing a directed change, it could never, by virtue of being a default rule, take precedence over the Immediate Cause Linking Rule. The relevant evidence comes from verbs of motion, assume position verbs, and internally caused verbs of change of state such as the Italian counterpart of *blush* and the Dutch counterpart of *bloom*. We will show that a similar argument can be constructed in favor of retaining the Existence Linking Rule.

4.2.1 Internally Caused Verbs of Change of State

We mentioned in chapter 3 that the notions of change of state and external causation do not always coincide. Although the majority of verbs of change of state are externally caused, there are some internally caused verbs of change of state. Such verbs are the perfect testing ground for the interaction between the Immediate Cause Linking Rule and the Directed Change Linking Rule since a priori they fall under the scope of both rules. If, as we propose, the Directed Change Linking Rule takes precedence over the Immediate Cause Linking Rule, then a verb denoting an internally caused change of state is predicted to be unaccusative. In this section we show that this prediction is borne out. In particular, we examine the Italian counterpart of English *blush*, *arrossire*, and the Dutch counterpart of English *bloom*, *bloeien*. This investigation will also once again demonstrate that verbs that are considered translation equivalents in two languages can differ in subtle ways, and yet conform to the lexical semantic categories that we have set out.

As we pointed out in section 1.2.1, the eventuality described by the English verb *blush* can be conceptualized as either a state or a change of state, and languages appear to make different choices about which conceptualization they choose. Dutch and Italian appear to have made different choices, according to the discussion in McClure 1990. McClure points out that the Italian verb *arrossire* 'blush' actually describes a change of state, a property that probably reflects its morphological shape: the verb literally means 'become red' (*rosso* is Italian for *red*). To support this proposal, McClure demonstrates that *arrossire* behaves like a telic verb with respect to time adverbials.

(64) a. *G è arrossito per 10 minuti.
        G is blushed for 10 minutes
    b. G è arrossito in un secondo.
        G is blushed in one second
        (McClure 1990:314, table 4)

But blushing is conceptualized as an internally caused eventuality, as shown by the fact that in Italian (and in English too, for that matter) this verb does not have a lexical causative; therefore, the Italian verb *arrossire* is an internally caused verb of change of state.

(65) *Il complimento/Mio padre mi ha arrossito.
     the compliment/my father me has blushed

If the Directed Change Linking Rule has precedence over the Immediate
Cause Linking Rule, then the Italian verb *arrossire* should be unaccusative. In fact, this verb does select only the unaccusative auxiliary *essere*
'be' and never selects the auxiliary *avere* 'have'.

McClure (1990) contrasts the Italian verb *arrossire* with its Dutch counterpart, *bloezen*, which he shows is compatible with durative phrases only,
suggesting that it lacks the change-of-state interpretation.

(66) a. J heeft een uur lang gebloosd.
         J has   one hour long blushed
     b. *J heeft in een uur gebloosd.
         J has   in one hour blushed
         (McClure 1990:314, table 4)

The Dutch verb *bloezen*, then, cannot fall under the scope of the Directed
Change Linking Rule, and, as an internally caused verb that is not a verb
of change of state, it should display unergative—and not unaccusative—
behavior, as it does. As (66a) shows, the Dutch verb takes the auxiliary
hebben 'have'. If the following examples of the *X's way* and cognate object
constructions are indicative, then English, like Dutch, treats the verb
blush as a 'be in state' verb with an unergative classification.

(67) My 92-year-old mother would blush her way through this
     particular collection of stories, jokes and rhymes. [V. G. Paley,
     "The Schoolyard Jungle," 43]

(68) a. Frederick, roused from his preoccupation, sprang to his feet,
         blushing the blush of shame. [P. G. Wodehouse, "Portrait of a
         Disciplinarian," 116]
     b. Catharine blushed a blush of anger. [1828 Scott, F. M. Perth III,
         53; cited in Visser 1963:417]

Thus, the verb *blush* describes an internally caused eventuality; however,
in some languages this eventuality is also considered to be a directed
change, so that the corresponding verb shows unaccusative behavior,
demonstrating that the Directed Change Linking Rule takes priority over
the Immediate Cause Linking Rule.

The near-synonymous English verbs *bloom*, *blossom*, and *flower* and
their counterparts in other languages are also internally caused verbs that
are sometimes open to a change-of-state interpretation. In particular,

bloom is ambiguous between a change-of-state reading (roughly 'come to be in bloom') and a reading in which the verb describes being in a state, specifically the state described by the phrase *in bloom*. In English the two readings can be distinguished through the use of the appropriate time adverbials. On its most salient reading, (69) means that the cactus was in the state described by the phrase *in bloom* for three days. However, this sentence may have an iterative change-of-state reading, where it means that the cactus kept producing new blossoms for three days.

(69) The cactus bloomed/blossomed for three days.

On the other hand, (70) can only have the change-of-state reading. In this example the state is reached at the end of three days.

(70) The cactus bloomed/blossomed in three days.

Although it is difficult to find diagnostics that will reveal the syntactic categorization of the different senses of *bloom* in English, evidence is available in Dutch.[8] The Dutch counterpart of *bloom*, *bloeien*, is an internally caused atelic verb, as shown by its compatibility with durative adverbs (see (71)). As expected, it takes the auxiliary *hebben*, compatible with the fact that internally caused verbs are not expected to be unaccusative if they are not verbs of directed change.

(71) Deze bloem heeft het hele   jaar gebloeid.
     this   flower has   the whole year bloomed
     'This flower bloomed for the whole year.'

However, there is a related particle verb *op-bloeien* (literally 'up-bloom'), which takes the auxiliary *zijn* 'be' and is used in a slightly different range of contexts than the verb *bloeien*.

(72) a. Hij bloeide helemaal   op toen ik hem zei dat
        he bloomed completely up when I him told that
        hij een goed artikel had geschreven.
        he a   good article had written
        'He cheered up/flourished completely when I told him that he
        had written a good article.'
     b. Hij is helemaal   op-gebloeid nadat hij van   baan is veranderd.
        he is completely up-bloomed after he from job   is changed
        'He completely cheered up/flourished after he changed his job.'

As these examples show, the verb *bloeien* cannot be applied to people directly, though the particle verb *op-bloeien* can. The verb *op-bloeien* not only takes the auxiliary *zijn* 'be', suggesting an unaccusative classification, but also has a change-of-state interpretation. The unaccusative classification is just what we would expect if it is an internally caused verb of change of state, and the Directed Change Linking Rule takes precedence over the Immediate Cause Linking Rule. The verb *op-bloeien* can also be applied to plants and flowers in a somewhat metaphorical sense (it does not mean that the plant has flowers) or to describe a transition to a booming economy, as in (73) and (74); again all of these interpretations involve a directed change.

(73) Het boompje is helemaal   op-gebloeid toen ik het
     the little tree is completely up-bloomed when I it
     regelmatig mest   gaf.
     regularly fertilizer gave
     'The little tree completely flourished when I regularly gave it
     fertilizer.'

(74) De economie bloeide   op.
     the economy bloomed up
     'The economy prospered.'

The unaccusative classification of the verb *op-bloeien* receives further confirmation. In Dutch, as in English, some unaccusative verbs can have related adjectival perfect participles although unergative verbs never can (Hoekstra 1984), and the verb *op-bloeien*, unlike *bloeien*, can be found as an adjectival perfect participle.

(75) *een gebloeid boompje
      a   bloomed tree

(76) En toen werd ik geconfronteerd met een volledig
     and then was I confronted   with a   completely
     op-gebloeide AIO.
     up-bloomed graduate student
     (AIO = Assistent In Opleiding 'assistant in training', i.e., graduate
     student)

4.2.2   Verbs of Inherently Directed Motion

A striking property of the verbs of inherently directed motion is that although they can be used either agentively or nonagentively, they consistently show unaccusative behavior. Of course, this property can be explained if, as we postulated above, the Directed Change Linking Rule takes precedence over the Immediate Cause Linking Rule, so that the latter rule will not apply to any verb to which the former applies. This property is most easily illustrated with data from Italian. The Italian verb *cadere* 'fall', although usually said to describe an action that is not under the control of the entity that moves, selects the unaccusative auxiliary *essere* 'be' even when used agentively.

(77) Luigi è caduto apposta.
    Luigi is fallen on purpose
    'Luigi fell on purpose.'
    (C. Rosen 1984:64, (76a))

Similarly, the Italian verb *salire* 'go up, climb' always takes the unaccusative auxiliary *essere* 'be', even though there is no reason not to think that it could be used agentively with an animate subject.[9]

(78) Sono (*ho) salito   sulla   montagna.
    am   have climbed on the mountain
    'I climbed/went up the mountain.'

We will show that the behavior of the verbs of inherently directed motion is in striking contrast to that of the *roll* verbs, just discussed in section 4.1.4. In section 5.3 we will show that when used agentively, the *roll* verbs are unergative, rather than unaccusative. Further extensive evidence from the behavior of verbs of motion for the ranking of the linking rules will be given in section 5.1.1.

4.2.3 Assume Position Verbs

As we noted in section 4.1.1.2, verbs of spatial configuration when predicated of agents can have one of two meanings: 'maintain a specific position' or 'assume a specific position'. We showed, further, that the linking rule that is relevant for the maintain position sense is the Immediate Cause Linking Rule. The assume position sense, on the other hand, involves an action that is both internally caused and a directed change. Given the evidence we presented in section 4.2.2 that the Directed Change Linking Rule takes precedence over the Immediate Cause Linking Rule, we would predict that verbs of spatial configuration in the assume position sense ought to be unaccusative.

The prepositional passive construction discussed in section 4.1.1.2 can be used to establish that in English these verbs are unergative in the maintain position sense and unaccusative in the assume position sense. We showed in that section that verbs like *sit* and *stand* can appear in the prepositional passive construction, as in (22), repeated here.

(79) a. This platform has been stood on by an ex-president.

    b. These chairs have been sat on by the Queen's children.

Although the active counterparts of these sentences, which are given in (80), are ambiguous between a maintain position and an assume position reading, it is striking that these verbs consistently resist the assume position interpretation when they are found in the prepositional passive construction.

(80) a. An ex-president stood on this platform.

    b. The Queen's children sat on those chairs.

The absence of this reading can be brought out: if a particle is added to the sentences in (80), then they become disambiguated, receiving only the assume position reading, as shown in (81). However, prepositional passives of these verbs are excluded in the presence of the particle, as in (82), showing definitively that no passive counterpart is available for the assume position reading.[10]

(81) a.   An ex-president stood up on this platform.

    b.   The Queen's children sat down on those chairs.

(82) a. *This platform has been stood up on by an ex-president.

    b. *These chairs have been sat down on by the Queen's children.

The lack of ambiguity exhibited in (79) is expected if these verbs are unaccusative on the assume position reading, since this reading would not be compatible with the prepositional passive.

    Further evidence for the unaccusative classification of assume position verbs comes from Italian. In Italian, assume position verbs are morphologically complex: they obligatorily appear with the reflexive clitic *si*, which is taken to be an indicator of unaccusative status when found with monadic verbs. Like all monadic verbs with the reflexive clitic, these verbs select the auxiliary *essere* 'be', which we take to be a sufficient condition for unaccusativity.

(83) Maria si   è seduta subito.

    Maria REFL is sat   right away

    'Maria sat down right away.'

4.2.4 Verbs of Existence

A further open question involving the precedence relations among the linking rules concerns the order of the Existence Linking Rule with respect to the other linking rules. There are two issues that need to be resolved: how is this rule ordered with respect to the Directed Change Linking Rule and the Immediate Cause Linking Rule, and is this ordering consistent with our claim that the Default Linking Rule is indeed a default rule?

We can provide a partial answer to these questions by adapting the argument from the previous section. Specifically, if agentivity can be shown to be irrelevant to the linking of the argument of a verb of existence, then we can conclude that the Existence Linking Rule has precedence over the Immediate Cause Linking Rule and that there is no reason to view the Default Linking Rule as anything more than its name suggests. In fact, when predicated of animates, verbs of existence can be used either agentively or nonagentively, but, like verbs of inherently directed motion, they consistently show unaccusative behavior. Again we illustrate this with an Italian example, which shows that the auxiliary *essere* 'be' is selected by the verb of existence *rimanere* 'remain' independent of agentivity.

(84) Gianni è rimasto   apposta.
     Gianni is remained on purpose
     'Gianni remained on purpose.'

This property is important for another reason. We suggested in section 3.3 that the distinctive properties of the verbs of existence and appearance might be attributable in part to the irrelevance of the notions of internal and external causation to the semantic characterization of these verbs. If the Immediate Cause Linking Rule had turned out to have precedence over the Existence Linking Rule (that is, if it had determined the classification of these verbs), this would have been at odds with this hypothesis concerning their semantic characterization.

We conclude that both the Directed Change and the Existence Linking Rules take precedence over the Immediate Cause Linking Rule, which in turn takes precedence over the Default Linking Rule. Next we must ask whether the Directed Change and Existence Linking Rules can be ordered with respect to each other. This is only an issue if their domains overlap, raising the more fundamental question of whether both rules are needed, a question we addressed in section 4.1.3. At this point we have not found any positive evidence that bears on this question, so we leave it for further study.

In his discussion of the semantic determinants of unaccusativity, Dowty (1991) briefly speculates that languages may weight telicity and agentivity differently in calculating the classification of individual verbs and that Italian may be a language that gives more weight to telicity than to agentivity. The results of this section may then be considered to provide empirical support for Dowty's speculation. However, it may be the case that there is parametric variation in this regard. That is, although we suspect that all languages make use of the same syntactically relevant components of meaning, it is possible that they vary in terms of which component takes precedence over another. Labelle (1990, 1992) offers very suggestive data from French that may indicate that here at least the Immediate Cause Linking Rule takes precedence over the Directed Change Linking Rule. She shows that there is a subtle difference in meaning between those intransitive verbs of change of state such as *se briser* 'break' that appear with the reflexive clitic *se* and select *être* 'be' as their auxiliary, suggesting that they are unaccusative, and those intransitive verbs of change of state such as *casser* 'break' that do not necessarily appear with the clitic *se* and select *avoir* 'have' as their auxiliary in these circumstances, suggesting that they are unergative. Specifically, Labelle distinguishes between "internally driven transformations of an entity" that unfold naturally "without control from external factors" (1992:393) and those changes that do not come about in such a way. This distinction is clearly reminiscent of the distinction between internally caused and externally caused changes of state used in this book. We leave it for future research to determine what parametric variation exists between languages in this area.

4.3 Comparison with Other Approaches

4.3.1 Aspectual Approaches
In this section we compare our analysis with previous attempts to predict on the basis of lexical semantic properties the class membership of intransitive verbs in particular and the syntactic expression of arguments in general. Agentivity was one of the first semantic notions implicated in the determination of verb status, as seen in Perlmutter's paper introducing the Unaccusative Hypothesis, where the major category of unergative verbs is characterized as "predicates describing willed or volitional acts" (1978:162). In recent years a number of researchers have claimed that lexical aspectual (Aktionsart) notions are most relevant for these purposes (Hoekstra 1984, B. Levin and Rappaport Hovav 1992, Martin 1991, Tenny 1987, Van Valin 1990, Zaenen 1993, among others).[11] The three

aspectual notions that have been most widely employed in studies of unaccusativity are agentivity, telicity, and stativity. We will compare our approach with approaches that have made use of these aspectual notions. Since Van Valin (1990) has provided the most explicit and thorough attempt to predict the class membership of verbs on the basis of lexical aspect, we focus on his analysis for the purposes of this comparison.

As we reviewed in chapter 2, Van Valin uses predicate decompositions based on the work of Dowty (1979) to represent verb meaning. The decompositions are assigned on the basis of the Vendler class to which a verb belongs. The decompositions Van Valin (1990:224) proposes for verbs in each of the Vendler classes are given in (85).

(85) a. STATE: **predicate′** (x) or (x, y)
      b. ACHIEVEMENT: BECOME **predicate′** (x) or (x, y)
      c. ACTIVITY ($+/-$ Agentive): (DO (x)) [**predicate′** (x) or (x, y)]
      d. ACCOMPLISHMENT: ϕ CAUSE ψ, where ϕ is normally an activity predicate and ψ an achievement predicate

Van Valin claims that unaccusative diagnostics are sensitive to those distinctions that reflect natural classes of verbs with respect to these decompositions. For example, he suggests that in Italian monadic activity verbs are unergative, whereas state, achievement, and accomplishment verbs are unaccusative. The relevant generalization is that the three types of verbs said to be unaccusative have lexical representations that include a state predicate, whereas the fourth type of verb, which is unergative, does not. Another distinction that can be captured naturally using these lexical representations is the telic/atelic distinction: only telic verbs have BECOME **predicate′** (x) or (x, y) in their lexical representations. In fact, Van Valin claims that the notion of telicity figures in the characterization of certain Dutch unaccusative phenomena, for example, auxiliary selection. In other languages, such as Acehnese and Tsova-Tush, the notion relevant to the classification of verbs is agentivity, rather than notions involving lexical aspect such as stativity and telicity. There may also be languages in which some constructions are sensitive to agentivity and others to telicity; Van Valin suggests that Dutch may be such a language. Dowty (1991) also stresses the centrality of the notions of telicity and agentivity in determining the class membership of intransitive verbs.

Our criticism of the aspectual approach will be threefold. We first discuss the advantage of taking agentivity to be subsumed under the notion of internal causation, as it is on our analysis (section 4.1.1). We illustrate the advantage of this approach in section 4.3.1.1 by examining the classification of verbs that are neither agentive nor telic. The behavior of these verbs, and in particular the fact that their behavior is not uniform, will indicate that telicity and agentivity are not sufficient for determining the class membership of all intransitive verbs. Next, in section 4.3.1.2, we show that the notion of stativity is not relevant for predicting class membership. Indeed, in our analysis, stativity does not play a role at all. Finally, in section 4.3.1.3, we show how our concept of "directed change," although similar to the concept of telicity, is preferred to the traditional aspectual notion of telicity.[12] In section 4.3.2 we compare aspects of our analysis with certain concepts that Dowty (1991) employs in his theory of argument selection.

4.3.1.1 Agentivity or Internal Causation? As mentioned above, both Dowty and Van Valin stress the importance of telicity and agentivity in determining class membership. Van Valin (1990) does not speculate on the status of verbs that are neither telic nor agentive, but from his analysis one would expect stativity to determine the status of such verbs, statives being unaccusative and nonstatives, perhaps, being unergative. Dowty (1991:608) speculates that the status of such verbs will depend on whether a particular language takes agentivity or the lack of it to be primary in verb classification, or whether it takes telicity or the lack of it to be primary. If the former, then nonagentive atelic verbs are expected to be unaccusative. If the latter, then such verbs are expected to be unergative. In any event, one would expect verbs that are neither telic nor agentive to display uniform behavior in any given language. Strikingly, however, this is not the case. We have shown that in English verbs of emission, which are atelic and nonagentive, show unergative behavior, whereas verbs from the *roll* class, which are also atelic and nonagentive, show unaccusative behavior. It is important to stress that this variation holds within a single language, so that it cannot be attributed to parametric variation between languages. Furthermore, the difference shows up in a single construction, namely, the resultative.

(86)   He had set an alarm, which rang at five thirty the following
       morning, shrilling them both awake. [R. Pilcher, *Voices in
       Summer*, 116]

(87)   *During the spring thaw, the boulders rolled the hillside bare.

The differing behavior of the *roll* verbs and the verbs of emission does find an explanation in our analysis, which appeals to the distinction between internally and externally caused verbs. Since verbs of emission are internally caused, the Immediate Cause Linking Rule will apply to their emitter argument. But since the *roll* verbs, when nonagentive, are externally caused, the Immediate Cause Linking Rule is not applicable to them, although the Default Linking Rule is. Since the single arguments of these two types of verbs fall under these different rules, they end up with different classifications.

4.3.1.2 Problems with Stativity Besides the notions of agentivity and telicity, Van Valin (1990) suggests that the notion "state" is relevant to verb classification. This proposal is based on Van Valin's observation that in Italian certain diagnostics of unaccusativity are sensitive to the distinction between activity verbs on the one hand and accomplishment, achievement, and stative verbs on the other. Given the lexical representations associated with these four types of verbs, Van Valin points out that the three classes that pattern together all have a state predicate in their lexical semantic representation (see (85)). In this section we show that contrary to Van Valin's proposal, the notion "state" is irrelevant to verb classification.

We turn first to the verbs of emission, which, as we have shown in section 4.1.1, are unergative. Most verbs of emission do not describe temporally bounded eventualities, so in principle these verbs could be classified as either stative or activity verbs. And in fact it seems to us that verbs of emission fall along a continuum of stativity, verbs of smell emission being the most stative, verbs of light emission being slightly less stative, and verbs of sound emission and substance emission being the most process-like. We focus on the two subclasses that we take to have the most stative members (and particularly on the most stative verbs within these subclasses) since these are the ones that will be the most relevant for assessing Van Valin's hypothesis: the verbs of smell emission and light emission.

Two definitional criteria have been used to isolate stative from nonstative verbs. (As Dowty (1979) has made clear, and as Lakoff (1966) himself acknowledges when he introduces his widely cited stativity tests, agentivity is *not* a criterion that distinguishes stative from nonstative verbs.) The first criterion, which is the more widely employed, is based on the notion of change. Stative verbs do not involve a change, whereas nonstative verbs do. This notion is essentially the one that Dowty (1979) resorts to in his revised verb classification. Dowty's original criterion for the distinction—that stative verbs, but not nonstatives, can be judged true at a single moment—proved not to be viable because of the existence of interval statives (our simple position verbs). This criterion is also used by Carter (1978) and Kearns (1991). Kearns writes, "The general observation is that states have no essential changes or transitions, from which it follows that they are continuous and are not essentially bounded" (1991:116). From the perspective of this criterion, certain verbs of emission such as *stink* (cited in Dowty 1979 as being a stative verb), *smell*, *gleam*, *glisten*, *glow*, and *shine* ought to be classified as stative since it is not apparent what kind of change they entail.[13] Comrie (1976a:48) presents a slightly different criterion. He suggests that nonstates, but not states, require an input of energy for the maintenance of the eventuality. This criterion would seem to class all verbs of light emission and smell emission as states.

Turning next to diagnostic tests for stativity, most purported stativity tests turn out to distinguish either agentive from nonagentive predicates or individual-level from stage-level predicates (see Carlson 1977, Dowty 1979, Lakoff 1966, among others, for some discussion). For example, it appears that the ability to be used in the present progressive is not a test for nonstativeness, but rather is a test for a nonmomentary predicate. Since the stage-level interval statives (i.e., the simple position verbs) are nonmomentary predicates, they can appear in the progressive. Most individual-level predicates are stative and most stage-level predicates are nonstative, but the examples in (88), cited by Dowty (1979), show that there are stage-level stative predicates.

(88) a.   New Orleans lies at the mouth of the Mississippi River.
           ??New Orleans is lying at the mouth of the Mississippi River.
           (Dowty 1979:174, (67a,a′))
     b.   My socks are lying under the bed. (Dowty 1979:173, (62a))
           ??My socks lie under the bed.

On the other hand, several of the tests that Lakoff (1966) cites for isolating stative verbs turn out to isolate agentive from nonagentive verbs. These tests are (i) only nonstatives can occur as imperatives, (ii) only nonstatives cooccur with adverbs like *deliberately* and *carefully*, and (iii) only nonstatives occur as complements of *force* and *persuade*. The drawbacks of these tests can be seen when they are applied to verbs with inanimate subjects, such as intransitive *roll*, which clearly does not describe a state. Yet as the examples in (89) show, this verb fails the tests; the sentences are only acceptable if the rock is anthropomorphized.

(89) a. *I persuaded the rock to roll down the hill.
     b. *The rock rolled down the hill carefully/deliberately.
     c. *Roll down the hill, rock!

The one stativity test cited by Dowty (1979) that does appear to correlate with the change/no change distinction is the ability of a verb to appear in *do* constructions. This property does not seem to be a reflection of agentivity, as shown by the examples in (90) with the verb *roll*.

(90) a. The marble rolled off the table and the ball did so too.
     b. What the rock did was roll down the hill.

One other test that seems to make the relevant distinction is Jackendoff's (1983) test for distinguishing states from what he terms "events" (i.e., nonstates): only nonstates appear in the frame *What happened/occurred/ took place was* .... Certain verbs of emission only marginally appear in the contexts described by Dowty and Jackendoff.

(91) a. ??What the spotlight did was shine on the parking lot.
     b. ??What Mary's face did was glow with excitement.
     c. ??What the garbage did was stink.

(92) a. ??What happened was the spotlight shone on the parking lot.
     b. ??What happened was Mary's face glowed with excitement.
     c. ??What happened was the garbage stank.

The sentences in (92) are really only acceptable on a reading where the onset of an event is described: the spotlight *began* to shine, Mary's face *began* to glow, and so on. Pulling together the results of this discussion, it appears that both from the perspective of definitional criteria and from the perspective of diagnostic tests, some verbs of emission are stative and some are not. Yet all of these verbs show uniform behavior with respect to the Unaccusative Hypothesis, suggesting that stativity is not relevant to their classification.

If the notion of state were a semantic determinant of unaccusativity, certain classes of verbs—unaccusative activity verbs and unergative stative verbs—would not be expected to exist. The stative verbs of emission illustrate the existence of unergative stative verbs, as do the maintain position verbs. Verbs of spatial configuration in the maintain position sense, though predicated of animates, are still stative—in fact, Dowty's name for this class is "interval statives"—but they are not unaccusative.[14] The nonagentive verbs of manner of motion such as *roll* illustrate the existence of unaccusative activity verbs. Such verbs behave like unaccusatives with respect to the diagnostics even though because of their aspectual classification as activity verbs they do not have a state predicate in the lexical representation that would be assigned to them under a Van Valin–style analysis.

4.3.1.3 Problems with Telicity Telicity has also been cited as a determinant of unaccusativity (Dowty 1991, Hoekstra 1984, Van Valin 1990, Zaenen 1993, among others). Telic intransitive verbs are typically unaccusative, as we have shown with verbs of change of state and verbs of inherently directed motion. However, our linking rule makes reference to the notion of directed change rather than telicity. This formulation was chosen because there are two classes of atelic verbs that behave like unaccusatives and seem to fall under the same linking rule as the telic verbs.

One class consists of the verbs that Dowty (1979) calls "degree achievement verbs" (see also Abusch 1985, 1986). This set includes the verbs *widen, harden, dim,* and *cool.* The degree achievement verbs are a subclass of the verbs of change of state, but are set apart from other verbs of change of state because they do not necessarily entail the achievement of an end state, although they entail a change in a particular direction. Thus, when a road widens, it becomes wider, but it need not necessarily become wide. To bring out the resemblance between these verbs and the second class of atelic verbs we will be examining in this section, we will refer to the degree achievements as *atelic verbs of change of state.* The second class of atelic verbs we consider consists of those verbs of inherently directed motion that we take to be the motional counterparts of the atelic verbs of change of state; we will refer to these as *atelic verbs of inherently directed motion.* This class includes verbs like *descend, rise,* and *fall,* which describe motion in a particular direction without necessarily entailing the attainment of a particular endpoint; thus, these verbs are not necessarily telic. The verbs in both classes display unaccusative behavior, even though they are not necessarily interpreted as telic (although they may be), as shown by their compatibility with durative *for* phrases, as well as punctual *at* phrases.

(93) a. The soup cooled for half an hour.
     b. The soup cooled at three o'clock.

(94) a. The plane descended for fifteen minutes.
   b. The plane descended at three o'clock.

(95) a. The temperature rose steadily for three hours.
   b. The temperature rose at one o'clock.

There are several types of evidence that atelic verbs of inherently directed motion like *rise* are unaccusative. The Italian counterparts of these verbs take the unaccusative auxiliary *essere* 'be'.

(96) è caduto 'has fallen', è disceso 'has descended'

The resultative construction cannot be used to test for the status of these verbs, because, as already mentioned, the resultative construction is incompatible with verbs of inherently directed motion. However, these verbs are also unable to occur in the *X's way* construction even though there are fewer restrictions on this construction than on the resultative construction, suggesting that they are unaccusative.

(97) a. *She rose her way to the presidency.
   b. *The oil rose its way to the surface.

Furthermore, they are not found with cognate objects.

(98) a. *The bird soared a graceful soar.
   b. *She rose a wobbly rise.

It is more difficult to find evidence bearing on the status of the atelic verbs of change of state. However, most of these verbs occur in the causative alternation. In line with the reasoning used in section 4.1.1.3 to explain why internally caused verbs such as *laugh* do not have causative uses, we can take the fact that these verbs *do* have causative uses as an indication that they are unaccusative.

(99) The soup cooled./I cooled the soup.

(100) The lights dimmed./I dimmed the lights.

The atelic verbs of change of state are also not found in the *X's way* construction, a property that is also consistent with an unaccusative analysis.

(101) a. *The soup cooled its way to room temperature.
   b. *The days lengthened their way to summer.

4.3.2 Comparison with Dowty's (1991) Approach
The theory of argument selection developed by Dowty (1991) may appear to differ in important ways from the theory being developed here. It

appears to us, however, that there is not much conflict between our general approach to linking and Dowty's approach. The fundamental innovative moves in Dowty's theory are two. First, there are only two thematic roles, agent and patient, relevant to argument expression (at least, for the expression of those arguments that are realized as subject or direct object). Second, these roles are not discrete but rather are considered to be cluster concepts. The thematic role borne by an argument is determined by the lexical entailments imposed on it by the verb, but none of these entailments is either necessary or sufficient for associating either the agent or the patient role to an argument. Dowty therefore refers to these roles as "Proto-Agent" and "Proto-Patient." For dyadic verbs the argument with the most Proto-Agent entailments is expressed as subject, and the argument with the most Proto-Patient entailments is expressed as direct object.

The linking rules we have presented can be seen as Proto-Agent and Proto-Patient entailments. It is likely that when the scope of our study is widened to deal with transitive verbs from a variety of classes, a more sophisticated method of calculating argument expression will be needed. Dowty suggests a simple method of calculation: "counting up" the Proto-Agent and Proto-Patient entailments of each argument. We have, however, found evidence that there is a precedence relation between certain linking rules, but there is in fact nothing in Dowty's theory of argument linking that would necessarily preclude giving certain entailments more weight than others in determining argument expression. Since the scope of Dowty's study is much broader than ours, his theory can be seen as an elaboration of ours, and ours can be seen to be a refinement of his in some ways. In this section we concentrate on the differences in the concepts we employ in our linking rules and those Dowty employs in his Proto-Patient entailments. The differences we find between the approaches, then, lie in the particular formulation of the linking rules or the entailments, rather than in the general conception of these rules. (As we discuss in section 5.2, however, we differ with Dowty in the treatment of variable behavior verbs.)

The concept in Dowty's work that should most obviously figure in such a comparison is *incremental theme;* it is a member of the set of Proto-Patient entailments. An incremental theme is an argument that stands in a homomorphic relation with the predicate of which it is an argument, in such a way that the part-whole relations of the theme with respect to some property can be mapped onto the part-whole relations of the event as a whole. To illustrate, Dowty uses the verb *mow*, whose direct object is an incremental theme. In *mow the lawn*, the "mowedness" of parts of the lawn can be mapped onto the parts of the event. When half of the lawn has been mowed, the event is halfway complete; when the entire lawn has been mowed, the entire event is complete.

It turns out that most arguments characterizable as incremental themes fall under our concept of directed change since they are entities that undergo a directed change. And yet, it is clear that the two concepts—incremental theme and argument undergoing a directed change—are not equivalent. Some arguments that undergo a directed change do not fall under Dowty's concept of incremental theme. These are the arguments of atelic verbs of inherently directed motion such as *rise* and atelic verbs of change of state such as *dim*. As Dowty himself points out, since these verbs involve what he calls an indefinite change of position or state, there is no clear endpoint to the event, and the argument that changes cannot stand in the relation to the event as a whole that is required for it to qualify as an incremental theme. The theme argument of a telic verb of directed motion such as *come* or directed motion *run*—the argument that undergoes a change of location—is also treated differently by the two accounts. Dowty argues that the path argument—and not the theme argument—of these verbs is the incremental theme. The reason for this is that if, for example, Jill goes halfway to the store, it is not the case that half of Jill goes to the store; instead, half the path to the store is traversed. However, the theme argument does fall under our notion of directed change. Directed change, then, picks out different arguments than Dowty's notion of incremental theme.

Nevertheless, all the arguments that fall under our Directed Change Linking Rule but do not count as incremental themes still have a Proto-Patient entailment in Dowty's system. Specifically, they undergo a change, whether definite or indefinite. The prediction in Dowty's system, as in ours, is that these arguments will be expressed as direct objects.

Are there, then, any empirical differences between our account and Dowty's? It turns out that there are. Consider first the telic verbs of inherently directed motion such as *come* and the telic uses of *run* in *Pat came to the house* and *Kelly ran to the school*. On our account the theme argument of these verbs falls under the same linking rule as the theme argument of telic verbs of change of state: the Directed Change Linking Rule. On Dowty's account the theme argument of the verbs of directed motion falls under the same Proto-Patient entailment as the theme argument of verbs like *roll* since the theme argument of *roll* and verbs like it also has the

Proto-Patient entailment of undergoing a change. For the purposes of comparing the two approaches, the question is whether or not the theme of a telic verb of inherently directed motion ought to be treated like the theme of a verb of change of state like *break* or like the theme of a verb like *roll*.

It appears to us that languages do treat the theme of a verb of inherently directed motion on a par with the theme of a verb of change of state and not on a par with the theme of verbs like *roll*. The relevant evidence was presented in section 4.2, where we showed that the Directed Change Linking Rule takes precedence over the Immediate Cause Linking Rule, since arguments that fall under both rules are expressed in accordance with the Directed Change Linking Rule. Specifically, internally caused verbs of change of state were shown to be unaccusative. But the same is true of verbs of inherently directed motion, as we showed in the same section: these verbs are unaccusative even when used agentively. Further extensive evidence for this point will be provided in chapter 5. There we will also show that verbs like *roll* work differently; these verbs are unergative when they are used agentively. For this reason we have formulated our linking rules so that the *roll* verbs fall under a distinct linking rule. This, then, is evidence that the theme of a verb like *come* ought to be treated on a par with the theme of a verb like *break* and not on a par with the theme of a verb like *roll*, contrary to Dowty's analysis.

It is more difficult to test the predictions of the two approaches concerning atelic verbs of change of state (i.e., the degree achievement verbs). We, of course, predict that such verbs will be unaccusative even if internally caused since the Directed Change Linking Rule takes precedence over the Immediate Cause Linking Rule. Likely candidates for such verbs —that is, internally caused atelic verbs of change of state—are the verbs that B. Levin (1993) has classed as "entity-specific verbs of change of state." One such verb is *decay*, which is not only an internally caused verb of change of state, but is also atelic. If it turns out that this is the appropriate semantic classification and that such verbs are unaccusative, then we have the relevant evidence. It appears, then, that our notion of directed change makes a better division among the verb classes than Dowty's notion of incremental theme.[15]

Does this mean that the notion of incremental theme has no place in the calculation of argument expression? We do not want to make this claim. Dowty makes use of this notion for predicting alternations in the expression of internal arguments of verbs such as *spray* and *load*. It is possible that when the scope of study is widened to include more verbs with more arguments, the notion of incremental theme will have a place in it. Furthermore, the notion of incremental theme is presumably used by Dowty to predict the selection of the direct object—which he analyzes as the incremental theme—in sentences like (102).

(102) The camel crossed the desert.

On the face of it, this example and others like it are problematic for the approach we have been developing since the argument entailed to undergo a directed change is not obviously expressed as a direct object. Other potentially problematic examples, which Dowty takes to have an incremental theme subject, are listed in (103).

(103) a. The train entered the station.
       b. The crowd exited the hall.
       c. The arrow pierced the target.

Dowty notes with skepticism the possibility of an unaccusative analysis for most of these verbs, which would be necessary to allow them to fall under our account. In fact, it appears to us that of the verbs involved, only *enter* and *exit* can plausibly be given an unaccusative analysis, and indeed in many other languages these verbs are not transitive, showing the hallmarks of unaccusative verbs. As for the other examples Dowty cites, it is just possible that in these instances there are two arguments that meet some criterion for expression as direct object, one that is entailed to undergo a directed change and another that is entailed to be an incremental theme. It is possible that, as with the verbs *spray* and *load*, these instances require a more elaborate system of argument selection that encompasses the notion of incremental theme. But what we hope to have shown is that the notion of incremental theme ought not to replace our notion of directed change.

4.4   Conclusion

In this chapter we have introduced four linking rules that essentially isolate three components of meaning relevant to the syntactic classification of verbs. We have also suggested that, at least in the languages we have examined, some of the rules are ordered with respect to each other. The theory of linking that we present in this chapter is not fully articulated. It is designed to deal with the problems raised by intransitive verbs. It is clear, however, that the linking rules ought to be applicable not just to intransitive verbs. We suspect that our rules are valid for transitive verbs as well; but once the scope of study is broadened, it is fairly clear that other syntactically relevant meaning components will also enter the picture. In that case it is possible that other precedence relations, like the one between the Directed Change Linking Rule and the Immediate Cause Linking Rule, will be found.

What we hope to have demonstrated here is that once the appropriate syntactically relevant meaning components are isolated, the syntactic expression of arguments turns out to be more systematic than it might have appeared to be. We also have tried to broaden the range of phenomena that need to be handled by any account of the syntactic expression of arguments. It is clear, however, that even in the domain of intransitive verbs, there are classes of verbs we have not yet fully scrutinized. To cite one example, among these classes are verbs like *swarm* that participate in the intransitive version of the locative alternation.

Chapter 5

Verbs with Multiple Meanings

In chapter 1 we stressed the importance of isolating those aspects of verb meaning that are relevant to the syntax. In evaluating whether the actual syntactic classification of a verb as unaccusative or unergative is the classification that is expected given its meaning, it is important to begin by carefully determining the meaning of the verb under consideration, especially with respect to the syntactically relevant aspects of meaning. Failure to do this has meant that some attempts to compare verbs from different languages that appear to be translation equivalents are flawed. As discussed in chapters 1, 3, and 4, verbs said to be translation equivalents may differ in just those aspects of meaning that are relevant to determining a verb's class membership. However, even in the analysis of the verbs of a single language, the same care must be taken in determining verb meaning: a single verb may be associated with a range of meanings differing from each other in precisely the syntactically relevant aspects of meaning, leading to different classifications of the verb on the different meanings.

It appears that all languages show—although to varying degrees—the phenomenon that Apresjan (1973, 1992) terms "regular polysemy": instances of polysemy that are consistently exhibited by words with certain types of meanings (see also Ostler and Atkins 1991). For instance, in English and Russian, at least, nouns such as *reel* and *cup* that name containers can often be used to refer to the quantity of a substance held by that container (*a reel of thread, a cup of milk*). Apresjan notes that there are instances of regular polysemy involving verbs as well. Atkins, Kegl, and B. Levin (1988) discuss one such example. They show that the verb *bake* can be associated with both a change-of-state meaning, as in *Max baked the potatoes*, and a creation meaning, as in *Max baked a pound cake*. Furthermore, these two meanings are associated with other verbs of cooking as well; thus, verbs of cooking manifest regular polysemy.

As mentioned in chapter 1, we call verbs that show regular polysemy "variable behavior verbs." This name is intended to emphasize the fact, illustrated in Atkins, Kegl, and B. Levin 1988, Laughren 1988, B. Levin 1991, B. Levin and Rappaport Hovav 1991, and Rappaport and B. Levin 1988, that verbs that are systematically associated with a range of meanings are also found in a range of syntactic configurations and display a range of patterns of syntactic behavior. These syntactic configurations and patterns of behavior are precisely the ones compatible with the various meanings associated with a given verb. Each meaning can be shown to be correlated with the appropriate syntactic behavior. Furthermore, as noted in chapter 1, this property of variable behavior verbs means that a careful consideration of the different meanings associated with such verbs can facilitate the isolation of the syntactically relevant aspects of verb meaning.

The ability of some verbs to be associated with multiple meanings can sometimes be used to explain their seemingly unexpected behavior with respect to the Unaccusative Hypothesis. This is true, for example, of some of the Italian verbs discussed by C. Rosen (1984) that select both the auxiliaries *avere* 'have' and *essere* 'be' (see section 1.2.1). In chapter 1 we showed how a single constant can often be associated with more than one lexical semantic template, and we have given additional examples of this process as it pertains to the variable behavior of certain verbs with respect to the causative alternation in the discussion of *buzz* and verbs like it in section 3.2.5 and in the discussion of the verbs of spatial configuration in section 3.3.3. If two or more lexical semantic representations sharing a single constant—and, thus, a common core element of meaning—differ from each other in exactly those meaning components that are relevant to the classification of verbs as unaccusative or unergative, and if, moreover, these lexical semantic representations are associated with the same name, then a single verb is actually predicted to exhibit variable behavior.

English is particularly rich in variable behavior verbs, although this may not be obvious since the morphological shape of the verbs themselves is constant across meanings. The absence of morphological clues often masks the fact that a single verb is associated with more than one meaning in English. In some languages, variations in verb meaning are signaled morphologically: verbs with related meanings share a verbal root, but are differentiated by affixes or changes in the shape of the root. For instance, in B. Levin and Rappaport 1988 we argue that the verbs found in the locative alternation (e.g., *spray paint on the wall/spray the wall with paint*) have different, but related, meanings associated with each of the argument expressions characteristic of the alternation despite the invariant morphological shape of the verb (see also Dowty 1991 and Pinker 1989 for analyses along similar lines). In contrast, the example of locative alternation in Russian in (1) shows the use of distinct perfective verb prefixes in the two variants. The use of verb prefixes to distinguish the verb forms in the two variants also characterizes this alternation in Hungarian, as the example in (2) shows.

(1) a. Kryst'jany   na-gruzili seno   na telegu.
       peasants (NOM) *na*-loaded hay (ACC) on cart-ACC
       'The peasants loaded hay on the cart.'
    b. Kryst'jany   za-gruzili telegu   senom.
       peasants (NOM) *za*-loaded cart-ACC hay-INST
       'The peasants loaded the cart with hay.'

(2) a. János rámázolta   a   festéket   a   falra.
       John onto-smeared-he-it the paint-ACC the wall-onto
       'John smeared paint on the wall.'
    b. János bemázolta   a   falat   festékkel.
       John in-smeared-he-it the wall-ACC paint-with
       'John smeared the wall with paint.'
       (Moravcsik 1978:257)

As the translations show, in English there is no change in the morphological shape of the verb in the locative alternation.

Knowledge of the possible multiple meanings that a verb can show and the factors that license them is an important part of the lexical knowledge of a language, and it figures prominently as part of knowledge of English, which, as just mentioned, is a language extremely rich in variable behavior verbs. Native speakers of a language are able to make judgments about possible and impossible multiple meanings for a verb and the syntactic behavior associated with these different meanings, suggesting that this phenomenon falls under the rubric of Plato's problem (Chomsky 1986b). Thus, this phenomenon can be considered central to knowledge of language, and a theory of language will not be complete without a full theory of variable behavior verbs.

Many interesting and important questions arise in the context of verbs with multiple meanings. If lexical syntactic properties are a projection of lexical semantic properties, as suggested by certain formulations of the Projection Principle (and as stipulated in the theory of c-selection and s-selection developed by Pesetsky (1982) and adopted by Chomsky (1986b)), then the fact that so many verbs can appear in a range of syntactic configurations, as happens with variable behavior verbs, may entail the wholesale proliferation of the lexical semantic representations associated with verbs. But the fact that knowledge of what are possible and impossible sets of multiple meanings for a verb seems to be part of core grammar suggests that multiple meanings are not merely listed in the lexical entries of verbs. If so, then an extremely important question arises: what is the source of the multiple meanings? In this chapter we describe two sources of multiple meanings, introducing them in the context of verbs that, because of their multiple meanings, alternate between unergative and unaccusative behavior. In section 5.1 we describe a type of polysemy that arises, we argue, from the existence of a lexical rule. In section 5.2 we contrast our approach to verbs showing this kind of polysemy with another approach that, although taking several forms, avoids lexical rules by attributing the multiple meanings of such verbs to their ability to be found in several constructions. In section 5.3 we highlight the properties of the type of polysemy discussed in section 5.1 by comparing it to a second type of polysemy, and we show that there is good reason to distinguish the two. We propose that the second type of polysemy, which has already been introduced in chapter 3 in the context of verbs of sound emission and verbs of spatial configuration, arises from the basic compatibility of particular constants with more than one lexical semantic template.

5.1   Rule-Governed Variable Behavior

In this section we discuss a range of verbs that qualify as internally caused verbs, but can acquire an additional meaning—that of a verb of directed motion—through the application of a lexical rule. Consequently, these verbs fall under either the Immediate Cause Linking Rule (on their basic meaning) or the Directed Change Linking Rule (on their directed motion meaning), giving rise to either an unergative or an unaccusative classification.

5.1.1   Verbs of Manner of Motion

Of the many variable behavior verbs found in English, the agentive verbs of manner of motion have probably received the most attention. As has often been pointed out (Hoekstra 1984, B. Levin and Rappaport Hovav 1992, L. Levin 1986, C. Rosen 1984, Talmy 1975, 1985, among many others), agentive verbs of manner of motion can regularly appear with directional phrases, resulting in the specification of both direction and manner of motion. The directed motion use of agentive verbs of manner of motion is found in some languages, but not in many others.[1]

Besides English, German and Modern Hebrew allow the directed motion use of agentive verbs of manner of motion, as shown in (3) and (4), respectively.

(3) a. Die Kinder liefen in   das   Zimmer (hinein).
       the children ran   into the-ACC room   (into)
       'The children ran into the room.'
    b. Die Kinder sind an das   andere Flußufer geschwommen.
       the children are to the-ACC other   riverbank swum
       'The children swam to the other side of the river.'

(4) a. Hu rakad   el mixuts la-xeder.
       he danced to outside to the-room
       'He danced out of the room.'
    b. Ha-saxyan   saxa la-gada   ha-šniya   šel ha-nahar.
       the-swimmer swam to the-side the-second of the-river
       'The swimmer swam to the other side of the river.'

In contrast, as Talmy (1975, 1985) has amply illustrated (see also Bergh 1948 and Carter 1988), most verbs of manner of motion in the Romance languages cannot take directional phrases (although see note 1 of this chapter); that is, they cannot be used as verbs of directed motion. (The Italian verb *correre* 'run', cited in section 1.2.1, is one of the few exceptions to this generalization in Italian; other exceptions are the verbs *saltare* 'jump' and *volare* 'fly'.) This contrasting behavior is illustrated by the English/French pair in (5). The English sentence in (5a) is ambiguous: the prepositional phrase *under the table* may be interpreted as the location of the motion or as the direction or goal of the motion. Its French translation in (5b) is unambiguous, the prepositional phrase receiving only the locative interpretation.

(5) a. The mouse is running under the table.
    b. La souris court sous la table.

To express the directional interpretation available to agentive verbs of manner of motion in English, languages such as French and Spanish must use a complex expression involving a verb of inherently directed motion, chosen to specify the direction, together with a prepositional, adverbial,

or gerundive phrase indicating the manner of motion, as in the French
examples in (6) and (7).

(6) Une vieille femme arriva en boitant de   l'arrière-boutique.
     an old woman arrived in limping from the back-store
     'An old woman hobbled in from the back.'
     (Vinay and Darbelnet 1958:105)

(7) Blériot traversa la Manche en avion.
     Blériot crossed the Channel by plane
     'Blériot flew across the Channel.'
     (Vinay and Darbelnet 1958:105)

In fact, work in comparative sylistics, noting the need for periphrastic
expression of the directed motion use of verbs of manner of motion, has
referred to this difference between the two types of languages as a "chassé
croisé," since there is a reversal between English and French with respect
to what is encoded in the verb and what in a subordinate phrase (Vinay
and Darbelnet 1958:105).

Some languages are intermediate between the English type and the Romance type, in that agentive verbs of manner of motion can be used as
verbs of directed motion only with the addition of a special morpheme.
For instance, Schaefer (1985) writes that in Tswana the morpheme -ɛ̀l-
must be adjoined to an agentive verb of manner of motion to convey the
idea of motion toward a goal.

(8)   Mò-símàné ó-tábóg-à fá-gòdímò gá-thàbà.
        CL.1-boy he-run-IMP NEARBY-top LOC-mountain
        'The boy is running on top of the mountain.'
        (Schaefer 1985:64, table II, 1)

(9)   *Mò-símàné ó-tábóg-à gòdímò gá-thàbà.
        CL.1-boy he-run-IMP top   LOC-mountain
        'The boy is running to the top of the mountain.'
        (Schaefer 1985:67, (4a))

(10)   Mò-símàné ó-tábóg-ɛ̀l-à kwá-gòdímò gá-thàbà.
        CL.1-boy he-run-to-IMP DISTANT-top LOC-mountain
        'The boy is running to the top of the mountain.'
        (Schaefer 1985:66, table III, 1)

Japanese also appears to instantiate the intermediate type of language.[2]
As examples (11) and (12) show, agentive verbs of manner of motion in

Japanese cannot take goal phrases directly; however, they may combine with the verb *iku* 'go' or another verb of inherently directed motion to form complex verbs that can take goal phrases.

(11) a. ?John-wa ekie-e   hashitta.
        John-TOP station-to ran
        (Yoneyama 1986:1, (1a))
     b. ?John-wa kishi-e   oyoida.
        John-TOP shore-to swam
        (Yoneyama 1986:1, (1b))

(12) a. John-wa ekie-e   hashitte-itta.
        John-TOP station-to running-went
        'John ran to the station.'
        (Yoneyama 1986:2, (3a))
     b. John-wa kishi-e   oyoide-itta.
        John-TOP shore-to swimming-went
        'John swam to the shore.'
        (Yoneyama 1986:2, (3b))

On their nondirected motion use agentive verbs of manner of motion, as internally caused verbs, fall under the Immediate Cause Linking Rule and are unergative as discussed in section 4.1.4. If, as suggested in chapter 4, the Directed Change Linking Rule takes precedence over the Immediate Cause Linking Rule, then we would expect agentive verbs of manner of motion to exhibit unaccusative behavior in the presence of directional phrases. Indeed, the pattern of auxiliary selection demonstrated by these verbs in Dutch, German, and Italian has been cited in support of this dual classification (Hoekstra 1984, L. Levin 1986, C. Rosen 1984, among others). In these languages, verbs of manner of motion typically select the auxiliary *have*, but they select the unaccusative auxiliary *be* in their directed motion use; this property is taken as an indication that the verbs are unaccusative in the directed motion use. This pattern of auxiliary selection is illustrated with the Dutch and Italian examples in (13) and (14); recall that the Italian verb *correre* 'run' is one of the few agentive verbs of manner of motion that shows a directed motion use in Italian.

(13) a. Hij heeft/*is gelopen.
        He has/is   run
        'He ran.'
        (Zaenen 1993:136, (22a))

    b. Hij is/?heeft naar huis gelopen.
        he is/has   to   home run
        'He ran home.'
        (Zaenen 1993:136, (22b))

(14) a. Ugo ha corso meglio ieri.
         Ugo has run   better yesterday
         'Ugo ran better yesterday.'
         (C. Rosen 1984:66, (86a))
     b. Ugo è corso a casa.
         Ugo is run   to home
         'Ugo ran home.'
         (C. Rosen 1984:67, (86b))

Although the evidence cited above is quite well known, there are two additional types of subtle evidence from English, not previously noted in the literature, that agentive verbs of manner of motion are unaccusative in the presence of directional phrases. We discuss these in turn in the following two sections.

5.1.1.1 The Resultative Construction   The first piece of evidence from English for the dual classification of agentive verbs of manner of motion comes from the resultative construction, which we analyzed in chapter 2. The agentive verbs of manner of motion show rather complicated behavior in the resultative construction. As noted by Simpson (1983b), these verbs may occur in the unaccusative resultative pattern with resultative phrases headed by one of a restricted group of adjectives, including *free* and *clear*, or by either of the intransitive directional elements *apart* and *together*.

(15) a. She danced/swam free of her captors.
     b. They slowly swam apart.
     c. However, if fire is an immediate danger, you must *jump clear of
         the vehicle.* [State of Illinois, *Rules of the Road*, 81; italics in
         original]

The agentive verbs of manner of motion in these examples are clearly found in the unaccusative resultative pattern: there is no apparent object, and the resultative phrase is predicated directly of the surface subject. The behavior of these verbs is particularly intriguing in light of the fact that the very same verbs can also appear in the unergative resultative pattern with a fake reflexive or nonsubcategorized object.

(16) a. He danced his feet sore.
    b. Don't expect to swim/jog yourself sober!

Thus, these verbs seem to be behaving both as unaccusative and as unergative verbs in the resultative construction.

A clue to solving this puzzle comes from comparing the resultative phrases in (15) and (16). The resultative phrases in the two types of resultative constructions cannot be interchanged, suggesting that they are drawn from distinct classes.

(17) a. *He danced sore.
    b. *Don't expect to swim/jog sober.

(18) a. *You must jump yourself clear of the vehicle.
    b. *They swam themselves apart.

The resultative phrases in (15) denote the result of a change in location, whereas those in (16) denote the result of a change of state. The adjective *clear* may describe a state, as in *a clear table*, but in the phrase *clear of the vehicle* found in (15c), this same adjective is to be interpreted as a location that is defined as being away from the vehicle. In fact, Talmy (1985:104) calls these types of adjectives and directional elements "paths," although clearly these particular elements describe a path by naming its endpoint. The difference in the types of resultative phrases selected in the two forms of the resultative construction is correlated with the interpretation of the verbs: (15) involves the directed motion use of agentive verbs of manner of motion and (16) involves the use of such verbs in which direction is not specified. These facts indicate that agentive verbs of manner of motion can indeed be associated with two related, though distinct, meanings, one consistent with an unaccusative and the other with an unergative classification of these verbs. Given this assumption, the odd behavior of these verbs in the resultative construction can be explained; they enter into different resultative patterns depending on whether they describe directed or nondirected motion.

5.1.1.2 The Causative Alternation Additional evidence from English that agentive verbs of manner of motion are unaccusative when they receive a directed motion interpretation comes from their behavior in the causative alternation. In chapter 3 we suggested that externally caused verbs are inherently dyadic and that the transitive use of prototypical causative alternation verbs is not the result of a process of lexical causativization. We also showed in chapter 4 that the Immediate Cause Linking Rule ensures that monadic internally caused verbs will not have transitive causative uses since such uses would involve two arguments competing for the same position in argument structure. Despite this, we also presented evidence in chapter 3 that certain agentive verbs of manner of motion do have causative uses, as shown in the examples repeated here.

(19) a.   The soldiers marched (to the tents).
     b.   The general marched the soldiers to the tents.
     c.   ??The general marched the soldiers.

(20) a.   The horse jumped (over the fence).
     b.   The rider jumped the horse over the fence.
     c.   The rider jumped the horse.

(21) a.   The mouse ran (through the maze).
     b.   We ran the mouse through the maze.
     c.   *We ran the mouse.

The existence of such uses can be explained given the assumption that these verbs are unaccusative in their directed motion sense. Thus, their single argument is a direct internal argument, and they do not take an external argument; therefore, the external argument position is left unfilled and can be filled by an external cause.[3] (We do not, however, formulate the rule that introduces the external cause.) Since the alternative linking that permits the introduction of an external cause is available only in the context of a directed motion interpretation, we have an explanation for the fact that a directional phrase is needed or, at the very least, must be understood when verbs of manner of motion are used causatively, as the examples above show.

As we argued in section 3.2.5, there is ample evidence that the causative pairs involving agentive verbs of manner of motion represent a different phenomenon from the causative pairs involving verbs of change of state such as *break*. The analysis we propose for the causative use of agentive verbs of manner of motion does in fact differ from our analysis of the causative use of a verb of change of state such as *break*. As we stressed in chapter 3, verbs of change of state do not undergo a process of causativization; they have a causative lexical semantic representation, reflecting the proposal that these verbs are externally caused.

Our account of why agentive verbs of manner of motion causativize capitalizes on properties of the lexical semantic representation of these verbs, so that this process would be expected to be productive. As the examples in (22) show, the phenomenon is more widespread than the few examples cited in the literature suggest, although its relatively limited use suggests that speakers of English are conservative about exercising this option; see also B. Levin and Rappaport Hovav 1994 for further discussion of the factors that may play a part in licensing such causative uses.[4]

(22) a. "... I promised Ms. Cain I would ride her around the ranch ..."
       [N. Pickard, *Bum Steer*, 92]
     b. ... several strong Teamsters ... shuffled Kit out of the room ...
       [L. Matera, *A Radical Departure*, 79]

Our account of the unaccusative and causative uses of such verbs also contrasts with our account of the same uses of the *roll* verbs, although both types of verbs are verbs of manner of motion. As we showed in section 4.1.4, the *roll* verbs are unaccusative when externally caused. The classification of these verbs is established by the Default Linking Rule independent of the presence of a directional phrase. Furthermore, as an externally caused verb, a *roll* verb is basically dyadic just like *break* and should allow for a causative counterpart whether or not a directional phrase is present. And in fact, the verb *roll*, unlike the verb *run*, can be used causatively even in the absence of a directional phrase.

(23) a. The bowling ball rolled (into the room).
     b. The bowler rolled the bowling ball (into the room).

The different pattern of causative uses associated with the two types of verbs supports the classification of the agentive verbs of manner of motion as unaccusative in their directed motion sense and unergative otherwise.

5.1.2 Verbs of Sound Emission

Members of a second class of English verbs—the verbs of sound emission—can also regularly become verbs of directed motion. These verbs, which constitute the largest subset of the verbs of emission discussed in chapters 3 and 4, describe the emission of sounds by either animate or inanimate entities. As the examples in (24) show, verbs of sound emission are frequently found with directional phrases in English, and in such uses they describe the directed motion of an entity, where the motion is necessarily characterized by the concomitant emission by that entity of a sound whose nature is lexicalized in the verb.

(24) a. ... the elevator wheezed upward. [M. Muller, *There's Nothing to Be Afraid Of*, 3]

b. At that moment, a flatbed truck bearing a load of steel rumbled
   through the gate. [M. Muller, *There's Nothing to Be Afraid Of*,
   39]
c. The kettle clashed across the metal grid. [S. Miller, *Family Pictures*, 34]

We showed in chapter 4 that verbs of sound emission, if internally caused, are unergative. The fact that these verbs in clearly internally caused uses appear with directional phrases suggests that English also allows verbs of sound emission to become verbs of directed motion. In fact, as we show in this section, verbs of sound emission with directional phrases show the range of unaccusative behavior expected if this meaning shift is allowed. To better illustrate this, we first present a semantic restriction on the meaning shift.

Not all verbs of sound emission can become verbs of directed motion. The source of this restriction is related to a striking property of verbs of sound emission: unlike the members of the other subclasses of verbs of emission, many of them can take animate agentive subjects, as well as inanimate nonagentive subjects. In this respect, the verbs of sound emission contrast with other unergative verbs, which generally only take animate subjects. In general, verbs of sound emission, when agentive, cannot become verbs of directed motion.

(25) a. *He yelled down the street.
         (cf. He yelled his way down the street.)
     b. *She shouted down the street.
         (cf. She shouted her way down the street.)
     c. *The frogs croaked to the pond.
         (cf. The frogs croaked their way to the pond.)

However, sometimes verbs of sound emission are found with both animate subjects and directional phrases.

(26) a. ... Sedgwick often clanked into town in sabre and spurs from
         the cavalry camp. [E. Thane, *Yankee Stranger*, 133]
     b. She rustled out of the room without waiting for a word from
         Lind. [M. Ostenso, *Wild Geese*, 30]

The verbs in the examples in (26), *clank* and *rustle*, specify sounds that are never emitted by the vocal tract; rather, they are emitted by contact between two surfaces. In fact, as M. Laughren has pointed out to us, the sounds in these particular examples are actually emitted by the clothes or accessories that the animate subject is wearing, though the sound is being attributed to the animate subject itself. In contrast, the verbs in (25) can be used solely to describe sounds emitted via the vocal tract by an animate entity; furthermore, *shout* and *yell* describe sounds that are often emitted specifically for the purpose of communication.

As discussed in B. Levin 1991 and B. Levin and Rappaport Hovav 1991, in order for a verb of sound emission to be used as a verb of directed motion, the sound must be emitted as a necessary concomitant of the motion. Thus, verbs of sound emission where the sound is emitted via the vocal tract would necessarily be precluded from taking directional phrases, as shown by the unacceptability of the examples in (25). Verbs of sound emission are found with animate subjects and directional phrases precisely when the associated sound is emitted through the actual motion of an animate entity; in the examples in (26) the subject, though animate, is treated no differently than the inanimate subjects in the examples in (24). When verbs that describe sounds that may or may not be emitted via the vocal tract are found with directional phrases, only the interpretation that does not involve the emission of the sound via the vocal tract is available. Thus, there are constraints that govern the shift in meaning displayed by verbs of sound emission, suggesting that this is a regular process. We turn now to evidence that the verbs of sound emission, like the agentive verbs of manner of motion, change classification as a consequence of this shift, as predicted by the linking rules of chapter 4.

5.1.2.1 The Resultative Construction Verbs of sound emission, like agentive verbs of manner of motion, can appear in the unaccusative resultative pattern illustrated in (27), a class of examples that was brought to our attention by R. D. Van Valin.

(27) a. ... the refrigerator door clicked open ... [M. E. Robertson, *Family Life*, 139]
   b. ... the curtains creak open and radiant evening light streams into the cluttered room. [S. Cheever, *Elizabeth Cole*, 70]
   c. The skylight thudded open with a shower of powdery plaster and some lopsided bricks. [M. Spark, *The Girls of Slender Means*, 158]
   d. The lid of the boiler clunked shut. [P. Lively, *The Road to Lichfield*, 52]

Furthermore, verbs of sound emission are found in such resultatives only under the restricted circumstances that allow them to be used as verbs of directed motion, namely, when they are predicated of inanimates (or animates regarded as inanimates) and the resultative phrase denotes a result location rather than a result state. (The resultative phrases in (27) do not denote the result of a change of location; rather, they denote the result of a change of position, which is probably a kind of change of location with no displacement.) Although the adjectives *open* and *shut* could denote result states, it is clear that in these examples they do not. Rather, they denote the positions associated with the states of being *open* or being *shut*. Indeed, comparable sentences with the same verbs become ungrammatical when the resultative phrases are replaced with resultative phrases that unambiguously denote result states rather than result locations.

(28) a. *The door banged to pieces.
     b. *The curtains creaked threadbare.
     c. *The skylight thudded to smithereens.
     d. *The lid clunked flat.

Verbs of sound emission are found in the unaccusative resultative pattern under the same conditions that allow them to be used as verbs of directed motion. That is, they must describe a sound that is a necessary concomitant of the motion of that entity, whether animate or inanimate.

(29) We splashed clear of the oncoming boat.

(30) ... the curtains creak open and radiant evening light streams into the cluttered room. [S. Cheever, *Elizabeth Cole*, 70]

As expected, verbs of sound emission cannot appear in the unaccusative resultative pattern when they describe any type of sound emitted by an animate entity via the vocal tract.[5]

(31) a. *He yelled clear of the falling rocks.
     b. *The frogs croaked apart.
     c. *They shouted free of their captors.

With such verbs, we find the unergative resultative pattern, just as might be expected, and, as with the agentive verbs of manner of motion, the resultative phrases clearly denote result states.

(32) a. We searched the woods and cliffs, yelled ourselves hoarse and imagined you drowned ... [M. Wesley, *A Sensible Life*, 327]
     b. Well, the conclusion was that my mistress grumbled herself calm. [E. Brontë, *Wuthering Heights*, 78]

The restrictions on which verbs of sound emission can be found in the unaccusative resultative pattern are the same as those on which of these verbs can take directional phrases, supporting the assignment of a common meaning to the verb in both instances.

We have demonstrated, then, that verbs of sound emission, when they show variable behavior, do so in a regular way. These basically unergative verbs show unaccusative behavior precisely when they are used as verbs of directed motion, causing the emitter argument to fall under the Directed Change Linking Rule. As with agentive verbs of manner of motion, the appearance of verbs of sound emission in the unaccusative resultative pattern with result locations is not unexpected, since such resultative constructions make use of the independently existing directed motion sense these verbs display.

5.1.2.2 The Causative Alternation In section 3.2.5 we proposed that certain verbs of sound emission can be either internally or externally caused and that the externally caused verbs of sound emission, as expected, show what can be characterized as "causative" uses, as in (33).

(33) a. The postman buzzed/rang the doorbell.
b. The impatient driver honked his horn.
c. Nora jingled the keys.
d. The cook clattered the dishes.

Although we have not been explicit about it, it is the internally caused verbs of sound emission that undergo the meaning shift to verbs of directed motion since only they are monadic. As a consequence of the meaning shift, these verbs become classified as unaccusative; thus, the possibility presents itself that internally caused verbs of sound emission should causativize in the presence of a directional phrase just as agentive verbs of manner of motion do. In fact, this type of causativization does seem to be attested, as in the examples in (34), although it seems to happen more sporadically than the comparable causativization of agentive verbs of manner of motion.

(34) a. Vrooooming his plane up and down ... Malcolm was holding onto whatever attention he could get ... [M. Grimes, *The Old Silent*, 225]
b. Slowly, they rumbled the Big Wheel across the sidewalk ... [R. Robinson, *Summer Light*, 28]
c. The driver roared/screeched the car down the driveway.

The examples in (35) show that the directional phrases are required in the causative examples in (34), suggesting that the directed motion use of these verbs is involved.

(35) a. *Malcolm vroomed his plane.
     b. *They rumbled the Big Wheel.
     c. *The driver roared/screeched the car.

Thus, the examples in (34) provide a striking contrast with those in (33), which show no directional phrase requirement. The existence of causatives with the directional phrase requirement, which suggests that such causatives are based on the directed motion use of verbs of sound emission, is also further evidence for the unaccusative classification of the directed motion use for the reasons discussed in section 5.1.1.2.

To recapitulate, we have just proposed that verbs of sound emission are found in two different types of causatives: one based on the internally caused verbs of sound emission and the other based on the externally caused verbs of sound emission. Since an internally caused verb of sound emission will only enter into causatives as a result of a shift in meaning to a verb of directed motion, such causatives will show a directional phrase requirement. Externally caused verbs of sound emission are dyadic by their very nature, so causatives involving such verbs will not show a directional phrase requirement. Although the existence of causatives of verbs of sound emission with and without a directional phrase requirement is precisely what we would expect given the two sources of causatives we have identified, our account of how the causatives arise makes another prediction: the directional phrases should only appear with causatives of internally caused verbs of sound emission, and, in fact, they must appear in such causatives. Thus, our account would receive strong support if we can show that the presence or absence of the directional phrase correlates appropriately with an internally or externally caused classification. Therefore, it is important that we clarify exactly where the directional phrase requirement arises in causative uses of verbs of sound emission.

Establishing such correlations is important for another reason. On the surface, it appears that verbs of sound emission, although internally caused, differ from agentive verbs of manner of motion in showing causative uses that lack a directional phrase requirement. In fact, this difference is only apparent. In discussing the directional phrase requirement, only the internally caused verbs of sound emission should be taken into consideration, since the meaning shift to verb of directed motion is relevant only to them. In this sense, internally caused verbs of sound emission are analogous to the agentive verbs of manner of motion and would be expected to show causative uses under the same conditions—that is, only in the presence of a directional phrase. In fact, we argue that if we restrict ourselves to these verbs, then we will find that they indeed causativize only in the presence of a directional phrase. Thus, once the appropriate comparison is made, the directional phrase requirement can be shown to extend to verbs of sound emission. What sets verbs of sound emission apart from agentive verbs of manner of motion is that certain verbs of sound emission can be either internally or externally caused. In contrast, agentive verbs of manner of motion are unable to describe externally caused eventualities, although there is a class of externally caused verbs of manner of motion—the *roll* verbs introduced in chapter 4. Verbs of sound emission with both internally and externally caused uses can be seen as combining the properties of the two types of verbs of manner of motion. We return to further similarities between the verbs of sound emission and the *roll* verbs in section 5.3.

Let us examine whether we can show the predicted correlation between the directional phrase and internal/external causation with verbs of sound emission. There are two possibilities to consider: verbs of sound emission that are only internally caused and verbs of sound emission that can be both internally and externally caused. We predict that those verbs of sound emission that are necessarily internally caused should show causatives only with directional phrases (and, then, only if they permit the meaning shift). For those verbs of sound emission that can be either internally or externally caused, we predict that the directional phrase requirement must surface in those uses where the verb is necessarily internally caused.

We begin by examining those verbs of sound emission that must receive an internally caused classification, such as *roar* and *screech*. Such verbs describe the sounds emitted by entities with "self-controlled" bodies, such as people, animals, vehicles, and machinery. Although we cannot exhaustively examine the causatives of such verbs, a survey of the examples of causatives of verbs of emission that we have found in texts suggests that this prediction is verified. The examples in (34) all involve such verbs, and a comparison of these examples with those in (35) shows that the directional phrase requirement holds for these particular verbs.

We turn next to those verbs of sound emission that are open to both internally and externally caused classifications. Such verbs describe sounds that can be externally caused by direct manipulation of the emitter, although they can also describe the emission of sounds under the emitter's own control, giving rise to the internally caused uses. As discussed in section 3.2.5, the externally caused use arises only if the emitter is manipulable. Thus, if we restrict ourselves to causative uses with non-manipulable emitters, these must involve internal causation, and we would predict that they would require a directional phrase. In fact, this prediction is difficult to test for the following reason: most verbs of sound emission that are both internally and externally caused describe sounds resulting from contact between two surfaces (e.g., the verbs *clatter* and *rattle*). Such sounds are almost always brought about by manipulable emitters, so it is almost impossible to find the relevant examples. Nevertheless, on the basis of the behavior of the necessarily internally caused verbs of sound emission, we suggest that not only agentive verbs of manner of motion, but also internally caused verbs of sound emission, require a directional phrase in their causative use, and that this requirement supports the unaccusative classification of the directed motion use of internally caused verbs of sound emission.[6]

To conclude this section, we point out that the behavior of verbs of sound emission with respect to resultatives and causatives provides support for the existence of parallels between certain verb classes that might not have been a priori obvious. It appears that agentive verbs of manner of motion behave more like verbs of sound emission than like verbs of inherently directed motion, though the latter are also verbs of motion. This observation shows that the components of meaning that determine syntactic behavior are not always the most obvious ones.

5.1.3   The Nature of the Meaning Shift

We have shown, then, that agentive verbs of manner of motion and internally caused verbs of sound emission regularly exhibit multiple meanings: all of these verbs can have directed motion senses. As we have foreshadowed throughout this book, we take this to be the result of a lexical rule. In this section we outline the reasons for assuming a lexical rule and discuss some of the characteristics of the lexical rule we are assuming. In section 5.2 we compare our approach with alternative approaches that do not posit lexical rules.

We assume that both agentive verbs of manner of motion and internally caused verbs of sound emission have basic classifications in which they are not verbs of directed motion. That is, the constants these verbs take their names from fairly well determine the lexical semantic template they are basically associated with, and this is the template of an internally caused verb rather than that of a verb of directed motion. However, we assume that English has a lexical rule that maps members of these two semantically coherent classes onto the class of verbs of directed motion. English makes use of this rule in a completely productive way, and, therefore, the availability of the multiple meanings does not have to be listed in the lexical entry of any individual verb. In fact, as far as we can tell, all agentive verbs of manner of motion and all internally caused verbs of sound emission where the sound emission is a necessary concomitant of the motion show both meanings.

The ability to show these multiple meanings appears to be rule-governed in two respects: first, as we have illustrated, it is productive over classes of verbs, and second, it is still restricted to certain classes of verbs. Garden-variety activity verbs cannot show this type of variable behavior, as illustrated in (36), again suggesting that a lexical statement of some kind is needed to restrict the domain of the rule.

(36) a. *Kelly laughed out of the room.
     (cf. Kelly went out of the room laughing.)
   b. *Dorothy sang out of the room.
     (cf. Dorothy went out of the room singing.)
   c. *Terry swore out of the room.
     (cf. Terry went out of the room swearing.)
   d. *Mildred exercised into the room.
     (cf. Mildred went into the room exercising.)
   e. *Kim hesitated out of the room.
     (cf. Kim went out of the room hesitating.)

Furthermore, this rule appears to be a rule that English makes use of, but other languages, such as the Romance languages, do not. Still other languages, like Tswana and Japanese, can lexicalize the additional component of meaning only when signaled by overt morphology.

Finally, the assumption that a lexical rule is involved in the meaning shift to verbs of directed motion can help explain a rather complicated set of facts regarding the behavior of these verbs. As already shown in section 2.2, the English resultative construction serves as a device for allowing the subject of an unergative verb to meet the Directed Change Linking Rule (there referred to as the Change-of-State Linking Rule) without any need for the verb to change its unergative classification. This is accomplished by the introduction of a postverbal NP (perhaps the subject of a small clause) that is either a reflexive pronoun coreferential with the subject or contains a body part bound to the subject, as in *She shouted herself hoarse* or *She cried her eyes blind*. The *X's way* construction introduced in chapter 4 serves as a similar device allowing English unergative verbs to express a change in the location of their subject while retaining their original unergative classification.

(37) a. Kelly laughed her way out of the room.
    b. Sing your way around the world!
    c. Sam joked his way into the meeting. (Jackendoff 1990:211, (1c))
    d. We ate our way across the U.S. (Jackendoff 1990:212, (8a))
    e. Mickey Mantle fanned his way into the Hall of Fame.
       (Jackendoff 1990:213, (11a))

On closer analysis, it is clear that the *X's way* construction is parallel in its essentials to the *Xself* and body part resultative constructions, a point also made by Marantz (1992). If the *X's way* phrase is assumed to involve an inalienably possessed head—the special noun *way*—so that it is on a par with the body part NPs in resultative constructions like *She cried her eyes blind*, then, just as in the resultative construction the properly bound body part can be used to allow the subject to meet the Directed Change Linking Rule, so can a phrase like *X's way*. The phrase *X's way* is obligatorily bound to the subject (**The children laughed the clown's way out of the room*). As a result of the binding relation, the PP predicated of this phrase is understood to be predicated of the subject. The PP describes a goal: typically an attained location, as in (37a), although it may receive a metaphorical or figurative interpretation, as in (37b).

Unlike the resultative construction, the *X's way* construction is not semantically restricted to a narrow class of verbs. Almost all unergative verbs can participate in the construction, as the examples in (37), as well as the corpus examples in (38), suggest; studies of this construction, particularly Salkoff's (1988), have illustrated its productivity by pointing to nonce uses involving denominal verbs—some of them even having compounds as bases—as in (39).

(38) a. The candidate off in the provinces, plotting and planning and
       dreaming his way to the nomination ... [R. Toner, "While
       Others Shrank from Race, Clinton Clung to Dream of
       Presidency," 14]

   b. Corporate executives wined, dined and golfed their way to a
      record $36.53 billion in expense account spending. [AP
      Newswire 1990, 45780080]
   c. ... volunteers sneezed, sniffled and coughed their way through
      years of tests ... [AP Newswire 1990, 23612106]
   d. ... Louis Rukeyser grins and winks his way into the homes of 10
      million television viewers every Friday ... [AP Newswire 1990,
      40311856]

(39) ... hoping to whistlestop his way to reelection. [CBS radio news, 27
     September 1992]

Jackendoff notes two semantic constraints on the verbs that can appear
in the *X's way* construction: "the verb must be capable of being construed
as a *process*" [italics in original] and, furthermore, "the verb must express
a process with some kind of internal structure" (1990:213). These properties of the *X's way* construction would predict that agentive verbs of
manner of motion and internally caused verbs of sound emission could
appear in this construction, and, as the examples in (40) and (41) show,
this prediction is borne out.

(40) a. ... young performers have sung and danced their way around
        the world many times since 1965. [AP Newswire 1990, 26684432]
     b. When they finally creep their way to the front of the line, a
        smiling mouseketeer named Brad manhandles them into the
        front seat of a boat ... [P. Klass, *Other Women's Children*, 29]
     c. "Now they are swimming their way toward Toronto." [AP
        Newswire 1990, 25826360]

(41) a. Then he watched as it gurgled its way into a whiskey tumbler.
        [M. Grimes, *The Five Bells and Bladestone*, 200]
     b. ... the train was soon shrieking and grinding its way toward St.
        Bridget. [F. Sullivan, *The Cape Anne*, 15]
     c. Above her flew a great gaggle of geese, honking their way south.
        [M. L'Engle, *An Acceptable Time*, 91]

The examples of the resultative construction given in (18) and repeated in
(42), which are ungrammatical with a reflexive, are rendered grammatical
by replacing the reflexive with an *X's way* phrase.

(42) a. *You must jump yourself clear of the vehicle.
     b. *They swam themselves apart.

(43) a. They jumped their way clear of the vehicle.

   b. They swam their merry way apart.

Thus, although most activity verbs can appear only in the unergative resultative construction, the agentive verbs of manner of motion and the internally caused verbs of sound emission can appear in either unergative or unaccusative resultative constructions. But even with these verbs, not just any resultative construction is possible. As the examples in (17) and (28) illustrate, verbs of manner of motion and verbs of sound emission can assume an unaccusative classification if the resultative phrase denotes a change of location, but not if it denotes a change of state. This restriction arises because the lexical rule that allows these verbs to undergo a class shift maps agentive verbs of manner of motion and internally caused verbs of sound emission onto verbs of directed motion, but not onto verbs of change of state. Thus, in order to predicate a change of state in the theme (i.e., moving entity) argument of a verb of manner of motion or the emitter argument of a verb of sound emission, the syntactic device available to unergative verbs for this purpose must be employed.

   The assumption, then, is that *They swam apart* involves a shift in the lexical classification of the verb, whereas *Pat swam her way across the Channel* does not. There is, in fact, support for this assumption. The evidence involves a difference in the interpretation of the two constructions. For ease of exposition we illustrate this point with agentive verbs of manner of motion, but the same point can be made with internally caused verbs of sound emission. Since we are assuming that verbs of manner of motion have a multiple *lexical* classification, we predict that they can predicate directional phrases of their subject in two ways. As unergative verbs, they can predicate directional phrases of their subject via the NP *X's way*. When they become verbs of directed motion via the lexical rule, not only do they change classification, becoming unaccusative, but they predicate a directional phrase of their surface subject directly without the need for an *X's way* NP. What is interesting is that there is often a subtle, but detectable, difference in interpretation between the two directed motion uses. For example, Jackendoff (1990:224) points out that the sentences in (44) show a slight difference in interpretation.

(44) a. Willy jumped into Harriet's arms.

   b. Willy jumped his way into Harriet's arms.

Whereas (44a) strongly implies a single jump, (44b) strongly implies a series of jumps. The sentences in (45) show a similar difference in interpretation.

(45) a. The passengers jumped clear of the burning bus.

   b. The passengers jumped their way clear of the burning bus.

It is significant that sentences like (44b) and (45b), in which agentive verbs of manner of motion retain their unergative classification, often involve a *series* of events, whereas the sentences in which the verbs show an unaccusative classification necessarily involve a single event. This difference in interpretation suggests that the distinction between inherent and derived aspect is relevant, and that it is inherent directed change, and not derived directed change, that determines unaccusative behavior. It appears that the unergative use of agentive verbs of manner of motion need not always involve multiple events, as the examples in (37a) and (37c), repeated in (46), illustrate, but the unaccusative use *must* never involve an iteration of events, always involving the directed motion use of the verb itself.

(46) a. Kelly laughed her way out of the room.

   b. Sam joked his way into the meeting. (Jackendoff 1990:211, (1c))

This difference is not surprising, since unaccusativity, on the theory we are proposing, is a *lexical* property and therefore should be determined by the lexical properties of a verb and not by sentence-level properties such as derived aspect.

This last point may actually shed some light on the distinction between derived and inherent aspect. In the literature on lexical aspect, it is usually suggested that the telic use of verbs of manner of motion involves derived aspect, precisely because verbs of manner of motion in isolation do not describe directed motion (Smith 1991, Verkuyl 1972, among others). However, if our approach is correct, then the shift is a lexical one. On our understanding of the phenomenon, the directed motion reading of unergative verbs in the *X's way* construction is derived compositionally in the syntax. For most unergative verbs, this is the only device available for achieving this interpretation. But for a subclass of unergative verbs, there is a second option, because these verbs have another lexical semantic representation.

The results of this section complement the results of chapter 2. There we noted that the explanation we gave for the syntax of the resultative construction implied that the resultative construction makes use of existing lexical entries and does not create new lexical entries. Initially, it might appear that this is not true of agentive verbs of manner of motion when they turn up in the unaccusative resultative pattern. That is, these verbs appear to change their lexical classification in the resultative construction.

However, in this section we showed that the agentive verbs of manner of motion are independently known to have multiple lexical classifications. English allows *Sally jumped clear of the car* for the same reason that it allows *Sally jumped out of the car*. English allows *Sally jumped clear of the car* but not **Sally jumped to exhaustion* because the latter sentence would involve an agentive verb of manner of motion becoming a verb of change of state, and English does not have such a lexical rule. Furthermore, although English permits agentive verbs of manner of motion to become verbs of directed motion, it does not permit most other verbs to undergo this shift. Therefore, English does not allow **The girls laughed apart* or **The children laughed clear of the oncoming car*, which it should allow if *laugh* were allowed to undergo a shift in lexical properties, for the same reason that it does not allow **Sally laughed out of the room*. Currently, we do not have any explanation for the fact that only verbs from certain semantic classes can become verbs of directed motion or for the fact that they can become verbs of directed motion but not verbs of change of state. These explanations must await a full theory of possible and impossible meaning shifts. What is important is that just those verbs that can independently become verbs of directed motion also can show a shift in syntax in the resultative construction. Although we do not have an explanation for this last fact, the correlation between the behavior of the verbs in the resultative construction and their behavior in isolation is most likely a principled one.

5.1.4 The Meaning Shifts in a Cross-Linguistic Context

Before concluding this section, we discuss the cross-linguistic aspect of the meaning shift phenomenon. Although we have not had the opportunity to explore in a systematic and thorough way the cross-linguistic availability and manifestation of the meaning shift with internally caused verbs of sound emission, it is striking that according to our preliminary investigations, the languages that allow verbs of sound emission to be used as verbs of directed motion are the same languages that allow agentive verbs of manner of motion to become verbs of directed motion. That is, just as the shift from verb of manner of motion to verb of directed motion is not manifested in all languages, neither is the shift from verb of sound emission to verb of directed motion. For example, the meaning shift involving verbs of sound emission is found in German and Modern Hebrew, both languages that resemble English in permitting agentive verbs of manner of motion to be used as verbs of directed motion, as shown in section 5.1.

The availability of the directed motion use of verbs of sound emission in German and Modern Hebrew is illustrated in (47) and (48), respectively.

(47) a. Die Kugel pfiff   durch   die   Luft.
        the bullet whistled through the-ACC air
        'The bullet whistled through the air.'
   b. Der Lastwagen rasselte den   Berg hinunter.
        the truck   rattled the-ACC hill   down
        'The truck rattled down the hill.'

(48) a. Ha-kadur šarak   le'evra.
        the-bullet whistled toward her
        'The bullet whistled toward her.'
   b. Ha-tankim ra'amu el me-ever la-gvul.
        the-tanks   roared to across   the-border
        'The tanks roared across the border.'

In contrast, Japanese, which does not allow verbs of manner of motion to be used as verbs of directed motion, also does not allow verbs of sound emission to be used as verbs of directed motion. Instead, to express the meanings that English can express using verbs of sound emission plus directional phrases, Japanese uses a verb of inherently directed motion together with adverbial phrases involving onomatopoeic nouns expressing sounds.

(49) Torakku-ga gatagatato   (oto-o   tatete)
    truck-NOM   rumbling sound (sound-ACC making)
    doraibuwei-ni haitte-kita.
    driveway-to   enter-came
    'The truck rumbled into the driveway.'

(50) Kanojo-wa kasakasato   oto-o   tatete heya-o   dete-itta.
    she-TOP   rustling sound sound-ACC making room-ACC exit-went
    'She rustled out of the room.'

In French, as in Japanese, verbs of sound emission resemble verbs of manner of motion: like them, they cannot be used as verbs of directed motion. In general, it is unnatural in French to attempt to mention a sound when the motion of an entity is being described. Meanings comparable to the English (a) sentences of (51) and (52) might be expressed periphrastically in French as in the (b) sentences, but even such translations would be considered poor and unnatural versions of the English sentences.[7]

(51) a. The car roared down the street.
    b. La voiture descendit   la   rue   en vrombissant.
      the car   went down the street in roaring

(52) a. The truck rumbled into the yard.
    b. Le camion entra   dans la   cour dans un grand fracas.
      the truck   entered in   the yard in   a big   din

Our preliminary investigations, then, suggest that if a language allows one class of verbs to shift, it will allow the other class to shift as well. Further study is necessary to determine not only the viability of this generalization but also whether the availability of meaning shifts reflects some deeper property of a language's lexical semantic organization. Certainly once the nature of these shifts is better understood, it should become possible to predict, at least to some extent, which languages will exhibit such shifts. If it turns out to be true that all languages that allow the shift for agentive verbs of manner of motion also allow the shift for verbs of sound emission, this strongly suggests that, as mentioned in section 1.4, whatever the lexical statement is that governs these shifts, it does not make direct reference to the classes of verbs, but instead refers to some more basic meaning component in terms of which these verb classes are defined.

Other considerations also suggest that direct reference to verb classes is not made in the lexical statement governing the meaning shifts. Agentive verbs of manner of motion and internally caused verbs of sound emission are not the only semantic classes of verbs that can become verbs of directed motion. Among intransitive verbs, verbs of body-internal motion, such as *flap, flutter,* and *wiggle,* also exhibit the shift, as in *The bird fluttered onto the branch.* The shift is also found among transitive verbs. For example, as noted in B. Levin and Rappaport Hovav 1991, the verbs *rub, sweep,* and *wipe,* and other verbs of contact through motion, whose removal sense was discussed in section 2.4.1, also show a verb-of-putting sense as a consequence of this meaning shift, as in *She swept the dust into the corner* or *I rubbed the oil into the furniture.* Verbs of exerting force, such as *pull* and *push,* are another type of transitive verbs that permit this shift: *They pushed the cart into the garage.* It is unlikely that the lexicon contains a rule that makes reference to all of these verb classes. It is more likely, as mentioned in section 1.4, that the statement makes reference to the meaning components in terms of which the relevant semantic classes are defined. This would be analogous to phonological rules, which are formulated not in terms of classes of phonemes but in terms of distinctive features that define these classes. Only further research on the cross-linguistic patterns of these shifts will allow the development of a predictive theory.

5.2 Consequences for Lexical Representation

In the previous section we investigated a number of verb classes where members are systematically associated with more than one meaning. We have informally referred to this phenomenon as "meaning shift." Although we have concentrated on those shifts that involve the multiple classifications of verbs as unergative and unaccusative, it is clear that the general phenomenon pervades the English verb lexicon and is not restricted to intransitive verbs. For example, we mentioned that, as discussed in Atkins, Kegl, and B. Levin 1988, verbs of cooking are systematically associated with more than one meaning. In section 2.4.1 we briefly discussed the phenomenon of verbs of contact through motion taking on the meaning of verbs of putting and removal (a phenomenon discussed in more depth in B. Levin and Rappaport Hovav 1991). What all these shifts have in common is that semantically coherent classes of verbs are systematically mapped into other existing semantically coherent classes of verbs.

In this section we compare the approach developed here with another one, which does not involve a lexical statement for the derivation of verbs with multiple meanings, but derives the meaning of a verb from the construction it appears in. Dowty (1991:608, fn. 41) writes, "Hypothesizing that a large semantically coherent group of verbs have duplicate categorization in unaccusative and unergative syntactic classes (and with corresponding different semantics in the two frames) would be missing the point, I argue." He suggests that if such duplicate categorization holds in general, this is evidence for the *semantic* approach to unaccusativity rather than the syntactic approach.[8] An analysis of the phenomenon of meaning shift in terms of the semantic approach would involve the assumptions that constructions are associated with different meanings and that variable behavior verbs by virtue of their core meaning are compatible with more than one construction. The meaning of a verb in a given construction is compositionally derived from the meaning of the predicates in the construction and the meaning of the construction itself. Since the semantic approach to unaccusativity does not take the unaccusative/unergative distinction to be a lexical property, the variable behavior of agentive verbs of manner of motion in the resultative construction, for example, would arise not from the existence of multiple lexical entries for these verbs but from the fact that these verbs are compatible with two different constructions, one (the unaccusative pattern) expressing only directed motion and the other (the unergative pattern) expressing either change of state (in the resultative construction) or directed motion (in the *X's way* construction).

Another, similar approach to variable behavior verbs, although one that still maintains that unaccusativity is syntactically encoded, is developed in work by Hoekstra (Hoekstra 1988, 1992, Hoekstra and Mulder 1990). Hoekstra explicitly denies that lexical rules are responsible for the multiple meanings associated with verbs. Rather, he suggests, verbs are free to project arguments of various semantic (and hence, syntactic) types; the meaning that a verb is ultimately associated with is determined by the construction it appears in. For example, Hoekstra and Mulder write, "The way in which the argument structure is projected onto the syntax contributes to (or determines within the limits set by the concept a predicate refers to) the meaning" (1990:7). They write further that "[c]ertain predicates vary, within limits, in their meaning, such that they take arguments of different types" (1990:75). The projection of verbs onto syntactic structure is constrained in two ways: (i) by the compatibility between the meaning of the predicator and the constructions that arise from the particular projections of arguments and (ii) by general syntactic principles. A further constraining factor would be the set of constructions that are available in any particular language. We have already compared our lexical approach to Hoekstra's approach in section 2.4.1, and we do so again in this section; we hope to show that the lexical approach is more plausible.

Although Dowty and Hoekstra differ in many ways in their conception of lexical structure, they both assume that there is no need for any kind of lexical statement in dealing with variable behavior verbs. Rather, verbs are projected fairly freely onto different syntactic configurations. We refer to this general approach as the *constructional* approach. (For a somewhat different version of the constructional approach to the problem of multiple meanings, see A. Goldberg 1992, 1994a.) Thus, if two languages have a particular construction, there should be no difference in the range of verbs that could enter into that construction. On the face of it, this is not correct. We are unaware of any language that lacks a means of expressing directed motion, yet languages vary with respect to which verbs can appear directly with a directional prepositional phrase. The fact that in

English this option is available to agentive verbs of manner of motion and internally caused verbs of sound emission cannot obviously be attributed merely to plausibility, since many other languages do not allow this option.

To extend the argument further, we consider how the lexical approach and the constructional approach would deal with the possibilities available to verbs in resultative constructions. Any analysis of the resultative construction will have to account for the fact that agentive verbs of manner of motion can appear in the unaccusative resultative pattern with an XP denoting a result location, but not with an XP denoting a result state, as illustrated by the following contrast:

(53) a. Bob jumped/ran clear of the car.
     b. *Bob jumped/ran into a frenzy.

The ungrammaticality of (53b) cannot be attributed to the fact that the unaccusative resultative pattern is always associated with a nonagentive reading, as (53a) indicates. Nor can it be said that the unaccusative pattern can only express a change of location, and not a change of state, as the following sentences show:

(54) a. The river froze solid.
     b. The bottle broke open.
     c. The soldiers starved to death.

If we wanted to derive these restrictions from the construction itself, we would have to distinguish unaccusative resultative constructions denoting changes of state from those denoting changes of location and propose that the former allow only nonagentive readings, whereas the latter allow agentive readings as well. But this would be missing the point entirely. It would make an unnatural division among the unaccusative resultative constructions only to capture a fact that needs to be independently stated in any event: agentive verbs of manner of motion can become verbs of directed motion, but not verbs of change of state.

The controversy over the representation of multiple meanings can be compared to the controversy over the existence of an independent morphological component. An issue that has received much attention in the area of morphology in recent years is whether there is a need for a morphological component with its own distinct set of principles or whether it is possible to reduce all morphological phenomena to independently established syntactic and phonological principles (for discussion, see

Aronoff 1994, Baker 1988b, Lieber 1992, Spencer 1991, among many others). Similarly, with respect to multiple meanings, the question is whether multiple meanings are handled via principles or rules specific to the lexicon or whether they can be shown to reduce to properties of syntactic configurations. There is no doubt that our understanding of multiple meanings will benefit from an explicit debate on these issues, just as our understanding of morphology has benefited from the debate over an independent morphological component. We see the study of multiple meanings—both in terms of developing a taxonomy of types and in terms of formulating a theory of their sources—as one of the most important open questions that has emerged in the course of our research on unaccusativity. Although we may not have resolved the issue conclusively, we would like to stress the importance of research into the problem of variable behavior verbs. No theory of linguistic competence will be complete without an account of such phenomena. Even if our discussion does not fully decide between available approaches, our discussion should at least show the kind of phenomena any theory will need to account for and clarify the types of predictions different theories make.

5.3 Variable Behavior That Is Not Rule-Governed

We have characterized variable behavior verbs as two verbs whose lexical semantic representations involve different lexical semantic templates that have a shared constant. In the previous sections we suggested that certain pairs of this type arise from a lexical rule of some sort. In this section we propose that other pairs do not arise from a lexical rule; instead, they arise simply because certain constants happen to be compatible with more than one lexical semantic template.

When we first introduced the *roll* verbs in section 4.1.4, we described them as the subclass of the verbs of manner of motion whose members are not necessarily agentive. As noted there, the members of this class are compatible with both animate and inanimate arguments; when these verbs take an animate argument, they permit both agentive and non-agentive interpretations, although the nonagentive interpretation, even with animate arguments, is perhaps the more natural. The availability of the two interpretations is reflected in the ambiguity of (55), which is discussed by Gruber (1965), Jackendoff (1972), and many others.

(55) Max rolled down the hill. (Jackendoff 1972:34, (2.46))

On one interpretation of this sentence, Max is an agent, rolling down the hill of his own volition; on the second interpretation, he is not an agent, but rolls down the hill because of some external cause, such as a push or, if he trips, gravity.

When the *roll* verbs take an animate argument, they can be viewed as describing an internally caused eventuality when agentive and an externally caused eventuality when nonagentive.[9] When they describe an internally caused eventuality, they are no different from agentive verbs of manner of motion such as *run* or *swim* and would be expected to behave like them. What sets a verb like *roll* and a verb like *run* apart is that the latter is necessarily agentive.[10] Presumably, this difference reflects the nature of the constant associated with the lexical semantic representation of each verb, which specifies the means or manner of motion unique to that verb. Not only does this component of meaning serve to distinguish one verb of manner of motion from another, but it also determines whether the verb will allow an agentive interpretation, a nonagentive interpretation, or both.

The linking rules predict that a member of the *roll* class will display unergative behavior when it takes an animate agentive argument and unaccusative behavior otherwise, since it will fall under the Immediate Cause Linking Rule if agentive and the Default Linking Rule otherwise. In fact, in English, when the verb *roll* takes an inanimate subject, it can be found in the unaccusative resultative pattern, as shown in (56), but not in the unergative pattern or the related *X's way* construction, as shown in (57); presumably, the examples in (57) are ungrammatical since the unaccusative verb cannot assign Case to its nonsubcategorized object.

(56) This time the curtain rolled open on the court of the Caesars ...
     [Olivia (D. Bussy), *Olivia*, 35]

(57) a. *The curtain rolled itself open.
     b. *During the spring thaw, the boulders rolled the hillside bare.
     c. *Because it was repeatedly opened and closed, the door rolled the groove in the floor smooth.
     d. *The pebbles rolled their way into the stream.

However, when it takes an animate agentive subject, the verb *roll* can be found in the unergative resultative pattern and in the *X's way* construction, as in (58). (The relevant reading of (58a) is the one where the children's own rolling causes the grass to become flat; there is also an irrelevant reading in which the children are using some sort of garden tool in order to make the grass flat.)

(58) a. The children rolled the grass flat.
     b. The children rolled their way across the field.

A further illustration of the variable behavior of the *roll* verbs in English comes from the prepositional passive construction. When the verb *roll* takes an animate agentive subject, it can be found in the prepositional passive construction, as in (59), as expected if in such instances the verb *roll* is internally caused and is therefore classified as unergative. In this respect, the verb *roll* is again behaving like the agentive verb of manner of motion *run*, which, as shown in (60), is also found in the prepositional passive.

(59) This carpet has been rolled on by three generations of children.

(60) This track has been run on by our finest young athletes.

There is also evidence from Italian for the variable behavior of the *roll* verbs. The Italian *roll* verbs were discussed briefly in section 4.1.4, where we pointed out that some can take the reflexive clitic *si* when intransitive. Those *roll* verbs whose Italian counterparts optionally take this clitic also show properties that fit in with the picture presented here concerning the source of the variable classification of these verbs. In the absence of *si*, these Italian verbs are compatible with the unaccusative auxiliary *essere* 'be', as well as with the auxiliary *avere* 'have', suggesting a dual classification. What is significant is that they are preferred with the unaccusative auxiliary *essere* 'be' if their argument is inanimate and therefore definitively nonagentive (B. Levin and Rappaport Hovav 1992)—that is, precisely in the circumstances where the verbs must clearly be externally caused.

In the discussion of lexical semantic representation in section 1.4 we proposed that the concept associated with a constant that a verb takes its name from usually determines the lexical semantic template that verb is basically associated with. This property gives the sense that there is a "basic" meaning to many verbs. For example, English speakers feel that the nondirected motion sense of *run* is more basic than the directed motion sense. However, not all verbs need have a single basic sense. In particular, it appears to us that the constant associated with the verb *roll*—the manner or means component of its meaning—can equally well be associated with the lexical semantic template of either an internally or an externally caused verb. Therefore, in formulating an account of the variable behavior of verbs like *roll*, there is no need to posit a lexical rule that will map the members of one semantically coherent verb class onto another, in this instance a rule mapping the nonagentive verbs of manner of motion onto the agentive verbs of manner of motion or vice versa. The variable behavior of certain verbs of manner of motion is simply the result of the existence of a lexical semantic constant that, by virtue of its nature, is basically compatible with more than one lexical semantic template.

We have previously proposed that certain constants are compatible with more than one lexical semantic template. For instance, we made this proposal in section 3.2.5 in order to explain the appearance of *buzz* and certain other verbs of sound emission in causative pairs that do not involve directional phrases, as in (61), repeated from chapter 3.

(61) a. The doorbell buzzed.
     b. The postman buzzed the doorbell.

Such behavior was considered problematic since the causative use of such verbs suggested an externally caused classification, yet we had initially characterized these verbs as internally caused, a characterization consistent with their unergative classification (see section 4.1.1.1). The explanation we offered for this behavior was the same as the one we have just given for the variable behavior of the *roll* verbs. We proposed that certain verbs of sound emission take their name from a lexical semantic constant that is compatible with two distinct lexical semantic templates, one associated with internal causation and the other with external causation. (This constant presumably represents the sound associated with a given verb of sound emission.) Causative uses of verbs of sound emission without directional phrases such as (61b), we argued, reflect the externally caused option. As support for this, note the existence of restrictions on the possible emitters observed for the causative use: the emitters must be directly manipulable, a property necessary if they are to be externally caused to emit a sound. This requirement explains why a verb like *buzz* is found in causative pairs only for certain choices of argument, as shown by contrasting (61) with another example repeated from chapter 3.

(62) a. The bees buzzed.
     b. *The postman buzzed the bees.

There is a difference, however, between the *roll* verbs and the verbs of sound emission. Unlike the *roll* verbs, externally caused verbs of sound emission generally show only the transitive, causative expression of their arguments. They do not detransitivize, showing unaccusative intransitive uses without directional phrases because the associated sound cannot be emitted spontaneously without the intervention of an agent. Thus, there are no externally caused verbs of sound emission that are found in the causative alternation. As discussed in section 3.2.5, we believe that apparent causative pairs such as (61) or *Sheila jingled the keys/The keys jingled* do not involve a derivational relation. Rather, the transitive use contains an externally caused verb and the intransitive use an internally caused verb, but the two verbs happen to share the same constant in their lexical semantic template and hence have the same name. They are instances of spurious causative pairs. Support for this analysis comes from the observation that if Sheila jingled the keys, it is not possible to say of the same event that the keys jingled; in contrast, if Pat breaks a window, it is possible to say of the same event that the window broke.

Having discussed the source of the causative uses of verbs of sound emission without directional phrases, we want to pull this discussion together with the discussion of the causative uses of these verbs with directional phrases in section 5.1.2.2, laying out the full picture that emerges concerning the possible meanings of verbs of sound emission. We have introduced four meanings for verbs of sound emission: an internally caused meaning, an externally caused meaning, a directed motion meaning, and a causative meaning related to the directed motion meaning. The first two meanings arise from the compatibility between certain constants associated with particular sounds and particular lexical semantic templates. The third meaning arises from a regular lexical rule of meaning shift that applies to the internally caused verbs of sound emission, and the fourth meaning arises from a process of causativization as applied to the third meaning. Which meanings are associated with the constant describing a given sound depends on the nature of the sound. Only sounds that can be both externally and internally caused, such as those associated with the verbs *buzz* and *honk*, will show both of the first two meanings. Only sounds that are emitted as necessary concomitants of motion such as *rumble* and *screech* will show the third and fourth meaning, in addition to the internally caused meaning. To show all four meanings, the sound must be able to be both internally and externally caused, and it must be a necessary concomitant of motion; clearly, only a limited set of sounds will have the appropriate properties.

The account of the variable behavior of verbs like *roll* and *buzz* leads to certain predictions that should, in principle, be verifiable. In examining the parametric variation that exists across languages in the behavior of agentive verbs of manner of motion and internally caused verbs of sound emission with respect to the ability to appear with directional phrases, we showed that languages vary systematically: either the option is available to the entire class of verbs, or it is completely unavailable (except, perhaps, to a handful of exceptions, as in Italian, where the verbs *correre* 'run', *saltare* 'jump', and *volare* 'fly' may take directional phrases, though in general agentive verbs of manner of motion cannot take such phrases). This pattern is expected if this behavior is rule-governed. In contrast, given the source of the variable behavior of the verbs *roll* and *buzz*, we predict that if there are differences among languages with respect to the variable behavior of such verbs, the differences will be associated with individual lexical items rather than with an entire class of verbs. For example, we could imagine that a language might exist with two verbs corresponding to the English verb *buzz:* one predicated of animals and other entities that buzz by their very nature—that is, an internally caused verb—and one used for doorbells and comparable devices—that is, an externally caused verb. What we would not expect to find is a language that does not allow for the possibility of a predicate that can have either an internally caused or an externally caused construal—that is, a language that cannot have any verbs like English *roll*, *buzz*, or *burn*. Indeed, we are unaware of the existence of such a language.

5.4 Conclusion

In this chapter we have examined a number of classes of verbs whose members can display both unaccusative and unergative behavior. We have shown that, far from undermining the idea that the syntactic classification of verbs is semantically determined, these verbs actually support this hypothesis, since in each instance the multiple syntactic classification is correlated with a multiple semantic classification in a manner consistent with the linking rules. The components of meaning we isolated as syntactically relevant in chapter 4 are precisely the aspects of meaning that determine the variable behavior of these verbs. Thus, these case studies lend further support to the linking rules introduced in chapter 4. We also presented some preliminary hypotheses concerning the nature and derivation of multiple meanings. The important questions left for future research concern the principles that determine and constrain the meaning shifts that were posited to account for the multiple semantic classifications and the exact way these meaning shifts are to be represented.

Chapter 6

The Problem of Locative Inversion

The unaccusative diagnostics that we have discussed so far are instances of what we called "deep unaccusative diagnostics" in chapter 1. That is, the D-Structure object of an unaccusative verb becomes an S-Structure subject, so that its underlying grammatical relation is obscured on the surface. In this chapter we present a detailed study of another widely cited diagnostic, the locative inversion construction, which has been taken to be one of two surface unaccusative diagnostics in English (the other being the *there*-insertion construction, which we will only mention briefly). That is, in the locative inversion construction the D-Structure object of an unaccusative verb does not become an S-Structure subject; instead, it maintains a postverbal position.

Locative inversion has been claimed to be a diagnostic for the unaccusative syntactic configuration (Bresnan and Kanerva 1989, Coopmans 1989, Hoekstra and Mulder 1990, L. Levin 1986, among others). Two kinds of evidence typically figure in arguments for its diagnostic status: evidence involving the set of verbs attested in the construction and evidence involving the syntax of the construction. The set of verbs that appears in the locative inversion construction bears a startling resemblance to the unaccusative verb class. The verb most frequently found in the locative inversion construction is the verb *be*, which we will not discuss here, but whose presence in the construction does not detract from an unaccusative analysis. More relevant to our concerns is the existence of an intransitivity constraint on this construction that is noted in traditional grammars. But even more striking, the intransitive verbs most commonly found in this construction—verbs such as *come*, *go*, and *appear*—are "prototypical" unaccusative verbs. Finally, passive transitive verbs, which are classed with unaccusative verbs in having no external argument, also figure prominently in the locative inversion construction, contrasting with the active form of the same verbs. Besides the nature of the verbs entering into the construction, certain aspects of the syntax of the construction are said to be explained by positing that the construction is restricted to verbs that lack an external argument—that is, unaccusative and passive verbs.

As we will show in section 6.2.2, however, there are problems with this initial characterization of locative inversion as an unaccusative diagnostic. First, only a semantically coherent subclass of the unaccusative verbs is represented in this construction. This restriction does not necessarily invalidate it as a diagnostic since most unaccusative diagnostics have semantic restrictions on them. More serious is the appearance of certain unergative verbs in this construction, a fact that is central to the analysis of locative inversion offered by Hoekstra and Mulder (1990). For example, as we discuss below, a corpus-based study of this construction shows that the presumably unergative verbs *work*, *chatter*, *glitter*, and *rumble* are all attested in the construction. In fact, some subclasses of the unergative class are extremely well represented among the verbs found in this construction. Thus, the appearance of these unergative verbs in the construction calls for an explanation.

There are several ways that the presence of unergative verbs in the locative inversion construction could be dealt with. One possibility is to simply deny that this construction is an unaccusative diagnostic and to find another explanation for its distributional properties. Rochemont and Culicover (1990) take this approach, although they have little to say about which verbs are found in the construction. A second possibility is to suggest that the unergative verbs found in this construction have two regularly related meanings, one compatible with an unaccusative analysis and the other with an unergative analysis, as we have suggested to account for certain unexpected instances of the resultative construction in chapter 5 and as implemented for locative inversion by Hoekstra and Mulder (1990).

In this chapter we opt for the first type of solution to the unergative verb dilemma. We argue that the locative inversion construction is not an unaccusative diagnostic in that it is not restricted only to verbs independently known to be unaccusative. Rather, we attribute its unaccusative-like distributional properties to the fact that this construction is associated with a particular discourse function, which in turn favors certain semantic classes of verbs. In particular, a subset of unaccusative verbs are shown to fit naturally with the discourse function of the construction, as does a certain class of passive verbs. We then argue that in the appropriate circumstances unergative verbs are also compatible with the discourse function of the construction.

We discuss several reasons for preferring this account to a multiple meaning account that allows the diagnostic status of the construction to be preserved. First, although we have explained the presence of unergative verbs in other constructions that diagnose unaccusativity by positing multiple meanings for the verbs involved, possibly arising from meaning shifts, the instances of locative inversion with unergative verbs do not show the properties associated with such meaning shifts. In particular, it is not easy to identify semantically coherent subclasses of the unergative verbs that map onto a single subclass of unaccusative verbs, allowing a simple statement of the meaning shift that might underlie the locative inversion data. This situation contrasts with the resultative construction, where, as we showed in chapter 5, it was possible to formulate an explicit rule of meaning shift: agentive verbs of manner of motion and internally caused verbs of sound emission become verbs of directed motion. We show that in general the restrictions on the verbs in locative inversion are different and depend on more than the properties of the verb in the construction. Then we show that the syntactic properties of the construction are not actually explained by positing that the verbs in the construction are unaccusative. As there are no compelling syntactic reasons for assuming the unaccusative analysis of locative inversion, there is no reason to resort to the process of meaning shift to explain the presence of unergative verbs in this construction. There remains, then, no motivation for the unaccusative analysis. To conclude this chapter, we suggest that the properties that set off locative inversion are properties of all "surface unaccusative" diagnostics across languages.

In concluding this introduction, we want to describe briefly the illustrative examples of the locative inversion construction used throughout this chapter. For the most part, these are naturally occurring examples taken from a corpus of close to 2,100 instances of the locative inversion construction collected by B. Birner, B. Levin, and G. Ward, with contributions from G. Green and L. Levin. (Although there is a substantial overlap between this corpus and the corpus of locative inversions discussed in Birner 1992, 1994, the two corpora are not the same.) No effort was made to select the tokens of the construction from a "balanced" collection of texts; in fact, we actively sought tokens from authors who showed a propensity for using the construction. Although the selectional criteria limit the types of conclusions that can be drawn from these tokens, they should not detract from our own primary goal: explaining the actual types of verbs found in locative inversion. Our corpus of locative inversions reveals clear trends concerning verb types, which we discuss throughout this chapter. Most striking of all, it demonstrates that common wisdom notwithstanding, the set of locative inversion verbs is quite large; we have found slightly more than 250 intransitive verbs and 130 passive verbs, which are listed in appendix B. Furthermore, the composition of the list of verbs suggests that the list would be expected to expand in certain areas if more data were available; we discuss this as appropriate throughout the chapter.

6.1 Locative Inversion: An Introduction

In this section we briefly sketch the hallmarks of the locative inversion construction. A typical instance of this construction is given in (1); in this and subsequent examples from the corpus, the relevant verb and any accompanying auxiliaries are given in small capital letters.

(1) In the distance APPEARED the towers and spires of a town which greatly resembled Oxford. [L. Bromfield, *The Farm*, 124]

The name given to this construction—locative inversion—reflects two properties of the construction. First, it is characterized by a noncanonical word order, "PP V NP," that appears to be the result of switching the positions of the NP and the PP in the canonical "NP V PP" word order, particularly since the inverted and noninverted sentences are near paraphrases of each other; for instance, (1) can be paraphrased by (2).

(2) The towers and spires of a town which greatly resembled Oxford appeared in the distance.

The second hallmark of this construction is the presence of a PP—typically a locative or directional PP—in preverbal position;[1] the construction takes its name from this PP. We will call this PP the *preverbal* PP. The preverbal PP in (1) corresponds to the postverbal PP in (2), the noninverted counterpart of this sentence. A third property of the construction will be central to our discussion. With rare exceptions, the verb in the locative inversion construction must be intransitive,[2] and it is this restriction, combined with the observation that not all intransitive verbs are found in this construction, that has led to the investigation of whether this construction is a possible unaccusative diagnostic.

Although the locative inversion construction could receive the analysis that its name suggests—that is, it could simply be derived by inverting the subject of an intransitive verb and a PP complement—such an analysis would have to be rejected as not being structure-preserving (Emonds 1976); in fact, locative inversion has figured in the debate over structure preservation. One appealing feature of the proposal that locative inversion is an unaccusative diagnostic is that a structure-preserving analysis becomes possible if the construction is restricted to unaccusative verbs. On this analysis, the D-Structure form of a locative inversion construction is most likely as schematized in (3), the PP moving to become the subject at S-Structure. (Alternatively, as Hoekstra and Mulder (1990) propose, the NP and PP could form a small clause; see section 6.7.)

(3) e [$_{VP}$ V NP PP]

On the unaccusative analysis, the postverbal NP is a D-Structure object of the verb. As the postverbal NP does not originate as the subject of the verb in the construction, the name "inversion" is no longer apt; nevertheless, we continue to refer to this construction using the established label "locative inversion."

An introduction to locative inversion would not be complete without a discussion of the similarities and differences between it and the *there*-insertion construction. This construction, which was discussed in section 4.1.3, is illustrated in (4) with a pair of sentences related to the locative inversion in (2). These two *there*-insertion sentences differ with respect to the placement of the PP; (4b) is an instance of the type of *there*-insertion referred to as an outside verbal.[3]

(4) a. In the distance there APPEARED the towers and spires of a town which greatly resembled Oxford.
     b. There APPEARED in the distance the towers and spires of a town which greatly resembled Oxford.

The hallmark of the *there*-insertion construction is the presence of *there* as the subject of the verb. Some researchers (see, for example, Kuno 1971, Postal 1977) have suggested that locative inversions are derived from *there*-insertion constructions of the form in (4a), where a PP precedes *there*, by dropping *there*, but Bresnan (1993) presents evidence against this analysis. Also of interest is that *there*-insertion has been argued to be an unaccusative diagnostic (Burzio 1986, L. Levin 1986, Stowell 1978, among others; see also section 4.1.3). Like locative inversion, it is rarely found with transitive verbs and shows the basic distributional properties of an unaccusative diagnostic. A further, particularly interesting similarity is that *there*-insertion is also found with a class of verbs that is both "too big" and "too small" in the same sense as the class found in locative inversion. Although there are some differences between the constructions, we believe that once the inside verbals discussed in section 4.1.3 are set aside, some form of the solution to the distributional dilemma for locative inversion can be extended to the remaining instances of *there*-insertion; for this reason, we will not systematically discuss *there*-insertion further in this chapter.[4]

6.2   The Verbs Found in Locative Inversion

In this section we review the verbs that enter into locative inversion, focusing first on the general distributional characteristics of the construction that have suggested that it is an unaccusative diagnostic and then turning to the properties that pose a problem for this analysis.

6.2.1   General Distributional Characteristics

The surface distribution of the locative inversion construction appears to justify the claim that it can serve as an unaccusative diagnostic. Locative inversion is found with intransitive verbs that are considered to be among the prototypical members of the unaccusative class, including certain verbs of appearance, as in (5), verbs of existence, as in (6), and verbs of inherently directed motion, as in (7). The verbs of existence that are attested in the construction include verbs of spatial configuration with inanimate subjects (i.e., in their simple position sense), as in (8).

(5) a. Over her shoulder APPEARED the head of Jenny's mother.
       [M. Spark, *The Prime of Miss Jean Brodie*, 27]

    b. From such optical tricks ARISE all the varieties of romantic
       hallucination ... [R. Goldstein, *The Late-Summer Passion of a
       Woman of Mind*, 167]

    c. ... from the lips of this poor soft-brained creature ISSUE a flow of
       beautiful words in the accent of some place that was certainly not
       Ballyderrig. [M. Laverty, *Never No More*, 20]

(6) a. At night, under the lights, and the rapt presence of forty or fifty
       guards in the corners and the corridors and the bus debarkation
       point, EXISTED that stricken awareness of a dire event to which the
       air itself can seem to be sensitive. [NMAN 187 (39); cited in H. H.
       Hartvigson and L. K. Jakobsen 1974:57]

b. Here and there FLOURISH groves of aged live oaks, planted to shadow the manor houses of the plantations that the road originally served. [C. von Pressentin Wright, "Plantation Mansions on the Mississippi," 14]

c. Far below the jagged spires and knife-edge ridges of the Dortmund range, smug and secure in the shadows of those glistening, snow-capped cathedrals, THRIVES the quaint town of Kringlewald. [W. Hjortsberg, *Alp*, 14]

(7) a. ... out of the house CAME a tiny old lady and three or four enormous people ... [L. Bromfield, *The Farm*, 1]

b. And when it's over, off WILL GO Clay, smugly smirking all the way to the box office, the only person better off for all the fuss. [R. Kogan, "Andrew Dice Clay Isn't Worth 'SNL' Flap," 4]

c. ... with him HAD ARRIVED hoards [*sic*] of workmen and carpenters ... [M. Piercy, *Summer People*, 235]

(8) a. ... from his hip pocket PROTRUDED a notebook with metal covers. [J. Steinbeck, *The Grapes of Wrath*, 240]

b. On the black lacquer top cf the piano PERCHED three brass-framed pictures ... [J. Olshan, *The Waterline*, 303–4]

c. Above the bed HANG two faded prints of men playing polo. [S. Cheever, *Elizabeth Cole*, 70]

In addition, verbs of manner of motion and, much less frequently, verbs of sound emission are found in locative inversion constructions when they take directional phrase complements, as in (9) and (10). This behavior is consistent with the arguments in chapter 5 that such verbs are unaccusative when they take directional complements.

(9) a. Down the dusty Chisholm Trail into Abilene RODE taciturn Spit Weaver, his lean brown face an enigma, his six-gun swinging idly from the pommel of Moisshe, the wonder horse. (Green 1980:590, (15c))

b. Into this heady atmosphere STRIDES Tucker Muldowney (Kirk Cameron), a maddeningly self-confident, gee-shucks freshman from Oklahoma who has entered Kenmont on a debating scholarship. [D. Kehr, "Resolved: 'Listen' Is a Boring Movie," 20]

c. Up the stairs BOUNDED Senator Dickerson, wearing an outlandish Hawaiian shirt. [R. Levitsky, *The Love That Kills*, 82]

d. Into this scene WALKED Corky's sister, Vera, eight years old,
who had been at a Brownies meeting, sewing a crayon pouch.
[A. Beattie, *Picturing Will*, 137]

(10) Through the orchards RATTLED the field station's Ford pickup,
bearing its two silent passengers. [R. Rothenberg, *The Bulrush
Murders*, 18]

As mentioned repeatedly throughout this book, the Unaccusative Hypothesis was prompted in part by the observation that the single argument of an unaccusative verb patterns like the object of a transitive verb or the subject of a passive verb with respect to certain phenomena. And in fact, the locative inversion construction is also found with passive verbs, as in (11).

(11) a. From this trench WERE RECOVERED sacrificial burials and
offerings dating to the final days of the Aztec empire. ["Lord of
the Wind: Aztec Offerings from Tlatelolco, Mexico," exhibit
sign]
    b. On the house roof HAS BEEN MOUNTED a copper lightning rod
oxidized green and an H-shaped television aerial, very tall to
catch the signals out here. [J. Updike, *Rabbit Is Rich*, 111]
    c. That spring she monopolized with her class the benches under
the elm from which COULD BE SEEN an endless avenue of dark
pink May trees, and HEARD the trotting of horses in time to the
turning wheels of light carts returning home empty by a hidden
lane from their early morning rounds. [M. Spark, *The Prime of
Miss Jean Brodie*, 104–5]

Although locative inversion is found with prototypical unaccusative and passive verbs, not all intransitive verbs appear to be compatible with this construction.

(12) a. Local residents shop at the supermarket on Main St.
    b. *At the supermarket on Main St. SHOP local residents.

(13) a. Many artists talk in the cafés of Paris.
    b. *In the cafés of Paris TALK many artists.

(14) a. Half a dozen newborn babies smile in the nursery.
    b. *In the nursery SMILE half a dozen newborn babies.

(15) a. Many disgruntled people complain in government offices.
    b. *In government offices COMPLAIN many disgruntled people.

As these examples suggest, the intransitive verbs that are not found in this construction fall into the semantic classes of verbs whose members are unergative. Most are internally caused agentive activity verbs. Finally, transitive verbs are not found in this construction (though see note 2).

(16) a. Archeologists recovered sacrificial burials from this trench. (cf. (11a))
      b. *From this trench RECOVERED archeologists sacrificial burials.
      c. *From this trench RECOVERED sacrificial burials archeologists.

(17) a. An electrician mounted a copper lightning rod on the house roof. (cf. (11b))
      b. *On the house roof MOUNTED an electrician a copper lightning rod.
      c. *On the house roof MOUNTED a copper lightning rod an electrician.

These distributional properties of the locative inversion construction are those expected of an unaccusative diagnostic: passive verbs and unaccusative verbs pattern differently from transitive verbs and unergative verbs. The former are set apart from the latter in having a direct internal argument, but no external argument.

6.2.2 Problematic Characteristics of the Distribution

Despite what the surface distributional characteristics suggest, the set of verbs found in the locative inversion construction is not precisely the expected set if this construction is a diagnostic that picks out all and only the unaccusative verbs. The class of verbs that is selected is both too small, in that not all unaccusative verbs are found in this construction, and too large, in that some purportedly unergative verbs are found in this construction. This pattern is not unfamiliar: we encountered similar patterns with both the resultative construction and the causative alternation. We will approach the comparable problems posed by the locative inversion construction bearing in mind the results of our studies of the other two constructions. We begin by illustrating the two problems for the claim that the locative inversion construction is an unaccusative diagnostic.

First, not all unaccusative verbs are found in the locative inversion construction. In particular, unaccusative verbs of change of state are typically not attested in the construction.

(18) a. *On the top floor of the skyscraper BROKE many windows.

   b. *On the streets of Chicago MELTED a lot of snow.

   c. *On backyard clotheslines DRIED the weekly washing.

Second, some verbs found in the locative inversion construction seem to be unergative verbs, a property that has also been observed and discussed by Hoekstra and Mulder (1990). The examples in (19) involve various types of activity verbs with animate subjects, including verbs that are taken to be prototypical members of the unergative class.

(19) a. Opposite the landing-place stood half-a-dozen donkeys with saddles on their backs and bunches of flowers in their bridles, and around them CHATTERED and SANG as many girls with the silver spadella stuck through their black tresses and a red handkerchief tied across their shoulders. [A. Munthe, *The Story of San Michele*, 1]

   b. On the third floor WORKED two young women called Maryanne Thomson and Ava Brent, who ran the audio library and print room. [L. Colwin, *Goodbye without Leaving*, 54]

   c. Behind the wheel LOUNGED a man uniformed with distinct nautical flavour. [A. W. Upfield, *The Widows of Broome*, 109]

   d. At one end, in crude bunks, SLEPT Jed and Henry ...
      [L. Bromfield, *The Farm*, 18]

   e. He thought of the free-form pool behind the bougainvillea hedge there, clogged with rafts of Styrofoam on which DOZED naked oily bathers lying on their backs wide open to that sun. [A. Marshall, *The Brass Bed*, 228]

Also problematic is the appearance of certain agentive verbs of manner of motion in the locative inversion construction with a locative PP as the preverbal PP.

(20) a. Above them PRANCED the horses on the Parthenon frieze ...
      [P. D. James, *A Taste for Death*, 352]

   b. Rainborough looked at these hangings. ... They were profusely covered with leaves and flowers among which RAN, FLEW, CRAWLED, fled, pursued, or idled an extraordinary variety of animals, birds, and insects. [IMFE 187 (51); cited in H. H. Hartvigson and L. K. Jakobsen 1974:58]

   c. Around her heaved and SHUFFLED the jeaned and T-shirted, apparently semidestitute crowd that peoples transatlantic aircraft. [P. Lively, *Perfect Happiness*, 17]

d. Inside SWAM fish from an iridescent spectrum of colors ...
[J. Olshan, *The Waterline*, 177]

As discussed in section 5.1.1, these verbs are basically unergative but behave like unaccusative verbs in the presence of directional PPs, so that the existence of locative inversion constructions with agentive verbs of manner of motion plus directional PPs, as in (9), would not be unexpected if this construction were an unaccusative diagnostic. However, since agentive verbs of manner of motion generally show unaccusative behavior only in the presence of directional PPs, the existence of locative inversion constructions with agentive verbs of manner of motion involving locative PPs such as those in (20) is problematic.

A survey of the corpus of locative inversion constructions shows another unexpected class of verbs that figures quite prominently in this construction: members of the class of verbs of emission. As discussed in section 4.1.1.1, there is substantial evidence that these verbs are unergative, yet members of this class—especially of some of its subclasses—are quite well represented among the verbs found in the locative inversion construction. We give examples with verbs of light emission in (21), verbs of sound emission in (22), and verbs of substance emission in (23); the corpus contains no attested examples involving the smallest of the subclasses, the verbs of smell emission. Verbs of light emission are probably the best represented, twelve of the twenty-one members of this set listed in B. Levin 1993 being attested.

(21) a. ... through the enormous round portal GLEAMED and GLISTENED a beautiful valley shining under sunset gold reflected by surrounding cliffs. [Z. Grey, *Riders of the Purple Sage*, 53]

b. On one hand FLASHES a 14-carat round diamond; on the other hand SPARKLES an 8-carat stone flanked by the diamond-studded initials WN. [*Philadelphia Inquirer*, "To the Top the Hard Way," 1-D]

c. On the folds of his spotless white clothing, above his left breast, GLITTERED an enormous jewel. [N. Lofts, *Silver Nutmeg*, 460]

(22) a. In the hall TICKED the long-case clock that had been a wedding present from her parents. [P. Lively, *Perfect Happiness*, 173]

b. And in their wake RUMBLED trucks to haul off the remains.
[S. Paretsky, *Burn Marks*, 157]

(23) Over a Bunsen burner BUBBLED a big, earthenware dish of stew.
[M. L'Engle, *A Wrinkle in Time*, 39]

Furthermore, the instances of verbs of sound emission in (22) are found with a locative PP, and there is no reason to associate this use, unlike the use with a directional PP as the preverbal PP seen in (10), with an unaccusative analysis. As unergative verbs found in the locative inversion construction, verbs of emission present a problem for the analysis of locative inversion.

One further easily distinguishable—though problematic—class of intransitive verbs is represented among the locative inversion verbs: a set of verbs that can be described as *verbs of body-internal motion*, a class we have not previously discussed in this book. These verbs describe movements of particular body parts, no displacement of the whole body necessarily being entailed. (Agentive verbs of manner of motion differ from these verbs in describing the movement of the whole body.) Members of this class are listed in (24).

(24) fidget, flap, flutter, gyrate, jiggle, pivot, rock, squirm, stir, sway,
     totter, twitch, wave, wiggle, wobble, wriggle, . . .

These verbs are occasionally found in the locative inversion construction.

(25) Black across the clouds FLAPPED the cormorant, screaming as it
     plummeted downward and disappeared into the wood.
     [M. L'Engle, *The Small Rain*, 332]

(26) . . . and in this lacey leafage FLUTTERED a number of grey birds with
     black and white stripes and long tails. [Z. Grey, *Riders of the Purple
     Sage*, 62]

Like agentive verbs of manner of motion and internally caused verbs of sound emission, these verbs are found in the locative inversion construction both with directional PPs as in (25) and with locative PPs as in (26). It is likely that these verbs resemble agentive verbs of manner of motion and internally caused verbs of sound emission in becoming verbs of directed motion in the presence of a directional phrase, so that the only problematic instances of locative inversion with these verbs are those such as (26) that involve locative PPs.

From the point of view of meaning, it is likely that these verbs are internally caused verbs. Typically, they take animate arguments that may, but need not, exert control over the action. Like other internally caused verbs, they do not regularly show transitive causative uses.[5]

(27) a. *The high heels tottered/wobbled the model.
     b. *The long lecture fidgeted/squirmed/wiggled the class.

If these verbs are indeed internally caused, then, by the Immediate Cause Linking Rule, they should be unergative. In fact, these verbs show certain properties that confirm an unergative classification. They are found in the *X's way* construction, as in (28). In addition, there are *-er* nominals related to these verbs, as in (29).

(28) a. He fidgeted his way out of her confessionals. [N. McKelvy, *Where's Ours?*, 162]

  b. ... people who could not possibly have squirmed their way into the rehearsals ... [Brown Corpus 894223]

  c. ... tapping their way along the pavement in the sort of high-heeled shoes that are supposed to go with attainment ... [A. Brookner, *A Friend from England*, 170]

  d. A heron flapping its way with lazy sweeps emphasised the emptiness as it left the estuary to travel inland. [M. Wesley, *A Sensible Life*, 9]

(29) flapper, rocker, wobbler, wriggler, ...

Thus, the appearance of these verbs in locative inversion constructions with locative PPs is problematic just as the appearance of agentive verbs of manner of motion in such constructions is.

The instances of locative inversion cited in this section involve representatives of several major subclasses of the unergative verbs. Their existence poses a problem if, as has been proposed in previous work, locative inversion is indeed a diagnostic for unaccusativity. One possible solution to this problem is to treat the problematic instances of locative inversion as exceptional. However, the phenomenon appears to be too pervasive for this approach to be viable. For instance, as noted above, just over half of the verbs of light emission listed in B. Levin 1993 are attested in this construction. In addition, a substantial number of agentive verbs of manner of motion occur in this construction without directional phrases. We suspect that an examination of additional corpus data would reveal that other members of these classes are eligible for locative inversion. And, although we do not go into details here, a study of naturally occurring instances of *there*-insertion shows a substantial overlap in the verbs occurring in this construction and locative inversion, also suggesting that the locative inversions with unergative verbs cannot simply be ignored. A second possibility is to propose that these unergative verbs allow a second meaning that is associated with an unaccusative analysis, possibly as a consequence of semantic class shift; a form of the multiple meaning approach is taken by Hoekstra and Mulder (1990), whose paper we discuss in section 6.7.

Here we argue for a third possibility, which involves dismissing the proposal that the locative inversion construction serves as an unaccusative diagnostic and proposing an alternative account of its unaccusative-like properties. We argue that it is the discourse function of the locative inversion construction that restricts the set of verbs attested in it. In section 6.3 we elaborate on the discourse function of the construction and show how it imposes constraints on the verb in the construction. In sections 6.4 and 6.5 we consider in more detail instances of locative inversion with various types of verbs and show how their properties are consistent with the demands imposed by the discourse function of this construction. In particular, we show that the demands of the discourse function can be met by a subclass of unaccusative verbs and, in the appropriate circumstances, by a wide variety of unergative verbs as well. Thus, the ability of a verb to be found in the unaccusative syntactic configuration is neither a necessary, nor a sufficient, condition for it to be found in the locative inversion construction. Then, in section 6.6 we show that the syntactic properties of the construction are not explained by appeal to an unaccusative syntactic analysis. Hence, no motivation remains for postulating an unaccusative analysis of the verbs in this construction.

6.3   The Discourse Function of Locative Inversion

Various researchers have noted that there are restrictions on the verbs found in the locative inversion construction. Bresnan (1993), for instance, proposes a restriction in terms of semantic roles. The locative inversion construction is available only to verbs that take theme and location arguments: "Locative inversion can occur just in case the subject can be interpreted as the argument of which the location, change of location, or direction expressed by the locative argument is predicated—a THEME in the sense of Gruber 1976 or Jackendoff 1972, 1976, 1987" (Bresnan 1993:10–11; small capitals in the original). One consequence of this restriction is that if a verb takes a locative adjunct, then it will not undergo locative inversion.

(30) a. *Among the guests was knitting my friend Rose. (Bresnan 1993, (10b))
      b. *Onto the ground had spit a few sailors. (Bresnan 1993, (11b))
      c. *On the corner smoked a woman. (Bresnan 1993, (14b))

Others, including Bolinger (1977) and Penhallurick (1984), characterize the set of locative inversion verbs as verbs of existence and appearance, a set of verbs that has been singled out as relevant to other linguistic phenomena, including in English *there*-insertion (Kimball 1973), extraposition from NP (Guéron 1980), and sentence accent (Faber 1987); see also Firbas 1966, 1992. There is an overlap between this characterization and Bresnan's, since verbs of existence and appearance generally describe the existence or appearance of a theme at a location, requiring verbs of this type to take precisely the set of arguments that Bresnan specifies.[6] But the real question is why this verb class is relevant to the construction. An answer to this question could provide insight into the wider class of verbs found in locative inversion.

The observed semantic restriction of locative inversion to verbs of existence and appearance has been linked to the discourse function of the construction (Birner 1992, 1994, Bolinger 1977, Bresnan and Kanerva 1989, Bresnan 1993, Guéron 1980, Penhallurick 1984, Rochemont 1986, among others). Although there have been different points of view concerning the precise discourse function of the construction, most commonly it has been said to be used for presentational focus; that is, it is used to introduce the referent of the postverbal NP on the scene (Bresnan 1993, Rochemont 1986, Rochemont and Culicover 1990, among others). On the assumption that the discourse function of locative inversion is presentational focus, Bresnan (1993:22–23) justifies the restriction that the verb be a verb of existence or appearance as follows: "In presentational focus, a scene is set and a referent is introduced on the scene to become the new focus of attention. In the core cases, a scene is naturally expressed as a location, and the referent as something of which location is predicated— hence, a theme. This imposes a natural selection of the ⟨th loc⟩ argument structure." Penhallurick (1984:42) makes a similar observation ("the verbs that do appear in the construction are appropriate for introducing an entity into the discourse"), going on to say that these are the verbs that Firbas (1966) characterizes as verbs expressing "existence or appearance on the scene."

However, based on an extensive corpus study of various types of English inversions, including locative inversion, Birner (1992, 1994) argues that calling the discourse function of this construction "presentational" is in some sense too strong. In particular, she shows that the postverbal NP need not always be discourse-new, as expected if its discourse function were purely presentational. Birner proposes instead that the discourse function of all inversions, locative inversion included, is to link "relatively unfamiliar information to the prior context via the clause-initial placement of information that is relatively familiar in the discourse" (1992:iii). On this analysis, which is supported by her corpus study, the information represented by the postverbal NP in a locative inversion must always be less familiar than the information represented by the NP in the preverbal PP; however, it need not be discourse-new. The presentational function often attributed to locative inversion is subsumed under Birner's characterization of the discourse function of the construction. Yet in that locative inversion does serve to introduce less familiar information in the context of more familiar information, the function of the construction is "presentational" in a broad sense. On the presentational focus account of locative inversion, the placement of the postverbal NP is attributed to its discourse function. The focus position is taken to be a VP-final adjoined position (Rochemont 1986). Although Birner's analysis does not claim that this NP is in presentational focus, there is no reason not to assume that an NP that is less familiar must occupy this special position if the discourse function of the construction is to be satisfied.

As mentioned above, Birner attributes a broader discourse function to the construction, which subsumes the presentational focus function. Thus, although verbs of existence and appearance are still expected to number among the locative inversion verbs, the class of locative inversion verbs might actually be larger. In fact, Birner further argues that "the verbs appearing in this construction represent evoked or inferrable information in context, and therefore contribute no new (i.e., discourse-new) information to the discourse" (1992:196), continuing "with the caveat that 'context' here appears to include the entire inversion as well as the prior linguistic and situational context" (1992:203–4). Stating this restriction somewhat differently, Birner, adopting a term introduced by Hartvigson and Jakobsen (1974), describes the verb in the locative inversion construction as "informationally light." The constraint on the verb follows from the discourse function of the construction. Presumably, if a verb in the locative inversion construction did contribute information that was not predictable from context, it would detract from the newness of the information conveyed by the postverbal NP. The discourse function of the construction would not be satisfied, and that instance of the construction would be excluded.

The restriction that the verb in a locative inversion be informationally light in context means that some types of verbs will be favored in this construction, but that quite a large range of verbs might be attested if the context could be appropriately manipulated. As we discuss in section 6.5, this aspect of the analysis explains why so many unergative verbs are found in the construction.

Here we turn back to the observation that the canonical locative inversion verbs are verbs of existence and appearance. Such verbs are inherently informationally light since they add no information to that provided by the preverbal PP, which, by setting a scene, suggests that something will exist on that scene; therefore, these verbs are expected in the locative inversion construction. In fact, verbs of existence can often be replaced by the copula without a noticeable change in sentence meaning, and Hoekstra and Mulder (1990) even describe locative constructions as copular constructions. There is another striking property of verbs of existence and appearance that contributes to their informational lightness: they typically have no lexicalized manner component. If these verbs did have a manner component, then they would not qualify as informationally light. As we will show in section 6.5, when a verb that does lexicalize a manner component is found in a locative inversion, certain constraints surface on the kind of postverbal NP that can appear in the construction. Roughly speaking, the postverbal NP must be chosen to counterbalance the effect of the verb's manner component, thus making the verb informationally light in context.

By characterizing the class of verbs found in the locative inversion construction as verbs of existence and appearance, many studies have excluded verbs of disappearance from the construction. On our account, there is no explicit ban on verbs of disappearance, although their absence does receive an explanation. Given the discourse function of the construction, it is unlikely that verbs of disappearance will be found in the construction. Usually, an entity whose disappearance is being described is likely to be central to the discourse and not discourse-new. However, if the discourse context could be appropriately manipulated, a verb of disappearance should be found in this construction. In fact, this prediction receives support from an instance of locative inversion with the verb *die;* we discuss this example further in note 8. (See also Kimball 1973 for a description of how the *there*-insertion construction might be manipulated to accommodate a verb of disappearance.)

We assume that the requirement that the verb be informationally light explains the virtual absence of transitive verbs from the locative inversion construction. Typically, in a sentence with a transitive verb new information about the subject is conveyed by the verb and object together. It is unlikely that the subject of such a sentence will represent the least familiar information, as the discourse function of the construction requires. (Such a sentence is likely to be what Guéron (1980) calls a "predication" rather than a "presentational" sentence.) The few reported or constructed instances of locative inversions with transitive verbs involve fixed phrases such as *take place* and *take root*, which have the type of meaning associated with a verb of existence. It is not surprising given the discourse function of the construction that only transitive verbs that participate in such phrases are found in locative inversion, and only when they are found as part of these phrases.[7]

Bresnan (1993) questions whether the discourse constraint on locative inversion can be formulated in terms of informational lightness. She suggests that the contrast in (31) and (32) involving the presence or absence of a cognate object cannot be explained by discourse considerations, writing that "it is hard to see how the cognate object *dance* lessens the informational lightness of (133b) [= (32b)], compared to (132b) [= (31b)]" (1993:63).

(31) a.   The women danced around the fire.

   b.   Around the fire danced the women. (Bresnan 1993:63, (132))

(32) a.   The women danced dances around the fire.

   b.   *Around the fire danced dances the women. (Bresnan 1993:63, (133))

In (32b), J. Bresnan (personal communication) notes that she has avoided a definite object precisely in order to affect the informational content of the sentence as little as possible. However, even the choice of an indefinite plural cognate object may well reduce informational lightness, since such an object gives the sentence an iterative derived aspectual interpretation that is lacking in (31). Although it might appear that cognate objects do not contribute new information, they in fact affect the aspectual interpretation of a sentence and semantically are best characterized as "result objects" (Macfarland 1994a, 1994b). Thus, it appears that the absence of cognate objects from locative inversion does not detract from the use of informational lightness in characterizing the discourse function of the construction.

6.4   Evidence from Various Verb Classes

In this section we provide further support for the restriction that the verb in the locative inversion construction be informationally light in context.

We limit ourselves in this section to examining the locative inversion behavior of various types of unaccusative and passive verbs attested in our corpus, turning to unergative verbs in the following section. Much of the evidence presented involves the disambiguation of verbs with multiple meanings when they are found in the locative inversion construction.

6.4.1 Verbs of Change of State

As demonstrated in chapter 3, most unaccusative verbs belong to one of two broad semantic classes: the verbs of existence and appearance or the externally caused verbs of change of state. These classes are also relevant to the distribution of locative inversion: the prevalence of locative inversions with verbs of existence and appearance contrasts with the virtual absence of locative inversions with externally caused verbs of change of state. For example, the verbs *melt*, *break*, and *dry*, cited in (18) as instances of unaccusative verbs not found in the locative inversion construction, are all externally caused verbs of change of state (although special circumstances that allow some of these verbs to be found in this construction are discussed below). The striking absence of externally caused verbs of change of state can be attributed to their semantic type. The fact that these verbs are not verbs of existence or appearance would be enough to exclude them from locative inversion on many accounts. But more important, the discourse function of locative inversion provides insight into why this should be the case. Externally caused verbs of change of state are not informationally light: by predicating an externally caused, and therefore unpredictable, change of state of their argument, these verbs themselves contribute discourse-new information and hence are not eligible for the construction. Thus, the fact that only a subset of the prototypical unaccusative verbs are found in locative inversion can be linked to its discourse function. Among the unaccusative verbs, only verbs of existence and verbs of appearance are inherently compatible with the discourse function of the construction.

Evidence for the strong restriction against having externally caused verbs of change of state in the locative inversion construction comes from the disambiguation of two verbs of this type when they are found in the construction. These are the verbs *break* and *open*. In addition to its well-known use as a verb of change of state, the verb *break* also has a use as a verb of coming into existence, as in *The war broke* or *The news broke*. What is relevant here is that it is attested in the locative inversion construction only in this sense and not in the change-of-state sense.

(33) "Then BROKE the war, on those awful days in August, and the face
of the world changed—I suppose forever." [E. Phillpotts, *The Red
Redmaynes*, 30]

Besides its change-of-state sense, where it is predicated of doors, windows,
and other apertures, the verb *open* has an appearance sense paraphrasable
as 'become visible'. This verb is found in the locative inversion construction only in this sense, as illustrated in (34).

(34) Underneath him OPENED a cavity with sides two hundred feet high.
[E. Phillpotts, *The Red Redmaynes*, 9]

Yet another instance of disambiguation that can be attributed to the semantic restriction on locative inversion is presented in (35). The verb *pop*
allows several interpretations: a verb-of-sound interpretation (*The corks
were popping*), a change-of-state interpretation (*The balloon popped*), and
a verb-of-appearance interpretation when used in the collocation *pop up*.
In (35) this verb is found in the locative inversion construction precisely in
this collocation.

(35) So up POPPED the name of T. W. Star, who was listed as the
ambassador of the steaming hot island of Nauru, the third smallest
country in the world after Vatican City and Monaco. [*Chicago
Tribune*, "Mr. Senior Diplomat, Sir, Where on Earth Were You?"
2]

Most externally caused verbs of change of state, such as *melt* and *dry*,
do not have an appearance sense, and they are not attested in the locative
inversion construction in the corpus we have collected. It appears that the
majority of externally caused verbs of change of state cannot be reinter-
preted as verbs of appearance. Presumably, this is because there is no
regular process of meaning shift from the class of externally caused verbs
of change of state to the class of verbs of existence and appearance. Thus,
only sporadic instances of such shifts such as the ones discussed here with
the verbs *break*, *open*, and *pop* are observed. What is interesting is that in
each of these instances the shift in meaning is accompanied by a "bleach-
ing" of the verb's meaning so that little more than the notion of appearance is left. In contrast, this property is not typical of the regular meaning
shifts discussed in chapter 5.

In this context, it is interesting to compare externally caused verbs of
change of state with the much smaller class of internally caused verbs of
change of state, discussed previously in sections 3.2.1 and 4.2.1. Internally

caused changes of state differ from externally caused changes of state in often characterizing the existence of an entity. Thus, flowers bloom and old wood decays in the natural course of events, but it is only incidental that glass breaks or that a door opens. This difference is part of what makes some changes of state internally caused and others externally caused. As mentioned earlier, unlike externally caused verbs of change of state, many internally caused verbs of change of state appear to describe states as well as changes of state. We have already pointed out that the internally caused verb of change of state *bloom* is ambiguous between the change-of-state reading 'come to be in bloom' and a state reading 'be in bloom'. Since by their very nature on their 'be in state' interpretation such verbs can characterize the existence of certain entities, they are informationally light; therefore, they would be expected to be compatible with the locative inversion construction. In fact, internally caused verbs of change of state are indeed observed in this construction in their 'be in state' interpretation.

(36) a. In the garden MAY BLOOM the Christmas plant Joel Roberts Poinsett brought back from Mexico during his difficult ambassadorship there in the 1840s. [AP Newswire 1990, 30823236]

   b. Next door, to the east, DECAYS Ablett Village, a half-vacant Camden Housing Authority project with as many windows of particle board as of glass. [*Philadelphia Inquirer*, "Apartment Dwellers Caught in Legal Tangle," 1-B]

An interesting example of the contrasting behavior of internally and externally caused verbs of change of state involves the verb *burn*, which, as discussed in chapter 3, can be used as either an internally caused or an externally caused verb, depending on what it is predicated of. This verb can be predicated of entities that can be consumed by fire such as paper, leaves, and wood. It can also be predicated of entities such as candles, lamps, fires, and other light or heat sources, which are designed to "burn" in order to emit light or heat. The first sense, but not the second, involves external causation. The verb *burn* is found in the locative inversion construction only when it is predicated of things that emit heat or light and whose existence is therefore characterized by burning.

(37) I was a rich boy, on my desk BURNT a thick candle. On the desk next to mine BURNT the thinnest candle in the whole class, for the mother of the boy who sat next to me was very poor. [A. Munthe, *The Story of San Michele*, 97]

There is good reason to believe that the verb *grow* is also an internally caused verb of change of state (B. Levin and Rappaport Hovav, in preparation). Like other internally caused verbs of change of state, this verb has a 'be in state' as well as a change-of-state reading, a property noted by Milsark (1974) in order to illustrate a restriction on the *there*-insertion construction to verbs of existence and appearance. The *there*-insertion construction has a discourse function that is similar, but not identical, to that of locative inversion (Bolinger 1977, Birner and Ward 1993, Ward and Birner 1993, among others), and the relevance of verbs of existence and appearance to this construction is explicitly stated by Kimball in describing the distribution of *there*-insertion: "the existential *there* can appear with a sentence if it expresses coming into being of some object, where this coming into being can include coming into the perceptual field of the speaker" (1973:265). Milsark (1974) points out that certain verbs are ambiguous between a change-of-state interpretation and an existence interpretation. For example, he cites the verb *grow*, which has both an existence interpretation, where it means 'live rootedly', as in (38a), and a change-of-state interpretation, as in (38b), where it means 'increase in size or maturity'.

(38) a. A plum tree grows in my backyard. ('live rootedly')
     b. Corn grows very slowly in Massachusetts. ('increase in size or maturity'; Milsark 1974:250, (11))

What Milsark points out is that when this verb is found in the *there*-insertion construction, as in (39), the only interpretation available is the existence interpretation, 'live rootedly'. The same type of disambiguation is observed when this verb appears in the locative inversion construction, as shown in (40a).

(39) There GREW some corn in our garden last year. ('live rootedly'; Milsark 1974:250, (14))

(40) a. In our garden GREW a very hardy and pest-resistant variety of corn. ('live rootedly')
     b. *In Massachusetts GROWS corn very slowly. ('increase in size or maturity')

This pattern of disambiguation is consistent with the discourse function of the construction: by contributing the information that the corn is getting taller and maturing the change-of-state sense of the verb is not informationally light. On the other hand, like other internally caused verbs of change of state, this verb has an existence sense, and it is found in the locative inversion construction in this sense.

The verb *grow* is one of the ten most frequently occurring verbs in our corpus of locative inversions; there are thirty-five tokens with this verb. Of the tokens that are predicated of plants, none involves the change-of-state interpretation. Of the remaining tokens, a few represent a third, extended sense of *grow* that might be paraphrased as 'develop' or 'come to be'; this sense is not predicated of plants. This sense qualifies as a verb-of-appearance sense, and it is also observed in the locative inversion construction.

(41) a. The hate filled Ellen then, and from that time GREW up in her a love for vengeance that would mark her life, a cruelty that gave her strength, a knife she always held close to her body. [M. Gordon, *The Other Side*, 94]

   b. In her GREW the conviction that a resolution to the problem would be found.

The presence of the particle *up* following the verb in (41a) emphasizes the telicity associated with the appearance sense, serving to disambiguate the verb.

6.4.2 Verbs of Emission

Under certain circumstances verbs of emission can be used in an appearance sense, and they are found in locative inversion in this sense, which has not been previously discussed and which is distinct from the sense discussed earlier in this chapter. Verbs of emission are often thought of as single-argument verbs, but in fact they are in some sense dyadic, taking as arguments the emitter and what is emitted. This observation is most evident with the verbs of substance emission. Most commonly, verbs of emission take the emitter as the subject as in (42a), the emittee being optionally expressed as the object. Some verbs of emission, particularly verbs of substance emission, allow an alternative realization of their arguments in which what is emitted is the surface subject, and the emitter is expressed in a *from* phrase, as in (42b).

(42) a. The bottle oozed (oil).
   b. Oil oozed from the bottle.

We propose that (42b) involves an unaccusative use of the verb. By the Existence Linking Rule, the emittee would be the internal argument, since it "appears" or "comes to exist" by virtue of being emitted. This mapping allows the emittee to be uniformly realized as an internal argument in both available realizations of the arguments of these verbs. There is also evidence for the unaccusative analysis of the emittee subject use from Italian auxiliary selection. In Italian at least some verbs of emission exhibit a similar ambiguity, as shown in (43) with the verb of sound emission *suonare* 'ring/sound'.

(43) a. Ha suonato il   campanello.
        has rung   the bell
        'The bell rang.'
     b. È appena suonata mezzanotte.
        is just   rung   midnight
        'It just struck midnight.'

This verb takes the auxiliary *avere* 'have' when it takes the emitter as subject, as in (43a), but it takes the unaccusative auxiliary *essere* 'be' when it takes the sound emitted as subject, as in (43b).

What is more relevant here is that verbs of emission would then be expected in the locative inversion construction in this second, emittee subject use since it involves the appearance on the scene of the emittee. In fact, our corpus attests instances of locative inversion that involve this sense of verbs of sound emission.

(44) a. From the speaker BOOMS the voice of Fox's ad sales head in Chicago. "Sold out!" [C. Stauth, "The Network Henhouse," 63]
     b. Out [of his throat] BOOMED the great vocal bell. [E. Bowen, *Eva Trout*, 251]

The presence of these verbs in locative inversion in this sense is consistent with the restriction that the verb be informationally light in context because sounds come to be on the scene by virtue of being emitted. Thus, by its very nature this sense of the verb allows the presentation of less familiar information via the postverbal NP in the context of more familiar information (the NP in the preverbal PP). We return in section 6.5 to the other, more often recognized sense of verbs of emission, which, as already mentioned, is problematic for the unaccusative analysis of locative inversion.

6.4.3 Verbs of Spatial Configuration

Another type of disambiguation that is found in the locative inversion construction involves verbs of spatial configuration such as *lie*, *sit*, and *stand.* Once again the disambiguation can be shown to arise because of the restriction that the verb in the locative inversion construction be informationally light. As discussed in chapter 3, in English these verbs typically show three noncausative senses: (i) the simple position sense, as in (45a), (ii) the maintain position sense, as in (45b), and (iii) the assume position sense, as in (45c).

(45) a. The book was sitting on the table.
     b. Sandy was sitting on the rickety old chair.
     c. Sandy sat hurriedly.

As noted by Bresnan (1993:13), when these verbs are found in the locative inversion construction, they do not allow the assume position interpretation; this is demonstrated by the nonambiguity of (46), as contrasted with the ambiguity of its noninverted counterpart in (47).

(46) Beside her SAT a little girl who bore a striking resemblance to Top
     o' the Evenin', her head a bit large and her eyes dark and piercing.
     [R. Levitsky, *The Love That Kills*, 209]

(47) A little girl sat beside her.

This observation is expected given the restriction that the verb in locative inversion be informationally light in context. In the assume position interpretation these verbs assert a property of their argument; thus, they present new information about their argument that is not predictable from context. Animate entities can assume one of a number of spatial configurations, and hence these verbs do not qualify as informationally light. We would expect that these verbs should be found in the locative inversion construction only in the simple position interpretation, the interpretation associated with a nonagentive, though not necessarily inanimate, argument. (In Bresnan's terms, these verbs take the ⟨*th loc*⟩ argument structure only on the simple position interpretation, but take only an agent argument on the assume position interpretation.) As we argued in section 3.3.3, in the simple position interpretation these verbs are basically verbs of existence and thus mean little more than 'be located'. A given simple position verb might appear to contribute information about the spatial orientation of the located entity since it lexicalizes a particular spatial configuration. But actually, the choice of verb is determined by properties of the located entity, and in this sense the verb is predictable from properties inherent to this entity and does not contribute information that could not be inferred from the postverbal NP. In those instances where an entity might be found in more than one spatial configuration—say, because it is animate—the PP and context often provide information that reduces the information that the verb contributes.

Many of the simple position verbs are attested in the locative inversion construction; the most common are *hang*, *lie*, *sit*, and *stand*. An examination of the tokens we have collected involving these verbs shows that they may be predicated of both inanimates, as in (48), and animates, as in (49).

(48) a. Behind a pale brick fence on the outskirts of the Iraqi village of Qurna SITS a small, gnarled apple tree with a double trunk. [E. Sciolino, "Iraq Yearns for Greatness—and an Identity," 1]

   b. On his lap LAY a vacation brochure from the Manitoba tourist bureau ... [E. S. Connell, *Mr. Bridge*, 224]

   c. On the kitchen dresser HUNG the quirkily-shaped pottery mug made by Tabitha in the school art class. [P. Lively, *Perfect Happiness*, 173]

(49) a. Outside some of the shops SAT old people gathered around wooden tables. [F. Cheong, *The Scent of the Gods*, 153]

   b. At the foot of the mountain SQUATTED two of Johnno's countrymen. [A. W. Upfield, *The Widows of Broome*, 175]

   c. On the floor before an open suitcase KNELT a now familiar figure. [M. Allingham, *The Fashion in Shrouds*, 157]

Our own intuition is that when these verbs are predicated of animates, they do not have the maintain position sense, the third sense, which is available only when these verbs are predicated of agentive animates. It is likely that this sense is ruled out for the same reasons as the assume position sense: the verb does not qualify as informationally light in context in these instances.

6.4.4 Verbs of Motion

Verbs of directed motion are well represented among locative inversion verbs, whether these are verbs of inherently directed motion such as *arrive*, *come*, and *go* or agentive verbs of manner of motion used as verbs of directed motion. We have found more tokens of the locative inversion construction with the verb *come* than with any verb other than *be;* roughly one-sixth of the examples collected involve *come*. As there is much independent evidence that verbs of directed motion are unaccusative, it would not be surprising that these verbs are attested in the locative inversion construction given an unaccusative analysis of the construction.

On our analysis, the appearance of these verbs in locative inversion would be sanctioned not by their unaccusativity, but by their ability to be used in conformance with the discourse function of the construction. We need to show, therefore, that these verbs are informationally light in context. We propose that they are found in locative inversions only when they can be viewed as verbs describing appearance on the scene.

We begin by examining the verb *come*, which, given its frequency, deserves its own discussion. As a verb of motion, the verb *come* takes a nonabstract NP, whether animate or inanimate, as its theme argument, as illustrated in (7a), repeated here.

(50) ... out of the house CAME a tiny old lady and three or four
enormous people ... [L. Bromfield, *The Farm*, 1]

This verb of inherently directed motion lexicalizes a particular deictic orientation for the motion. Simplifying somewhat, the verb *come* describes motion onto the scene identified with or by the speaker. Because of this deictic orientation, this verb naturally can be used to describe appearance on the scene, and thus provides a context for the presentation of less familiar information via the postverbal NP in the context of more familiar information (the NP in the preverbal PP). But in many of its uses in our corpus of locative inversions, *come* takes as its argument an inanimate abstract NP—an NP that is not capable of moving or being moved —as in (51); in these uses the NP in the preverbal PP is often abstract as well.

(51) The sweetness and the richness is disappearing and instead in their
place COMES a new sourness, an after-taste which may be the wine
or the fetid aftermath of an over-satisfied anticipation. [C. Clewlow,
Keeping the Faith, 64]

In these uses the verb is not used as a verb of motion strictly speaking; it seems simply to describe appearance on the scene, losing any sense of motion, though retaining its telicity. (In fact, one could ask whether this verb and possibly some of the other verbs of inherently directed motion are better viewed as verbs of appearance in all their uses.) The verb *come* acts like little more than a copula; the only extra contribution is a sense of appearance on the scene that is not associated with the copula. The availability of the pure appearance sense of *come* probably follows from the inherent telicity and deictic orientation of this verb. It is likely that the particular deictic orientation of this verb explains why it is so often found in the locative inversion construction and why we have collected almost seven times more tokens for it than for the verb of inherently directed motion *go*, which typically describes movement directed away from the scene identified with or by the speaker.[8]

An examination of the instances of locative inversion with other verbs of inherently directed motion suggests that these verbs can also receive an appearance interpretation in this construction. Consider the following example with the verb *rise*, which does not have a deictic component of meaning, though it does lexicalize an inherent direction:

(52) Out of the trees below them ROSE a large night bird with a great flapping of wings ... [M. L'Engle, *The Small Rain*, 331]

Our claim is that these verbs are used with an appearance interpretation in the locative inversion construction. In principle, such verbs can be used to describe motion into or out of the scene; however, these verbs are not found in locative inversions when what is being described is movement out of the scene. For instance, it is clear that (52) describes motion onto the scene: even though the prepositional phrase describes the source of the motion, the scene is set outside of the source, as is made clear within the prepositional phrase itself (*out of the trees below them*). The context of the example shows that the postverbal NP is less familiar than the NP in the preverbal PP, as required for the discourse function of the construction to be met. The restriction to an appearance interpretation shows that being a verb of inherently directed motion is not sufficient for these verbs to appear in the construction; for the same reason, this shows that unaccusativity is not sufficient to license their presence in the construction.

This observation extends to the directed motion sense of agentive verbs of manner of motion. As mentioned in section 6.2.2, the existence of instances of the locative inversion construction involving agentive verbs of manner of motion used with a directional phrase is not incompatible with an unaccusative analysis of locative inversion; in fact, their existence has been taken as evidence for this analysis, as in Coopmans 1989. As we discussed in chapter 5, agentive verbs of manner of motion may have a directed motion sense; this use, which is identifiable by the presence of a directional PP, receives an unaccusative analysis. Again it turns out that being a verb of directed motion is not sufficient. The construction must also be used to present less familiar information in the context of more familiar information, and consistent with this the verb itself must be informationally light in context. In fact, there is evidence that in locative inversions with the directed motion sense of agentive verbs of manner of motion, as in those with verbs of inherently directed motion, not only must the postverbal NP be less familiar than the NP in the preverbal PP, but the PP must be chosen to convey appearance on the scene.

A survey of locative inversions with agentive verbs of manner of motion used as verbs of directed motion reveals that these inversions all have an appearance interpretation, suggesting a constraint against using such locative inversions to describe movement out of the scene. This constraint is particularly striking since agentive verbs of manner of motion do not lexicalize a direction of motion, so that in their directed motion sense any information about direction of motion is contributed by the PP. In principle, these verbs could appear with PPs that specify movement either into or out of the scene. Yet a survey of the tokens of locative inversions with agentive verbs of manner of motion plus directional PPs in the corpus shows that they include contexts with goal PPs that clearly describe appearance on the scene, as in (9a) and (9b), as well as in (53).

(53) Into the room WALKED Sylvia Tucker, with Zahid walking behind her like a puppet. [A. Hosain, *Sunlight on a Broken Column*, 52]

But what makes this point in a particularly forceful way is the interpretation that locative inversions receive when one of these verbs is used with a source PP, as in (54). In these sentences the object of the source preposition (or the implied object when none is expressed, as in (54a)) describes the prior location of the postverbal NP.

(54) a. In the climactic scene, the expert, a tiny woman with her hair in a bun, delicately opens the closet door and out RUSHES a wild, screaming, fire-breathing monster ... [T. L. Friedman, *From Beirut to Jerusalem*, 47]

   b. ... from out its hole CRAWLED a gigantic monarch iguana, six feet in length, moving slowly with deceptive sluggishness. [A. W. Upfield, *The Sands of Windee*, 106]

   c. They had scarcely exchanged greetings with each other when out of an open carriage at the gate, STEPPED Mrs. Duff-Scott on her way to that extensive kettledrum which was held in the Exhibition at this hour. [A. Cambridge, *The Three Miss Kings*, 237]

Such examples receive an interpretation in which the relevant scene is not defined by the location described by the object of the preposition, but rather is set outside of this location. It would not be possible to use the examples above if the scene were set inside the closet, the iguana's hole, or the carriage, although corresponding noninverted sentences may be: the sentence *The monster rushed out of the closet* could be used whether the scene was set inside or outside of the closet. In fact, a closer look at locative inversions where such verbs occur with goal PPs shows an analogous effect: the location denoted by the PP must name the current scene. Consider (53), which could not be used if the room were not the current scene.

To summarize, when PPs denoting sources and goals are used with agentive verbs of manner of motion in locative inversions, they are used from a perspective that allows the sentence as a whole to receive an appearance interpretation. Although these verbs describe a manner of motion and thus might be considered to have a component of meaning that could contribute unpredictable information, when they appear in their directed motion sense in a locative inversion the overall appearance interpretation associated with the construction serves to minimize the verb's actual contribution and makes the interpretation of the locative inversion as a whole compatible with its discourse function. More generally, for a verb to be a verb of directed motion, it is not sufficient for it to be found in the locative inversion construction; rather, such a verb must be used to describe appearance on the scene. In this way, the verb in the construction is informationally light in context, allowing the discourse function of the construction to be met by the appropriate choice of preverbal PP and postverbal NP.

To conclude this section, we consider an additional stative sense that some verbs of motion can show. As noted by Jackendoff (1990) and Dowty (1991), among others, certain agentive verbs of manner of motion can be used as verbs describing the location of a physical object with extent, as in *The railway tracks run along the stream*. Verbs of inherently directed motion can also show such senses, as in *The road dropped down into the valley* or *The mountains rise behind the village*. In these instances the verbs are used statively to describe the existence of a physical object at a particular location. The choice of verb depends on finding a fit between properties of the motion characteristic of the verb and properties of the located object. For example, the vertical extension of mountains makes them compatible with the verb *rise*, which lexicalizes motion upward. As a consequence, there is a redundancy between the verb and the located object in these uses, making the verb informationally light. As long as the preverbal PP and the postverbal NP are in the appropriate relation so that the discourse function of the locative inversion construction is met, these verbs should be found in the construction. Indeed, both agentive verbs of manner of motion and verbs of inherently directed motion are observed in the locative inversion construction in such senses.

(55) a. One crossed a little valley through which RAN the brook called Toby's Run. [L. Bromfield, *The Farm*, 137]

    b. On their left, far-distant and hazy, MARCHED a range of impassable-looking mountains. [R. Pilcher, *September*, 193]

(56) a. Before him ASCENDED a gradual swell of smooth stone. [Z. Grey, *Riders of the Purple Sage*, 51]

    b. Behind the house opened a narrow coomb and DESCENDED a road to the dwelling. [E. Phillpotts, *The Red Redmaynes*, 70]

6.4.5 Evidence from Passive Verbs

Given the discourse constraints on the locative inversion construction, only some passive verbs are expected to be found in this construction, even though on an unaccusative analysis all verbal passives would meet its syntactic constraints. In fact, both Bolinger (1977) and Bresnan (1993) discuss restrictions on the passive verbs found in the locative inversion construction. Bresnan, in particular, points out that instances of the locative inversion construction with passive verbs must meet the same restriction on possible verbs as instances of the locative inversion construction with intransitive verbs. Given her statement of the restriction, this means that only passive verbs that have theme and location arguments are eligible. As noted above, we assume that Bresnan's restriction is subsumed under the verb of existence and appearance constraint, which we subsume in turn under the requirement that the verb be informationally light in context. We will show that the passive verbs found in the construction satisfy this requirement.

A survey of the passive verbs found in our corpus of locative inversions reveals several readily identifiable semantic subclasses. These classes are listed in (57), and a locative inversion with a member of each is given in (58).

(57) a. Verbs of putting: display, embed, heap, locate, place, put, range, situate, store, . . .

    b. Verbs of putting in a spatial configuration: hang, lay, mount, perch, seat, suspend, . . .

   c. Verbs of attachment: glue, hook, lace, paste, pin, staple, . . .

   d. Verbs of image impression: engrave, imprint, inscribe, scrawl, scribble, stamp, write, . . .

   e. Verbs of creation: build, carve, cook, erect, . . .

   f. Verbs of perception: discern, glimpse, hear, realize, see, . . .

(58) a. Here and there over Jeff's Station's map WERE PLACED tiny red flags. [A. W. Upfield, *The Sands of Windee*, 124]

     b. Around him WERE HUNG photorealistic paintings of enlarged cash-register receipts . . . [A. Beattie, *Picturing Will*, 73–74]

     c. To each side of the straw-stuffed pack WERE HOOKED the saddle-bags and water-drums. [A. W. Upfield, *Man of Two Tribes*, 37–38]

     d. . . . on either side of the water WERE BUILT the humpies of tree-boughs and bags of bark . . . [A. W. Upfield, *No Footprints in the Bush*, 56]

     e. . . . a badge of yellow on which WERE STAMPED in gold letters the words "Aid to the Committee." [L. Bromfield, *The Farm*, 285]

     f. . . . through the gap COULD BE SEEN a section of the flower garden beyond, a square of hazy blues and greens and golds . . . [P. Lively, *Treasures of Time*, 177]

As might be expected, there are minimal pairs where an intransitive verb and the passive of its transitive causative counterpart (where one exists) are both found in locative inversions. Compare (58b), which uses the passive form of transitive *hang*, with (8c), repeated as (59), which uses intransitive *hang*.

(59) Above the bed HANG two faded prints of men playing polo. [S. Cheever, *Elizabeth Cole*, 70]

Although there are undoubtedly locative inversions based on verbal passives, the majority of locative inversions with passive verbs appear to us to involve adjectival passives. Unfortunately, the passive locative inversions do not have any of the explicit diagnostic features of adjectival passives discussed by Wasow (1977). For instance, it is well known that both adjectival passives and verbal passives can be found with the verb *be*, so the passive auxiliary provides no clue. Our classification of certain passives as adjectival, therefore, is based on our assessment of their meaning, which in many instances is the "statal" interpretation associated with adjectival passives, as in (58d) and (58e). These two examples do not describe the actual process of building or stamping, as a verbal passive would. Instead, they describe the results: the existence of the created artifacts. In contrast, the following examples seem to be more likely candidates for verbal passives.

(60) a. Then WAS COMMITTED that great crime, memorable for its singular atrocity, memorable for the tremendous retribution by which it was followed. [CLIVE, 513, b.; cited in Poutsma 1904:252]

  b. ... and from under it WAS THRUST forth a narrow, snake-like head from the jaws of which flickered a long, fine, blue tongue. [A. W. Upfield, *Wings above the Diamantina*, 109]

Below we will show that the discourse function of the locative inversion construction provides insight into why so many locative inversions with passive verbs tend to involve adjectival passives.

We turn now to a consideration of how passive locative inversions meet the discourse function of the construction. Bresnan (1993) notes that if passivization suppresses the agent argument of a verb, the passive form of a verb with agent, theme, and location arguments qualifies for locative inversion, since it has the argument structure ⟨*th loc*⟩—the argument structure that is associated with a verb of existence or appearance. This characterization alone suggests that a passive verb should be compatible with the discourse function of locative inversion. Nevertheless, we would like to consider in more detail exactly how passivization creates verbs that satisfy the discourse condition we have stated on verbs in locative inversion: that the verb should be informationally light in context. Putting aside for the moment the verbs of perception, the subclasses of transitive verbs found in the passive in the locative inversion construction all can be described as verbs of causing something to exist or appear. A survey of the attested verbs confirms that they have meanings that can be characterized as 'cause to come to be' or 'cause to be'—it is arguable which,[9] but either meaning is consistent with the requirement that the verb be informationally light. We consider some of these subclasses in more detail.

A prominent subclass of verbs found in the passive in locative inversion consists of verbs whose meaning involves a notion of creation, including a few that are inherently verbs of creation such as *build* and *erect;* a number that have extended senses as verbs of creation, primarily verbs of image impression, as in (61); and some drawn from various other semantic classes, such as the cooking verb *bake*, to which we return below.

(61) a. Across the face of the top letter WAS WRITTEN in The Old Man's
         handwriting, "not to be forgotten." [L. Bromfield, *The Farm*,
         262]
     b. He wears a silver ring he bought in Egypt—it cost all of forty
        cents, he told me—and on it ARE ENGRAVED three pyramids.
        [G. Ehrlich, *Heart Mountain*, 266]

Verbs of creation are accomplishment verbs. As mentioned in chapter 3,
such verbs have a complex event structure consisting of a process and a
result state. Verbs of creation are verbs of causing something to come to
exist, and, therefore, the result state describes the existence of the created
object at some location. Passivization "removes" the agent argument of a
verb, but, even more important, the adjectival passive of an accomplishment verb simply describes the state resulting from the action described by
that verb. With adjectival passives of verbs of creation the result state is a
state of existence, precisely the type of meaning that makes the adjectival
passive an appropriate predicate for a locative inversion construction. It
is not surprising, therefore, that such adjectival passives are often found
in locative inversions.

Verbs of putting, verbs of putting in a spatial configuration, and verbs
of attachment, like verbs of creation, are accomplishment verbs, and like
them will have a complex event structure consisting of a process and a
result state. With these verbs, the result state describes the attained location of some physical object. Given this, in the adjectival passive form
these verbs are also expected in locative inversions.

There are verbs with more than one sense that are disambiguated when
they appear in locative inversion in the passive. The nature of the disambiguation lends support to our characterization of the types of verbs
expected in locative inversion. Some verbs have a creation sense, in addition to another sense that appears to be more basic. When these verbs are
found in the locative inversion construction, they show only the creation
sense. Consider, for example, a verb like *scratch*. This verb can describe an
activity involving a particular type of contact by impact, taking as its
direct object a surface (location), as in *I scratched the record*, or it can be
used as an accomplishment verb to describe the creation of a particular
image through that type of contact. The creation sense is an extended
sense: the contact results in the creation of marks—possibly words or
images—on a surface. (Since creation senses are regularly associated with
verbs of this type, it is possible that this sense may arise through a lexical
rule of the type described in chapter 5, although nothing in our discussion

in this section hinges on this.) The verb *scratch* is found in the locative inversion construction only in the creation sense.

(62) ... on it [= the knife handle] HAD BEEN SCRATCHED a symbol that looked like a tick-tack-toe box with the extensions on the left and the top missing. [S. Dunlop, *Karma*, 41]

It does not seem possible to construct a locative inversion that involves the contact-by-impact sense. Consider, for example, (63).

(63) On the old wooden tabletop HAD BEEN SCRATCHED a record.

This sentence cannot receive the interpretation that a (phonograph) record got scratched through contact with an old table; the only possible interpretation is a verb-of-creation interpretation in which a written record has been cut into the tabletop. The unavailability of the contact-by-impact sense can be attributed to the verb's not being informationally light in this sense; see the discussion below of transitive verbs that are not found in passive locative inversions. When verbs that are not basically verbs of creation are found in locative inversions in a creation sense, the additional information content of the verb that can be attributed to its basic sense is predictable because the basic sense describes a process used to create the particular artifact that is denoted by the postverbal NP.

Similar examples can be constructed from the subset of verbs of image impression such as *engrave* and *inscribe*, which show alternative expressions of their arguments (see B. Levin 1993) as in (64).

(64) a. The jeweler engraved the name on the ring.
     b. The jeweler engraved the ring with the name.

What is interesting is that when these verbs are found in locative inversions, the locative inversion construction is based on the variant with the locative PP (that is, (64a)). The created object is expressed in both variants of the alternation, but a locative inversion based on the *with* variant would contain the created image or writing, which is necessarily discourse-new, as the preverbal PP, thus violating the discourse function of the construction requiring that the NP in the preverbal PP be less familiar.

The presence of verbs of perception in passive locative inversions may seem harder to explain, but these verbs can also be shown to be construable as verbs of existence in the adjectival passive. In their active use these verbs describe the act of perceiving a state or an event. Frequently, the state asserts the existence of a physical object at some location. In the adjectival passive these verbs describe the fact that some entity or event impinges (adjectival passive) or comes to impinge (verbal passive) on the senses, and by virtue of this it is possible to infer that the entity exists at some location or that the event has taken place. Consequently, in the passive these verbs can be seen as having an appearance or existence interpretation, sanctioning their appearance in locative inversions.

(65) a. From the dining-room now COULD BE HEARD the sounds of Hoovering. [R. Pilcher, *September*, 514]

    b. ... through the gap COULD BE SEEN a section of the flower garden beyond, a square of hazy blues and greens and golds ... [P. Lively, *Treasures of Time*, 177]

The importance of the appearance interpretation in verbal passives with verbs of perception can be seen in (65a), where, as in the examples with verbs of directed motion, a source PP is possible only on the interpretation that the scene is set outside of the location described in that PP.

Some transitive verbs cannot be viewed as having a lexical semantic representation that embeds a state of existence. Consequently, their passive forms are less likely to yield passives that are informationally light in context, and instances of passive locative inversion with such verbs are much worse than the attested examples, as the following attempts to construct such examples show:

(66) a. *In the kitchen WERE CHOPPED pounds and pounds of mushrooms.

    b. *To the tourists WERE SOLD the most garish souvenirs.

    c. *At that movie WERE FRIGHTENED a lot of little children.

    d. *In that museum WERE ADMIRED many Impressionist paintings.

A subset of the excluded verbs should be singled out. Consistent with the discourse function of the construction is the apparent exclusion from locative inversion of the passive forms of the causative externally caused verbs of change of state such as transitive *dry*, *melt*, and *break*.

(67) a. *On the top floor of the skyscraper WERE BROKEN many windows.

    b. *On the streets of Chicago WAS MELTED a lot of snow.

    c. *On backyard clotheslines WAS DRIED the weekly washing.

The passive forms of these verbs are not informationally light, just like their intransitive counterparts. Again, the exclusion of these verbs from locative inversions is brought out by instances of disambiguation. Some verbs, including many cooking verbs, can be used as verbs of change of state or verbs of creation (Atkins, Kegl, and B. Levin 1988). Thus, the verb *bake* can be used to describe a particular change of state, as in *The cook baked the potatoes and apples*, or to describe the creation of baked goods through that change of state, as in *The cook baked ten loaves of rye bread.* Interestingly, the sole attested example of a verb of cooking in the locative inversion construction, cited in (68), involves the creation sense: the postverbal NP is a conjunction, whose components name a range of baked goods rather than their source (dough or batter).

(68) In it [= the kitchen] WERE COOKED the puddings, the pies, the cakes, the waffles, and the pancakes which filled the table meal after meal. [L. Bromfield, *The Farm*, 125]

It is also significant that the locative phrase in this sentence refers to the kitchen rather than the oven. If the locative phrase referred to the oven, it is more likely that the emphasis would be on the change of state from dough or batter to baked goods rather than on the creation of the baked goods. When the locative phrase refers to the kitchen, the shift in emphasis is not quite so likely. In fact, informants judge (69) to be worse than (68).

(69) In the oven WERE COOKED the pies, the cakes, the breads, and the cookies which filled the table meal after meal.

6.4.6 Summary

The discourse function of the locative inversion construction explains why some unaccusative verbs are favored in locative inversion and why others are not found at all. In this section we looked closely at a variety of unaccusative and passive verbs and showed that they are found in the locative inversion construction when they are informationally light; being unaccusative or passive is not sufficient. We also showed that the discourse function of the construction explains certain instances of disambiguation. In the next section we investigate why some apparently unergative verbs are found in the locative inversion construction.

6.5 Unergative Verbs in Locative Inversion

As the discussion in section 6.2.2 shows, a variety of apparently unergative verbs can turn up in the locative inversion construction. These include internally caused verbs of emission, agentive verbs of manner of motion,

verbs of body-internal motion, and a scattering of other activity verbs
such as *work*, *chatter*, *sing*, and *doze*. These data are of particular interest
because on the one hand, the fact that more members of some unergative
subclasses than others are found in locative inversions suggests the existence of some constraints, but on the other hand, members of enough
distinct subclasses are found in the construction to cast doubt on the
feasibility of referring to particular subclasses in the statement of any
constraints on their occurrence.

We begin by looking at a solution to the unergative verb dilemma that
appeals to a notion of semantic class shift along the lines used to solve
other problems posed by variable behavior verbs in chapter 5. That is, we
could posit a process that turns certain unergative verbs into verbs of
existence; by virtue of this additional semantic class membership, these
verbs will be classified as unaccusative on this sense. In the instances of
meaning shifts that we described in chapter 5, it was possible to formulate
rules that detail how verbs from one class map into a second class; however, it is very difficult to come up with comparable rules for locative
inversion. Because of the wide variety of unergative verbs found in locative inversion, any statement of meaning shift would have to contain an
elaborate disjunction of verb classes (internally caused verbs of emission,
verbs of body-internal motion, agentive verbs of manner of motion, and
miscellaneous other agentive activity verbs). If the set of unergative verbs
found in this construction is not to be characterized disjunctively, then we
are left with a very broad and potentially not very informative characterization of the class: the class of internally caused monadic predicates. In
principle, then, any internally caused monadic verb would be a candidate
for locative inversion, since this is the common semantic denominator of
the problem verbs. Yet this broad common denominator needs to be
balanced against the observation that verbs from some subclasses of the
internally caused verbs are more likely to be found in locative inversion
than verbs from other subclasses. The meaning shift approach does not
provide any insight into this observation. Presumably, the variation in
distribution could be attributed to specific aspects of the meaning of individual verbs that license their occurrence in locative inversion. Ideally,
the factors that determine the differential distribution within the classes
attested in locative inversion should also be the factors that exclude most
activity verbs from the construction. Nor does the broad characterization
that would be necessary allow for the other factors, such as the relationship between the postverbal NP and the verb, which we will show in this

section to be important to determining whether locative inversion is possible. In the instances of meaning shifts we discussed in chapter 5, the mappings between classes were much cleaner; they were not dependent on such additional factors. Furthermore, all the instances of meaning shifts in chapter 5 involved a change in telicity, whereas verbs do not show a change in telicity when they are found in the locative inversion construction (unless it is independently attributable to the factors detailed in the meaning shifts described in chapter 5). For these reasons, we do not feel that a meaning shift account is appropriate for locative inversion.

If, on the other hand, the unergative verbs in the locative inversion construction were used in such a way that the discourse function of the construction were met, then there would be no reason to resort to such a meaning shift. In fact, the explanation in terms of the discourse function actually does all the work, since, as we show in section 6.6, there is no compelling syntactic reason to assume that the locative inversion construction involves unaccusative syntax. What would it take for a locative inversion with an unergative verb to satisfy the construction's discourse function? The postverbal NP would have to be less familiar than the NP in the preverbal PP. In addition, the verb must not contribute information that is newer than the postverbal NP; that is, it must be informationally light in context. To meet this requirement, an unergative verb, like a verb of existence, cannot contribute additional information beyond the fact that the entity it is predicated of exists. The key to explaining how this is possible with unergative verbs comes from the observation, which we substantiate below, that in locative inversions with unergative verbs the verb and postverbal NP are mutually predictable and therefore conform to the discourse function of the construction.

Following proposals by Bolinger (1977) for several English constructions including locative inversion and by Babby (1978, 1980) in reference to the genitive of negation in Russian, which also shows similar properties, we propose that the informational lightness requirement can be satisfied if the activity or process that the verb describes is characteristic of the entity the verb is predicated of (see also Birner 1992). Babby writes that the "lexical verbs used in ES's [= existential sentences] normally denote the subject noun's most typical action from the point of view of the speaker, i.e., they denote the action through which human beings identify or encounter the subject noun's referent in the real world" (1978:27). Similarly, Bolinger writes, "Fairly common is the use of a verb that represents a normal or customary action of a thing to suggest that the thing is there" (1977:97), citing examples of VP-inversion, including those in (70), though his observation also extends to locative inversion, which he discusses in the same paper.

(70) a.   Waving gaily was a bright flag. (Bolinger 1977:97, (55))
     b.   ?Burning merrily was an enemy flag. (Bolinger 1977:97, (56))

Thus, waving is the normal motion associated with a flag, so that it in some sense characterizes the existence of the flag. The verb, then, can be used simply to characterize that a flag exists without asserting anything more about it. In contrast, burning in the 'be consumed by fire' sense intended in (70b) does not characterize the existence of a flag; hence the oddness of this example. The use of *burn* in (70b) is an externally caused use. As already discussed, this verb also has an internally caused use when it is predicated of light and heat sources. In this use the verb describes the emission of light or heat, and, indeed, a VP-inversion that uses the internally caused sense of the verb, such as *Burning slowly was a tall beeswax candle*, is perfectly acceptable. In fact, Firbas, in more general studies of presentational contexts, observes that the relationship between the verb and its argument is often one of "semantic affinity" (1966:244, 1992:60).

In the remainder of the section we show that in locative inversions with unergative verbs, the activity or process that the verb describes is characteristic of the entity that the verb is predicated of. We discuss two properties of the locative inversions in our corpus that support this proposal: (i) the unergative verbs found in the locative inversion construction include those that impose strict selectional restrictions on their argument and (ii) even those verbs that do not do this are found in locative inversions with a restricted range of arguments. The second property has not to our knowledge been discussed elsewhere; the other has been discussed, but in more limited contexts. To conclude the section, we comment on the proposal that verbs in this construction that take animate subjects are in some sense "deagentivized."

Although the unergative verbs observed in locative inversions are drawn from different subclasses of the unergative class, these verbs share a common property, which can be shown to correlate with the observation that verbs from some of these subclasses are more likely to be found in locative inversions than verbs from others. Many of the unergative verbs found in locative inversions, particularly the verbs of emission and verbs of body-internal motion, impose very strict selectional restrictions on their arguments as discussed in section 3.2.1, and, probably related to this, many of them are the types of verbs that describe the characteristic activities of the NPs that meet their selectional restrictions. Consequently, when these verbs are found in the locative inversion construction, there is a relationship of mutual predictability between the verb and the argument.

We illustrate this relationship first with verbs of body-internal motion. For instance, the typical things that flutter are flags and bird wings, and conversely, the typical thing that flags and bird wings do is flutter. And in fact, the occurrences of *flutter* in the locative inversion corpus have flags and birds as their postverbal NPs.

(71) a. ... before the front there stretched a plateau whereon stood a flagstaff and spar, from the point of which FLUTTERED a red ensign. [E. Phillpotts, *The Red Redmaynes*, 70]
b. ... in this lacey leafage FLUTTERED a number of grey birds with black and white stripes and long tails. [Z. Grey, *Riders of the Purple Sage*, 62]

Returning to Bolinger's example (70a), the only naturally occurring instance of the verb *wave* that we have found involves its being predicated of a clump of tall thin plants, which is consistent with the requirement that the verb describe a characteristic activity: tall thin plants in windy places wave.

(72) Out of the precipice behind WAVED a profusion of feathery rock-lilies ... [R. Praed, *Outlaw and Lawmaker*, 259]

The relationship of mutual predictability extends to verbs of light emission and sound emission. Only things like jewels, certain metals, and glass flash, sparkle, or glitter. Similarly, clocks tick, but trucks rumble.

(73) a. On one hand FLASHES a 14-carat round diamond; on the other hand SPARKLES an 8-carat stone flanked by the diamond-studded initials WN. [*Philadelphia Inquirer*, "To the Top the Hard Way," 1-D]
b. On the folds of his spotless white clothing, above his left breast, GLITTERED an enormous jewel. [N. Lofts, *Silver Nutmeg*, 460]

(74) a. In the hall TICKED the long-case clock that had been a wedding present from her parents. [P. Lively, *Perfect Happiness*, 173]
b. And in their wake RUMBLED trucks to haul off the remains. [S. Paretsky, *Burn Marks*, 157]

As verbs describing characteristic activities of their argument's referent, these verbs do not contribute new information and qualify as informationally light in context, explaining their occurrence in locative inversions.

We can now begin to speculate why more members of some classes than others are found in locative inversions. Almost by their very nature, verbs of emission show the property of mutual predictability, explaining their prevalence in locative inversions. What may be more difficult to explain is why so many more verbs of light emission are attested than verbs of sound emission. This may simply reflect that visual perception is more frequently used than aural perception to take in a scene, suggesting that less familiar information is more likely to be apprehended using a visual than an aural modality.

The proposal that unergative verbs in locative inversions qualify as informationally light because they are predictable from the postverbal NP also receives support from instances of locative inversions involving unergative verbs that do not exert such strict selectional restrictions on their argument. When such verbs are found in locative inversions, they are still found with arguments that are prototypically characterized by the activity or process described by the verb, although this constraint does not hold when these verbs are not used in this construction. For instance, the locative inversion involving the verb *chatter*, given in (19a) and repeated here, takes *girls* as the postverbal NP, whereas the one involving the verb *doze*, given in (19e) and also repeated here, takes *bathers*.

(75) a. Opposite the landing-place stood half-a-dozen donkeys with saddles on their backs and bunches of flowers in their bridles, and around them CHATTERED and SANG as many girls with the silver spadella stuck through their black tresses and a red handkerchief tied across their shoulders. [A. Munthe, *The Story of San Michele*, 1]

   b. He thought of the free-form pool behind the bougainvillea hedge there, clogged with rafts of Styrofoam on which DOZED naked oily bathers lying on their backs wide open to that sun. [A. Marshall, *The Brass Bed*, 228]

In particular, these uses do not take the name of a particular person as the postverbal NP; if this were the case, then it is likely that the verb would be contributing information about the activity of that particular person and would not meet the requirement that it be informationally light.

Agentive verbs of manner of motion can also be used to illustrate this point. We have seen that when these verbs take a directional phrase complement, the appropriate choice of PP allows them to be used to describe appearance on the scene. It is this directional PP that sanctions their use in locative inversion in conformance with the requirement that the verb be informationally light. As long as the postverbal NP introduces less familiar information than the NP in the preverbal PP, its referent does not have to be something whose characteristic activity is movement in the manner described by the verb in the construction. But we will show that when the preverbal PP is locative, the verb must also describe an activity characteristic of the existence of the postverbal NP, thus restricting the range of possible postverbal NPs. This relationship between the verb and the postverbal NP is illustrated in (20d), repeated here as (76): swimming is a kind of motion that is characteristic of the existence of fish, so that this sentence really conveys little more than the fact that colorful fish are inside the tank.

(76) Inside SWAM fish from an iridescent spectrum of colors ...
    [J. Olshan, *The Waterline*, 177]

We predict that in the presence of a directional PP an agentive verb of manner of motion will not show the same restrictions on the postverbal NP as it does when it occurs with a locative PP. A survey of the postverbal NPs found in locative inversions with verbs of manner of motion when the preverbal PP is directional and when it is locative shows that they are quite different. For example, the verb *fly*, which occurs ten times in our corpus, is found with both directional and locative preverbal PPs. As illustrated in (77), when the PP is locative, the postverbal NPs for the relevant senses of *fly* include birds (eagles, geese) and insects (butterflies).

(77) a. Above her FLEW a great gaggle of geese, honking their way south. [M. L'Engle, *An Acceptable Time*, 91]
    b. Above it FLEW a flock of butterflies, the soft blues and the spring azures complemented by the gold and black of the tiger swallowtails. [M. L'Engle, *A Swiftly Tilting Planet*, 197]

There are two instances of the verb *hop*, one with a locative PP and the other with a directional PP; the first use has a postverbal NP that specifies a set of rabbits, and the second involves the NP *two sleek young men*.

(78) In the enclosure, among the chicks, HOPPED the most recent children of Nepomuk and Snow White. They were the second rabbit litter this year. [M. Benary, *Rowan Farm*, 287]

(79) ... out HOPPED two sleek young men dressed all in white carrying
     dozens of large white paper boxes. [L. Colwin, *Goodbye without
     Leaving*, 240]

Although some agentive verbs of manner of motion are found with
both directional and locative PPs, others are not found with both types of
PPs in our corpus, and it is not always clear to us that this is completely
attributable to limitations stemming from the size or composition of the
corpus. Among the agentive verbs of manner of motion that are not
observed with locative PPs are *walk*, which occurs eighteen times in our
corpus, and *rush*, which occurs six times. (Most of the other agentive
verbs of manner of motion occur one or at most two times.) Both verbs
always occur with directional phrases in locative inversions, probably because walking and rushing are not considered characteristic motions of a
particular type of entity. On the other hand, in our corpus the verb *sail* is
found only in locative inversions with locative PPs with postverbal NPs
such as eagles, clouds, and fog.[10] Presumably, this verb could be found in
locative inversions with directional PPs in the sense of 'sailing a boat' and
would take humans as the postverbal NP.

To summarize, the set of postverbal NPs found when agentive verbs of
manner of motion are used with directional PPs and locative PPs are
different, the NPs found with the latter being constrained to entities
whose characteristic motion is that described by the verb. Furthermore,
verbs that describe types of motion that are unlikely to be characteristic
of particular entities, such as *rush* and *walk*, are not found in locative
inversions with locative PPs because the verb, not being predictable from
the postverbal NP, will never be informationally light. We can now understand why agentive verbs of manner of motion are so well represented
among the unergative verbs found in locative inversions. These verbs can
be found in locative inversions when used as verbs of directed motion. In
addition, many of these verbs can describe characteristic motions of some
entity and are thus candidates for locative inversions with locative PPs.

Discussions of verbs that are not inherently verbs of existence or appearance, but are found in the *there*-insertion and locative inversion constructions, have noted that aspects of the meaning of these verbs are
deemphasized when they are found in these constructions. In describing
the genitive of negation in Russian, which appears to have similar restrictions, Babby notes that the Russian literature on genitive of negation
describes the verb in this construction as being "desemanticized" (1978:
17–18), and it appears that this characterization is equally apt for the

locative inversion construction. Ljung goes further, stating that the verb in the locative inversion construction is "nonreferring" (1980:135). A stronger proposal along these lines is made by Kirsner in discussing the *there*-insertion construction; he argues that the verb is "deagentivized" (1973:111), a proposal that might be extended to the locative inversion construction, since analogues of Kirsner's arguments can be constructed for this construction. For locative inversion, the claim would be based on the contrast in (80), which is the locative inversion analogue of the *there*-insertion constructions Kirsner presents in support of his point; these constructions are also discussed by Jenkins (1975).

(80) a. From the flagpole waved a tattered banner.
     b. *From the roof waved a bearded student.
         (cf. Kirsner 1973:110, (12c,d))

The verb *wave* has two senses: an agentive sense where the verb means 'greet' or 'beckon' and a nonagentive sense where it characterizes the type of motion made by flags and certain other types of objects when moved by the wind. Only this second sense, which, when it holds of flags, characterizes their existence, is found in the locative inversion construction. The only interpretation possible for (80b) would be one where the student is waving in the way a flag would wave. On the basis of this observation, Kirsner proposes that the NP loses its agentiveness. We feel that Kirsner is not quite right here: if the postverbal NP in a locative inversion is something that can typically be agentive, then it does not seem plausible that an agentive verb would not be necessarily informationally light if it denotes a characteristic activity of the NP. We have given such an example in (75a). An example such as (80b) is problematic precisely because the verb is not informationally light in that context: there is no sense in which waving is a characteristic activity of a student. Kirsner also takes the oddness of certain adverbs such as *voluntarily* and *stubbornly* in *there*-insertions as evidence for his deagentivization claim; such adverbs are often odd in locative inversions as well. We attribute the restrictions on such adverbs to their being incompatible with the discourse function of the construction: they typically assert information about the postverbal NP that is incompatible with the relative newness of this NP.

We hope to have shed light on the reasons why many unergative verbs might be found in locative inversions, as well as on the varying prevalence of locative inversion across a range of semantically coherent subclasses of the unergative class. It is now possible to understand why Milsark, in writing about the *there*-insertion construction, which shows a similar, though not identical, discourse function (Birner and Ward 1993), notes that this construction involves "a bewildering variety of verbs. The list is immense and may in fact comprise a majority of the intransitive verbs in English" (1974:247). Although we would exclude externally caused verbs of change of state, at least for locative inversion, we otherwise find Milsark's observation equally applicable to locative inversion. In light of the factors that we have shown to sanction the presence of unergative verbs in locative inversions, we can expect to continue to encounter new verbs in this construction.

6.6 The Syntax of Locative Inversion: Is an Unaccusative Analysis Necessary?

Having argued that the set of verbs found in locative inversion can be explained without taking this construction to be an unaccusative diagnostic, in this section we reassess the syntactic evidence presented in other work in favor of this position and show that it is weak. However suggestive the attested verbs are of an unaccusative analysis for this construction—and we have argued that, appearances to the contrary, they do not force such an analysis—this in itself is not sufficient reason to take the construction to be an unaccusative diagnostic. In order to argue convincingly that a construction *is* an unaccusative diagnostic, its properties need to be tied to the unaccusative syntactic configuration. We have found that the attempts to accomplish this with locative inversion are not compelling. We conclude that locative inversion is not an unaccusative diagnostic, especially in light of the fact that there is another explanation for the appearance of so many unaccusative verbs in this construction.

In sections 6.6.1 and 6.6.2 we review the best argument that we are able to construct that the syntactic properties of locative inversion in English call for an unaccusative analysis; we assume that this is the argument implicitly used to justify the unaccusative analysis in some other studies. This argument proceeds in two steps: (i) there is strong evidence—much of it presented or reviewed in Bresnan 1993—that the preverbal PP is a subject at some level of linguistic representation, and (ii) once this is established, it becomes possible to argue, given certain theory-internal assumptions, that the postverbal NP must be a D-Structure object. However, the second step in this argument is questionable since it makes use of an assumption that is no longer universally accepted given the introduction of the VP-Internal Subject Hypothesis. Thus, the argument as a whole loses its force. We review this argument below and explain why it can no longer be maintained. We show, furthermore, that no other convincing evidence exists that the postverbal NP is a direct object. If this is the case, there is no reason to assume that the subjects of unergative verbs found in locative inversion are anything other than subjects. Then, in the remainder of the section we argue that other evidence that has been taken as supporting an unaccusative analysis of the construction actually does not support such an analysis.

6.6.1   The Preverbal PP Is a Subject

In a paper on the locative inversion construction in English and Chicheŵa, Bresnan (1993) argues convincingly that the preverbal PP is a subject at some level of linguistic representation; specifically, she argues that it is a subject at LFG's f-structure, analogous in relevant respects to the GB framework's S-Structure. Bresnan argues against a variety of alternative analyses of the status of this PP and also presents a substantial amount of evidence in favor of this position, including evidence from subject raising, tag questions, subject extraction, and extraction from coordinate constituents; we review some of her arguments below. We argue that the preverbal PP does not originate as the subject of the verb and hence is not the external argument of the verb—but rather moves from a VP-internal position to subject position (and may subsequently topicalize).

The first piece of evidence for the subject status of the PP comes from the *that*-trace effect (Perlmutter 1971), which is discussed with respect to locative inversion by Bresnan (1977, 1993) and Stowell (1981), among others. Bresnan shows that extraction of the preverbal PP in the locative inversion construction patterns with extraction of subjects in showing the *that*-trace effect, even though extraction of VP-internal PPs does not lead to the effect. The *that*-trace effect is present only when the PP is extracted from a locative inversion construction, not when it is extracted from its noninverted counterpart. This contrast is illustrated in the examples below (these examples are given by Bresnan (1993), who bases them on her earlier work (Bresnan 1977)). The first pair of sentences, in (81), involves the extraction of a PP in an embedded locative inversion construction, and the second pair, in (82), involves the extraction of the PP in the noninverted counterpart of the embedded clause in (81).

(81) a.   It's in these villages that we all believe _____ can be found the
          best examples of this cuisine.
     b.   *It's in these villages that we all believe that _____ can be found
          the best examples of this cuisine.
          (Bresnan 1993:31, (62))

(82) a.   It's in these villages that we all believe the finest examples of
          this cuisine can be found _____.
     b.   It's in these villages that we all believe that the finest examples
          of this cuisine can be found _____.
          (Bresnan 1993:31, (63))

This pattern suggests that the PP is indeed a subject, since extraction from
VP-internal positions does not trigger this effect.

Additional evidence that the preverbal PP is a subject comes from the
interaction of locative inversion with raising, as discussed by Bresnan
(1993), L. Levin (1986), and Postal (1977), among others. When the locative inversion construction is embedded under a subject-raising verb, the
preverbal PP raises to become the surface subject of the matrix verb. In
(83) the embedded verb is passive; in (84) it is intransitive.

(83) In this spot, well toward the center and front of the vast herd,
      appeared about to BE ENACTED a battle between a monarch and his
      latest rival for supremacy. [Z. Grey, *The Thundering Herd*, 331]

(84) ... and to the cone were made to ADHERE bushy sprigs of mint of
      marjoram which Otto seized from the pile of green fodder beside
      him ... [IMIG 38 (65); cited in H. H. Hartvigson and L. K.
      Jakobsen 1974:59]

As the subject of the noninverted counterparts of these sentences, the NP
can also raise, as shown in (85). (We are assuming that *adhere* is an unaccusative verb.)

(85) a.   A battle$_i$ appeared [t_i about to be enacted t_i in this spot].
     b.   Bushy sprigs$_i$ were made [t_i to adhere t_i to the cone].

Yet nonsubjects do not typically raise, and, as shown in (86), the PPs do
not raise when the embedded verb has a subject.

(86) a.   *In this spot$_i$ appeared [a battle$_j$ about to be enacted t_j t_i].
     b.   *To the cone$_i$ were made [bushy sprigs$_j$ to adhere t_j t_i].

In fact, given the theory-internal assumptions of the GB framework, raising can only take place from subject position. As these examples illustrate, the interaction of locative inversion with raising also suggests that the preverbal PP is a subject.

In most of the literature on locative inversion it is usually simply assumed without argument that the PP cannot have originated as the subject of the verb. In fact, there is good reason to make this assumption. For instance, it receives support from the presence of passive verbs in locative inversion.

(87) Next to these, in a wooden cabinet of some antiquity, WAS KEPT a quantity of papers, handed down to the Institute by some long-vanished department of the (then) Colonial Office. [H. Holt, *A Lot to Ask: A Life of Barbara Pym*, 157]

Presumably, in (87) the PP is selected by the verb *keep* both when it is passive and when it is active. When the verb is active, it can take an external argument as well as the PP. Consequently, the PP cannot be an external argument when the verb is used in its active form and, therefore, it cannot be an external argument in the passive use of the verb, since active and passive forms of the same verb differ only with respect to their external argument. As there is no reason to assume a different analysis of locative inversions with intransitive verbs, there is no reason to expect that the PP is the external argument with such verbs either.

There is a difference of opinion concerning whether the preverbal PP in a locative inversion is actually in subject position at S-Structure (i.e., Spec, IP position), as proposed by Hoekstra and Mulder (1990), or whether it is in some other sentence-initial position, having moved there from subject position (i.e., Spec, CP position or a position created by adjunction to IP or CP), as proposed by Stowell (1981) and Coopmans (1989), among others. Although not proposing a movement account, Bresnan (1993), following Stowell, argues that the preverbal PP is a subject at LFG's f-structure, though it is topicalized at c-structure. Hoekstra and Mulder (1990) argue that the PP is in subject position, pointing out that locative inversion constructions can be embedded in sentences with *wh*-complementizers, so that it could not occupy Spec, CP position.

(88) We suddenly saw how into the pond jumped thousands of frogs.
     (Hoekstra and Mulder 1990:32, (72))

Hoekstra and Mulder also provide evidence from questions formed on locative inversions against the proposal that the preverbal PP is adjoined to IP. We do not take a stand on whether the locative PP is an S-Structure subject or whether, despite Hoekstra and Mulder's arguments to the contrary, it is in some other sentence-initial position, leaving a trace in subject position. As will become apparent in the next section, it is sufficient for our purposes to establish that the PP is a subject at some point in the derivation.

6.6.2   The Status of the Postverbal NP

We turn now to the second and more questionable step in the argument that locative inversion is an unaccusative diagnostic. Assuming that the preverbal PP is indeed a subject at some point in the derivation, the θ-Criterion and Projection Principle (Chomsky 1981, 1986b) can be used to argue that a verb found in the locative inversion construction must be an unaccusative verb or a passive verb; that is, the verb must not have an external argument—the property that unaccusative and passive verbs share. If the verb in a locative inversion construction were an unergative verb and therefore did have an external argument, then the subject position would be a θ-position, and the PP would not be expected to occupy this position without violating the θ-Criterion and Projection Principle.[11]

This line of argument for an unaccusative analysis of locative inversion loses its force with the introduction of the VP-Internal Subject Hypothesis. This hypothesis, proposed in the work of Fukui and Speas (1986), Koopman and Sportiche (1991), Kuroda (1988), Sportiche (1988), Zagona (1982), among others, suggests that all surface subjects, whether of transitive, unergative, or unaccusative verbs, originate inside VP, but then move to the Spec, IP position. The VP-Internal Subject Hypothesis does not render the unaccusative/unergative distinction unnecessary; rather, the external argument of transitive and unergative verbs would originate in Spec, VP, but the direct internal argument of an unaccusative verb would still originate as the sister of V. However, if the VP-Internal Subject Hypothesis is adopted, then the argument that unergative verbs are excluded from the locative inversion construction given in the previous paragraph does not go through. On the VP-internal subject analysis, the external argument of an unergative verb is generated within the VP, so that a PP complement of the verb could move into the Spec, IP position without violating the θ-Criterion and Projection Principle. Thus, with the adoption of the VP-Internal Subject Hypothesis, there is no reason that unergative verbs would be precluded from the locative inversion construction.

Assuming the VP-Internal Subject Hypothesis, once the PP moves into Spec, IP position, this position is no longer available for the external argument of an unergative verb. The external argument would move to a position to the right of the verb, presumably to a VP-adjoined position of the type that has been posited for focus (Rochemont 1986, Samek-Lodovici 1993). We assume that this movement is required because of the discourse function of the locative inversion construction. In (89) we sketch a possible derivation of a locative inversion with an unergative verb.[12]

(89) a. D-Structure: $[_{IP}\ e\ [_{I'}\ I\ [_{VP}\ NP\ [_{V'}\ V\ PP]]]]$
    b. S-Structure: $[_{IP}\ PP_i\ [_{I'}\ V_j+I\ [_{VP}\ [_{VP}\ t_k\ [_{V'}\ t_j\ t_i]]\ NP_k]]]$

Given this analysis, a locative inversion with an unergative verb does not violate structure preservation (cf. section 6.1). A locative inversion construction containing an unaccusative verb would involve the following structures:

(90) a. D-Structure: $[_{IP}\ e\ [_{I'}\ I\ [_{VP}\ [_{V'}\ V\ NP\ PP]]]]$
    b. S-Structure: $[_{IP}\ PP_i\ [_{I'}\ V_j+I\ [_{VP}\ [_{VP}\ [_{V'}\ t_j\ t_k\ t_i]]\ NP_k]]]$

The major difference between locative inversion constructions with unaccusative and unergative verbs involves the D-Structure location of the postverbal NP. In addition, this syntactic analysis allows transitive verbs to occur in the locative inversion construction. In fact, such constructions, though rare, are attested; their rarity on our account follows from the discourse function of locative inversion.

Even in the unaccusative accounts of locative inversion there is some discussion concerning whether the postverbal NP is in fact an S-Structure object, or whether it actually occupies some other position to the right of object position at S-Structure, possibly as a consequence of its discourse function, as in the structures we have proposed (see also Bresnan 1993). As noted by Coopmans (1989), it is not easy to discriminate between these two options a priori. One type of evidence that may be relevant to choosing between them involves the placement of the postverbal NP with respect to a postverbal PP in a construction with a bona fide unaccusative verb; this type of evidence has been discussed by Burzio (1986) with respect to *there*-insertion and is reviewed in section 4.1.3. If the postverbal NP in a locative inversion with an unaccusative verb could occur outside a PP, then it could not be occupying its D-Structure position. This would open up the possibility that even when the NP appears to be directly postverbal, it might nevertheless not be in object position. Although such evidence is difficult to find since it would require an unaccusative verb cooccurring with two PPs—an unlikely situation—we have found several instances of locative inversion with clear unaccusative verbs where the NP is to the right of a postverbal PP, as in (91).

(91) Out of the mud-brick ruins of temples and ziggurats HAVE EMERGED over the last century the traces of cities whose names evoke the rise of human civilization: Babylon and Kish, Nimrud and Nippur, Ur and Uruk. [J. N. Wilford, "To Endangered List in Gulf, Add Archeology," 1]

Such examples confirm that the postverbal NP in a locative inversion with an unaccusative verb can be in a position to the right of the object position. All things being equal, there is no reason not to consider that this is the case for all locative inversions with unaccusative verbs. Furthermore, there is no reason to believe that the postverbal NP in a locative inversion with an unergative verb is in a different position.

We have also found a locative inversion token with a clear unaccusative verb where the NP occurs to the left of a postverbal, but apparently VP-internal, PP.

(92) From one cottage EMERGED Ian with a spade, rubber boots and an enthusiastic expression. [R. Billington, *Loving Attitudes*, 60]

As shown in (93), tests for VP constituency applied to the noninverted counterpart of (92) suggest that the PP is inside the VP in (92). There is no reason, then, to posit rightward movement of the postverbal NP in this instance.

(93) a. ??Ian emerged from the cottage with a spade and Phil did so with a rake.
    b. ??Ian said that he would emerge from the cottage with a spade and emerge he did with a spade.

However, it is interesting that in this particular token, the verb is a verb of appearance and hence is trivially compatible with the discourse function of the construction; this may explain why the postverbal NP has not moved out of object position. It is likely that discourse considerations typically require such movement and that this type of example is exceptional and arises because the verb itself is a verb of appearance. Whatever the ultimate explanation for this example might be, what is important for our account is that there are no comparable examples with verbs that are independently known to be unergative. With unergative verbs the post-verbal NP originates in the VP-internal subject position and is moved to the right to a VP-adjoined position; the NP is never in object position and thus would not be expected to be found inside the PP.

6.6.3   Verbs Taking Sentential Complements

Bresnan (1993) argues that the unaccusative analysis of locative inversion is necessary to account for the data in (94), which were brought to her attention by D. Pesetsky.[13]

(94) a.   The cure for cancer was discovered in this very room. ∼
           In this very room was discovered the cure for cancer.
           (Bresnan 1993, (107a))

   b.   That cancer was caused by eating too many tomatoes was
        discovered in this very room. ∼
        *In this very room was discovered that cancer was caused by
        eating too many tomatoes.
        (Bresnan 1993, (107b))

These examples show that sentential complements cannot undergo locative inversion. Bresnan writes that an account such as hers, which relies on an unaccusative analysis of locative inversion, can explain this fact: "This contrast is precisely what we expect if objects in English occupy NP positions that exclude *that* and *for* complements, and the inverted theme arguments of locative inversions are objects" (1993:48). More specifically, she writes that "postverbal CP complements ... are disallowed: they cannot fill the c-structure object position to satisfy the verb" (1993:62). She suggests that an account such as ours has no natural explanation for this fact.

   Recall, however, that on our account, as on most others, the postverbal NP is in VP-adjoined position, and not in the direct object position. Therefore, the restriction against the appearance of CP in the direct object position could just as easily be formulated as a restriction against CPs appearing in the VP-adjoined position. It is well known that object position is not the only position that is reserved exclusively for NPs. Emonds (1976), Grimshaw (1982), Koster (1978), Stowell (1981), and others have pointed out that the subject position is also an NP position; that is, non-NPs are excluded from this position. In the GB framework, such restrictions have been attributed to Case theory (Stowell 1981), but any theory, LFG included, will have to give some account of why CPs are excluded from certain positions. Pursuing this for a moment, since the exclusion of

CPs from certain positions has been attributed to Case theory in the GB framework, we would have to maintain that the VP-adjoined position is a Case position in order to explain the contrast in (94). We would have to state that this position is a Case position independently, precisely because the NPs that are found in this position will need to get Case. The post-verbal NP in a locative inversion cannot get Case in its position within the VP: VP-internal subjects are not in a Case position, and unaccusative verbs do not assign Case to their objects. We do not set out exactly how the postverbal NP would receive Case here; since our goal is understanding the constraints on the verbs in locative inversion, we have explored the syntax of the construction only to the extent that it impinges on this issue. We simply note that Case assignment is also a problem facing any analysis of the locative inversion construction; see Coopmans 1989 and Hoekstra and Mulder 1990 for particular proposals.

There is some support for taking the VP-adjoined position in locative inversion to be an NP position. Specifically, another effect that has been associated with NP positions is manifested in this position. Although the subject position is generally considered to be an NP position only, as J. Grimshaw (personal communication) has pointed out, it is well known that *wh*-CPs can sometimes be found in subject position even though *that*-CPs cannot. As evidence for this, note that *wh*-CPs pattern with NPs, rather than with *that*-CPs, with respect to subject-aux inversion.

(95) a.   Does Pat's arrival continue to surprise you?
     b.   ?Does why Pat came continue to surprise you?
     c.   *Does that Pat came continue to surprise you?

This fact suggests that *wh*-CPs, unlike *that*-CPs, can be found in what are said to be NP positions. If the postverbal position in a locative inversion is an NP position in the same sense as the subject position, then we might expect to find *wh*-CPs in this position. Indeed, it appears that a *wh*-CP can be the postverbal element in a locative inversion.

(96) a.   In this very room was discovered the cure for cancer.
     b.   In this very room was discovered why smoking causes cancer.
     c.   *In this very room was discovered that smoking causes cancer.

It seems to us and to other speakers we have consulted that the locative inversion with the *wh*-CP is close to perfect. This supports our proposal that the CP data that Bresnan presents should be explained in terms of grammatical categories rather than grammatical function.

Finally, it is worth pointing out that the absence of *that*-CPs cannot be attributed to the discourse function of the construction. It is certainly possible to introduce new or less familiar information in a sentential complement. It is also possible to focus sentential complements when they are found in those positions that are open to them using devices such as sentence accent. Furthermore, as pointed out by B. Birner (personal communication), the exclusion of *that*-CPs from locative inversion is an instance of a more general phenomenon. Such CPs are also excluded from a variety of inversions in English, as shown by the examples in (97), which Birner provided.

(97) a. The findings were surprising. #Also surprising was that tomatoes cure cancer.
   b. In that church they teach that life is an illusion. #Also taught there is that knowledge is evil.
   c. The children arrived at school, but the door was locked. ?On the wall was posted that the district had run out of funding.

And again, in each instance, we believe there is an improvement when a *wh*-CP is used instead of a *that*-CP.

(98) a. Their findings were surprising. Also surprising was why tomatoes cure cancer.
   b. In that church they teach that life is an illusion. Also taught there is why knowledge is evil.
   c. The children arrived at school, but the door was locked. On the wall was posted why the district couldn't keep the school open any longer.

The sentential complement problem, then, is not a problem that involves a particular grammatical function; rather, it is a problem involving the grammatical category that can instantiate a particular grammatical function.

6.6.4 The Locative Alternation

As part of this discussion, we want to briefly note that the intransitive form of the locative alternation, which might appear to further support the unaccusative classification of some of the apparently unergative verbs found in locative inversions, does not. Perusal of the extensive list of verbs appearing in the intransitive form of the locative alternation given by Salkoff (1983) shows that many of the unergative verbs found in the locative inversion construction also figure in the intransitive form of the locative alternation. This alternation is illustrated in (99) with a verb of light emission.

(99) a. Fireflies glowed in the field. (locative variant)
     b. The field glowed with fireflies. (*with* variant)

This overlap might appear to further support the availability of a second, unaccusative classification for some unergative verbs because of the "holistic" interpretation associated with the subject of the *with* variant of the intransitive locative alternation. Both the transitive and intransitive locative alternations show this effect (Anderson 1971, Schwartz-Norman 1976, among others): the attribution of the property of being wholly affected to the location argument in the *with* variant (i.e., when it is not expressed in a PP). However, the expression of the location argument in this variant is different in the transitive and intransitive forms of the alternation: it is the object in the transitive form (*The farmer loaded the truck with hay*), but the subject in the intransitive form (as in (99b)). Nevertheless, on the assumption that the verb in the intransitive form of the alternation is unaccusative, it becomes possible to give a unified account of this effect in terms of the notion of D-Structure object, since the location argument will be the D-Structure object in the *with* variant in both forms of the alternation.

Given the near-paraphrase relation between the two variants of the intransitive locative alternation, it might seem natural to extend the unaccusative analysis to the locative variant—the variant that is the "base" of any locative inversions involving the alternating verbs. However, Hoekstra and Mulder (1990) point out that there is not necessarily support for this move. In particular, the holistic interpretation is associated only with the *with* variant. Thus, although the holistic effect might motivate an unaccusative analysis for the verb in the *with* variant, it does not motivate an unaccusative analysis for the verb in the locative variant; in fact, Hoekstra and Mulder assume that this variant does not receive an unaccusative analysis for all verbs. The desirability of an unaccusative analysis of the locative variant depends on the analysis of the semantic relationship between the two variants, a topic that we leave for further research.

6.6.5 Evidence from Passive Verbs

Locative inversions with passive verbs provide independent support for the proposal that locative inversion is not an unaccusative diagnostic. The presence of passive verbs in the locative inversion construction has often been taken as evidence for the unaccusative analysis of this construction. On closer examination, however, it appears that at least some instances of locative inversions with passive verbs argue against the unaccusative analysis. The reason is that, as discussed in section 6.4.5, many instances of locative inversion with passive verbs appear to involve adjectival rather than verbal passives. If the passives are adjectival, then they receive an unergative analysis since adjectival passives are formed by lexical externalization (rather than movement) of the direct internal argument of a verbal passive (B. Levin and Rappaport 1986). Thus, the existence of adjectival passives in locative inversions is a problem for the unaccusative analysis of the locative inversion construction.

To summarize, in this section we have argued against an unaccusative analysis of the locative inversion construction. Specifically, we have shown that although there is convincing evidence in English that the preverbal PP is a subject at some level of linguistic representation, there is no equally strong evidence that the postverbal NP is an object. We have sketched an alternative analysis in which the postverbal NP is in a VP-adjoined position, allowing both unaccusative and unergative verbs to be found in the construction.

6.7   An Alternative Account

In this section we briefly consider an alternative syntactic account, proposed by Hoekstra and Mulder (1990), of the presence of unergative verbs in the locative inversion construction. This account, like the meaning shift account discussed briefly in section 6.5, posits two meanings for the unergative verbs found in locative inversion: one meaning that is compatible with an unaccusative classification of the verb and is associated with its appearance in locative inversion and a second that is compatible with an unergative classification. This account allows an unaccusative analysis of the locative inversion construction to be maintained, a property that is not necessarily in its favor given the discussion in section 6.6. The source of the multiple meanings on this account is not a rule of meaning shift, but the compatibility of certain verbs with two different syntactic projections of their arguments, each representing a distinct meaning. In this sense, the analysis instantiates the constructional approach discussed in chapter 5, applying it to the variable behavior of verbs in locative inversion.

Hoekstra and Mulder (1990) take locative inversion to be an unaccusative diagnostic, but they depart from some other accounts by proposing that the NP and the PP form a small clause, which is itself the internal argument of the verb, as in (100); either the NP or the PP then moves to subject position, giving rise to the noninverted or inverted construction, schematized in (101a) and (101b), respectively.

(100) e [$_{VP}$ V [$_{SC}$ NP PP]]

(101) a. NP$_i$ [$_{VP}$ V [$_{SC}$ t_i PP]]
       b. PP$_i$ [$_{VP}$ V [$_{SC}$ NP t_i]]

The small clause analysis is motivated in part by a desire to maintain a binary-branching structure (see also the discussion of Hoekstra's (1988) account of the resultative construction in section 2.4.1). This analysis is also supposed to represent the fact that the referent of the NP is located (or comes to be located) at the place denoted by the PP, a relation that can be represented as a relation of predication: the PP is predicated of the NP. For Hoekstra and Mulder, a predication relation must always be represented via a clausal structure, providing further motivation for the small clause analysis. As independent support for the small clause analysis, Hoekstra and Mulder suggest that there is evidence that the verb does not impose selectional restrictions on the NP, as would be expected on this analysis since the NP is not an argument of the verb; however, later in this section we discuss evidence that suggests otherwise. What is most important is that the small clause analysis would also require that the verb in the locative inversion construction not take an external argument; if it did, the movement of an NP or PP to the subject position would not be possible. Therefore, for the reasons that were spelled out in section 6.6.2, the verb must be unaccusative.

Hoekstra and Mulder's (1990) explanation of the presence of unergative verbs in the locative inversion construction resembles the meaning shift account in assuming that a second meaning is available for these verbs. As discussed in chapter 5, they propose that "[c]ertain predicates vary, within limits, in their meaning, such that they may take arguments of different types" (1990:75). As applied to the problem posed by locative inversion, verbs that typically select an individual realized as an NP as the external argument, and thus can receive an activity interpretation, can instead select a state of affairs, realized as a small clause internal argument, thus becoming verbs of existence.

(102) a. NP [$_{VP}$ V]
       b. e [$_{VP}$ V [$_{SC}$ NP PP]]

This approach differs from the meaning shift approach, however, in denying the existence of lexical rules of meaning shift. As the discussion in section 6.5 shows, the ability of an unergative verb to be found in a locative inversion construction does not depend solely on the verb. It seems to us that positing that a verb can have two meanings does not help in understanding the complicated interacting factors that determine which unergative verbs actually tend to manifest the second meaning (or argument selection option in Hoekstra and Mulder's terms) or, to the extent that this option is manifested by some verbs, what circumstances favor it. This does not mean that Hoekstra and Mulder's approach could not be modified to take the discourse function of the construction into account, but it is likely that any attempt to do this would not gain much from having two meanings available for these verbs.

One facet of Hoekstra and Mulder's account is at odds with our observation in section 6.5 that the verb in a locative inversion is in some sense predictable from the postverbal NP. As just mentioned, Hoekstra and Mulder propose that the verb in a locative inversion construction is an unaccusative verb taking a small clause complement, as schematized in (102b). They note that on their analysis the verb should not exert any selectional restrictions on the postverbal NP in a locative inversion; rather, it should exert selectional restrictions only on the small clause as a whole. As support for this analysis, they cite examples like those in (103), some of which involve verbs of manner of motion, and point out that the subjects in these examples are not selected by the verb.

(103) a. My skin turned red.
     b. John flew into a rage.
     c. The well ran dry.
     d. They fell in love.
     (Hoekstra and Mulder 1990:11, (19))

As we have shown, the relationship between the verb and the postverbal NP that appears to license the use of unergative verbs in locative inversions seems incompatible with the predictions of Hoekstra and Mulder's small clause analysis. The examples discussed in section 6.5 show a very close connection between the verb and the postverbal NP in locative inversions with unergative verbs: either the verb takes a limited range of arguments to begin with or it is found with a limited set of arguments in the construction. This dependence is not expected on a small clause analysis, raising questions about its ultimate viability.

As for the examples in (103) that Hoekstra and Mulder cite in favor of the small clause analysis, it is clear that they represent idiomatic uses of the verbs. The verbs are semantically "bleached": they have lost basic elements of their meaning, including any sense of motion. In fact, all of the examples describe changes of state and hence none of them have locative inversion analogues. When the same verbs are found in locative inversions, the central elements of their meaning may be deemphasized, but they are not lost. This is evident, for instance, from an examination of the locative inversions with the verb *fly*, cited in (77). Although Hoekstra and Mulder's examples may require a small clause analysis, their distinctive properties do not make them the right examples to use to address the issue of selectional restrictions in locative inversion. Rather, the behavior of unergative verbs in locative inversion supports an analysis in which such verbs do not take a single argument realized as a small clause, further weakening the reasons for positing two meanings for the unergative verbs in the locative inversion construction. Hoekstra and Mulder's reasons for positing an unaccusative analysis are also rendered less compelling; as pointed out above, it was the small clause structure that led to an unaccusative analysis.

6.8   The Larger Picture

To conclude this chapter, we look briefly at some wider implications of our study of locative inversion. We began our discussion of this construction by noting that at least on the surface, it shows properties that are distinct from those of other unaccusative diagnostics. Most important, the argument of the verb is found postverbally, suggesting that if the construction were an unaccusative diagnostic, it wears its unaccusativity on its sleeve. We called such diagnostics "diagnostics of surface unaccusativity." However, in the course of this chapter we argued that the reasons for considering locative inversion to be an unaccusative diagnostic are not all that strong, attributing some of the properties that suggested otherwise to its discourse function. The question that arises is, What are the implications of our study of locative inversion for purported diagnostics of surface unaccusativity more generally?

Although we have been unable to carry out in-depth investigations of constructions that might qualify as diagnostics for surface unaccusativity in other languages, it appears that candidate constructions are found with a class of verbs that is "too big" in exactly the same sense as the class of verbs found in the locative inversion construction. (Most of this work does not examine the question of whether all unaccusative verbs can show the relevant phenomena, so it is more difficult without further research to know whether the class of verbs is also "too small" in the same way, though the examples illustrating verbs found in these constructions suggests that this is probably the case.) We mention several examples. The Russian genitive of negation has been argued to be an unaccusative diagnostic (Pesetsky 1982), but Babby's (1978, 1980) data concerning its distribution suggest that the class of verbs found in this construction also includes some of the same types of unergative verbs as are found in English locative inversion. And, as mentioned above, Babby's characterization of the factors that allow verbs that are not verbs of existence or appearance to occur in the construction is equally apt for English. Torrego (1989) discusses the distribution of postverbal bare plurals in Spanish, and from her discussion it seems that their distribution shows certain properties that are reminiscent of the distribution of locative inversion.

The additional diagnostic for surface unaccusativity that we are most familiar with is *ne*-cliticization in Italian. Its status as an unaccusative diagnostic was established by Belletti and Rizzi (1981) and by Burzio (1986), among others, who linked its distribution to properties of the syntactic configuration in which it is found. Furthermore, it has often been claimed that this construction is found only with verbs that take the auxiliary *essere* 'be', reinforcing its classification as an unaccusative diagnostic. However, Lonzi (1985) points out that a variety of verbs that take the auxiliary *avere* 'have' do permit *ne*-cliticization, but only when they are found in a simple tense; *ne*-cliticization is not possible when these verbs are found in a complex tense in which the auxiliary is expressed.

(104) a. *Non ne   ha trillato forte   nessuna (di sveglie).
           not of them has trilled loudly none   (of alarm clocks)
           (complex tense, *avere* selected; Lonzi 1985:112, (60b))
       b. Non ne   trilla forte   nessuna (di sveglie).
           not of them trills loudly none   (of alarm clocks)
           (simple tense; Lonzi 1985:112, (60a))

(105) a. *Ne   ha   camminato tanta, di gente, su
           of them have walked   many of people on
           quei marciapiedi.
           those sidewalks
           (complex tense, *avere* selected; Lonzi 1985:112, (64b))

b. Ne   cammina tanta, di gente, su quei
    of them walks   many of people on those
    marciapiedi.
    sidewalks
    (simple tense; Lonzi 1985:112, (64a))

Lonzi's data raise questions about the validity of *ne*-cliticization as a diagnostic, despite Belletti and Rizzi's and Burzio's arguments. In section 6.6.2 we showed that the arguments linking locative inversion to the unaccusative syntactic configuration do not hold in the context of the VP-Internal Subject Hypothesis. We might ask whether Belletti and Rizzi's and Burzio's arguments that *ne*-cliticization is an unaccusative diagnostic can be maintained, and in fact, Saccon (1992) raises the same question.[14]

Lonzi proposes that the availability of *ne*-cliticization is governed by discourse considerations; her statement of these factors suggests that they are not too different from the ones that we have discussed for locative inversion. A preliminary investigation of our own suggests that unergative verbs are found in this construction under circumstances similar to those that sanction the appearance of English unergative verbs in locative inversion—that is, in contexts where the verb describes a characteristic activity or process of the entity it is predicated of. Additional examples can be constructed to illustrate this.

(106) a. *Di ragazze, ne   hanno lavorato molte nelle
           of girls   of them have   worked many in the
           fabbriche di Shanghai.
           factories of Shanghai
           (complex tense, *avere* selected)
      b. Di ragazze, ne   lavorano molte nelle   fabbriche
          of girls   of them work   many in the factories
          di Shanghai.
          of Shanghai
          (simple tense)

(107) a. *Di ragazzi, ne   hanno russato molti nel
           of boys   of them have   snored many in the
           corridoio del   treno.
           corridor of the train
           (complex tense, *avere* selected)

b. Di ragazzi, ne   russavano molti nel   corridoio
   of boys   of them snore   many in the corridor
   del   treno.
   of the train
   (simple tense)

Lonzi makes one particularly interesting comment concerning the following example:

(108) Ti accorgerai che in quest'ufficio ne   telefonano
      you'll realize that in this office   of them telephone
      davvero molti, di stranieri.
      really   many of foreigners
      (Lonzi 1985:113, (71b))

She points out that the preferred interpretation of this sentence is the one where the telephone calls come into the office, rather than the one where the telephone calls originate in the office. This comment brings to mind the observation in section 6.4.4 on verbs of motion, where appearance-like interpretations are favored.

Based on our preliminary investigations of phenomena said to involve "surface unaccusativity" in other languages, we speculate that such phenomena are not unaccusative diagnostics strictly speaking, but rather to a large extent receive their explanation from discourse considerations. We leave this question and its implications to further study.

Afterword

The primary goal of this book has been to substantiate the thesis that unaccusativity is semantically determined and syntactically encoded. Although this thesis is not new—as mentioned in chapter 1, it is essentially the original version of the Unaccusative Hypothesis proposed by Perlmutter (1978)—it has proved remarkably difficult to support in detail, since so much about the behavior of verbs has not been understood. It is not surprising, then, that in the course of trying to determine the lexical semantic underpinnings of unaccusativity, a variety of issues concerning the nature of the lexical semantic representation of verbs were touched upon, and certain insights into such representations have emerged.

Virtually all generative theories developed over the last fifteen years have taken major aspects of the syntax of sentences to be directly projected from the lexical properties of verbs and other predicators. Within the GB framework, this idea finds its expression in the various formulations of the Projection Principle (Chomsky 1981). In order to implement the Projection Principle, verbs must have structured lexical representations, whose structure can then determine major aspects of the syntax of a sentence. These representations may take the form of an argument structure, or they may be more semantic in nature, taking the form of a lexical semantic representation of some type.

One of the challenges facing theories that include a principle like the Projection Principle is the fact that many verbs can appear in a bewildering range of syntactic contexts. If this kind of variety turns out to be the rule rather than the exception, then maintaining the Projection Principle may entail a wholesale proliferation of lexical entries for verbs. On the other hand, it is possible to reject the basic insight behind the Projection Principle. A fundamental motivation behind the instantiation of the constructional approach developed by Hoekstra (1992) (see also Hoekstra and Mulder 1990) is precisely the desire to deny the existence of structured lexical representations. On the constructional approach, a verb is associated with some basic concept that has no internal linguistic structure. Arguments are projected freely onto basic syntactic structures made available by languages; the exact meaning of a verb in a particular syntactic configuration is determined by the concept the verb is associated with in conjunction with the meaning associated with the syntactic structure. The meanings associated with these syntactic structures are similar in many respects to the meanings associated with the primitive predicates most commonly proposed in theories of predicate decomposition of meaning.

If the conclusions we have been drawing throughout the book are correct, then the central thesis of the constructional approach—that there are no structured lexical representations determining the syntax of a sentence —is not correct. First, our analysis of the resultative construction strongly suggests that verbs are basically paired with a particular number of arguments. Second, our analysis of the phenomenon of meaning shifts suggests that the regular association of verbs with multiple lexical entries is governed by some sort of lexical statement. Finally, our discussion of locative inversion suggests that unergative verbs do not project their arguments differently in this construction.

Whatever the final resolution of this particular issue turns out to be, certain other results emerge clearly from the study presented here. By far the most important is the isolation of a set of syntactically relevant meaning components. It is clear that progress in lexical semantics has been hampered by a failure to distinguish those aspects of meaning that are syntactically relevant from those that are not. We take it as an encouraging sign that the meaning components that we have isolated in this book bear a strong resemblance to the meaning components isolated by other researchers working in the same area. Although we do not presume to have said the final word on this topic, we hope to have presented a methodology for studying the lexical semantics–syntax interface, developed in the course of our work on unaccusativity, that can in the future be applied to other areas of the verb lexicon.

Appendix A
Verb Classes and Their Members

In this appendix we list the members of the major intransitive verb classes discussed in this book. The lists given are those for the corresponding verb classes in B. Levin 1993. The section number identifying the verb class in Levin 1993 is given in parentheses following the class name. Where the name or composition of a class as used in this book differs from the usage in Levin 1993, we have noted this following the section number.

(1) *Verbs of emission* (43)

    a. *Verbs of light emission* (43.1): beam, blaze, blink, burn, flame, flare, flash, flicker, glare, gleam, glimmer, glint, glisten, glitter, glow, incandesce, scintillate, shimmer, shine, sparkle, twinkle

    b. *Verbs of sound emission* (43.2): babble, bang, beat, beep, bellow, blare, blast, blat, boom, bubble, burble, burr, buzz, chatter, chime, chink, chir, chitter, chug, clack, clang, clank, clap, clash, clatter, click, cling, clink, clomp, clump, clunk, crack, crackle, crash, creak, crepitate, crunch, cry, ding, dong, explode, fizz, fizzle, groan, growl, gurgle, hiss, hoot, howl, hum, jangle, jingle, knell, knock, lilt, moan, murmur, patter, peal, ping, pink, pipe, plink, plonk, plop, plunk, pop, purr, putter, rap, rasp, rattle, ring, roar, roll, rumble, rustle, scream, screech, shriek, shrill, sing, sizzle, snap, splash, splutter, sputter, squawk, squeak, squeal, squelch, strike, swish, swoosh, thrum, thud, thump, thunder, thunk, tick, ting, tinkle, toll, toot, tootle, trill, trumpet, twang, ululate, vroom, wail, wheeze, whine, whir, whish, whistle, whoosh, whump, zing

    c. *Verbs of smell emission* (43.3): reek, smell, stink

    d. *Verbs of substance emission* (43.4): belch, bleed, bubble, dribble, drip, drool, emanate, exude, foam, gush, leak, ooze, pour, puff, radiate, seep, shed, slop, spew, spill, spout, sprout, spurt, squirt, steam, stream, sweat

(2) *Verbs of inherently directed motion* (51.1): advance, arrive, ascend, ?climb, come, ?cross, depart, descend, enter, escape, exit, fall, flee, go, leave, plunge, recede, return, rise, tumble

(3) *Verbs of manner of motion* (51.3, Levin's "manner-of-motion verbs")

    a. Roll *verbs* (51.3.1): bounce, coil, drift, drop, float, glide, move, revolve, roll, rotate, slide, spin, swing, turn, twirl, twist, whirl, wind

    b. *Agentive verbs of manner of motion* (51.3.2, Levin's "*run* verbs"): amble,
backpack, bolt, bounce, bound, bowl, canter, carom, cavort, charge,
clamber, climb, clump, coast, crawl, creep, dart, dash, dodder, drift, file,
flit, float, fly, frolic, gallop, gambol, glide, goosestep, hasten, hike, hobble,
hop, hurry, hurtle, inch, jog, journey, jump, leap, limp, lollop, lope,
lumber, lurch, march, meander, mince, mosey, nip, pad, parade,
perambulate, plod, prance, promenade, prowl, race, ramble, roam, roll,
romp, rove, run, rush, sashay, saunter, scamper, scoot, scram, scramble,
scud, scurry, scutter, scuttle, shamble, shuffle, sidle, skeddadle, skip,
skitter, skulk, sleepwalk, slide, slink, slither, slog, slouch, sneak,
somersault, speed, stagger, stomp, stray, streak, stride, stroll, strut,
stumble, stump, swagger, sweep, swim, tack, tear, tiptoe, toddle, totter,
traipse, tramp, travel, trek, troop, trot, trudge, trundle, vault, waddle,
wade, walk, wander, whiz, zigzag, zoom

(4) *Verbs of existence and appearance*

    a. *Verbs of existence* (47.1, only Levin's "*exist* verbs" are listed here):
coexist, ?correspond, ?depend, dwell, endure, exist, extend, flourish,
languish, linger, live, loom, lurk, overspread, persist, predominate,
prevail, prosper, remain, reside, shelter, stay, survive, thrive, tower, wait

    b. *Verbs of appearance* (48.1.1, only Levin's "*appear* verbs" are listed here):
appear, arise, awake, awaken, break, burst, come, dawn, derive, develop,
emanate, emerge, erupt, evolve, exude, flow, form, grow, gush, issue,
materialize, open, plop, result, rise, spill, spread, steal, stem, stream,
supervene, surge, wax

    c. *Verbs of occurrence* (48.3): ensue, eventuate, happen, occur, recur,
transpire

(5) *Verbs of spatial configuration* (47.6): balance, bend, bow, crouch, dangle,
flop, fly, hang, hover, jut, kneel, lean, lie, loll, loom, lounge, nestle, open,
perch, plop, project, protrude, recline, rest, rise, roost, sag, sit, slope, slouch,
slump, sprawl, squat, stand, stoop, straddle, swing, tilt, tower

(6) *Verbs of disappearance* (48.2): die, disappear, expire, lapse, perish, vanish

(7) *Externally caused verbs of change of state* (45, only relevant subclasses of
Levin's "verbs of change of state" are listed)

    a. Break *verbs* (45.1): break, chip, crack, crash, crush, fracture, rip, shatter,
smash, snap, splinter, split, tear

    b. Bend *verbs* (45.2): bend, crease, crinkle, crumple, fold, rumple, wrinkle

    c. *Cooking verbs* (45.3): bake, barbecue, blanch, boil, braise, broil, brown,
charbroil, charcoal-broil, coddle, cook, crisp, deep-fry, French fry, fry,
grill, hardboil, heat, microwave, oven-fry, oven-poach, overcook, pan-
broil, pan-fry, parboil, parch, percolate, perk, plank, poach, pot-roast,
rissole, roast, sauté, scald, scallop, shirr, simmer, softboil, steam, steam-
bake, stew, stir-fry, toast

    d. *Other alternating verbs of change of state* (45.4): abate, advance, age, air,
alter, atrophy, awake, balance, blast, blur, burn, burst, capsize, change,

char, chill, clog, close, collapse, collect, compress, condense, contract, corrode, crumble, decompose, decrease, deflate, defrost, degrade, diminish, dissolve, distend, divide, double, drain, ease, enlarge, expand, explode, fade, fill, flood, fray, freeze, frost, fuse, grow, halt, heal, heat, hush, ignite, improve, increase, inflate, kindle, light, loop, mature, melt, multiply, overturn, pop, quadruple, rekindle, reopen, reproduce, rupture, scorch, sear, short, short-circuit, shrink, shrivel, singe, sink, soak, splay, sprout, steep, stretch, submerge, subside, taper, thaw, tilt, tire, topple, triple, unfold, vary, warp

Zero-related to adjective: blunt, clean, clear, cool, crisp, dim, dirty, double, dry, dull, empty, even, firm, level, loose, mellow, muddy, narrow, open, pale, quiet, round, shut, slack, slim, slow, smooth, sober, sour, steady, tame, tense, thin, triple, warm

Change of color: blacken, brown, crimson, gray, green, purple, redden, silver, tan, whiten, yellow

-en verbs: awaken, brighten, broaden, cheapen, coarsen, dampen, darken, deepen, fatten, flatten, freshen, gladden, harden, hasten, heighten, lengthen, lessen, lighten, loosen, moisten, neaten, quicken, quieten, ripen, roughen, sharpen, shorten, sicken, slacken, smarten, soften, steepen, stiffen, straighten, strengthen, sweeten, tauten, thicken, tighten, toughen, waken, weaken, widen, worsen

-ify verbs: acetify, acidify, alkalify, calcify, carbonify, dehumidify, emulsify, fructify, gasify, humidify, intensify, lignify, liquefy, magnify, nitrify, ossify, petrify, purify, putrefy, silicify, solidify, stratify, vitrify

-ize verbs: americanize, caramelize, carbonize, crystallize, decentralize, demagnetize, democratize, depressurize, destabilize, energize, equalize, fossilize, gelatinize, glutenize, harmonize, hybridize, iodize, ionize, magnetize, neutralize, oxidize, polarize, pulverize, regularize, stabilize, unionize, vaporize, volatilize, westernize

-ate verbs: accelerate, agglomerate, ameliorate, attenuate, coagulate, decelerate, deescalate, degenerate, desiccate, deteriorate, detonate, disintegrate, dissipate, evaporate, federate, granulate, incubate, levitate, macerate, operate, proliferate, propagate, ulcerate, vibrate

(8) *Internally caused verbs of change of state* (45.5, Levin's "verbs of entity-specific change of state"): blister, bloom, blossom, burn, corrode, decay, deteriorate, erode, ferment, flower, germinate, molder, molt, rot, rust, sprout, stagnate, swell, tarnish, wilt, wither

Appendix B

Verbs Found in the Locative Inversion Construction

In this appendix we list the verbs that we have found in the locative inversion construction. As we mention in chapter 6, the corpus of locative inversion that formed the basis of our research was collected opportunistically, and no effort was made to limit our study to the set of locative inversions found in a "balanced" sample of English texts. Since our goal was an understanding of unaccusativity, we were particularly interested in the range of verbs found in this construction, whatever the nature of the text they were found in. We list the verbs we have found in the construction in this appendix for two reasons: to dispel the misconception that the set of verbs found in this construction is small and to provide future researchers with a list of verbs to work from. The list is split into two parts: the intransitive verbs found in the construction and the passive verbs found in the construction. In addition, we found the following transitive verb plus object combinations in the construction: *take place* and *take root*. This list should not be considered to be a complete list of the verbs that can be found in the construction. Furthermore, as we discuss in chapter 6, a careful examination of this list suggests that some types of additional verbs are more likely to be encountered in the future than others.

(1) *Intransitive verbs*: adhere, alight, amble, appear, apply, arise, arrive, ascend, await, beat, begin, behold, belch, belong, blaze, bloom, blossom, bob, boom, bound, break, bubble, bulge, burn, burst, cascade, chatter, climb, cling, come, commence, crawl, creep, crouch, curl, dance, dangle, dash, dawn, decay, depend, derive, descend, die, dilute, doze, drain, drift, drip, droop, drop, dwell, echo, emanate, emerge, ensue, enter, erupt, evolve, exist, extend, exude, fall, fall out, fan, fester, figure, flap, flash, flee, flicker, float, flood, flop, flourish, flow, flower, flutter, fly, follow, gallop, gather, get, gleam, glimmer, glisten, glitter, gloom, go, grow, hang, happen, hatch, head, heave, hide, highlight, hobble, hop, hover, hulk, hurry, hurtle, idle, issue, jerk, jump, kneel, labour, laze, lean, leap, lie, linger, live, look, loom, lounge, lurk, march, mill, mingle, mount, move, nestle, occur, open, operate, originate, parachute, parade, pass, peep, peer, perch, persist, plop, pop, pour, prance, preside, project, protrude, puff, pull, purl, pursue, radiate, ramble, range, rattle, read, reappear, rear, recline, reign, remain, repose, reside, rest,

revolve, ride, ring, ripple, rise, roil, roll, romp, rotate, rove, rumble, run, rush, sail, scamper, scintillate, scurry, scuttle, seep, seethe, sheer, shelter, shine, shiver, shoot, show, shriek, shuffle, sing, sit, sleep, slide, slip, slope, slouch, soar, sound, sparkle, speak, speed, spill, splash, sprawl, spread, spring, sprout, squat, stagger, stand, stare, steal, stem, step, stick out, straddle, stray, stream, stretch, stride, stroll, strut, succeed, surface, sweep, swim, swing, swirl, swoop, thrive, throne, throng, tick, toil, tower, trail, trickle, trot, trudge, tumble, twinkle, twist, unroll, waft, wait, walk, waltz, war, wave, well, wheel, whirl, work, yawn

(2) *Passive verbs*: be added, be appended, be arranged, be arrayed, be assembled, be attached, be balanced, be blended, be born, be brocaded, be built, be buried, be burned, be carried, be carved, be clipped, be clustered, be clutched, be collected, be committed, be concealed, be concentrated, be cooked, be coupled, be described, be directed, be discerned, be discovered, be discussed, be displayed, be draped, be drawn, be driven, be dropped, be embedded, be enacted, be engraved, be entombed, be erected, be exiled, be exploded, be expressed, be extinguished, be fastened, be fired, be fixed, be flung, be folded, be found, be gathered, be given, be glimpsed, be glued, be gotten, be grouped, be heaped, be heard, be hidden, be hooked, be housed, be hung, be imprinted, be included, be inscribed, be interspersed, be kept, be laced, be laid, be left, be lined up, be listed, be located, be lodged, be meant, be mined, be mingled, be mounted, be outlined, be painted, be parked, be pasted, be perched, be piled, be pinned, be placed, be put, be raised, be ranged, be realized, be recovered, be reflected, be related, be represented, be scattered, be scratched, be scrawled, be scribbled, be seated, be seen, be served, be set, be shelved, be shown, be situated, be slung, be sounded, be spawned, be spelled, be spread, be stacked, be stamped, be stapled, be stored, be stowed, be strapped, be strewn, be stuck, be subsumed, be sunk, be suspended, be tattooed, be thrown, be thrust, be trained, be trapped, be tucked, be understood, be washed, be wound, be woven, be written

Notes

Chapter 1

1. See Pullum 1988 for a brief overview of the development of this hypothesis and similar hypotheses. Although Perlmutter's paper provided the impetus for recent explorations of the syntactic properties associated with members of the intransitive verb class, Hall 1965 probably contains the earliest proposal that there is a subclass of intransitive verbs whose surface subjects are underlyingly objects, as both Pullum (1988) and Dowty (1991) point out.

2. The syntactic encoding of unaccusativity does not necessarily have to be a configurational encoding, as it is in the GB framework. The approach to unaccusativity in Lexical Functional Grammar (LFG) as presented in Bresnan and Zaenen's (1990) analysis of the resultative construction is also one in which unaccusativity is syntactically encoded, even though LFG does not have a level of syntactic representation comparable to GB's D-Structure. LFG's a-structure, which is not configurational like GB's D-Structure, still allows a syntactic distinction between unergative and unaccusative verbs. In a-structure the argument that surfaces as the object of a transitive verb and the single argument of an unaccusative verb both receive the syntactic feature specification $[-r]$ (unrestricted syntactic function); this feature sets these arguments apart from the arguments that surface as subjects of unergative and transitive verbs, which receive the syntactic feature specification $[-o]$ (nonobjective syntactic function) at a-structure.

3. In fact, unaccusative verbs may differ from each other in another way as well: some may select one internal argument—a direct argument—whereas others may select more than one. The same holds of unergative verbs: some may and some may not select indirect internal arguments; however, an unergative verb never selects a direct internal argument.

4. There is no generally accepted account of how the inability of a verb to assign structural Case can be reduced to the unaccusative D-Structure configuration. For some attempts, see Everaert 1986, Laka 1993, and J. Levin and Massam 1985, among others. More recent work has suggested a need to reexamine the part of Burzio's Generalization that states that if a verb does not take an external argument, it cannot assign structural Case. Although this generalization appears to be

valid in English and some other languages, and we will take advantage of its validity in this book, several studies have reported phenomena in various languages involving a verb that lacks an external argument but is nevertheless able to assign structural Case; for example, see Sobin 1985 on the Ukrainian passive. Phenomena such as these make clear that the relationship between lack of an external argument and structural Case assignment is more complex than Burzio's Generalization suggests. It is most likely that the inability to assign structural Case is to be taken not as a defining property of unaccusative verbs but as a derived property. A full account of the relationship between lack of external argument and structural Case assignment is needed for a full account of unaccusativity.

5. The two definitions diverge in their classification of verbs with neither an external nor a direct internal argument, a set of verbs that does not really concern us. The major set of verbs that appear to meet this characterization are the weather verbs (e.g., *drizzle, rain, snow*). With respect to Burzio's definition, weather verbs qualify as unaccusative verbs. It is not so clear how they would be classified with respect to the definition in terms of direct internal argument, since they have neither an external argument nor a direct internal argument. If, as Ruwet (1991) argues, these verbs are unaccusative verbs, then there is empirical evidence bearing on the proper definition; however, the arguments that Ruwet cites in favor of this position need to be reassessed in light of the methodological considerations stressed throughout this chapter. The question of the classification of weather verbs is further complicated by claims that in English the *it* that turns up as their subject is a quasi argument (Chomsky 1981, Pesetsky 1995, Zubizarreta 1982; see also Bolinger 1972); if so, these verbs take an external argument and would have to be analyzed as unergative verbs.

6. C. Rosen (1984) cites the dual auxiliary verbs as disproving what she terms the "Little Alignment Hypothesis," formulated as follows: "For any one predicate in any one language, there is a fixed mapping which aligns each semantic role with an initial GR [= grammatical relation]. The alignment remains invariant for all clauses with that predicate" (1984:53). It should be noted that this hypothesis is not the same as the hypothesis that the syntactic expression of arguments is determinable on the basis of meaning, since it imposes the additional requirement that a given semantic role will always be associated with the same syntactic expression for each use of a predicator. One could imagine that the syntactic expression of the arguments of a predicator could be predictable, while still varying across different uses of that predicator. For example, suppose that the syntactic expression of the theme argument of a verb of change of state were characterized as follows: the theme is expressed as direct object when the verb is used transitively but as subject when the verb is used intransitively. Given such a statement, the syntactic expression of a theme, although variable, is nevertheless predictable. Such a statement, however, would not be allowed by Rosen's Little Alignment Hypothesis.

Rosen's Little Alignment Hypothesis also relies on the assumption that the syntactically relevant aspects of verb meaning remain constant across different uses of a verb; furthermore, it assumes that the semantic roles remain constant across uses. Therefore, even devising a way to test the validity of this hypothesis would first require doing a certain amount of lexical semantic investigation as groundwork. This point is important since the Little Alignment Hypothesis seems to be the precursor of Baker's (1988a) Uniformity of θ Assignment Hypothesis, although research that makes use of Baker's hypothesis often does not show an awareness of these ramifications.

7. See section 4.2.1 for further discussion of the verb *blush*. There we cite evidence from McClure 1990 that the "translation equivalent" of *blush* in Dutch is an activity verb, accounting for a difference in the classification of this verb in Italian and Dutch.

8. See Everaert 1992 for further discussion of the ramifications of such data for the theory of auxiliary selection. In fact, the question arises whether telicity is even a necessary condition for unaccusativity in Dutch in light of the existence of the verb *blijven* 'remain', which takes the auxiliary *zijn* 'be', but is not telic. It appears to us from all the material we have read on auxiliary selection in Dutch that a fully accurate descriptive generalization of this phenomenon has not yet been offered for this language.

9. The specific phenomena that Martin (1991) discusses have also been discussed under the heading of "split intransitivity." This label is used by Merlan (1985) to describe patterns of case marking or verb agreement in various languages that subdivide intransitive verbs into two classes. Since then the label has sometimes been applied to any phenomenon that distinguishes among intransitive verbs, including phenomena that are cited as unaccusative diagnostics, as in Van Valin 1990. Merlan's study, which surveys split intransitivity in its original narrow sense in a range of languages and evaluates a range of semantic notions that might be responsible for the splits, suggests that split intransitivity is sometimes merely semantic. More extensive studies are needed to evaluate the exact relation between the phenomena typically cited under the label "split intransitivity" and the phenomena cited as unaccusative diagnostics.

10. In this context, we mention *ne*-cliticization, whose status as an unaccusative diagnostic was established by Belletti and Rizzi (1981), Burzio (1986), Perlmutter (1989), and C. Rosen (1984), among others. Although *ne*-cliticization has remained one of the most cited and least questioned of the unaccusative diagnostics, several researchers have suggested that it may not be a diagnostic after all (Lonzi 1985, Saccon 1992). In our own research we have found that in every instance where we examined a surface unaccusative diagnostic, questions about that diagnostic's validity arose. We conclude that further study of these diagnostics as a class is needed to assess the significance of these phenomena for the nature of unaccusativity. For additional discussion, see section 6.8.

11. If the VP-Internal Subject Hypothesis (Koopman and Sportiche 1991, Kuroda 1988, Fukui and Speas 1986, Sportiche 1988, Zagona 1982, among others) is adopted, the notion of external argument will need to be refined. Presumably, the internal arguments would be those realized within V′ and the external argument would be the one realized external to V′.

12. Since it is not relevant to the point under discussion, we do not consider whether the meaning of a verb of putting is more accurately characterized as

'cause to be at a location' (i.e., the causative of a stative) or 'cause to come to be at a location' (i.e., the causative of a verb of change), as in (21). See Carter 1976, 1978 for arguments in favor of analyzing all causative verbs as causatives of verbs of change. See also section 3.3.3 for some related discussion.

13. We leave aside the issue of additional meanings attributable to metaphorical extension that develop once the basic pairing of a meaning and a phonological form is in place. See Hale and Keyser 1993 for another approach to the problem of the pairing of verb meanings and verb names based on the incorporation of constants into empty verbal heads.

14. In some languages one of these two verbs is morphologically complex. Interestingly, in such languages *sell* is usually morphologically analyzable as 'cause to buy'. The association of morphologically complex forms with particular meanings is not arbitrary since morphemes have associated meanings, though such associations would benefit from examination in the context of the questions posed here.

Chapter 2

1. Since we will show in section 2.2.1 that not all postverbal NPs that have resultative XPs predicated of them are necessarily analyzed as objects, we refer to those NPs whose status as objects is in question as *postverbal NPs* in this section. However, we continue for the sake of convenience to refer to the restriction on the distribution of resultative phrases as the Direct Object Restriction.

2. As J. Grimshaw has pointed out to us, some speakers find a gradation in acceptability between the three types of resultative constructions based on unergative verbs, preferring the constructions with fake reflexives to those with nonsubcategorized NPs with possessive pronouns, and in turn preferring those to the resultative constructions with other nonsubcategorized NPs. Even this last kind of resultative, however, is extensively represented in the examples we have collected.

3. Pustejovsky (1991b) suggests that resultative phrases that appear with unaccusatives can only provide a further specification of the result that is lexically encoded in the verb to which the resultative phrase is added. This proposal cannot be true in general since this property holds of the examples in (19a–c) but not of the examples in (19d–e).

4. Reliance on Burzio's Generalization as an explanation of these examples is perhaps a weak point in our analysis, since, as mentioned, an explanation for this generalization is still lacking, and its absolute validity has been called into question. However, it is a fact of English that unaccusative verbs cannot be followed by bare NPs. Furthermore, this phenomenon does not appear to be reducible to any semantic generalization. Therefore, we are still justified in attributing the ungrammaticality of these examples to a syntactic property of unaccusative verbs.

5. A. Zaenen has pointed out to us that the differing status of the examples in (26) and (27) does not necessarily have to be attributed to the status of the posthead NPs as arguments or nonarguments, since there may be other explanations for the contrasting behavior. Although this is strictly speaking true, the fact that our

explanation is not the only explanation available does not detract from its validity. In any event, we are not aware of an explicit alternative account for the contrast.

6. We have checked these judgments with several informants, and the judgments that we obtained correspond to Rothstein's.

7. Given that they can be predicated of subjects, depictive phrases raise a more fundamental question about the validity of the mutual c-command requirement on predication. All accounts of depictive phrases that we are aware of seek to preserve this requirement, which we take to be valid. Roberts (1988) takes the data involving depictive phrases as support for VP-internal subjects. Rothstein (1989) accounts for the data using a theory of predicate merger.

8. This rule is relevant to the expression of the arguments of a verb. It is possible, and even likely, that predicators of different lexical categories map their arguments to syntax differently. In particular, the argument of an adjective that denotes a result state may not be subject to the requirement that it be governed by the adjective. Therefore, the fact that resultative phrases can be predicated of nonderived subjects of adjectival passives, as mentioned in section 2.2.1, is not necessarily a problem. A diagnostic should not be used blindly; rather, the explanation for the diagnostic must always be sought and taken into account.

9. Carrier and Randall (in press) note the existence of some idioms that have the syntactic form of a resultative construction, such as *bleed ... white, eat ... out of house and home, work one's fingers to the bone.* The existence of such idioms is not precluded by the proposal that the meaning of the resultative construction is compositionally derived. All idioms have the syntactic properties of constructions that typically are associated with compositionally derived meanings, so the existence of idioms that take the form of the resultative construction but do not have compositional meanings should be no surprise. These constructions would presumably take on idiomatic meanings in the same way as any other construction would. What is more important is that most resultative constructions are instances of innovative constructions with compositional meanings.

10. There also appear to be no lexically simple verbs that mean 'cause to become ADJECTIVE', where ADJECTIVE is individual-level (see section 3.2.1 for discussion). Thus, the absence of resultative phrases headed by individual-level predicates might be attributed to the fact that the resultative construction cannot create a verb type that is not capable of being a lexical verb.

11. Simpson (1983a) notes the restriction on resultative phrases with verbs of motion and formulates a similar restriction in terms of the notions of change of state and change of location. A. Goldberg's (1991) Unique Path Constraint is yet another formulation of this restriction.

12. A resultative construction such as *clean something clean* is rather odd. This oddness can probably be attributed to the fact that the verb *clean* itself lexicalizes the precise result state that the adjective specifies so that the adjective *clean* here does not contribute additional information. In such instances, the two result states —the one lexicalized in the verb and the one expressed via the resultative phrase— can be considered redundant. In fact, the resultative construction *clean something*

spotless is considerably better; here the adjective does have a contribution to make.

13. The unacceptability of resultative constructions in which the resultative phrase is predicated of the object of a preposition, as in *The silversmith pounded on the metal flat*, would have a similar explanation. The resultative phrase would again have to be part of a small clause headed by a PRO controlled by the object of the preposition, and this PRO would again be governed by the verb, violating the PRO Theorem.

14. We have found a similar phenomenon involving experiencer-object psych-verbs, as in (i) and (ii). Although we originally took these examples to be instances of transitive resultative constructions with a nonsubcategorized postverbal NP, as shown by the unacceptability of (iii) and (iv), we now believe that an alternative analysis should be possible that shows some broad similarity to the one we propose for the *wash* sentences.

(i)   ... but Miss Chancellor made him feel that she was in earnest, and that idea frightened the resistance out of him ... [H. James, *The Bostonians*, 167]

(ii) The journalist ... has made it big by charming intimate truths out of powerful interview subjects. [M. Gallagher, review of *Best Intentions* by K. Lehrer, 16]

(iii) *The idea frightened the resistance.

(iv) *The journalist charmed intimate truths.

Again the NP that would ordinarily be expected to be the object of the verb in isolation—with these verbs, the experiencer argument—is expressed in these constructions, although as the object of a preposition. These constructions describe a change in the state of the experiencer that results in depriving the experiencer of what is described by the postverbal NP. It remains to be seen whether a verb-of-removal analysis is also desirable here or whether an alternative account is preferable.

15. Although Van Valin claims that his account is a semantic one, the notions of actor and undergoer are not really semantic notions, as we have already pointed out in chapter 1, since, as Van Valin himself stresses, the terms cannot be reduced to or equated with any semantic notion such as agent or patient. We disregard this point here and concentrate simply on the viability of Van Valin's account. And, in fact, the notion of undergoer is not really crucial to Van Valin's analysis since reference to a particular LS substructure can replace this notion, as we discuss here.

16. It seems to us that in Van Valin's approach it may be difficult to explain the inability of resultative phrases to be predicated of the object of a preposition, as in *The blacksmith pounded on the metal flat*. It is possible that this sentence is excluded since it does not have an undergoer for the resultative phrase to be predicated of, assuming that an undergoer cannot be expressed as the object of a preposition.

17. This amounts to saying that resultative phrases can only be added to verbs that in isolation describe some change: either a change of location or a change of state. This generalization is not true, since resultative phrases can follow verbs of contact by impact such as *hammer* and *pound*, which in isolation do not describe any change. We disregard this point here and continue to develop the analysis, but it should be clear that this fact already detracts from its viability.

Chapter 3

1. The unaccusative status of verbs of change of state, especially those that participate in the causative alternation, has been assumed by linguists working on unaccusativity beginning with Perlmutter (1978), who included them among the semantic classes of unaccusative verbs on the basis of their behavior with respect to impersonal passivization. In Italian these verbs pass the standard unaccusative tests, including selection of the auxiliary *essere* 'be'. In English these verbs can appear in the unaccusative resultative pattern and cannot assign accusative Case, as shown by their inability to take various types of nonsubcategorized objects. We defer a systematic demonstration of the unaccusativity of these verbs until chapter 4, where we also present the linking rules that determine their unaccusative status. The verbs *laugh*, *play*, and *speak*, cited below as unergative verbs, are representative of the intransitive agentive activity verbs that are taken to be the prototypical unergative verbs cross-linguistically in Perlmutter 1978 and subsequent work. This classification is based on the behavior of these verbs with respect to standard unaccusative diagnostics.

2. Some English intransitive verbs without transitive causative counterparts are used transitively in the resultative construction discussed in chapter 2, but in this construction the verbs do not have the transitive causative meaning associated with the alternating verbs. Consider the verb *laugh* in the resultative construction *The crowd laughed the candidate off the stage*. This resultative example does not mean that the crowd made the candidate laugh, which would be the interpretation that would parallel the intended interpretation of (4b); it can only mean that the crowd laughed.

3. In languages that form the equivalent of the English periphrastic (i.e., *make*) causative through the use of a causative morpheme, these verbs will systematically have causatives. But this type of causative usually involves a different type of causation from the type associated with the alternating verbs, which is termed "direct" (or, sometimes, manipulative, contact, or immediate) causation, contrasting with English periphrastic causatives, which allow an "indirect," as well as a direct, causation interpretation (Comrie 1976b, Cruse 1972, Nedyalkov and Silnitsky 1973, Shibatani 1976, among others). The type of causative expressed with alternating verbs in English is not available to all verbs, unlike the type of causative expressed by the periphrastic causative construction in English, which is productive. In some languages both direct and indirect causation are morphologically encoded, but in such languages the two typically involve distinct morphological devices. We refer to the kind of causative we are focusing on here as the

"lexical causative," since it is typically formed using the lexical resources of a language and shows the hallmarks of a lexical process (Wasow 1977).

4. Chierchia (1989) also takes the transitive variant of an alternating verb to be basic, but he takes the presence of reflexive morphology on the intransitive unaccusative variant in Italian and other languages seriously, proposing that the unaccusative use is derived by a lexical operation of reflexivization, which identifies the internal argument of a dyadic causative verb such as *break* with its external argument. Chierchia proposes that the causative interpretation associated with the dyadic variant of most of these verbs carries over in some sense to the monadic variant: the reflexivization process is associated with a particular kind of "static" causative interpretation. To illustrate, the verb *sink* is taken to be a basically dyadic causative verb. Its intransitive unaccusative form is derived from the transitive form by the process of reflexivization, a sentence like *The boat sank* being given the interpretation 'a property of the boat causes the boat to sink' (Chierchia 1989:19). As evidence for this aspect of his analysis, Chierchia notes that unaccusative verbs are commonly associated with reflexive morphology across languages. This property is explained on his analysis since these verbs are explicitly derived by a process of reflexivization. Although we agree with Chierchia that the causative variant is in some sense basic, we do not commit ourselves to the reflexivization part of Chierchia's analysis.

5. Our investigation of selectional restrictions was inspired by Rothemberg's (1974) study of French verbs with transitive and intransitive uses. This study includes examples of many verbs whose transitive and intransitive uses have diverging selectional restrictions.

6. Of course, there are some languages where the reverse type of morphology is used to create a dyadic causative predicate from the monadic predicate. Nine of the sixty languages in Nedjalkov's sample show this property. However, it is difficult to tell from Nedjalkov's paper whether the morpheme used to form transitive *break* is the same one used to derive causatives in general in the languages concerned, although the data Nedjalkov cites in an appendix suggest that in the majority of these languages it is at least not the morpheme used to form the causative of *laugh*.

7. Nedjalkov (1969) notes that in those languages where the verb *laugh* has both transitive and intransitive uses, this verb typically means 'laugh at' rather than 'make laugh' when used transitively.

8. More comprehensive inventories of the members of the four groups, together with extensive descriptions of their properties, can be found in B. Levin 1993; see also B. Levin 1991 for a study focusing on the verbs of sound emission. Many of the verbs of sound emission have agentive uses; in this section we are concerned only with their nonagentive uses (see section 5.1.2 for some discussion of the agentive uses).

All the verbs of emission take the emitter as the subject; however, the verbs of substance emission differ from the other subclasses in showing more variety in the expression of their arguments (see B. Levin 1993). One of these other possible expressions of arguments is discussed in section 6.4.2.

9. Agentive internally caused verbs like *run* can appear with the adverbial *by itself* under the 'without outside help' interpretation, as in *Carrie ran by herself today*. This interpretation, however, is only available under very restricted circumstances, say, if Carrie suffered an injury and as a result of much physical therapy she finally was able to run unaided.

10. We have restricted our attention here to verbs that are syntactically intransitive. It may be that there are internally caused verbs that are syntactically transitive. We leave this question for future research, which will explore the nature of these representations more fully.

11. Actually, with the exception of the verb *blush*, which interestingly takes an animate subject, the internally caused verbs of change of state cited here have both a change-of-state interpretation and a 'be in state' interpretation. The two interpretations can be brought out using the following pair of sentences: *The flower bloomed for three days*, *The flower bloomed in a day*.

12. See Brousseau and Ritter 1991 for further discussion of the circumstances that allow verbs to take both instruments and agents as subjects. See Hale and Keyser 1993 for some similar ideas on how the specification of a manner or means can impede detransitivization.

13. There is an interesting gap in the set of observed verb meanings, which is probably significant: although there are verbs such as *break* that describe the bringing about of a specified change of state by an unspecified activity, there are no verbs that describe the bringing about of an unspecified change of state by a specified activity.

14. Our account shows some similarity to the account proposed by van Voorst (1993), which also ties detransitivization to whether or not a verb specifies properties of an argument. Unfortunately, this manuscript came to our attention too late to be able to include a full discussion of it.

15. Some researchers include the verb *walk*, which is found in pairs such as *The visitor walked to the museum/Lisa walked the visitor to the museum*, among the agentive verbs of manner of motion that can be causativized. The interpretation of the transitive *walk* sentence differs crucially from that of the causative (b) sentences in (66)–(68). Unlike these sentences, the transitive *walk* sentence lacks any sense of coercion. It is unclear to us whether the behavior of *walk* is representative of a general pattern.

16. There may be some disagreement about whether the directional phrases are absolutely necessary in the transitive causative uses of these verbs, particularly with the verb *jump*. But even if these phrases need not be expressed in certain circumstances, they are always understood in the transitive causative use. For example, sentence (70c) cannot mean that the rider made the horse jump in place; rather, it must receive a directional interpretation, where the horse jumps, say, over a fence. We provide an explanation for this property in section 5.1.1.2.

17. In fact, it is also possible that unaccusative verbs that are not externally caused will develop transitive causative variants. In such instances we would predict, once again, that the relationship between the two variants in such causative

pairs will not be the same as the one that holds in the *break*-type causative pairs. We illustrate this phenomenon in section 3.3.3.

18. The Modern Hebrew causative pairs involving agentive verbs of manner of motion do not show the directional phrase restriction manifested in the comparable English pairs. In chapter 5 we present an analysis of the English pairs in which the directional phrase in some sense licenses the position needed for the external cause. We assume that the causative affix in Modern Hebrew has its own argument structure, which includes an external cause, so that Modern Hebrew need not have recourse to the English strategy.

19. We acknowledge that occasionally a restricted and specialized transitive causative use of one of these verbs does arise and might even gain general currency, as in the recent transitive use of the verb *disappear*, which has emerged in connection with certain political events in South America. However, these are idiosyncratic causative pairs of the type illustrated with the verb *burp* in section 3.2.5. The idiosyncratic nature of the causative use of *disappear* is reflected in the absence of a comparable use of its near synonym, the verb *vanish* (**The police vanished the activists*).

20. The greater number of verbs of existence and appearance with the reflexive morpheme in Russian than in Italian or French might be attributable to the rather different distribution of this morpheme in Russian, and concomitantly to the different function that this different distribution reflects. As discussed in B. Levin 1985, in Russian this morpheme is even found with some unergative verbs and seems to signal inability to assign accusative Case, rather than lack of an external argument. (The unergative verbs that do occur with *-sja* are never paired with transitive causative variants without this morpheme, contrasting with the suffixed unaccusative verbs of change of state.) In French and Italian the reflexive morpheme need not signal inability to assign accusative Case, as sentences such as the Italian *Maria si è lavata i capelli* 'Maria washed her hair' show. Rather, it is taken to signal the existence of a binding relation between the subject and an argument inside the VP (Burzio 1986, C. Rosen 1984, among others). It is only when a verb does not have an external argument that, by Burzio's Generalization, it is unable to assign accusative Case.

21. The facts are actually more complicated. At least in English, the interpretation of the adverbial *by itself* relevant to Chierchia's argument—the 'without outside help' interpretation—is found in the following sentence: *The explosion occurred/happened by itself*. This example, as well as the other problematic examples we have found, involve verbs of occurrence, a subset of the larger set of verbs of existence and appearance whose members take events, rather than entities, as arguments. Perhaps their distinctive behavior arises because events are themselves caused and thus can license the adverbial phrase on the 'without outside help' interpretation. Nevertheless, it is worth pointing out that only some verbs in this class appear felicitously with the adverbial. Contrast the previous example with **The riot ensued by itself*, ??*The infection recurred by itself*.

22. The exact function of these completive particles deserves further investigation.

It appears that in the progressive these particles are compatible with the maintain position sense as well.

23. A reviewer questions our inclusion of the verb *balance*, suggesting that it can be used intransitively. Our own intuition, which appears to be supported by corpus evidence, is that *balance* can be used intransitively only with an animate agentive subject, as in *She could balance on one foot for hours*—hence, in the maintain position sense and not in the simple position sense, the sense that is relevant here. The verb *mount* also has a transitive noncausative, though agentive, use, as in *She mounted the horse;* this use seems to involve something resembling the assume position sense. Finally, we note that we have also included the verb *perch* among the verbs used to illustrate this point, although there appears to be dialectal variation involving its use; some speakers can use it intransitively with inanimate subjects, and others cannot. For the latter speakers, *perch* patterns precisely like *balance:* it can have only the maintain position sense when intransitive, giving rise to the animacy restriction.

Chapter 4

1. We have formulated the linking rules in terms of the argument structure notions "external argument" and "direct internal argument" since we see these rules as mapping the lexical semantic representation into the lexical syntactic representation or argument structure. The external argument and direct internal argument are then "projected" into the syntax as the D-Structure grammatical relations of subject and object, respectively. It would also have been possible to formulate the linking rules in terms of the corresponding D-Structure grammatical relations.

2. These verbs have also been argued to be unergative in Italian on the basis of their failure to permit *ne*-cliticization. Given the questions concerning whether *ne*-cliticization is indeed a true unaccusative diagnostic (see note 10 of chapter 1 and section 6.8), we have decided not to cite *ne*-cliticization as an unaccusative diagnostic either here or at any of the other points in chapters 4 and 5 where this might have been possible.

3. We recognize, however, that the viability of the impersonal passive diagnostic is still controversial. For instance, it needs to be further scrutinized in view of observations such as those made by Zaenen (1993) that suggest that in certain circumstances some unaccusative verbs are found in impersonal passive constructions. In the final analysis, the status of this construction as an unaccusative diagnostic depends in part on showing that the syntactic properties of unaccusative verbs explain the lack of impersonal passive constructions containing these verbs. See Marantz 1984 and Baker, Johnson, and Roberts 1989 for possible explanations along these lines. If these explanations are indeed valid, as we feel they are, then the data that Zaenen discusses must be reevaluated.

In some languages, including Lithuanian, all predicates can undergo impersonal passivization (Baker, Johnson, and Roberts 1989, Marantz 1984, Timberlake 1982). Following Baker, Johnson, and Roberts (1989), we assume that their existence does not invalidate the impersonal passive test and the related English prepositional passive test introduced in section 4.1.1.2 in languages like English and Dutch, but rather indicates that there is something special about the passive construction in languages like Lithuanian.

4. Couper-Kuhlen (1979) presents a careful large-scale study of a wide range of verbs aimed at isolating the semantic factors that determine whether an English verb allows the prepositional passive. The results of this study confirm the existence of an animacy restriction.

5. As our analysis stands, the Immediate Cause Linking Rule applies both to the external cause of an externally caused verb and to the internal cause of an internally caused verb. However, these two types of arguments do not correspond to any one position in lexical semantic representation: the external cause is the argument of a CAUSE predicate; the argument of an internally caused verb is not. It remains to be seen whether or not this is a disadvantage of the proposed approach.

6. There is, however, a fundamental difference in the way the two linking rules are formulated: the Change-of-State Linking Rule is formulated in terms of D-Structure positions, and the Directed Change Linking Rule is formulated in terms of argument structure positions. We stated the Change-of-State Linking Rule in terms of D-Structure syntactic positions in chapter 2 because it was intended to encompass the postverbal NP in resultative constructions based on unergative verbs even though on our analysis that NP is not part of the argument structure of the verb in the construction. We believe that the Change-of-State Linking Rule can be nonetheless dispensed with in favor of the Directed Change Linking Rule once additional facets of the analysis of the resultative construction are elaborated. It is likely that a fully worked out analysis of this construction will involve the formation of a complex predicate, along the lines suggested by Neeleman and Weerman (1993). If so, the postverbal NP will be the argument of the complex predicate, allowing this NP to fall under the Directed Change Linking Rule as applied to the arguments of the complex predicate, allowing the fundamental insight of the analysis in chapter 2 to be maintained. Specifically, the complex predicate analysis does not require positing that the verb in the resultative construction acquires a new argument structure; instead, the arguments of the verb in isolation are input to the rule of complex predicate formation, which creates a new predicate with its own arguments. The linking rules would then apply to the arguments of the complex predicate.

7. It is interesting that there is no need to subdivide the verbs of inherently directed motion according to internal and external causation in order to account for their properties. In fact, the meaning of these verbs seems to leave open whether they are to be understood as denoting internally or externally caused eventualities. It is likely that, as suggested in B. Levin and Rappaport Hovav 1992, this property is to be attributed to the element of meaning lexicalized by these verbs or, from the perspective in section 1.4, the element of meaning that these verbs take their name from. These verbs lexicalize a direction, rather than a means or manner. Means or manner, when lexicalized in the verb, can determine whether or not a verb will be agentive, and hence whether the verb can describe an internally caused eventual-

ity, but direction, it seems, does not have this effect. In this respect these verbs are more like verbs of existence and appearance.

8. In fact, Centineo (1986), Martin (1991), and Van Valin (1990) have all cited *fiorire*, the Italian counterpart of English *bloom*, *blossom*, and *flower*, as being a verb that can select either the auxiliary *avere* 'have' or the auxiliary *essere* 'be'. It may be that this verb is open to both the state and change-of-state interpretations in Italian, and that the variation in auxiliary selection correlates with the variation in meaning.

9. The Italian verb *salire*, though sometimes glossed with English *climb*, has a purely directed motion sense. That is, it corresponds to *climb* only in the sense of 'go up', not in the manner-of-motion 'clamber' sense.

10. The unacceptability of these sentences cannot be attributed simply to the presence of a particle in the prepositional passive. There are well-formed prepositional passives that include a particle, such as *This kind of behavior is looked down on by everyone*.

11. Although agentivity and the related notion of protagonist control are not aspectual notions strictly speaking, they have continued to figure in aspectual accounts of the semantic underpinnings of unaccusativity, presumably because the verbs most often used to illustrate activities have agentive subjects (e.g., *jog*, *laugh*, *shout*, *work*). As pointed out by Verkuyl (1989), the existence of nonagentive activity verbs casts doubt on the use of agentivity and protagonist control as indicators of aspectual status. Indeed, agentivity is not really directly related to the internal temporal constituency of a predicate: as Dowty (1979) shows, there are both agentive and nonagentive verbs in all the traditional aspectual classes.

12. We do not, of course, deny the important role telicity plays in the aspectual analysis of sentences. Legendre (1991) also presents a critique of Van Valin's account that is based on a large-scale study of French intransitive verbs. She finds that, with the possible exception of the notion of activity, the components of meaning that Van Valin employs are not very effective for classifying a verb.

13. It is important to distinguish the emitter from what is emitted: in graphic representations, odor exuded and light emitted are typically depicted as flowing from the emitter, although the emitter itself is not represented as undergoing a change. In fact, some verbs of emission can take the emittee as subject (*Water oozed out of the crack*) and in this use show clearly unaccusative behavior (see section 6.4.2). The very term "emission" suggests a kind of change, although again with respect to what is emitted and not the emitter. This duality may account for the fact that the sentences in (92), which are intended to illustrate the stativity of these verbs, are not completely unacceptable.

14. Although it is possible to deny that these verbs are stative, as Carter (1978) does, they are considered stative under most definitions of stativity. This is certainly true by the definitional criteria we cited. Sitting and lying do not involve any change, nor do they ordinarily require any input of energy to maintain.

15. Punctual verbs such as *die* also do not fall under Dowty's notion of incremental theme, just as they do not technically fall under Tenny's (1987, 1992) related

notion "measuring out." It seems to us that the argument of a verb such as *die* ought to fall under the same linking rule as the other arguments that undergo a directed change, but at this point we have no direct evidence for this.

Chapter 5

1. In the recent generative literature this observation about differences between languages is generally attributed to Talmy, but it has been made previously (although sometimes in a less general form), particularly in the work of traditional grammarians and comparative stylisticians (Bergh 1948, Malblanc 1968, Vinay and Darbelnet 1958, among others). In particular, Bergh (1948) provides a careful and thorough descriptive study of differences in the expression of direction in French, and to a lesser extent Italian and Spanish, on the one hand, and Swedish, English, and German, on the other. Talmy's important contribution has been to articulate the significance of these observations, synthesizing them into a typology of lexicalization patterns. Following up on Talmy's influential papers, other investigators have continued to explore the lexicalization of motion and direction in other languages (see, for example, Aske 1989, Choi and Bowerman 1991, Olsen 1991, Schaefer 1985, Tsujimura 1991, 1993, Yoneyama 1986). Bergh's work, taken together with these other studies, suggests that the patterns of behavior in the Romance languages are less clear than Talmy's work suggests and that Talmy's typology of the possible lexicalizations of verbs of motion across languages needs refinement. Specifically, our own impression is that certain properties of the prepositional system of a language—particularly the expression of the notions of location and goal—interact with the lexicalization patterns that a language makes available to give rise to the different patterns of behavior found across languages. We hope to look more closely at these issues in future work.

2. The lexicalization patterns of verbs of motion in Japanese have been the subject of some controversy. Tsujimura (1991) argues that, despite a claim to the contrary by L. Levin, Mitamura, and Mahmoud (1988), Japanese is an English-type, and not a Romance-type, language. On the basis of further, more recent investigations, Tsujimura (1993) finds that the evidence bearing on the status of Japanese is more complicated than she suggested in her earlier paper and that as a first approximation Yoneyama's (1986) analysis, which we present here, is a reasonable description of the lexicalization patterns of verbs of motion in Japanese. It is interesting that the disagreement concerning whether Japanese is like English or not stems from differences of opinion about what constitutes a goal phrase in Japanese. Thus, as foreshadowed in note 1, a full understanding of Japanese's place in a typology of the lexicalization of motion requires a deeper understanding of the means of expressing goals and locations in Japanese.

3. The absence of an external argument must be viewed as a necessary, but not a sufficient, condition on the ability of a verb to introduce an external cause to its representation because there are two classes of unaccusative verbs, verbs of existence and appearance and internally caused verbs of change of state, that do not allow the introduction of an additional external cause, as noted in chapter 3, except in occasional novel coinages.

4. It is clear from the full context of (22a) that the riders are on separate horses, so that the example cannot be dismissed as having the accompaniment interpretation found in sentences such as *The boy walked his dog,* which might be argued to represent a distinct phenomenon (see note 15 of chapter 3).

5. Because of differences in the selectional properties of the adjectives that head them, the resultative phrases that can be predicated of animates are typically headed by the adjectives *free* and *clear,* whereas those predicated of inanimates are typically headed by *open, closed,* and *shut.*

6. S. Pinker (personal communication) has pointed out to us that there is a preference for a directional phrase when some verbs of light emission are used causatively: *The stagehand shone the light across the stage.* We assume that this is just another instantiation of the same phenomenon in which the meaning shift to verb of directed motion licenses a causative use of the verb.

7. Some notes about the French examples. In (51b) the French verb *vrombir,* unlike the English verb *roar,* is very literary. In (52b) the French noun *fracas,* like the English noun *din,* can be used for a range of loud noises and thus does not capture any of the properties that make the sound associated with the verb *rumble* different from those associated with other verbs describing loud sounds.

8. Nonetheless, Dowty (1991) does attribute the two uses of locative alternation verbs like *spray* and *load* to the existence of two lexical entries for these verbs, possibly related by a lexical rule.

9. The *roll* verbs could also be internally caused for certain choices of inanimate arguments that can be viewed as self-propelled such as certain types of vehicles or machines. For purposes of simplicity we will ignore this possibility and restrict ourselves to those inanimate arguments for which this is not the case.

10. This is not strictly true since there are nonagentive uses of *run,* as in *The machine is running.* However, this is clearly not a basic use of the verb. In contrast, there is no sense in which either the agentive or the nonagentive use of *roll* can be said to be nonbasic.

Chapter 6

1. More often than not the preverbal PPs found in the locative inversion construction are locative with verbs of existence and directional with verbs of appearance (typically, a source or goal PP). When they are not locative or directional, they tend to be temporal PPs since some verbs such as *occur* and *happen* locate events in time; these temporal PPs can be regarded as locative PPs since an analogy can be made between time and space. The only exceptions are the "comitative"-like PPs headed by *with,* which are found almost exclusively with the verbs *come* and *go,* and most often in their purely nonmotional appearance sense. And even with these verbs, benefactive, manner, and instrumental phrases are never found.

2. In the few instances of locative inversion involving transitive verbs, the NP that is understood as the subject of the verb turns up after the object of the verb, rather than in immediately postverbal position, as in *In this room took place a meeting*

between several famous kings. However, locative inversion is found extremely infrequently with transitive verbs. Those transitive verbs that are found in the construction often form fixed phrases with their objects (e.g., *take place* in the example just given); these phrases are understood to be predicates of existence or appearance, thus not interfering with the discourse function of locative inversion introduced in section 6.3.

3. There is a third possible position for the PP: following an immediately post-verbal NP. This order would instantiate precisely the type of *there*-insertion construction referred to as an inside verbal. This option does not seem particularly acceptable with the example in (1), possibly because of the heaviness of the NP.

4. A study of *there*-insertion must explain the different positions that the PP can occupy, as well as which of these positions are open for different choices of verbs. Various studies (Aissen 1975, Burzio 1986, Milsark 1974, among others) have noted that there is some correlation between the verb in the construction and the possible placement of the PP, but a thorough analysis remains to be carried out.

5. The actual behavior of these verbs is more complex than the discussion here suggests. Like the verbs of sound emission described in sections 3.2.5 and 5.3, some of these verbs have an externally caused meaning as well as the internally caused meaning that is of interest here. This externally caused meaning, like that of the verbs of sound emission, is found with manipulable entities and involves a transitive, causative use of the verb, as in *The soldier waved the flag.* In addition, some of these verbs may take a second argument on their internally caused use; with these verbs, this second argument is the body part manifesting the motion, as in *The bird fluttered its wings.* We believe that these uses are not true causative uses (e.g., **The child fluttered the parakeet's wings*), but we leave their precise analysis as a topic for further research. See section 6.4.2 for a brief discussion of somewhat similar, dyadic uses of verbs of emission.

6. As discussed in chapter 3, there are a few exceptions: the most "canonical" verbs of existence and appearance—*appear, develop, happen, occur,* and *exist*—do not require a locative PP, as in *An accident occurred,* although it seems to us that even in these instances a location or a time—which is simply a location on a temporal dimension—is understood.

7. The fact that verbs that are syntactically dyadic (i.e., transitive) but semantically monadic (i.e., they are paraphrasable by an intransitive verb in these phrases) appear in the locative inversion construction strongly suggests that the constraint is semantic rather than syntactic. This situation contrasts with auxiliary selection in Dutch, where, as described in section 1.2.2, verbs that are semantically consistent with the selection of the auxiliary *zijn* 'be' (i.e., they are telic in certain phrases) but syntactically inconsistent with the selection of this auxiliary (i.e., they are transitive) cannot, in fact, take it. We took this to be evidence that there are syntactic factors that determine auxiliary selection.

8. Actually, this characterization of *go*'s inherent deictic orientation is not quite accurate. Studies of this verb show that it is quite complicated to characterize the actual direction of motion described in sentences using *go,* since it depends on multiple factors. For some discussion, see Fillmore 1971 and Jensen 1982.

Interestingly, the verb *go* is the only verb of motion that is found in instances of locative inversion that at first glance might seem to have a disappearance rather than an appearance sense.

(i) There are no more horses there and the stable itself has been pulled down. With it HAVE GONE those wonderful, dark, smelly conveyances known as cabs which conveyed the citizenry with dignity to and from funerals and weddings. [L. Bromfield, *The Farm*, 220]

Although we would like to understand why this interpretation is possible with this verb and not others and believe that the key lies in a more careful analysis of the inherent deictic orientation of this verb, we point out once again that on our account verbs of disappearance are not a priori ruled out from occurring in the locative inversion construction if the construction's discourse function can be met (see section 6.3). An examination of the NPs in such locative inversions with *go* suggests that these inversions do link less familiar to more familiar information, so that the basic discourse requirement of the construction is indeed satisfied. In fact, the one locative inversion we have found with a verb of disappearance—the verb *die*—satisfies the basic discourse requirement of locative inversion. This example, which is cited in (ii), could have had the verb *die* replaced by the verb *go* without a change in meaning.

(ii) With the demise of Dennis Conner as defender of the America's Cup this year also DIED the possibility of turning the cup races into an advertising campaign. [G. McKay, "America's Cup '92 + Love, Beauty, and Science," 29]

As in the locative inversions that involve the disappearance sense of the verb *go*, the inverted PP in (ii) is headed by the preposition *with*. We believe that this shared property will turn out to be important to a full understanding of such locative inversions.

9. As mentioned in note 12 of chapter 1 in the context of verbs of putting, it is difficult to tell whether a transitive causative verb such as *put* means 'cause to come to be at a location' (i.e., cause to appear) or 'cause to be at a location' (i.e., cause to exist). There may be good reason for choosing the first option, given Carter's (1976, 1978) arguments that all causative verbs are causatives of verbs of change. Although Carter does not discuss verbs of creation, his arguments could be extended to such verbs, supporting lexical semantic representations in which they do not embed a state predicate directly. Since these verbs are accomplishments, Carter's representations resemble in this respect the aspectually motivated predicate decompositions that these verbs would be assigned by Dowty (1979).

10. Clouds and fog, though not animate agents, can be conceived of as having self-controlled bodies so that when they are the arguments of *sail*, the verb is still internally caused. As already mentioned, agentive verbs of manner of motion might be more accurately described as internally caused verbs of manner of motion since some do permit nonagentive, though self-controlled, arguments.

11. A near analogue of the argument that the verb in the locative inversion construction must be an unaccusative or passive verb can be constructed within LFG.

A theme argument may be realized as a subject or an object, whereas an agent argument must be realized as a subject; thus, an agent argument, but not a theme argument, would compete with a location argument for the subject grammatical function, preventing locative inversion. It is precisely for this reason that it is important that a locative inversion have the ⟨*th loc*⟩ argument structure associated with unaccusative or passive verbs, rather than the ⟨*ag*⟩ argument structure associated with unergative verbs. See Bresnan 1993 and Bresnan and Kanerva 1989.

12. We have put the PP inside the V′, but it is possible that with unergative verbs the PP should be outside the V′ and either inside the VP or adjoined to the VP, since it is not selected by the verb. To keep the structure simpler, we have also not shown the movement of the PP to Spec, CP position, proposed by some researchers.

13. Our discussion of Bresnan's analysis of locative inversion here and throughout this chapter is based on Bresnan 1993, which appeared as Bresnan 1994 while this book was in press. The published paper maintains the basic analysis of the earlier version, refining certain aspects of it. However, Bresnan 1994 does not include the discussion of locative inversion with sentential complement-taking verbs included in Bresnan 1993 and discussed here; such locative inversions are discussed in a recent paper (Bresnan 1995), which also came to our attention while this book was in press. We mention also that Bresnan 1994 moves beyond Bresnan 1993 in dealing with the problem of unergative verbs in locative inversion. Bresnan proposes that a theme-location analysis can be "overlaid" on an unergative verb precisely when the verb's sole argument can be located by locating the event the verb denotes, thus allowing locative inversion.

We thank B. Birner, J. Grimshaw, and D. Pesetsky for discussion of the material in this section.

14. Not only does Saccon (1992) adopt the VP-Internal Subject Hypothesis in her analysis of *ne*-cliticization, but she further assumes that the unaccusative/unergative distinction is not syntactically represented. She does not give a reason for this assumption; it may be based on the data showing that *ne*-cliticization is not sensitive to this distinction. Our own understanding is that the VP-Internal Subject Hypothesis does not preclude an unaccusative analysis of some verbs, but simply forces unergative verbs to have their external argument within the VP. Although *ne*-cliticization may not after all be an unaccusative diagnostic, other evidence has been cited for the unaccusative/unergative distinction in Italian, and we believe that much of it will hold up even if the VP-Internal Subject Hypothesis is adopted for Italian.

References

Abusch, D. 1985. "On Verbs and Time." Doctoral dissertation, University of Massachusetts, Amherst.

Abusch, D. 1986. "Verbs of Change, Causation, and Time." Report CSLI-86-50, Center for the Study of Language and Information, Stanford University, Stanford, Calif.

Aissen, J. 1975. "Presentational-*There* Insertion: A Cyclic Root Transformation." In *Papers from the Eleventh Regional Meeting, Chicago Linguistic Society*, 1–14. Chicago Linguistic Society, University of Chicago, Chicago, Ill.

Anderson, S. R. 1971. "On the Role of Deep Structure in Semantic Interpretation." *Foundations of Language* 7:387–96.

Anderson, S. R. 1977. "Comments on the Paper by Wasow." In Culicover, Wasow, and Akmajian 1977, 361–77.

Andrews, A. 1982. "A Note on the Constituent Structure of Adverbials and Auxiliaries." *Linguistic Inquiry* 13:313–17.

Apresjan, J. D. [Apresjan, Y. D.] 1973. "Regular Polysemy." *Linguistics*, no. 142:5–32.

Apresjan, Y. D. 1992. *Lexical Semantics: User's Guide to Contemporary Russian Vocabulary*. Ann Arbor, Mich.: Karoma.

Aronoff, M. 1994. *Morphology by Itself*. Cambridge, Mass.: MIT Press.

Aske, J. 1989. "Path Predicates in English and Spanish: A Closer Look." In *Proceedings of the Fifteenth Annual Meeting of the Berkeley Linguistics Society*, 1–14. Berkeley Linguistics Society, University of California, Berkeley.

Atkins, B. T., J. Kegl, and B. Levin. 1988. "Anatomy of a Verb Entry: From Linguistic Theory to Lexicographic Practice." *International Journal of Lexicography* 1:84–126.

Aulestia, G., and L. White. 1990. *English-Basque Dictionary*. Reno, Nev.: University of Nevada Press.

Babby, L. H. 1978. "Lexical Functions and Syntactic Constructions: Russian Existential Sentences." In *Papers from the Parasession on the Lexicon*, 26–33. Chicago Linguistic Society, University of Chicago, Chicago, Ill.

Babby, L. H. 1980. *Existential Sentences and Negation in Russian*. Ann Arbor, Mich.: Karoma.

Baker, M. 1983. "Objects, Themes, and Lexical Rules in Italian." In L. Levin, Rappaport, and Zaenen 1983, 1–45.

Baker, M. 1988a. *Incorporation: A Theory of Grammatical Function Changing*. Chicago, Ill.: University of Chicago Press.

Baker, M. 1988b. "Morphology and Syntax: An Interlocking Independence." In *Morphology and Modularity*, ed. M. Everaert, A. Evers, R. Huybregts, and M. Trommelen, 9–32. Dordrecht: Foris.

Baker, M., K. Johnson, and I. Roberts. 1989. "Passive Arguments Raised." *Linguistic Inquiry* 20:219–52.

Belletti, A. 1988. "The Case of Unaccusatives." *Linguistic Inquiry* 19:1–34.

Belletti, A., and B. Levin. 1985. "Speculations on θ-Role Assignment and the V PP Construction." Ms., Center for Cognitive Science, MIT, Cambridge, Mass.

Belletti, A., and L. Rizzi. 1981. "The Syntax of *Ne:* Some Theoretical Implications." *The Linguistic Review* 1:117–54.

Bergh, L. 1948. "Moyens d'exprimer en français l'idée de direction: Étude fondée sur une comparaison avec les langues germaniques, en particulier le suédois." Doctoral dissertation, University of Gothenburg.

Berman, R. A. 1978. *Modern Hebrew Structure*. Tel Aviv: University Publishing Projects.

Berman, R. A. 1980. "Child Language as Evidence for Grammatical Description: Preschoolers' Construal of Transitivity in the Verb System of Hebrew." *Linguistics* 18:677–701.

Birner, B. J. 1992. "The Discourse Function of Inversion in English." Doctoral dissertation, Northwestern University, Evanston, Ill.

Birner, B. J. 1994. "Information Status and Word Order: An Analysis of English Inversion." *Language* 70:233–59.

Birner, B. J., and G. Ward. 1993. "*There*-Sentences and Inversion as Distinct Constructions: A Functional Account." In *Proceedings of the Nineteenth Annual Meeting of the Berkeley Linguistics Society*, 27–39. Berkeley Linguistics Society, University of California, Berkeley.

Bolinger, D. 1972. "Ambient *It* Is Meaningful Too." *Journal of Linguistics* 9:261–70.

Bolinger, D. 1977. *Form and Meaning*. London: Longman.

Bolozky, S. 1982. "Strategies of Modern Hebrew Verb Formation." *Hebrew Annual Review* 6:69–79.

Bolozky, S., and G. N. Saad. 1983. "On Active and Non-Active Causativizable Verbs in Arabic and Hebrew." *Zeitschrift für Arabische Linguistik* 10:71–79.

Bresnan, J. 1977. "Variables in the Theory of Transformations." In Culicover, Wasow, and Akmajian 1977, 157–96.

Bresnan, J. 1980. "Polyadicity: Part I of a Theory of Lexical Rules and Representations." In Hoekstra, van der Hulst, and Moortgat 1980, 97–121. Also in Bresnan 1982, 149–72.

Bresnan, J., ed. 1982. *The Mental Representation of Grammatical Relations.* Cambridge, Mass.: MIT Press.

Bresnan, J. 1993. "Locative Inversion and the Architecture of UG." Ms., Stanford University, Stanford, Calif.

Bresnan, J. 1994. "Locative Inversion and the Architecture of Universal Grammar." *Language* 70:72–131.

Bresnan, J. 1995. "Category Mismatches." In *Theoretical Approaches to African Linguistics,* ed. A. Akinlabi. (Trends in African Linguistics 1.) Princeton, N.J.: Africa World Press.

Bresnan, J., and J. M. Kanerva. 1989. "Locative Inversion in Chicheŵa: A Case Study of Factorization in Grammar." *Linguistic Inquiry* 20:1–50.

Bresnan, J., and A. Zaenen. 1990. "Deep Unaccusativity in LFG." In Dziwirek, Farrell, and Mejías-Bikandi 1990, 45–57.

Brinton, L. J. 1988. *The Development of English Aspectual Systems: Aspectualizers and Post-Verbal Particles.* Cambridge: Cambridge University Press.

Brousseau, A.-M., and E. Ritter. 1991. "A Non-Unified Analysis of Agentive Verbs." In *Proceedings of the Tenth West Coast Conference on Formal Linguistics,* 53–64. Stanford, Calif.: CSLI Publications. Distributed by University of Chicago Press, Chicago, Ill.

Burzio, L. 1981. "Intransitive Verbs and Italian Auxiliaries." Doctoral dissertation, MIT, Cambridge, Mass. Revised as Burzio 1986.

Burzio, L. 1986. *Italian Syntax: A Government-Binding Approach.* Dordrecht: Reidel.

Carlson, G. N. 1977. "Reference to Kinds in English." Doctoral dissertation, University of Massachusetts, Amherst.

Carrier, J., and J. H. Randall. 1992. "The Argument Structure and Syntactic Structure of Resultatives." *Linguistic Inquiry* 23:173–234.

Carrier, J., and J. H. Randall. In press. *From Conceptual Structure to Syntax.* Berlin: Mouton de Gruyter.

Carter, R. J. 1976. "Some Constraints on Possible Words." *Semantikos* 1:27–66.

Carter, R. J. 1978. "Arguing for Semantic Representations." *Recherches Linguistiques* 5–6:61–92. Université de Paris VIII, Vincennes. Reprinted in Carter 1988, 139–66.

Carter, R. J. 1988. *On Linking: Papers by Richard Carter,* ed. B. Levin and C. Tenny. Lexicon Project Working Papers 25, Center for Cognitive Science, MIT, Cambridge, Mass.

Centineo, G. 1986. "A Lexical Theory of Auxiliary Selection in Italian." In *Davis Working Papers in Linguistics* 1, 1–35. Linguistics Program, University of California, Davis.

Chierchia, G. 1989. "A Semantics for Unaccusatives and Its Syntactic Consequences." Ms., Cornell University, Ithaca, N.Y.

Choi, S., and M. Bowerman. 1991. "Learning to Express Motion Events in English and Korean: The Influence of Language-Specific Lexicalization Patterns." *Cognition* 41:83–121. Also in B. Levin and Pinker 1992, 83–121.

Chomsky, N. 1970. "Remarks on Nominalization." In Jacobs and Rosenbaum 1970, 184–221.

Chomsky, N. 1973. "Conditions on Transformations." In *A Festschrift for Morris Halle*, ed. S. Anderson and P. Kiparsky, 232–86. New York: Holt, Rinehart and Winston.

Chomsky, N. 1981. *Lectures on Government and Binding*. Dordrecht: Foris.

Chomsky, N. 1986a. *Barriers*. Cambridge, Mass.: MIT Press.

Chomsky, N. 1986b. *Knowledge of Language: Its Nature, Origin, and Use*. New York: Praeger.

Clark, E. V. 1978. "Locationals: Existential, Locative, and Possessive." In Greenberg 1978, 85–126.

Clark, E. V., and H. H. Clark. 1979. "When Nouns Surface as Verbs." *Language* 55:767–811.

Comrie, B. 1976a. *Aspect*. Cambridge: Cambridge University Press.

Comrie, B. 1976b. "The Syntax of Causative Constructions: Cross-Language Similarities and Divergences." In Shibatani 1976, 261–312.

Coopmans, P. 1989. "Where Stylistic and Syntactic Processes Meet: Locative Inversion in English." *Language* 65:728–51.

Couper-Kuhlen, E. 1979. *The Prepositional Passive in English*. Tübingen: Niemeyer.

Cruse, D. A. 1972. "A Note on English Causatives." *Linguistic Inquiry* 3:522–28.

Cruse, D. A. 1973. "Some Thoughts on Agentivity." *Journal of Linguistics* 9: 11–23.

Culicover, P., T. Wasow, and A. Akmajian, eds. 1977. *Formal Syntax*. New York: Academic Press.

Davidson, D. 1967. "The Logical Form of Action Sentences." In *The Logic of Decision and Action*, ed. N. Rescher, 81–95. Pittsburgh, Pa.: University of Pittsburgh Press.

Davies, W. D. 1981. "Choctaw Clause Structure." Doctoral dissertation, University of California, San Diego.

Declerck, R. 1979. "Aspect and the Bounded/Unbounded (Telic/Atelic) Distinction." *Linguistics* 17:761–94.

DeLancey, S. 1985. "Agentivity and Syntax." In *Papers from the Parasession on Causatives and Agentivity at the Twenty-First Regional Meeting*, 1–12. Chicago Linguistic Society, Chicago, Ill.

Diesing, M. 1992. *Indefinites*. Cambridge, Mass.: MIT Press.

Dixon, R. M. W. 1982. *Where Have All the Adjectives Gone? and Other Essays in Semantics and Syntax*. Berlin: Mouton.

Doron, E. 1991. Talk presented at Bar Ilan University, Ramat Gan.

Dowty, D. R. 1979. *Word Meaning and Montague Grammar*. Dordrecht: Reidel.

Dowty, D. R. 1981. "Quantification and the Lexicon: A Reply to Fodor and Fodor." In *The Scope of Lexical Rules*, ed. M. Moortgat, H. van der Hulst, and T. Hoekstra, 79–106. Dordrecht: Foris.

Dowty, D. R. 1991. "Thematic Proto-Roles and Argument Selection." *Language* 67:547–619.

Dubinsky, S., and C. Rosen. 1987. "A Bibliography on Relational Grammar through May 1987 with Selected Titles on Lexical-Functional Grammar." Bloomington, Ind.: Indiana University Linguistics Club.

Dziwirek, K., P. Farrell, and E. Mejías-Bikandi, eds. 1990. *Grammatical Relations: A Cross-Theoretical Perspective*. Stanford, Calif.: CSLI Publications. Distributed by University of Chicago Press, Chicago, Ill.

Emonds, J. 1976. *A Transformational Approach to English Syntax*. New York: Academic Press.

Everaert, M. 1986. "The Syntax of Reflexivization." Doctoral dissertation, University of Utrecht.

Everaert, M. 1992. "Auxiliary Selection in Idiomatic Constructions." Ms., Research Institute for Language and Speech, University of Utrecht.

Faber, D. 1987. "The Accentuation of Intransitive Sentences in English." *Journal of Linguistics* 23:341–58.

Fillmore, C. J. 1968. "The Case for Case." In *Universals in Linguistic Theory*, ed. E. Bach and R. T. Harms, 1–88. New York: Holt, Rinehart and Winston.

Fillmore, C. J. 1970. "The Grammar of *Hitting* and *Breaking*." In Jacobs and Rosenbaum 1970, 120–33.

Fillmore, C. J. 1971. *Santa Cruz Lectures on Deixis*. Bloomington, Ind.: Indiana University Linguistics Club.

Firbas, J. 1966. "Non-Thematic Subjects in Contemporary English." *Travaux Linguistiques de Prague* 2:239–56.

Firbas, J. 1992. *Functional Sentence Perspective in Written and Spoken Communication*. Cambridge: Cambridge University Press.

Fodor, J. A., and J. D. Fodor. 1980. "Functional Structures, Quantifiers, and Meaning Postulates." *Linguistic Inquiry* 11:759–70.

Foley, W. A., and R. D. Van Valin, Jr. 1984. *Functional Syntax and Universal Grammar*. Cambridge: Cambridge University Press.

Fukui, N., and M. Speas. 1986. "Specifiers and Projection." In *MIT Working Papers in Linguistics 8: Papers in Theoretical Linguistics*, 128–72. Department of Linguistics and Philosophy, MIT, Cambridge, Mass.

Gladney, F. 1993. "Russian *stanóvitsja* 'stands up' and *+i* Imperfective Thematization." *Journal of Slavic Linguistics* 1:61–79.

Glinert, L. 1989. *The Grammar of Modern Hebrew*. Cambridge: Cambridge University Press.

Gołab, Z. 1968. "The Grammar of Slavic Causatives." In *American Contributions to the Sixth International Congress of Slavists*, Vol. 1, ed. H. Kučera, 71–94. The Hague: Mouton.

Goldberg, A. E. 1991. It Can't Go Down the Chimney Up: Paths and the English Resultative. In *Proceedings of the Seventeenth Annual Meeting of the Berkeley Linguistics Society*, 368–78. Berkeley Linguistics Society, University of California, Berkeley.

Goldberg, A. E. 1992. "The Inherent Semantics of Argument Structure: The Case of the English Ditransitive Construction." *Cognitive Linguistics* 3:37–74.

Goldberg, A. E. 1994a. *Constructions: A Construction Grammar Approach to Argument Structure*. Chicago, Ill.: University of Chicago Press.

Goldberg, A. E. 1994b. "Making One's Way through the Data." In *Complex Predicates*, ed. A. Alsina, P. Sells, and J. Bresnan. Stanford, Calif.: CSLI Publications. Distributed by University of Chicago Press, Chicago, Ill.

Green, G. 1980. "Some Wherefores of English Inversions." *Language* 56:582–601.

Greenberg, J. H., ed. 1978. *Universals of Human Language: Syntax 4*. Stanford, Calif.: Stanford University Press.

Grimshaw, J. 1982. "Subcategorization and Grammatical Relations." In *Subjects and Other Subjects*, ed. A. Zaenen, 35–55. Bloomington, Ind.: Indiana University Linguistics Club.

Grimshaw, J. 1987. "Unaccusatives—An Overview." In *Proceedings of NELS 17*, 244–59. GLSA, University of Massachusetts, Amherst.

Grimshaw, J. 1990. *Argument Structure*. Cambridge, Mass.: MIT Press.

Grimshaw, J. 1993. "Semantic Structure and Semantic Content in Lexical Representation." Ms., Rutgers University, New Brunswick, N.J.

Grimshaw, J. 1994. "Lexical Reconciliation." *Lingua* 92:411–30.

Grimshaw, J., and S. Vikner. 1993. "Obligatory Adjuncts and the Structure of Events." In *Knowledge and Language II: Lexical and Conceptual Structure*, ed. E. Reuland and W. Abraham, 143–55. Dordrecht: Kluwer.

Gropen, J., S. Pinker, M. Hollander, and R. Goldberg. 1991. "Affectedness and Direct Objects: The Role of Lexical Semantics in the Acquisition of Verb Argument Structure." *Cognition* 41:153–95. Also in B. Levin and Pinker 1992.

Gruber, J. S. 1965. "Studies in Lexical Relations." Doctoral dissertation, MIT, Cambridge, Mass. Also published in Gruber 1976.

Gruber, J. S. 1976. *Lexical Structures in Syntax and Semantics*. Amsterdam: North-Holland.

Guéron, J. 1980. "On the Syntax and Semantics of PP Extraposition." *Linguistic Inquiry* 11:637–78.

Guerssel, M. 1986. "On Berber Verbs of Change: A Study of Transitivity Alternations." Lexicon Project Working Papers 9, Center for Cognitive Science, MIT, Cambridge, Mass.

Guerssel, M., K. Hale, M. Laughren, B. Levin, and J. White Eagle. 1985. "A Cross-Linguistic Study of Transitivity Alternations." In *Papers from the Parasession on Causatives and Agentivity*, 48–63. Chicago Linguistic Society, University of Chicago, Chicago, Ill.

Hale, K., and S. J. Keyser. 1986. "Some Transitivity Alternations in English." Lexicon Project Working Papers 7, Center for Cognitive Science, MIT, Cambridge, Mass.

Hale, K., and S. J. Keyser. 1987. "A View from the Middle." Lexicon Project Working Papers 10, Center for Cognitive Science, MIT, Cambridge, Mass.

Hale, K., and S. J. Keyser. 1988. "Explaining and Constraining the English Middle." In *Studies in Generative Approaches to Aspect*, ed. C. Tenny, 41–58. Lexicon Project Working Papers 24, Center for Cognitive Science, MIT, Cambridge, Mass.

Hale, K., and S. J. Keyser. 1993. "On Argument Structure and the Lexical Expression of Syntactic Relations." In *The View from Building 20: Essays in Linguistics in Honor of Sylvain Bromberger*, ed. K. Hale and S. J. Keyser, 53–109. Cambridge, Mass.: MIT Press.

Hall [Partee], B. 1965. "Subject and Object in English." Doctoral dissertation, MIT, Cambridge, Mass.

Halliday, M. A. K. 1967. "Notes on Transitivity and Theme in English Part I." *Journal of Linguistics* 3:37–81.

Hartvigson, H. H., and L. K. Jakobsen. 1974. *Inversion in Present-Day English*. Odense: Odense University Press.

Haspelmath, M. 1993. "More on the Typology of Inchoative/Causative Verb Alternations." In *Causatives and Transitivity*, ed. B. Comrie and M. Polinsky, 87–120. Amsterdam: John Benjamins.

Higginbotham, J. T. 1985. "On Semantics." *Linguistic Inquiry* 16:547–93.

Hoekstra, T. 1984. *Transitivity*. Dordrecht: Foris.

Hoekstra, T. 1988. "Small Clause Results." *Lingua* 74:101–39.

Hoekstra, T. 1992. "Aspect and Θ Theory." In Roca 1992, 145–74.

Hoekstra, T., and R. Mulder. 1990. "Unergatives as Copular Verbs: Locational and Existential Predication." *The Linguistic Review* 7:1–79.

Hoekstra, T., H. van der Hulst, and M. Moortgat, eds. 1980. *Lexical Grammar*. Dordrecht: Foris.

Hubbard, P. L. 1980. "The Syntax of the Albanian Verb Complex." Doctoral dissertation, University of California, San Diego.

Jackendoff, R. S. 1972. *Semantic Interpretation in Generative Grammar*. Cambridge, Mass.: MIT Press.

Jackendoff, R. S. 1976. "Toward an Explanatory Semantic Representation." *Linguistic Inquiry* 7:89–150.

Jackendoff, R. S. 1983. *Semantics and Cognition*. Cambridge, Mass.: MIT Press.

Jackendoff, R. S. 1987. "The Status of Thematic Relations in Linguistic Theory." *Linguistic Inquiry* 18:369–411.

Jackendoff, R. S. 1990. *Semantic Structures*. Cambridge, Mass.: MIT Press.

Jacobs, R., and P. Rosenbaum, eds. 1970. *Readings in English Transformational Grammar*. Waltham, Mass.: Ginn.

Jenkins, L. 1975. *The English Existential*. Tübingen: Niemeyer.

Jensen, J. B. 1982. "Coming and Going in English and Spanish." In *Readings in Spanish-English Contrastive Linguistics*, Vol. 3, ed. R. Nash and D. Belaval, 37–65. San Juan: Inter American University Press.

Jespersen, O. 1927. *A Modern English Grammar on Historical Principles. Part 3: Syntax, Second Volume*. Heidelberg: Carl Winter.

Junker, M.-O. 1988. "Transitive, Intransitive and Reflexive Uses of Adjectival Verbs in French." In *Advances in Romance Linguistics*, ed. D. Birdsong and J.-P. Montreuil, 189–99. Dordrecht: Foris.

Kayne, R. S. 1984. *Connectedness and Binary Branching*. Dordrecht: Foris.

Kearns, K. S. 1991. "The Semantics of the English Progressive." Doctoral dissertation, MIT, Cambridge, Mass.

Keyser, S. J., and T. Roeper. 1984. "On the Middle and Ergative Constructions in English." *Linguistic Inquiry* 15:381–416.

Kimball, J. P. 1973. "The Grammar of Existence." In *Papers from the Ninth Regional Meeting, Chicago Linguistic Society*, 262–70. Chicago Linguistic Society, University of Chicago, Chicago, Ill.

Kirsner, R. S. 1973. "Natural Focus and Agentive Interpretation: On the Semantics of Dutch Expletive *er*." In *Stanford Occasional Papers in Linguistics* 3, 101–14. Committee on Linguistics, Stanford University, Stanford, Calif.

Koopman, H., and D. Sportiche. 1991. "The Position of Subjects." *Lingua* 85: 211–58.

Koster, J. 1978. "Why Subject Sentences Don't Exist." In *Recent Transformational Studies in European Languages*, ed. S. J. Keyser, 53–64. Cambridge, Mass.: MIT Press.

Kratzer, A. 1989. "Stage-Level and Individual-Level Predicates." In *Papers on Quantification*, ed. E. Bach, A. Kratzer, and B. Partee. NSF Report, University of Massachusetts, Amherst.

Kučera, H., and W. N. Francis. 1967. *Computational Analysis of Present-Day American English*. Providence, R.I.: Brown University Press.

Kuno, S. 1971. "The Position of Locatives in Existential Sentences." *Linguistic Inquiry* 2:333–78.

Kuroda, S.-Y. 1988. "Whether We Agree or Not." *Lingvisticae Investigationes* 12:1–47.

Labelle, M. 1990. "Unaccusatives and Pseudo-Unaccusatives in French." In *Proceedings of NELS 20*, 303–17. GLSA, University of Massachusetts, Amherst.

Labelle, M. 1992. "Change of State and Valency." *Journal of Linguistics* 28:375–414.

Lafitte, P. 1979. *Grammaire Basque (Navarro-Labourdin Littéraire)*. Donostia: Elkar.

Laka, I. 1993. "Unergatives That Assign Ergative, Unaccusatives That Assign Accusative." In *MIT Working Papers in Linguistics 18: Papers on Case and Agreement 1*, 149–72. Department of Linguistics and Philosophy, MIT, Cambridge, Mass.

Lakoff, G. 1966. "Stative Adjectives and Verbs in English." In *Mathematical Linguistics and Automatic Translation*, ed. A. G. Oettinger, I-1–I-16. Report NSF-17, The Computation Laboratory, Harvard University, Cambridge, Mass.

Lakoff, G. 1968. "Some Verbs of Change and Causation." In *Mathematical Linguistics and Automatic Translation*, ed. S. Kuno. Report NSF-20, Aiken Computation Laboratory, Harvard University, Cambridge, Mass.

Lakoff, G. 1970. *Irregularity in Syntax*. New York: Holt, Rinehart and Winston.

Laughren, M. 1988. "Towards a Lexical Representation of Warlpiri Verbs." In W. Wilkins 1988, 215–42.

Legendre, G. 1991. "Split Intransitivity: A Reply to Van Valin (1990)." Ms., University of Colorado, Boulder.

Levin, B. 1983. "On the Nature of Ergativity." Doctoral dissertation, MIT, Cambridge, Mass.

Levin, B. 1985. "Case Theory and the Russian Reflexive Affix." In *Proceedings of the Fourth West Coast Conference on Formal Linguistics*, 178–89. Stanford Linguistics Association, Stanford University, Stanford, Calif.

Levin, B. 1989. "The Basque Verbal Inventory and Configurationality." In *Configurationality*, ed. L. Maracz and P. Muysken, 39–62. Dordrecht: Foris.

Levin, B. 1991. "Building a Lexicon: The Contribution of Linguistic Theory." *International Journal of Lexicography* 4:205–26. Also in *Challenges in Natural Language Processing*, ed. M. Bates and R. Weischedel, 1993, 76–98. Cambridge: Cambridge University Press.

Levin, B. 1993. *English Verb Classes and Alternations: A Preliminary Investigation*. Chicago, Ill.: University of Chicago Press.

Levin, B. 1994. "Approaches to Lexical Semantic Representation." In *Automating the Lexicon*, ed. D. Walker, A. Zampolli, and N. Calzolari, 53–91. Oxford: Oxford University Press.

Levin, B., and S. Pinker, eds. 1992. Reprint. *Lexical and Conceptual Semantics*. Oxford: Blackwell. Original edition, *Cognition* 41, 1991.

Levin, B., and T. Rapoport. 1988. "Lexical Subordination." In *Papers from the Twenty-Fourth Regional Meeting, Chicago Linguistic Society*, 275–89. Chicago Linguistic Society, University of Chicago, Chicago, Ill.

Levin, B., and M. Rappaport. 1986. "The Formation of Adjectival Passives." *Linguistic Inquiry* 17:623–61.

Levin, B., and M. Rappaport. 1988. "Non-event *-er* Nominals: A Probe into Argument Structure." *Linguistics* 26:1067–83.

Levin, B., and M. Rappaport. 1989. "An Approach to Unaccusative Mismatches." In *Proceedings of NELS 19*, 314–28. GLSA, University of Massachusetts, Amherst.

Levin, B., and M. Rappaport Hovav. 1991. "Wiping the Slate Clean: A Lexical Semantic Exploration." *Cognition* 41:123–51. Also in B. Levin and Pinker 1992, 123–51.

Levin, B., and M. Rappaport Hovav. 1992. "The Lexical Semantics of Verbs of Motion: The Perspective from Unaccusativity." In Roca 1992, 247–69.

Levin, B., and M. Rappaport Hovav. 1994. "A Preliminary Analysis of Causative Verbs in English." *Lingua* 92:35–77.

Levin, B., and M. Rappaport Hovav. In preparation. "External and Internal Causation." Ms., Northwestern University, Evanston, Ill., and Bar Ilan University, Ramat Gan.

Levin, J., and D. Massam. 1985. "Surface Ergativity: Case/Theta Relations Reexamined." In *Proceedings of NELS 15*, 286–301. GLSA, University of Massachusetts, Amherst.

Levin, L. 1986. "Operations on Lexical Forms: Unaccusative Rules in Germanic Languages." Doctoral dissertation, MIT, Cambridge, Mass.

Levin, L., T. Mitamura, and A. T. Mahmoud. 1988. "Lexical Incorporation and Resultative Secondary Predicates." Handout of a paper presented at the 63rd Annual Meeting of the LSA, New Orleans, La.

Levin, L., M. Rappaport, and A. Zaenen, eds. 1983. *Papers in Lexical-Functional Grammar*. Bloomington, Ind.: Indiana University Linguistics Club.

Levin, L., and J. Simpson. 1981. "Quirky Case and the Structure of Icelandic Lexical Entries." In *Papers from the Seventeenth Regional Meeting, Chicago Linguistic Society*, 185–96. Chicago Linguistic Society, University of Chicago, Chicago, Ill.

Lieber, R. 1992. *Deconstructing Morphology: Word Formation in Syntactic Theory*. Chicago, Ill.: University of Chicago Press.

Ljung, M. 1980. *Reflections on the English Progressive*. Gothenburg: University of Gothenburg.

Lonzi, L. 1985. "Pertinenza della struttura tema-rema per l'analisi sintattica." In *Theme-Rheme in Italian*, ed. H. Stammerjohann, 99–120. Tübingen: Gunter Narr.

Lyons, J. 1967. "A Note on Possessive, Existential and Locative Sentences." *Foundations of Language* 3:390–96.

Macfarland, T. 1994a. "Argument and Event Structure of Cognate Objects." *ConSole 1 Proceedings*, 165–182. The Hague: Holland Academic Graphics.

Macfarland, T. 1994b. "Cognate Objects in English: Events or Results." Paper presented at the 68th Annual Meeting of the LSA, Boston, Mass.

Malblanc, A. 1968. *Stylistique comparée du français et de l'allemand.* Paris: Didier.

Manzini, M. R. 1983. "On Control and Control Theory." *Linguistic Inquiry* 14: 421–46.

Marantz, A. P. 1984. *On the Nature of Grammatical Relations.* Cambridge, Mass.: MIT Press.

Marantz, A. P. 1992. "The *Way* Construction and the Semantics of Direct Arguments in English." In Stowell and Wehrli 1992, 179–88.

Marchand, H. 1969. *The Categories and Types of Present-Day English Word-Formation.* 2d ed. Munich: C. H. Beck.

Martin, J. B. 1991. "The Determination of Grammatical Relations in Syntax." Doctoral dissertation, University of California, Los Angeles.

McClure, W. 1990. "A Lexical Semantic Explanation for Unaccusative Mismatches." In Dziwirek, Farrell, and Mejías-Bikandi 1990, 305–18.

McLendon, S. 1978. "Ergativity, Case, and Transitivity in Eastern Pomo." *International Journal of American Linguistics* 44:1–9.

Merlan, F. 1985. "Split Intransitivity: Functional Oppositions in Intransitive Inflection." In *Grammar Inside and Outside the Clause*, ed. J. Nichols and A. C. Woodbury, 324–62. Cambridge: Cambridge University Press.

Milsark, G. 1974. "Existential Sentences in English." Doctoral dissertation, MIT, Cambridge, Mass.

Moorcroft, R. 1985. "The Role of Semantic Restrictions in German Passive Formation." In *Germanic Linguistics: Papers from a Symposium at the University of Chicago*, ed. J. T. Faarlund, 157–70. Bloomington, Ind.: Indiana University Linguistics Club.

Moravcsik, E. A. 1978. "On the Case Marking of Objects." In Greenberg 1978, 249–90.

Mulder, R., and P. Wehrmann. 1989. "Locational Verbs as Unaccusatives." In *Linguistics in the Netherlands 1989*, ed. H. Bennis and A. van Kemenade, 111–22. Dordrecht: Foris.

Napoli, D. J. 1988. "Review of L. Burzio: *Italian Syntax.*" *Language* 64:130–42.

Nedjalkov, V. P. [Nedyalkov, V. P.] 1969. "Nekotorye verojatnostnye universalii v glagol'nom slovoobrazovanii." In *Jazykovye universalii i lingvističeskaja tipologija*, ed. I. F. Vardul', 106–14. Moscow: Nauka.

Nedyalkov, V. P., and G. G. Silnitsky. 1973. "The Typology of Morphological and Lexical Causatives." In *Trends in Soviet Theoretical Linguistics*, ed. F. Kiefer, 1–32. Dordrecht: Reidel.

Neeleman, A., and F. Weerman. 1993. "The Balance between Syntax and Morphology: Dutch Particles and Resultatives." *Natural Language & Linguistic Theory* 11:433–75.

Olsen, M. B. 1991. "Lexical Semantic Typology of Motion Verbs: Insight from Translation." In *Papers from the Second Annual Meeting of the Formal Linguistic Society of Midamerica*, 255–71. Program in Linguistics, University of Michigan, Ann Arbor.

Ostler, N. D. M., and B. T. S. Atkins. 1991. "Predictable Meaning Shift: Some Linguistic Properties of Lexical Implication Rules." In *Lexical Semantics and Knowledge Representation*, ed. J. Pustejovsky and S. Bergler, 76–87. ACL SIG Workshop Proceedings. Association for Computational Linguistics, Morristown, N.J.

Parsons, T. 1990. *Events in the Semantics of English*. Cambridge, Mass.: MIT Press.

Penhallurick, J. 1984. "Full-Verb Inversion in English." *Australian Journal of Linguistics* 4:33–56.

Perlmutter, D. M. 1971. *Deep and Surface Structure Constraints in Syntax*. New York: Holt, Rinehart and Winston.

Perlmutter, D. M. 1978. "Impersonal Passives and the Unaccusative Hypothesis." In *Proceedings of the Fourth Annual Meeting of the Berkeley Linguistics Society*, 157–89. Berkeley Linguistics Society, University of California, Berkeley.

Perlmutter, D. M. 1989. "Multiattachment and the Unaccusative Hypothesis: The Perfect Auxiliary in Italian." *Probus* 1:63–119.

Perlmutter, D. M., and P. M. Postal. 1984. "The 1-Advancement Exclusiveness Law." In Perlmutter and C. Rosen 1984, 81–125.

Perlmutter, D. M., and C. Rosen, eds. 1984. *Studies in Relational Grammar 2*. Chicago, Ill.: University of Chicago Press.

Pesetsky, D. 1982. "Paths and Categories." Doctoral dissertation, MIT, Cambridge, Mass.

Pesetsky, D. 1995. *Zero Syntax. Experiencers and Cascades*. Cambridge, Mass.: MIT Press.

Pinker, S. 1989. *Learnability and Cognition: The Acquisition of Argument Structure*. Cambridge, Mass.: MIT Press.

Postal, P. M. 1977. "About a 'Nonargument' for Raising." *Linguistic Inquiry* 8:141–55.

Poutsma, H. 1904. *A Grammar of Late Modern English*. Groningen: P. Noordhoff.

Prince, A. 1975. "The Phonology and Morphology of Tiberian Hebrew." Doctoral dissertation, MIT, Cambridge, Mass.

Pullum, G. K. 1988. "Citation Etiquette beyond Thunderdome." *Natural Language & Linguistic Theory* 6:579–88.

Pustejovsky, J. 1991a. "The Generative Lexicon." *Computational Linguistics* 17:409–41.

Pustejovsky, J. 1991b. "The Syntax of Event Structure." *Cognition* 41:47–81. Also in B. Levin and Pinker 1992, 47–81.

Rapoport, T. R. 1987. "Copular, Nominal, and Small Clauses: A Study of Israeli Hebrew." Doctoral dissertation, MIT, Cambridge, Mass.

Rapoport, T. R. 1990. "Secondary Predication and the Lexical Representation of Verbs." *Machine Translation* 4:31–55.

Rapoport, T. R. 1991. "Adjunct-Predicate Licensing and D-Structure." In *Syntax and Semantics 25: Perspectives on Phrase Structure: Heads and Licensing*, ed. S. Rothstein, 159–87. San Diego, Calif.: Academic Press.

Rappaport, M. 1979. "Morphological Regularities in the Hebrew Verb Paradigm." Ms., CUNY, New York.

Rappaport, M., and B. Levin. 1988. "What to Do with Θ-Roles." In W. Wilkins 1988, 7–36.

Rappaport Hovav, M., and B. Levin. 1992. "*-er* Nominals: Implications for a Theory of Argument Structure." In Stowell and Wehrli 1992, 127–53.

Rappaport Hovav, M., and B. Levin. In press. "Classifying Single Argument Verbs." In *Lexical Specification and Lexical Insertion*, ed. P. Coopmans, M. Everaert, and J. Grimshaw. Hillsdale, N.J.: Lawrence Erlbaum Associates.

Reinhart, T. 1991. "Lexical Properties of Ergativity." Paper presented at the Workshop on Lexical Specification and Lexical Insertion, Research Institute for Language and Speech, University of Utrecht.

Roberts, I. G. 1987. *The Representation of Implicit and Dethematized Subjects.* Dordrecht: Foris.

Roberts, I. G. 1988. Predicative APs. *Linguistic Inquiry* 19:703–10.

Roca, I. M., ed. 1992. *Thematic Structure: Its Role in Grammar.* Berlin: Mouton de Gruyter.

Rochemont, M. S. 1986. *Focus in Generative Grammar.* Amsterdam: John Benjamins.

Rochemont, M. S., and P. Culicover. 1990. *English Focus Constructions and the Theory of Grammar.* Cambridge: Cambridge University Press.

Roeper, T. 1987. "Implicit Arguments and the Head-Complement Relation." *Linguistic Inquiry* 18:267–310.

Rosen, C. 1981. "The Relational Structure of Reflexive Clauses: Evidence from Italian." Doctoral dissertation, Harvard University, Cambridge, Mass.

Rosen, C. 1984. "The Interface between Semantic Roles and Initial Grammatical Relations." In Perlmutter and C. Rosen 1984, 38–77.

Rosen, S. T. 1989. "Argument Structure and Complex Predicates." Doctoral dissertation, Brandeis University, Waltham, Mass.

Rosen, S. T. 1993. "Verb Classes and the Acquisition of Verb Arguments." Ms., University of Kansas, Lawrence.

Rothemberg, M. 1974. *Les verbes à la fois transitifs et intransitifs en français contemporain.* The Hague: Mouton.

Rothstein, S. 1983. "The Syntactic Forms of Predication." Doctoral dissertation, MIT, Cambridge, Mass.

Rothstein, S. 1989. "Predicate Linking and Predicate Absorption." Ms., Bar Ilan University, Ramat Gan.

Rothstein, S. 1992. "Case and NP Licensing." *Natural Language & Linguistic Theory* 10:119–39.

Ruwet, N. 1991. *Syntax and Human Experience*. Chicago, Ill.: University of Chicago Press.

Saccon, G. 1992. "VP-Internal Arguments and Locative Subjects." In *Proceedings of NELS 22*, 383–97. GLSA, University of Massachusetts, Amherst.

Salkoff, M. 1983. "Bees Are Swarming in the Garden." *Language* 59:288–346.

Salkoff, M. 1988. "Analysis by Fusion." *Lingvisticae Investigationes* 12:49–84.

Samek-Lodovici, V. 1993. "Italian's Postverbal Focus Position and Its Role in Postverbal *Wh*-Extraction." Ms., Rutgers University, New Brunswick, N.J.

Sato, H. 1987. "Resultative Attributes and GB Principles." *English Linguistics* 4:91–106.

Schaefer, R. P. 1985. "Motion in Tswana and Its Characteristic Lexicalization." *Studies in African Linguistics* 16:57–87.

Schein, B. 1982. "Non-Finite Complements in Russian." In *MIT Working Papers in Linguistics 4: Papers in Syntax*, 217–43. Department of Linguistics and Philosophy, MIT, Cambridge, Mass.

Schein, B. 1985. "Event Logic and the Interpretation of Plurals." Doctoral dissertation, MIT, Cambridge, Mass.

Schlyter, S. 1978. "German and French Movement Verbs: Polysemy and Equivalence." In *Papers from the Fourth Scandinavian Conference of Linguistics*, 349–54. Odense: Odense University Press.

Schlyter, S. 1981. "*De-à/von-zu* avec les verbes de mouvement cursifs et transformatifs." In *Analyse des prépositions*, ed. C. Schwarze, 171–89. Tübingen: Niemeyer.

Schwartz-Norman, L. 1976. "The Grammar of 'Content' and 'Container.'" *Journal of Linguistics* 12:279–87.

Shannon, T. F. 1987. "On Some Recent Claims of Relational Grammar." In *Proceedings of the Thirteenth Annual Meeting of the Berkeley Linguistics Society*, 247–63. Berkeley Linguistics Society, University of California, Berkeley.

Shibatani, M., ed. 1976. *Syntax and Semantics 6: The Grammar of Causative Constructions*. New York: Academic Press.

Shibatani, M. 1976. "The Grammar of Causative Constructions: A Conspectus." In Shibatani 1976, 1–40.

Simpson, J. 1983a. "Resultatives." In L. Levin, Rappaport, and Zaenen 1983, 143–57.

Simpson, J. 1983b. "Adjuncts." Ms., MIT, Cambridge, Mass.

Smith, C. S. 1970. "Jespersen's 'Move and Change' Class and Causative Verbs in English." In *Linguistic and Literary Studies in Honor of Archibald A. Hill. Vol. 2: Descriptive Linguistics*, ed. M. A. Jazayery, E. C. Polomé, and W. Winter, 101–9. The Hague: Mouton.

Smith, C. S. 1991. *The Parameter of Aspect*. Dordrecht: Kluwer.

Sobin, N. 1985. "Case Assignment in Ukrainian Morphological Passive Constructions." *Linguistic Inquiry* 16:649–62.

Spencer, A. 1991. *Morphological Theory: An Introduction to Word Structure in Generative Grammar*. Oxford: Blackwell.

Sportiche, D. 1988. "A Theory of Floating Quantifiers and Its Corollaries for Constituent Structure." *Linguistic Inquiry* 19:425–49.

Stowell, T. 1978. "What Was There before There Was There." In *Papers from the Fourteenth Regional Meeting, Chicago Linguistic Society*, 457–71. Chicago Linguistic Society, University of Chicago, Chicago, Ill.

Stowell, T. 1981. "Origins of Phrase Structure." Doctoral dissertation, MIT, Cambridge, Mass.

Stowell, T. 1991. "Small Clause Restructuring." In *Principles and Parameters in Comparative Grammar*, ed. R. Freidin, 182–218. Cambridge, Mass.: MIT Press.

Stowell, T., and E. Wehrli, eds. 1992. *Syntax and Semantics 26: Syntax and the Lexicon*. San Diego, Calif.: Academic Press.

Stroik, T. 1992. "Middles and Movement." *Linguistic Inquiry* 23:127–37.

Talmy, L. 1975. "Semantics and Syntax of Motion." In *Syntax and Semantics 4*, ed. J. P. Kimball, 181–238. New York: Academic Press.

Talmy, L. 1985. "Lexicalization Patterns: Semantic Structure in Lexical Forms." In *Language Typology and Syntactic Description 3: Grammatical Categories and the Lexicon*, ed. T. Shopen, 57–149. Cambridge: Cambridge University Press.

Talmy, L. 1991. "Path to Realization: A Typology of Event Integration." In *Buffalo Papers in Linguistics 91-01*, 147–87. Department of Linguistics, State University of New York, Buffalo.

Tenny, C. 1987. "Grammaticalizing Aspect and Affectedness." Doctoral dissertation, MIT, Cambridge, Mass.

Tenny, C. 1992. "The Aspectual Interface Hypothesis." In *Lexical Matters*, ed. I. A. Sag and A. Szabolcsi, 1–27. Stanford, Calif.: CSLI Publications. Distributed by University of Chicago Press, Chicago, Ill. An earlier version appeared in *Proceedings of NELS 18*, 490–508. GLSA, University of Massachusetts, Amherst.

Timberlake, A. 1982. "The Impersonal Passive in Lithuanian." In *Proceedings of the Eighth Annual Meeting of the Berkeley Linguistics Society*, 508–24. Berkeley Linguistics Society, University of California, Berkeley.

Torrego, E. 1989. "Unergative-Unaccusative Alternations in Spanish." In *MIT Working Papers in Linguistics 10: Functional Heads and Clause Structure*, 253–72. Department of Linguistics and Philosophy, MIT, Cambridge, Mass.

Townsend, C. E. 1970. *Continuing with Russian*. New York: McGraw-Hill.

Tsujimura, N. 1991. "On the Semantic Properties of Unaccusativity." *Journal of Japanese Linguistics* 13:91–116.

Tsujimura, N. 1993. "Manner of Motion Verbs and Resultatives in Japanese." Ms., Indiana University, Bloomington, Ind.

Van Valin, R. D., Jr. 1990. "Semantic Parameters of Split Intransitivity." *Language* 66:221–60.

Van Valin, R. D., Jr. 1993. "A Synopsis of Role and Reference Grammar." In *Advances in Role and Reference Grammar*, ed. R. D. Van Valin, Jr., 1–164. Amsterdam: John Benjamins.

Vendler, Z. 1957. "Verbs and Times." *Philosophical Review* 56:143–60. Also in *Linguistics in Philosophy*, by Z. Vendler, 1967, 97–121. Ithaca, N.Y.: Cornell University Press.

Verkuyl, H. J. 1972. *On the Compositional Nature of the Aspects*. Dordrecht: Reidel.

Verkuyl, H. J. 1989. "Aspectual Classes and Aspectual Composition." *Linguistics and Philosophy* 12:39–94.

Vikner, S. 1991. "*Be* Is Selected over *Have* If and Only If It Is Part of an A-Chain." In *Issues in Germanic Syntax*, ed. W. Abraham, W. Kosmeijer, and E. Reuland, 365–81. Berlin: Mouton de Gruyter.

Vinay, J.-P., and J. Darbelnet. 1958. *Stylistique comparée du français et de l'anglais*. Paris: Didier.

Voorst, J. G. van. 1993. "The Semantic Structure of Causative Constructions." Ms., Université du Québec à Montréal.

Ward, G., and B. J. Birner. 1993. "*There*-Sentences and Information Status." In *Northwestern University Working Papers in Linguistics* 5, 51–68. Department of Linguistics, Northwestern University, Evanston, Ill.

Wasow, T. 1977. "Transformations and the Lexicon." In Culicover, Wasow, and Akmajian 1977, 327–60.

Wasow, T. 1985. "Postscript." In *Lectures on Contemporary Syntactic Theories*, by P. Sells, 193–205. Stanford, Calif.: CSLI Publications. Distributed by University of Chicago Press, Chicago, Ill.

Wilkins, D. P., and R. D. Van Valin, Jr. 1993. "The Case for a Case Reopened: Agents and Agency Revisited." Technical Report 93–2, Center for Cognitive Science, State University of New York, Buffalo.

Wilkins, W., ed. 1988. *Syntax and Semantics 21: Thematic Relations*. San Diego, Calif.: Academic Press.

Williams, E. 1980. "Predication." *Linguistic Inquiry* 11:203–38.

Williams, E. 1981. "Argument Structure and Morphology." *The Linguistic Review* 1:81–114.

Williams, E. 1982. "Another Argument That Passive Is Transformational." *Linguistic Inquiry* 13:160–63.

Williams, E. 1983. "Against Small Clauses." *Linguistic Inquiry* 14:287–308.

Yoneyama, M. 1986. "Motion Verbs in Conceptual Semantics." In *Bulletin of the Faculty of Humanities 22*, 1–15. Seikei University, Tokyo.

Young, R. W., and W. Morgan. 1980. *The Navajo Language: A Grammar and Colloquial Dictionary*. Albuquerque, N.M.: University of New Mexico Press.

Zaenen, A. 1993. "Unaccusativity in Dutch: Integrating Syntax and Lexical Semantics." In *Semantics and the Lexicon*, ed. J. Pustejovsky, 129–61. Dordrecht: Kluwer.

Zagona, K. 1982. "Government and Proper Government of Verbal Projections." Doctoral dissertation, University of Washington, Seattle.

Zubizarreta, M. L. 1982. "On the Relationship of the Lexicon to Syntax." Doctoral dissertation, MIT, Cambridge, Mass.

Zubizarreta, M. L. 1987. *Levels of Representation in the Lexicon and in the Syntax*. Dordrecht: Foris.

Sources of Examples

Aiken, J. 1990. *Jane Fairfax*. New York: St. Martin's Press.

Allingham, M. 1985. Reprint. *The Fashion in Shrouds*. New York: Bantam. Original edition, 1938.

Andrews, P. 1986. "Abandoned in Iran." *New York Times Book Review*. 7 December.

Bagnold, E. 1954. *The Squire*. In *The Girl's Journey*. Garden City, N.Y.: Doubleday.

Bailey, J. 1991. *Bagged*. New York: St. Martin's Press.

Baker, R. 1992. "The '92 Follies." *New York Times Magazine*. 1 November.

Beattie, A. 1989. *Picturing Will*. New York: Random House.

Benary, M. 1955. *Rowan Farm*. Translated by R. and C. Winston. London: Macmillan.

Billington, R. 1988. *Loving Attitudes*. New York: William Morrow.

Bowen, E. 1982. Reprint. *Eva Trout*. Harmondsworth: Penguin. Original edition, New York: Knopf, 1968.

Brennan, C. 1991. *Headhunt*. New York: Carroll and Graf.

Bromfield, L. 1933. *The Farm*. New York: Grosset and Dunlap.

Brontë, E. 1965. Reprint. *Wuthering Heights*. London: Penguin English Library. Original edition, 1847.

Brookner, A. 1987. *A Friend from England*. New York: Pantheon.

Brown, P. L. 1990. "Dodging Hippos on the Zambezi." *New York Times*. 29 July.

Cambridge, A. 1987. Reprint. *The Three Miss Kings*. London: Virago. Original edition, Heinemann, 1891.

Cancogni, A. 1988. "A Widow's Dream." *New York Times Book Review*. 26 June.

Cheever, S. 1989. *Elizabeth Cole*. New York: Farrar, Straus and Giroux.

Cheong, F. 1991. *The Scent of the Gods*. New York: Norton.

Chicago Tribune. 1989. "'Mr. Senior Diplomat, Sir, Where on Earth Were You?'" 28 June.

Chute, P. 1987. *Castine*. Garden City, N.Y.: Doubleday.

Clewlow, C. 1988. *Keeping the Faith*. New York: Poseidon.

Colwin, L. 1990. *Goodbye without Leaving*. New York: Poseidon.

Connell, E. S. 1981. Reprint. *Mr. Bridge*. San Francisco: North Point. Original edition, New York: Knopf, 1969.

Dark, E. 1959. *Lantana Lane*. London: Collins.

Drake, M. R. 1990. "A Message from the Director." *Northwestern Perspective*. Department of University Relations, Northwestern University, Evanston, Ill. Summer.

Dunlop, S. 1991. Reprint. *Karma*. New York: Dell. Original edition, 1981.

Ehrlich, G. 1988. *Heart Mountain*. New York: Viking Penguin.

Eliot, G. 1979. Reprint. *Daniel Deronda*. New York: Signet. Original edition, 1876.

Friedman, T. L. 1989. *From Beirut to Jerusalem*. New York: Farrar, Straus and Giroux.

Gallagher, M. 1987. Review of *Best Intentions* by K. Lehrer. *New York Times Book Review*. 16 August.

Goldstein, R. 1989. *The Late-Summer Passion of a Woman of Mind*. New York: Farrar, Straus and Giroux.

Gordon, M. 1989. *The Other Side*. New York: Viking.

Grey, Z. 1980. *Riders of the Purple Sage*. In *Z. Grey: Five Complete Novels*. New York: Avenel.

Grey, Z. 1980. *The Thundering Herd*. In *Z. Grey: Five Complete Novels*. New York: Avenel.

Grimes, M. 1987. *The Five Bells and Bladestone*. Boston: Little, Brown.

Grimes, M. 1989. *The Old Silent*. Boston: Little, Brown.

Haire-Sargeant, L. 1992. *H.—*. New York: Pocket Books.

Hartvigson, H. H., and L. K. Jakobsen. 1974. *Inversion in Present-Day English*. Odense: Odense University Press.

Hedges, C. 1992. "Heavy Snow in Israel Helps the Trains, Sort Of." *New York Times*. 1 March.

Hjortsberg, W. 1969. *Alp*. New York: Simon and Schuster.

Holt, H. 1991. *A Lot to Ask: A Life of Barbara Pym*. New York: Dutton.

Hosain, A. 1988. Reprint. *Sunlight on a Broken Column*. London: Virago. Original edition, London: Chatto and Windus, 1961.

James, H. 1986. Reprint. *The Bostonians*. London: Penguin Classics. Original edition, New York: Macmillan, 1886.

James, P. D. 1986. *A Taste for Death*. London: Faber and Faber.

Kehr, D. 1989. "Resolved: 'Listen' Is a Boring Movie." *Chicago Tribune*. 8 May.

Klass, P. 1990. *Other Women's Children*. New York: Random House.

Kogan, R. 1990. "Andrew Dice Clay Isn't Worth 'SNL' Flap." *Chicago Tribune*. 11 May.

Laverty, M. 1989. Reprint. *Never No More*. London: Virago. Original edition, Longmans, 1942.

Lehmann, B. 1987. Reprint. *Rumour of Heaven*. London: Virago. Original edition, Methuen, 1934.

Leimbach, D. 1990. "Wunderbar!" *New York Times Magazine*. September 30.

L'Engle, M. 1962. *A Wrinkle in Time*. New York: Farrar, Straus and Giroux.

L'Engle, M. 1978. *A Swiftly Tilting Planet*. New York: Farrar, Straus and Giroux.

L'Engle, M. 1984. Reprint. *The Small Rain*. New York: Farrar, Straus and Giroux. Original edition, Vanguard Press, 1945.

L'Engle, M. 1989. *An Acceptable Time*. New York: Farrar, Straus and Giroux.

Levitsky, R. 1991. *The Love That Kills*. New York: Scribner's.

Lindkvist, K.-G. 1976. *A Comprehensive Study of Conceptions of Locality*. Stockholm: Almqvist and Wiksell.

Lively, P. 1980. *Treasures of Time*. Garden City, N.Y.: Doubleday.

Lively, P. 1985. Reprint. *Perfect Happiness*. London: Penguin. Original edition, Heinemann, 1983.

Lively, P. 1988. *Moon Tiger*. New York: Grove.

Lively, P. 1991. *The Road to Lichfield*. New York: Grove Weidenfeld.

Lofts, N. 1968. Reprint. *Silver Nutmeg*. London: Corgi. Original edition, Michael Joseph, 1947.

"Lord of the Wind: Aztec Offerings from Tlatelolco, Mexico." 1989–1990. Exhibit sign. Museum of Natural History, Denver. 18 October 1989–28 January 1990.

Marshall, A. 1986. *The Brass Bed*. New York: Doubleday.

Mason, B. A. 1983. "A New-Wave Format." In *Shiloh and Other Stories*. London: Chatto and Windus.

Matera, L. 1991. Reprint. *A Radical Departure*. New York: Ballantine. Original edition, 1988.

McKay, G. 1992. "America's Cup '92 + Love, Beauty, and Science." *New York Times*. 19 May.

McKelvy, N. 1987. *Where's Ours?* Chicago, Ill.: Academy Chicago.

Miller, S. 1990. *Family Pictures*. New York: Harper and Row.

Muir, W. 1987. *Imagined Corners*. Reprint. Edinburgh: Canongate Classics. Original edition, Martin Secker, 1935.

Muller, M. 1985. *There's Nothing to Be Afraid Of*. New York: St. Martin's Press.

Munthe, A. 1929. *The Story of San Michele*. John Murray.

Oates, J. C. 1992. *Black Water*. New York: Dutton.

Olivia (D. Bussy). 1949. *Olivia*. London: Hogarth Press.

Olshan, J. 1989. *The Waterline*. New York: Doubleday.

Ostenso, M. 1961. Reprint. *Wild Geese*. Toronto: New Canadian Library. Original edition, Dodd, Mead, 1925.

Paley, V. G. 1993. "The Schoolyard Jungle." *New York Times Book Review*. 16 May.

Paretsky, S. 1988. *Blood Shot*. New York: Dell.

Paretsky, S. 1990. *Burn Marks*. New York: Delacorte.

Pesetsky, B. 1991. *The Late Night Muse*. New York: HarperCollins.

Philadelphia Inquirer. 1983. "To the Top the Hard Way." 16 September.

Philadelphia Inquirer. 1984. "Apartment Dwellers Caught in Legal Tangle." 7 May.

Phillpotts, E. 1922. *The Red Redmaynes*. New York: Macmillan.

Pickard, N. 1990. *Bum Steer*. New York: Pocket Books.

Piercy, M. 1989. *Summer People*. New York: Summit.

Pilcher, R. 1984. *Voices in Summer*. New York: St. Martin's Press.

Pilcher, R. 1990. *September*. New York: St. Martin's Press.

Poutsma, H. 1904. *A Grammar of Late Modern English*. Groningen: P. Noordhoff.

Praed, R. 1988. Reprint. *Outlaw and Lawmaker*. London: Pandora. Original edition, 1898.

Pryce-Jones, D. 1986. *The Afternoon Sun*. New York: Weidenfeld and Nicolson.

Robertson, M. E. 1989. Reprint. *Family Life*. New York: Penguin. Original edition, New York: Atheneum, 1987.

Robinson, R. 1988. *Summer Light*. New York: Viking.

Rothenberg, R. 1991. *The Bulrush Murders*. New York: Carroll and Graf.

Sciolino, E. 1990. "Iraq Yearns for Greatness—and an Identity." The Week in Review Section. *New York Times*. 26 August.

Smith, D. 1989. *Remember This*. New York: Henry Holt.

Spark, M. 1962. *The Prime of Miss Jean Brodie*. Philadelphia and New York: Lippincott.

Spark, M. 1963. *The Girls of Slender Means*. New York: Knopf.

Stallard, D. 1987. "The Logical Analysis of Lexical Ambiguity." In *Proceedings of the 25th Annual Meeting*. Association for Computational Linguistics.

State of Illinois. 1989. *Rules of the Road*.

Stauth, C. 1990. "The Network Henhouse." *New York Times Magazine*. July 15.

Steinbeck, J. 1969. Reprint. *The Grapes of Wrath*. Harmondsworth: Penguin. Original edition, New York: Viking, 1939.

Stern, G. B. 1925. *The Matriarch*. New York: Knopf.

Sullivan, F. 1989. Reprint. *The Cape Anne*. New York: Penguin. Original edition, Crown, 1988.

Tan, A. 1989. *The Joy Luck Club*. New York: G. P. Putnam and Sons.

Thane, E. 1944. *Yankee Stranger*. Chicago, Ill.: People's Book Club.

Thurm, M. 1991. *The Way We Live Now*. New York: Bantam.

Toner, R. 1992. "While Others Shrank from Race, Clinton Clung to Dream of Presidency." *New York Times*. 12 July.

Updike, J. 1981. *Rabbit Is Rich*. New York: Knopf.

Upfield, A. W. 1985. Reprint. *The Sands of Windee*. New York: Collier. Original edition, 1931.

Upfield, A. W. 1985. Reprint. *The Widows of Broome*. New York: Collier. Original edition, 1950.

Upfield, A. W. 1986. Reprint. *The Bachelors of Broken Hill*. New York: Collier. Original edition, 1950.

Upfield, A. W. 1986. Reprint. *Man of Two Tribes*. New York: Collier. Original edition, 1956.

Upfield, A. W. 1986. Reprint. *No Footprints in the Bush*. New York: Collier. Original edition, 1940.

Upfield, A. W. 1986. Reprint. *Sinister Stones*. New York: Collier. Original edition, 1954.

Upfield, A. W. 1986. Reprint. *Wings above the Diamantina*. New York: Collier. Original edition, 1936.

Visser, F. Th. 1963. *An Historical Syntax of the English Language. Part One: Syntactical Units with One Verb*. Leiden: E. J. Brill.

von Pressentin Wright, C. 1991. "Plantation Mansions on the Mississippi." Travel Section. *New York Times*. 10 February.

Wesley, M. 1990. *A Sensible Life*. New York: Viking.

Wilford, J. N. 1990. "To Endangered List in Gulf, Add Archeology." *New York Times*. 16 September.

Wodehouse, P. G. 1977. "Portrait of a Disciplinarian." In *Meet Mr. Mulliner*. New York: Ballantine.

Index